Digital Media and
Communication

Digital Media and Communication

Edited by
Alfred White

 Larsen & Keller
www.larsen-keller.com

Digital Media and Communication
Edited by Alfred White
ISBN: 978-1-63549-009-1 (Hardback)

 Larsen & Keller

Published by Larsen and Keller Education,
5 Penn Plaza,
19th Floor,
New York, NY 10001, USA

Cataloging-in-Publication Data

Digital media and communication / edited by Alfred White.
    p. cm.
Includes bibliographical references and index.
ISBN 978-1-63549-009-1
1. Digital media--Textbooks. 2. Communication--Textbooks.
I. White, Alfred.
HM851 .D54 2017
302.231--dc23

The publisher's policy is to use permanent paper from mills that operate a sustainable forestry policy. Furthermore, the publisher ensures that the text paper and cover boards used have met acceptable environmental accreditation standards.

Printed and bound in the United States of America.

For more information regarding Larsen and Keller Education and its products, please visit the publisher's website www.larsen-keller.com

Table of Contents

Preface

The progress of technology has integrated the digital world in all sectors of industry as well as daily life. The field of digital media and communication is one such field which has significantly emerged as a distinct field of study. This textbook is written in a comprehensive student-friendly language to make the understanding of even the most complex topics of this subject as easy and informative as possible. The book encapsulates the current approaches, tools and techniques revolving around digital media and communication in a detailed manner to provide incredible insights to the readers.

To facilitate a deeper understanding of the contents of this book a short introduction of every chapter is written below:

Chapter 1- The field of digital media is expanding at a fast pace. Therefore, to keep up with the progress of the field, extensive reading is mandatory. This chapter provides in-depth detail about the various aspects in the area of digital media and communication. It also introduces the students to the basic and the complex introductory theories of this subject.

Chapter 2- This chapter will discuss some of the important topics related to digital media. It will elaborate in detail, topics like information age, mass media, digital electronics, information society, cognitive-cultural economy and computer-mediated communication. It will trace their progression, relation to economics and other factors and will also discuss related technological aspects.

Chapter 3- The field of media is ever evolving and digital media has transformed the media industry in the past decade. New techniques, methods and technologies are being regularly introduced. This chapter will discuss the various new techniques being used in content creation and also elaborate the technologies in new media. It will help students gain complete knowledge about this subject.

Chapter 4- This chapter is designed to introduce the students to the various tools and techniques that are used in digital media and communication. Some of the topics discussed in the chapter are data, image, audio and video with respect to digital media. It also introduces relatively nascent forms of digital communication such as instant messaging, social media, Facebook, YouTube, viral marketing and blog, among others. The aim of this chapter is to provide students with a comprehensive knowledge of this field.

Chapter 5- Communication helps in addressing a large audience at once using diverse mediums such as television, radio, etc. This chapter focuses on the digital means of communication which have revolutionized the field of communication. The topics elaborated herein include digital radio, internet, online newspaper, etc.

Finally, I would like to thank the entire team involved in the inception of this book for their valuable time and contribution. This book would not have been possible without their efforts. I would also like to thank my friends and family for their constant support.

Editor

Introduction to Digital Media and Communication

The field of digital media is expanding at a fast pace. Therefore, to keep up with the progress of the field, extensive reading is mandatory. This chapter provides in-depth detail about the various aspects in the area of digital media and communication. It also introduces the students to the basic and the complex introductory theories of this subject.

Hard drives store information in binary form and so are considered a type of physical digital media.

Digital media are any media that are encoded in a machine-readable format. Digital media can be created, viewed, distributed, modified and preserved on digital electronics devices. Computer programs and software; digital imagery, digital video; video games; web pages and websites, including social media; data and databases; digital audio, such as mp3s; and e-books are examples of digital media. Digital media are frequently contrasted with print media, such as printed books, newspapers and magazines, and other traditional or analog media, such as pictures, film or audio tape.

Combined with the Internet and personal computing, digital media has caused disruption in publishing, journalism, entertainment, education, commerce and politics. Digital media has also posed new challenges to copyright and intellectual property laws, fostering an open content movement in which content creators voluntarily give up some or all of their legal rights to their work. The ubiquity of digital media and its effects on society suggest that we are at the start of a new era in industrial history, called the Information Age, perhaps leading to a paperless society in which all media are produced and consumed on computers. However, challenges to a digital transition remain, including outdated copyright laws, censorship, the digital divide, and the specter of a digital dark age, in which older media becomes inaccessible to new or upgraded information systems. Digital media has a significant, wide-ranging and complex impact on society and culture.

History

Before Electronics

Analog computers, such as Babbage's Difference Engine, use physical, i.e. tangible, parts and actions to control operations

Machine-readable media predates the Internet, modern computers and electronics. Machine-readable codes and information were first conceptualized by Charles Babbage in the early 1800s. Babbage imagined that these codes would provide instructions for his Difference Engine and Analytical Engine, machines he designed to solve the problem of error in calculations. Between 1822 and 1823, Ada Lovelace, a mathematician, wrote the first instructions for calculating numbers on Babbage's engines. Lovelace's instructions are now believed to be the first computer program.

Though the machines were designed to perform analytical tasks, Lovelace anticipated the potential social impact of computers and programming, writing, "For, in so distributing and combining the truths and the formulae of analysis, that they may become most easily and rapidly amenable to the mechanical combinations of the engine, the relations and the nature of many subjects in that science are necessarily thrown into new lights, and more profoundly investigated... there are in all extensions of human power, or additions to human knowledge, various collateral influences, besides the main and primary object attained." Other early machine-readable media include the instructions for player pianos and jacquard looms.

Digital Computers

01010111 01101001 01101011
01101001 01110000 01100101
01100100 01101001 01100001

Digital codes, like binary, can be changed without reconfiguring mechanical parts

Though they used machine-readable media, Babbage's engines, player pianos, jacquard looms and many other early calculating machines were themselves analog computers, with physical, mechanical parts. The first truly digital media came into existence with the rise of digital computers. Digital computers use binary code and Boolean logic to store and process information, allowing one machine in one configuration to perform many different tasks. The first modern, programmable, digital computers, the Manchester Mark 1 and the EDSAC, were independently invented between 1948 and 1949. Though different in many ways from modern computers, these machines had digital software controlling their logical operations. They were encoded in binary, a system of ones and zeroes that are combined to make hundreds of characters. The 1s and 0s of binary are the "digits" of digital media.

"As We May Think"

While digital media came into common use in the early 1950s, the *conceptual* foundation of digital media is traced to the work of scientist and engineer Vannevar Bush and his celebrated essay "As We May Think," published in the *Atlantic Monthly* in 1945. Bush envisioned a system of devices that could be used to help scientists, doctors, historians and others, store, analyze and communicate information. Calling this then-imaginary device a "memex", Bush wrote:

The owner of the memex, let us say, is interested in the origin and properties of the bow and arrow. Specifically he is studying why the short Turkish bow was apparently superior to the English long bow in the skirmishes of the Crusades. He has dozens of possibly pertinent books and articles in his memex. First he runs through an encyclopedia, finds an interesting but sketchy article, leaves it projected. Next, in a history, he finds another pertinent item, and ties the two together. Thus he goes, building a trail of many items. Occasionally he inserts a comment of his own, either linking it into the main trail or joining it by a side trail to a particular item. When it becomes evident that the elastic properties of available materials had a great deal to do with the bow, he branches off on a side trail which takes him through textbooks on elasticity and tables of physical constants. He inserts a page of longhand analysis of his own. Thus he builds a trail of his interest through the maze of materials available to him.

Bush hoped that the creation of this memex would be the work of scientists after World War II. Though the essay predated digital computers by several years, "As We May Think," anticipated the potential social and intellectual benefits of digital media and provided the conceptual framework for digital scholarship, the World Wide Web, wikis and even social media. It was recognized as a significant work even at the time of its publication.

Impact

The Digital Revolution

In the years since the invention of the first digital computers, computing power and storage capacity have increased exponentially. Personal computers and smartphones put the ability to access, modify, store and share digital media in the hands of billions of people. Many electronic devices, from digital cameras to drones have the ability to create, transmit and view digital media. Combined with the World Wide Web and the Internet, digital media has transformed 21st century society in a way that is frequently compared to the cultural, economic and social impact of the printing press. The change has been so rapid and so widespread that it has launched an economic transition from an industrial economy to an information-based economy, creating a new period in human history known as the Information Age or the digital revolution.

The transition has created some uncertainty about definitions. Digital media, new media, multimedia, and similar terms all have a relationship to both the engineering innovations and cultural impact of digital media. The blending of digital media with other media, and with cultural and social factors, is sometimes known as new media or "the new media." Similarly, digital media seems to demand a new set of communications skills, called transliteracy, media literacy, or digital literacy. These skills include not only the ability to read and write—traditional literacy—but the ability to navigate the Internet, evaluate sources , and create digital content. The idea that we are moving toward a fully digital, "paperless" society is accompanied by the fear that we may soon—or currently—be facing a digital dark age, in which older media are no longer accessible on modern devices or using modern methods of scholarship. Digital media has a significant, wide-ranging and complex effect on society and culture.

Disruption in Industry

Compared with print media, the mass media, and other analog technologies, digital media are easy to copy, store, share and modify. This quality of digital media has led to significant changes in many industries, especially journalism, publishing, education, entertainment, and the music business. The overall effect of these changes is so far-reaching that it is difficult to quantify. For example, in movie-making, the transition from analog film cameras to digital cameras is nearly complete. The transition has economic benefits to Hollywood, making distribution easier and making it possible to add high-quality digital effects to films. At the same time, it has affected the analog special effects, stunt, and animation industries in Hollywood. It has imposed painful costs on small movie theaters, some of which did not or will not survive the transition to digital. The effect of digital media on other media industries is similarly sweeping and complex.

In journalism, digital media and citizen journalism have led to the loss of thousands of jobs in print media and the bankruptcy of many major newspapers. But the rise of digital journalism has also created thousands of new jobs and specializations. E-books and self-publishing are changing the book industry, and digital textbooks and other media-inclusive curricula are changing primary and secondary education. In academia, digital media has led to a new form of scholarship, called digital scholarship, and new fields of study, such as digital humanities and digital history. It has changed the way libraries are used and their role in society. Every major media, communications and academic endeavor is facing a period of transition and uncertainty related to digital media.

Individual as Content Creator

Digital media has also allowed individuals to be much more active in content creation. Anyone with access to computers and the Internet can participate in social media and contribute their own writing, art, videos, photography and commentary to the Internet, as well as conduct business online. This has come to be known as citizen journalism. This spike in user created content is due to the development of the internet as well as the way in which users interact with media today. The release of technologies such mobile devices allow for easier and quicker access to all things media. Many media production tools that were once only available to a few are now free and easy to use.

The cost of devices that can access the internet is dropping steadily, and now personal ownership of multiple digital devices is becoming standard. These elements have significantly affected political participation. Digital media is seen by many scholars as having a role in Arab Spring, and crackdowns on the use of digital and social media by embattled governments are increasingly common. Many governments restrict access to digital media in some way, either to prevent obscenity or in a broader form of political censorship.

User-generated content raises issues of privacy, credibility, civility and compensation for cultural, intellectual and artistic contributions. The spread of digital media, and the wide range of literacy and communications skills necessary to use it effectively, have deepened the digital divide between those who have access to digital media and those who don't.

Web Only News

As the internet becomes more and more prevalent, more companies are beginning to distribute content through internet only means. Prime time audiences have dropped 23% for News Corp, the worlds largest broadcasting channel. With the loss of viewers there is a loss of revenue but not as bad as what would be expected. While the dollar amount dropped roughly 2%, overall cable revenue was up about 5% which is slower growth than what was expected. Cisco Inc released its latest forecast and the numbers are all trending to internet news to continue to grow at a rate where it will be quadruple by 2018.

As of 2012, the worlds largest internet only media company, The Young Turks, are averaging 750,000 users per day, and are continuing to grow, currently having over 2 billion views across all The Young Turks controlled channels, which covers world news, sports, movie reviews, college focused content and a round table style discussion channel.

Digital media pose many challenges to current copyright and intellectual property laws. The ease of creating, modifying and sharing digital media makes copyright enforcement a challenge, and copyright laws are widely seen as outdated. For example, under current copyright law, common Internet memes are probably illegal to share in many countries. Legal rights are at least unclear for many common Internet activities, such as posting a picture that belongs to someone else to a social media account, covering a popular song on a YouTube video, or writing fanfiction. Over the last decade the concept of fair use has been applied to many online medias.

To resolve some of these issues, content creators can voluntarily adopt open or copyleft licenses, giving up some of their legal rights, or they can release their work to the public domain. Among the most common open licenses are Creative Commons licenses and the GNU Free Documentation License, both of which are in use on Wikipedia. Open licenses are part of a broader open content movement that pushes for the reduction or removal of copyright restrictions from software, data and other digital media.

Additional software has been developed in order to protect digital media. Digital Rights Management (DRM) is used to digitally copyright material and allows users to use that media for specific cases. For example, DRM allows a movie producer to rent a movie at a lower price than selling the movie, restricting the movie rental license length, rather than only selling the movie at full price. Additionally, DRM can prevent unauthorized sharing or modification of media.

Digital Media is numerical, networked and interactive system of links and databases that allows us to navigate from one bit of content or webpage to another.

One form of Digital media that is becoming a phenomenon is in the form of a digital magazine. What exactly is a digital magazine? Due to the economic importance of digital magazines, the Audit Bureau of Circulations integrated the definition of this medium in its latest report (March 2011): a digital magazine involves the distribution of a magazine content by electronic means; it may be a replica. This is the out dated definition of what a digital magazine is. A digital magazine should not be, in fact, a replica of the print magazine in PDF, as was common practice in recent years. It should, rather, be a magazine that is, in essence, interactive and created from scratch to a digital platform (Internet, mobile phones, private networks, iPad or other device). The barriers for digital magazine distribution are thus decreasing. At the same time digitizing platforms are broadening the scope of where digital magazines can be published, such as within websites and on smartphones. With the improvements of tablets and digital magazines are becoming visually enticing and readable magazines with it graphic arts.

References

- *Pavlik, John; McIntosh, Shawn. Converging Media (Fourth ed.). Oxford University Press. pp. 237–239. ISBN 978-0-19-934230-3. "Digital Media" (PDF). Technology Brief. University of Guelph. September 2006. Retrieved 28 March 2014.*

- *Dewar, James A. (1998). "The information age and the printing press: looking backward to see ahead". RAND Corporation. Retrieved 29 March 2014.*

- *Koehl, Sean (15 May 2013). "We need to act now to prevent a digital 'dark age'". Wired. Retrieved 29 March 2014.*

- *O'Carroll, Eoin (10 December 2012). "Ada Lovelace: what did the first computer program do?". Christian Science Monitor. Retrieved 29 March 2014.*

- *Copeland, B. Jack (Fall 2008). "The modern history of computing". The Stanford Encyclopedia of Philosophy. Stanford University. Retrieved 31 March 2014.*

- *Simpson, Rosemary; Allen Renear; Elli Mylonas; Andries van Dam (March 1996). "50 years after "As We May Think": the Brown/MIT Vannevar Bush symposium" (PDF). Interactions. pp. 47–67. Retrieved 29 March 2014.*

- *Mynatt, Elizabeth. "As we may think: the legacy of computing research and the power of human cognition". Computing Research Association. Retrieved 30 March 2014.*

- *Bazillion, Richard (2001). "Academic libraries in the digital revolution" (PDF). Educause Quarterly. Retrieved 31 March 2014.*

- *Ito, Mizuko; et al. (November 008). "Living and learning with the new media: summary of findings from the digital youth project" (PDF). Retrieved 29 March 2014.*

- *Cusumano, Catherine (18 March 2013). "Changeover in film technology spells end for age of analog". Brown Daily Herald. Retrieved 31 March 2014.*

- *McCracken, Erin (5 May 2013). "Last reel: Movie industry's switch to digital hits theaters -- especially small ones -- in the wallet". York Daily Record. Retrieved 29 March 2014.*

- *Kirchhoff, Suzanne M. (9 September 2010). "The U.S. newspaper industry in transition" (PDF). Congressional Research Service. Retrieved 29 March 2014.*

- *Zara, Christopher (2 October 2012). "Job growth in digital journalism is bigger than anyone knows". International Business Times. Retrieved 29 March 2014.*

- *Cohen, Cathy J.; Joseph Kahne (2012). "Participatory politics: new media and youth political action" (PDF). Retrieved 29 March 2014.*

- *Kelley, Peter (13 June 2013). "Philip Howard's new book explores digital media role in Arab Spring". University of Washington. Retrieved 30 March 2014.*

- *Rininsland, Andrew (16 April 2012). "Internet censorship listed: how does each country compare?". The Guardian. Retrieved 30 March 2014.*

- *Crawford, Susan P. (3 December 2011). "Internet access and the new digital divide". The New York Times. Retrieved 30 March 2014.*

Significant Topics of Digital Media and Communication

2

This chapter will discuss some of the important topics related to digital media. It will elaborate in detail, topics like information age, mass media, digital electronics, information society, cognitive-cultural economy and computer-mediated communication. It will trace their progression, relation to economics and other factors and will also discuss related technological aspects.

Information Age

The Information Age (also known as the Computer Age, Digital Age, or New Media Age) is a period in human history characterized by the shift from traditional industry that the Industrial Revolution brought through industrialization, to an economy based on information computerization. The onset of the Information Age is associated with the Digital Revolution, just as the Industrial Revolution marked the onset of the Industrial Age.

During the information age, the phenomenon is that the digital industry creates a knowledge-based society surrounded by a high-tech global economy that spans over its influence on how the manufacturing throughput and the service sector operate in an efficient and convenient way. In a commercialized society, the information industry is able to allow individuals to explore their personalized needs, therefore simplifying the procedure of making decisions for transactions and significantly lowering costs for both the producers and buyers. This is accepted overwhelmingly by participants throughout the entire economic activities for efficacy purposes, and new economic incentives would then be indigenously encouraged, such as the knowledge economy.

The Information Age formed by capitalizing on computer microminiaturization advances. This evolution of technology in daily life and social organization has led to the fact that the modernization of information and communication processes has become the driving force of social evolution.

Internet

The Internet was conceived as a fail-proof network that could connect computers together and be resistant to any single point of failure. It is said that the Internet cannot be totally destroyed in one event, and if large areas are disabled, the information is easily rerouted. It was created mainly by DARPA on work carried out by British scientists like Donald Davies; its initial software applications were e-mail and computer file transfer.

Though the Internet itself has existed since 1969, it was with the invention of the World Wide Web in 1989 by British scientist Tim Berners-Lee and its introduction in 1991 that the Internet became an easily accessible network. The Internet is now a global platform for accelerating the flow of information and is pushing many, if not most, older forms of media into obsolescence.

Progression

Library Expansion

Library expansion was calculated in 1945 by Fremont Rider to double in capacity every 16 years, if sufficient space were made available. He advocated replacing bulky, decaying printed works with miniaturized microform analog photographs, which could be duplicated on-demand for library patrons or other institutions. He did not foresee the digital technology that would follow decades later to replace analog microform with digital imaging, storage, and transmission media. Automated, potentially lossless digital technologies allowed vast increases in the rapidity of information growth. Moore's law, which was formulated around 1965, calculated that the number of transistors in a dense integrated circuit doubles approximately every two years.

The proliferation of the smaller and less expensive personal computers and improvements in computing power by the early 1980s resulted in a sudden access to and ability to share and store information for increasing numbers of workers. Connectivity between computers within companies led to the ability of workers at different levels to access greater amounts of information.

Information Storage

The world's technological capacity to store information grew from 2.6 (optimally compressed) exabytes in 1986 to 15.8 in 1993, over 54.5 in 2000, and to 295 (optimally compressed) exabytes in 2007. This is the informational equivalent to less than one 730-MB CD-ROM per person in 1986 (539 MB per person), roughly 4 CD-ROM per person of 1993, 12 CD-ROM per person in the year 2000, and almost 61 CD-ROM per person in 2007. It is estimated that the world's capacity to store information has reached 5 zettabytes in 2014. This is the informational equivalent of 4,500 stacks of printed books from the earth to the sun.

Information Transmission

The world's technological capacity to receive information through one-way broadcast networks was 432 exabytes of (optimally compressed) information in 1986, 715 (optimally compressed) exabytes in 1993, 1.2 (optimally compressed) zettabytes in 2000, and 1.9 zettabytes in 2007 (this is the information equivalent of 174 newspapers per person per day). The world's effective capacity to exchange information through two-way telecommunication networks was 281 petabytes of (optimally compressed) information in 1986, 471 petabytes in 1993, 2.2 (optimally compressed) exabytes in 2000, and 65 (optimally compressed) exabytes in 2007 (this is the information equivalent of 6 newspapers per person per day). In the 1990s, the spread of the Internet caused a sudden leap in access to and ability to share information in businesses and homes globally. Technology was developing so quickly that a computer costing $3000 in 1997 would cost $2000 two years later and $1000 the following year.

Computation

The world's technological capacity to compute information with humanly guided general-purpose computers grew from 3.0×10^8 MIPS in 1986, to 4.4×10^9 MIPS in 1993, 2.9×10^{11} MIPS in 2000 to 6.4×10^{12} MIPS in 2007. A article in the recognized Journal Trends in Ecology and Evolution reports that by now digital technology "has vastly exceeded the cognitive capacity of any single human being and has done so a decade earlier than predicted. In terms of capacity, there are two measures of importance: the number of operations a system can perform and the amount of information that can be stored. The number of synaptic operations per second in a human brain has been estimated to lie between 10^{15} and 10^{17}. While this number is impressive, even in 2007 humanity's general-purpose computers were capable of performing well over 10^{18} instructions per second. Estimates suggest that the storage capacity of an individual human brain is about 10^{12} bytes. On a per capita basis, this is matched by current digital storage (5×10^{21} bytes per 7.2×10^{9} people)".

Relation to Economics

Eventually, Information and Communication Technology—computers, computerized machinery, fiber optics, communication satellites, Internet, and other ICT tools—became a significant part of the economy. Microcomputers were developed and many businesses and industries were greatly changed by ICT.

Nicholas Negroponte captured the essence of these changes in his 1995 book, *Being Digital*. His book discusses similarities and differences between products made of atoms and products made of bits. In essence, a copy of a product made of bits can be made cheaply and quickly, and shipped across the country or internationally quickly and at very low cost.

The Information Age has affected the workforce in several ways. It has created a situation in which workers who perform tasks which are easily automated are being forced to find work which involves tasks that are not easily automated. Workers are also being forced to compete in a global job market. Lastly, workers are being replaced by computers that can do their jobs faster and more effectively. This poses problems for workers in industrial societies, which are still to be solved. However, solutions that involve lowering the working time are usually highly resisted.

Jobs traditionally associated with the middle class (assembly line workers, data processors, foremen and supervisors) are beginning to disappear, either through outsourcing or automation. Individuals who lose their jobs must either move up, joining a group of "mind workers" (engineers, doctors, attorneys, teachers, scientists, professors, executives, journalists, consultants), or settle for low-skill, low-wage service jobs.

The "mind workers" are able to compete successfully in the world market and receive high wages. Conversely, production workers and service workers in industrialized nations are unable to compete with workers in developing countries and either lose their jobs through outsourcing or are forced to accept wage cuts. In addition, the internet makes it possible for workers in developing countries to provide in-person services and compete directly with their counterparts in other nations.

This has had several major consequences, including increased opportunity in developing countries and the globalization of the workforce.

Workers in developing countries have a competitive advantage which translates into increased opportunities and higher wages. The full impact on the workforce in developing countries is complex and has downsides.

In the past, the economic fate of workers was tied to the fate of national economies. For example, workers in the United States were once well paid in comparison to the workers in other countries. With the advent of the Information Age and improvements in communication, this is no longer the case. Because workers are forced to compete in a global job market, wages are less dependent on the success or failure of individual economies.

Automation, Productivity, and Job Loss

The Information Age has affected the workforce in that automation and computerization have resulted in higher productivity coupled with net job loss. In the United States for example, from January 1972 to August 2010, the number of people employed in manufacturing jobs fell from 17,500,000 to 11,500,000 while manufacturing value rose 270%.

Although it initially appeared that job loss in the industrial sector might be partially offset by the rapid growth of jobs in the IT sector, the recession of March 2001 foreshadowed a sharp drop in the number of jobs in the IT sector. This pattern of decrease in jobs continued until 2003.

Data has shown that overall, technology creates more jobs than it destroys even in the short run.

Rise of Information-Intensive Industry

Industry is becoming more information-intensive and less labor and capital-intensive. This trend has important implications for the workforce; workers are becoming increasingly productive as the value of their labor decreases. However, there are also important implications for capitalism itself; not only is the value of labor decreased, the value of capital is also diminished. In the classical model, investments in human capital and financial capital are important predictors of the performance of a new venture. However, as demonstrated by Mark Zuckerberg and Facebook, it now seems possible for a group of relatively inexperienced people with limited capital to succeed on a large scale.

Innovations

The Information Age was enabled by technology developed in the Digital Revolution, which was itself enabled by building on the developments in the Technological Revolution.

Computers

Before the advent of electronics, mechanical computers, like the Analytical Engine in 1837, were designed to provide routine mathematical calculation and simple decision-making capabilities. Military needs during World War II drove development of the first electronic computers, based on vacuum tubes, including the Z3, the Atanasoff–Berry Computer, Colossus computer, and ENIAC.

The invention of the transistor in 1947 enabled the era of mainframe computers (1950s – 1970s), typified by the IBM 360. These large room-sized computers provided data calculation and manipulation that was much faster than humanly possible, but were expensive to buy and maintain, so were initially limited to a few scientific institutions, large corporations and government agencies. As transistor technology rapidly improved, the ratio of computing power to size increased dramatically, giving direct access to computers to ever smaller groups of people.

Along with electronic arcade machines and home video game consoles in the 1980s, the development of the personal computers like the Commodore PET and Apple II (both in 1977) gave individuals access to the computer. But data sharing between individual computers was either non-existent or largely manual, at first using punched cards and magnetic tape, and later floppy disks.

Data

The first developments for storing data were initially based on photographs, starting with microphotography in 1851 and then microform in the 1920s, with the ability to store documents on film, making them much more compact. In the 1970s, electronic paper allowed digital information appear as paper documents.

Early information theory and Hamming codes were developed about 1950, but awaited technical innovations in data transmission and storage to be put to full use. While cables transmitting digital data connected computer terminals and peripherals to mainframes were common, and special message-sharing systems leading to email were first developed in the 1960s, independent computer-to-computer networking began with ARPANET in 1969. This expanded to become the Internet (coined in 1974), and then the World Wide Web in 1989.

Public digital data transmission first utilized existing phone lines using dial-up, starting in the 1950s, and this was the mainstay of the Internet until broadband in the 2000s. The introduction of wireless networking in the 1990s combined with the proliferation of communications satellites in the 2000s allowed for public digital transmission without the need for cables. This technology led to digital television, GPS, and satellite radio through the 1990s and 2000s.

Computers continued to become smaller and more powerful, to the point where they could be carried. In the 1980s and 1990s, laptops first allowed computers to become portable, and PDAs allowed use while standing or walking. Pagers existing since the 1950s, were largely replaced by mobile phones beginning in the 1990s, giving mobile networking ability to a few at first. These have now become commonplace, and include digital cameras. Starting in the late 1990s, tablets and then smartphones combined and extended these abilities of computing, mobility, and information sharing.

Mass Media

The mass media is a diversified collection of media technologies that reach a large audience via mass communication. The technologies through which this communication takes place include a variety of outlets.

Broadcast media transmit information electronically, via such media as film, radio, recorded music, or television. Digital media comprises both Internet and mobile mass communication. Internet media comprise such services as email, social media sites, websites, and Internet-based radio and television. Many other mass media outlets have an additional presence on the web, by such means as linking to or running TV ads online, or distributing QR Codes in outdoor or print media to direct mobile users to a website. In this way, they can utilise the easy accessibility and outreach capabilities the Internet affords, as thereby easily broadcast information throughout many different regions of the world simultaneously and cost-efficiently. Outdoor media transmit information via such media as AR advertising; billboards; blimps; flying billboards (signs in tow of airplanes); placards or kiosks placed inside and outside of buses, commercial buildings, shops, sports stadiums, subway cars, or trains; signs; or skywriting. Print media transmit information via physical objects, such as books, comics, magazines, newspapers, or pamphlets. Event organizing and public speaking can also be considered forms of mass media.

The organizations that control these technologies, such as movie studios, publishing companies, and radio and television stations, are also known as the mass media.

The mass media system is one of the ten function systems of modern societies.

Issues With Definition

In the late 20th century, mass media could be classified into eight mass media industries: books, the Internet, magazines, movies, newspapers, radio, recordings, and television. The explosion of digital communication technology in the late 20th and early 21st centuries made prominent the question: what forms of media should be classified as "mass media"? For example, it is controversial whether to include cell phones, computer games (such as MMORPGs), and video games in the definition. In the 2000s, a classification called the "seven mass media" became popular. In order of introduction, they are:

1. Print (books, pamphlets, newspapers, magazines, etc.) from the late 15th century

2. Recordings (gramophone records, magnetic tapes, cassettes, cartridges, CDs, and DVDs) from the late 19th century

3. Cinema from about 1900

4. Radio from about 1910

5. Television from about 1950

6. Internet from about 1990

7. Mobile phones from about 2000

Each mass medium has its own content types, creative artists, technicians, and business models. For example, the Internet includes blogs, podcasts, web sites, and various other technologies built atop the general distribution network. The sixth and seventh media, Internet and mobile phones, are often referred to collectively as digital media; and the fourth and fifth, radio and TV, as broadcast media. Some argue that video games have developed into a distinct mass form of media.

While a telephone is a two-way communication device, mass media communicates to a large group. In addition, the telephone has transformed into a cell phone which is equipped with Internet access. A question arises whether this makes cell phones a mass medium or simply a device used to access a mass medium (the Internet). There is currently a system by which marketers and advertisers are able to tap into satellites, and broadcast commercials and advertisements directly to cell phones, unsolicited by the phone's user. This transmission of mass advertising to millions of people is another form of mass communication.

Video games may also be evolving into a mass medium. Video games (for example massively multiplayer online role-playing games (MMORPGs, such as *RuneScape*) provide a common gaming experience to millions of users across the globe and convey the same messages and ideologies to all their users. Users sometimes share the experience with one another by playing online. Excluding the Internet however, it is questionable whether players of video games are sharing a common experience when they play the game individually. It is possible to discuss in great detail the events of a video game with a friend one has never played with, because the experience is identical to each. The question, then, is whether this is a form of mass communication.

Characteristics

Five characteristics of mass communication have been identified by sociologist John Thompson of Cambridge University:

- "[C]omprises both technical and institutional methods of production and distribution" - This is evident throughout the history of mass media, from print to the Internet, each suitable for commercial utility

- Involves the "commodification of symbolic forms" - as the production of materials relies on its ability to manufacture and sell large quantities of the work; jas radio stations rely on their time sold to advertisements, so too newspapers rely on their space for the same reasons

- "[S]eparate contexts between the production and reception of information"

- Its "reach to those 'far removed' in time and space, in comparison to the producers"

- "[I]nformation distribution" - a "one to many" form of communication, whereby products are mass-produced and disseminated to a great quantity of audiences

Mass vs. Mainstream and Alternative

The term "mass media" is sometimes erroneously used as a synonym for "mainstream media". Mainstream media are distinguished from alternative media by their content and point of view. Alternative media are also "mass media" outlets in the sense that they use technology capable of reaching many people, even if the audience is often smaller than the mainstream.

In common usage, the term "mass" denotes not that a given number of individuals receives the products, but rather that the products are available in principle to a plurality of recipients.

Mass vs. Local and Speciality

Mass media are distinguished from local media by the notion that whilst mass media aims to reach a very large market, such as the entire population of a country, local media broadcasts to a much smaller population and area, and generally focuses on regional news rather than global events. A third type of media, speciality media, provide for specific demographics, such as specialty channels on TV (sports channels, porn channels, etc.). These definitions are not set in stone, and it is possible for a media outlet to be promoted in status from a local media outlet to a global media outlet. Some local media, which take an interest in state or provincial news, can rise to prominence because of their investigative journalism, and to the local region's preference of updates in national politics rather than regional news. *The Guardian*, formerly known as the *Manchester Guardian*, is an example of one such media outlet; once a regional daily newspaper, *The Guardian* is currently a nationally respected paper.

Forms of Mass Media

Broadcast

A family listening to a crystal radio in the 1920s

The sequencing of content in a broadcast is called a schedule. With all technological endeavours a number of technical terms and slang have developed.

Radio and television programs are distributed over frequency bands that in the United States are highly regulated. Such regulation includes determination of the width of the bands, range, licensing, types of receivers and transmitters used, and acceptable content.

Cable television programs are often broadcast simultaneously with radio and television programs, but have a more limited audience. By coding signals and requiring a cable converter box at individual recipients' locations, cable also enables subscription-based channels and pay-per-view services.

A broadcasting organisation may broadcast several programs simultaneously, through several channels (frequencies), for example BBC One and Two. On the other hand, two or more organisations may share a channel and each use it during a fixed part of the day, such as the Cartoon Network/Adult Swim. Digital radio and digital television may also transmit multiplexed programming, with several channels compressed into one ensemble.

When broadcasting is done via the Internet the term webcasting is often used. In 2004, a new phenomenon occurred when a number of technologies combined to produce podcasting. Podcasting is an asynchronous broadcast/narrowcast medium. Adam Curry and his associates, the *Podshow*, are principal proponents of podcasting.

Film

The term 'film' encompasses motion pictures as individual projects, as well as the field in general. The name comes from the photographic film (also called filmstock), historically the primary medium for recording and displaying motion pictures. Many other terms exist: *motion pictures* (or just *pictures* and "picture"), *the silver screen, photoplays, the cinema, picture shows, flicks*, and commonly *movies*.

Films are produced by recording people and objects with cameras, or by creating them using animation techniques and/or special effects. Films comprise a series of individual frames, but when these images are shown in rapid succession, an illusion of motion is created. Flickering between frames is not seen because of an effect known as persistence of vision, whereby the eye retains a visual image for a fraction of a second after the source has been removed. Also of relevance is what causes the perception of motion: a psychological effect identified as beta movement.

Film is considered by many to be an important art form; films entertain, educate, enlighten, and inspire audiences. Any film can become a worldwide attraction, especially with the addition of dubbing or subtitles that translate the film message. Films are also artifacts created by specific cultures, which reflect those cultures, and, in turn, affect them.

Video Games

A video game is a computer-controlled game in which a video display, such as a monitor or television, is the primary feedback device. The term "computer game" also includes games which display only text (and which can, therefore, theoretically be played on a teletypewriter) or which use other methods, such as sound or vibration, as their primary feedback device, but there are very few new games in these categories. There always must also be some sort of input device, usually in the form of button/joystick combinations (on arcade games), a keyboard and mouse/trackball combination (computer games), a controller (console games), or a combination of any of the above. Also, more esoteric devices have been used for input, e.g., the player's motion. Usually there are rules and goals, but in more open-ended games the player may be free to do whatever they like within the confines of the virtual universe.

In common usage, an "arcade game" refers to a game designed to be played in an establishment in which patrons pay to play on a per-use basis. A "computer game" or "PC game" refers to a game that is played on a personal computer. A "Console game" refers to one that is played on a device specifically designed for the use of such, while interfacing with a standard television set. A "video game" (or "videogame") has evolved into a catchall phrase that encompasses the aforementioned along with any game made for any other device, including, but not limited to, advanced calculators, mobile phones, PDAs, etc.

Audio Recording and Reproduction

Sound recording and reproduction is the electrical or mechanical re-creation and/or amplification of sound, often as music. This involves the use of audio equipment such as microphones, recording devices, and loudspeakers. From early beginnings with the invention of the phonograph using purely mechanical techniques, the field has advanced with the invention of electrical recording, the mass production of the 78 record, the magnetic wire recorder followed by the tape recorder, the vinyl LP record. The invention of the compact cassette in the 1960s, followed by Sony's Walkman, gave a major boost to the mass distribution of music recordings, and the invention of digital recording and the compact disc in 1983 brought massive improvements in ruggedness and quality. The most recent developments have been in digital audio players.

An album is a collection of related audio recordings, released together to the public, usually commercially.

The term record album originated from the fact that 78 RPM Phonograph disc records were kept together in a book resembling a photo album. The first collection of records to be called an "album" was Tchaikovsky's *Nutcracker Suite*, release in April 1909 as a four-disc set by Odeon records. It retailed for 16 shillings—about £15 in modern currency.

A music video (also promo) is a short film or video that accompanies a complete piece of music, most commonly a song. Modern music videos were primarily made and used as a marketing device intended to promote the sale of music recordings. Although the origins of music videos go back much further, they came into their own in the 1980s, when Music Television's format was based on them. In the 1980s, the term "rock video" was often used to describe this form of entertainment, although the term has fallen into disuse.

Music videos can accommodate all styles of filmmaking, including animation, live action films, documentaries, and non-narrative, abstract film.

Internet

The Internet (also known simply as "the Net" or less precisely as "the Web") is a more interactive medium of mass media, and can be briefly described as "a network of networks". Specifically, it is the worldwide, publicly accessible network of interconnected computer networks that transmit data by packet switching using the standard Internet Protocol (IP). It consists of millions of smaller domestic, academic, business, and governmental networks, which together carry various information and services, such as email, online chat, file transfer, and the interlinked web pages and other documents of the World Wide Web.

Contrary to some common usage, the Internet and the World Wide Web are not synonymous: the Internet is the system of interconnected *computer networks*, linked by copper wires, fiber-optic cables, wireless connections etc.; the Web is the contents, or the interconnected *documents*, linked by hyperlinks and URLs. The World Wide Web is accessible through the Internet, along with many other services including e-mail, file sharing and others described below.

Toward the end of the 20th century, the advent of the World Wide Web marked the first era in which most individuals could have a means of exposure on a scale comparable to that of mass media. Anyone with a web site has the potential to address a global audience, although serving to high levels of web traffic is still relatively expensive. It is possible that the rise of peer-to-peer technologies may have begun the process of making the cost of bandwidth manageable. Although a vast amount of information, imagery, and commentary (i.e. "content") has been made available, it is often difficult to determine the authenticity and reliability of information contained in web pages (in many cases, self-published). The invention of the Internet has also allowed breaking news stories to reach around the globe within minutes. This rapid growth of instantaneous, decentralized communication is often deemed likely to change mass media and its relationship to society.

"Cross-media" means the idea of distributing the same message through different media channels. A similar idea is expressed in the news industry as "convergence". Many authors understand cross-media publishing to be the ability to publish in both print and on the web without manual conversion effort. An increasing number of wireless devices with mutually incompatible data and screen formats make it even more difficult to achieve the objective "create once, publish many".

The Internet is quickly becoming the center of mass media. Everything is becoming accessible via the internet. Rather than picking up a newspaper, or watching the 10 o'clock news, people can log onto the internet to get the news they want, when they want it. For example, many workers listen to the radio through the Internet while sitting at their desk.

Even the education system relies on the Internet. Teachers can contact the entire class by sending one e-mail. They may have web pages on which students can get another copy of the class outline or assignments. Some classes have class blogs in which students are required to post weekly, with students graded on their contributions.

Blogs (Web Logs)

Blogging, too, has become a pervasive form of media. A blog is a website, usually maintained by an individual, with regular entries of commentary, descriptions of events, or interactive media such as images or video. Entries are commonly displayed in reverse chronological order, with most recent posts shown on top. Many blogs provide commentary or news on a particular subject; others function as more personal online diaries. A typical blog combines text, images and other graphics, and links to other blogs, web pages, and related media. The ability for readers to leave comments in an interactive format is an important part of many blogs. Most blogs are primarily textual, although some focus on art (artlog), photographs (photoblog), sketchblog, videos (vlog), music (MP3 blog), audio (podcasting) are part of a wider network of social media. Microblogging is another type of blogging which consists of blogs with very short posts.

Rss Feeds

RSS is a format for syndicating news and the content of news-like sites, including major news sites like Wired, news-oriented community sites like Slashdot, and personal blogs. It is a family of Web feed formats used to publish frequently updated content such as blog entries, news headlines, and podcasts. An RSS document (which is called a "feed" or "web feed" or "channel") contains either a summary of content from an associated web site or the full text. RSS makes it possible for people to keep up with web sites in an automated manner that can be piped into special programs or filtered displays.

Podcast

A podcast is a series of digital-media files which are distributed over the Internet using syndication feeds for playback on portable media players and computers. The term podcast, like broadcast, can refer either to the series of content itself or to the method by which it is syndicated; the latter is also called podcasting. The host or author of a podcast is often called a podcaster.

Mobile

Mobile phones were introduced in Japan in 1979 but became a mass media only in 1998 when the first downloadable ringing tones were introduced in Finland. Soon most forms of media content were introduced on mobile phones, tablets and other portable devices, and today the total value of media consumed on mobile vastly exceeds that of internet content, and was worth over 31 billion dollars in 2007 (source Informa). The mobile media content includes over 8 billion dollars worth of mobile music (ringing tones, ringback tones, truetones, MP3 files, karaoke, music videos, music streaming services etc.); over 5 billion dollars worth of mobile gaming; and various news, entertainment and advertising services. In Japan mobile phone books are so popular that five of the ten best-selling printed books were originally released as mobile phone books.

Similar to the internet, mobile is also an interactive media, but has far wider reach, with 3.3 billion mobile phone users at the end of 2007 to 1.3 billion internet users (source ITU). Like email on the internet, the top application on mobile is also a personal messaging service, but SMS text messaging is used by over 2.4 billion people. Practically all internet services and applications exist or have similar cousins on mobile, from search to multiplayer games to virtual worlds to blogs. Mobile has several unique benefits which many mobile media pundits claim make mobile a more powerful media than either TV or the internet, starting with mobile being permanently carried and always connected. Mobile has the best audience accuracy and is the only mass media with a built-in payment channel available to every user without any credit cards or PayPal accounts or even an age limit. Mobile is often called the 7th Mass Medium and either the fourth screen (if counting cinema, TV and PC screens) or the third screen (counting only TV and PC).

Print Media

Magazine

A magazine is a periodical publication containing a variety of articles, generally financed by advertising and/or purchase by readers.

Magazines are typically published weekly, biweekly, monthly, bimonthly or quarterly, with a date on the cover that is in advance of the date it is actually published. They are often printed in color on coated paper, and are bound with a soft cover.

Magazines fall into two broad categories: consumer magazines and business magazines. In practice, magazines are a subset of periodicals, distinct from those periodicals produced by scientific, artistic, academic or special interest publishers which are subscription-only, more expensive, narrowly limited in circulation, and often have little or no advertising.

Magazines can be classified as:

- General interest magazines (e.g. *Frontline, India Today, The Week, The Sunday Times* etc.)

- Special interest magazines (women's, sports, business, scuba diving, etc.)

Newspaper

A newspaper is a publication containing news and information and advertising, usually printed on low-cost paper called newsprint. It may be general or special interest, most often published daily or weekly. The first printed newspaper was published in 1605, and the form has thrived even in the face of competition from technologies such as radio and television. Recent developments on the Internet are posing major threats to its business model, however. Paid circulation is declining in most countries, and advertising revenue, which makes up the bulk of a newspaper's income, is shifting from print to online; some commentators, nevertheless, point out that historically new media such as radio and television did not entirely supplant existing.

Outdoor Media

Outdoor media is a form of mass media which comprises billboards, signs, placards placed inside and outside of commercial buildings/objects like shops/buses, flying billboards (signs in tow of airplanes), blimps, skywriting, AR Advertising. Many commercial advertisers use this form of mass media when advertising in sports stadiums. Tobacco and alcohol manufacturers used billboards and other outdoor media extensively. However, in 1998, the Master Settlement Agreement between the US and the tobacco industries prohibited the billboard advertising of cigarettes. In a 1994 Chicago-based study, Diana Hackbarth and her colleagues revealed how tobacco- and alcohol-based billboards were concentrated in poor neighbourhoods. In other urban centers, alcohol and tobacco billboards were much more concentrated in African-American neighborhoods than in white neighborhoods.

Purposes

A panel in the Newseum in Washington, D.C., shows the September 12 headlines in America and around the world

Mass media encompasses much more than just news, although it is sometimes misunderstood in this way. It can be used for various purposes:

- Advocacy, both for business and social concerns. This can include advertising, marketing, propaganda, public relations, and political communication.

- Entertainment, traditionally through performances of acting, music, sports, and TV shows along with light reading; since the late 20th century also through video and computer games.

- Public service announcements and emergency alerts (that can be used as political device to communicate propaganda to the public).

Professions Involving Mass Media

Journalism

Journalism is the discipline of collecting, analyzing, verifying and presenting information regarding current events, trends, issues and people. Those who practice journalism are known as journalists.

News-oriented journalism is sometimes described as the "first rough draft of history" (attributed to Phil Graham), because journalists often record important events, producing news articles on short deadlines. While under pressure to be first with their stories, news media organizations usually edit and proofread their reports prior to publication, adhering to each organization's standards of accuracy, quality and style. Many news organizations claim proud traditions of holding government officials and institutions accountable to the public, while media critics have raised questions about holding the press itself accountable to the standards of professional journalism.

Public Relations

Public relations is the art and science of managing communication between an organization and its key publics to build, manage and sustain its positive image. Examples include:

- Corporations use marketing public relations to convey information about the products they manufacture or services they provide to potential customers to support their direct sales efforts. Typically, they support sales in the short and long term, establishing and burnishing the corporation's branding for a strong, ongoing market.

- Corporations also use public relations as a vehicle to reach legislators and other politicians, seeking favorable tax, regulatory, and other treatment, and they may use public relations to portray themselves as enlightened employers, in support of human-resources recruiting programs.

- Nonprofit organizations, including schools and universities, hospitals, and human and social service agencies, use public relations in support of awareness programs, fund-raising programs, staff recruiting, and to increase patronage of their services.

- Politicians use public relations to attract votes and raise money, and, when successful at the ballot box, to promote and defend their service in office, with an eye to the next election or, at career's end, to their legacy.

Publishing

Publishing is the industry concerned with the production of literature or information – the activity of making information available for public view. In some cases, authors may be their own publishers.

Traditionally, the term refers to the distribution of printed works such as books and newspapers. With the advent of digital information systems and the Internet, the scope of publishing has expanded to include websites, blogs, and the like.

As a business, publishing includes the development, marketing, production, and distribution of newspapers, magazines, books, literary works, musical works, software, other works dealing with information.

Publication is also important as a legal concept; (1) as the process of giving formal notice to the world of a significant intention, for example, to marry or enter bankruptcy, and; (2) as the essential precondition of being able to claim defamation; that is, the alleged libel must have been published.

Software Publishing

A software publisher is a publishing company in the software industry between the developer and the distributor. In some companies, two or all three of these roles may be combined (and indeed, may reside in a single person, especially in the case of shareware).

Software publishers often license software from developers with specific limitations, such as a time limit or geographical region. The terms of licensing vary enormously, and are typically secret.

Developers may use publishers to reach larger or foreign markets, or to avoid focussing on marketing. Or publishers may use developers to create software to meet a market need that the publisher has identified.

History

Early wooden printing press, depicted in 1520.

The history of mass media can be traced back to the days when dramas were performed in various ancient cultures. This was the first time when a form of media was "broadcast" to a wider audience. The first dated printed book known is the "Diamond Sutra", printed in China in 868 AD, although it is clear that books were printed earlier. Movable clay type was invented in 1041 in China. However, due to the slow spread of literacy to the masses in China, and the relatively high cost of paper there, the earliest printed mass-medium was probably European popular prints from about 1400. Although these were produced in huge numbers, very few early examples survive, and even most known to be printed before about 1600 have not survived. The term "mass media" was coined with the creation of print media, which is notable for being the first example of mass media, as we use the term today. This form of media started in Europe in the Middle Ages.

Johannes Gutenberg's invention of the printing press allowed the mass production of books to sweep the nation. He printed the first book, a Latin Bible, on a printing press with movable type in 1453. The invention of the printing press gave rise to some of the first forms of mass communication, by enabling the publication of books and newspapers on a scale much larger than was previously possible. The invention also transformed the way the world received printed materials, although books remained too expensive really to be called a mass-medium for at least a century after that. Newspapers developed from about 1612, with the first example in English in 1620; but they took until the 19th century to reach a mass-audience directly. The first high-circulation newspapers arose in London in the early 1800s, such as The Times, and were made possible by the invention of high-speed rotary steam printing presses, and railroads which allowed large-scale distribution over wide geographical areas. The increase in circulation, however, led to a decline in feedback and interactivity from the readership, making newspapers a more one-way medium.

The phrase "the media" began to be used in the 1920s. The notion of "mass media" was generally restricted to print media up until the post-Second World War, when radio, television and video were introduced. The audio-visual facilities became very popular, because they provided both information and entertainment, because the colour and sound engaged the viewers/listeners and because it was easier for the general public to passively watch TV or listen to the radio than to actively read. In recent times, the Internet become the latest and most popular mass medium. Information has become readily available through websites, and easily accessible through search engines. One can do many activities at the same time, such as playing games, listening to music, and social networking, irrespective of location. Whilst other forms of mass media are restricted in the type of information they can offer, the internet comprises a large percentage of the sum of human knowledge through such things as Google Books. Modern day mass media includes the internet, mobile phones, blogs, podcasts and RSS feeds.

During the 20th century, the growth of mass media was driven by technology, including that which allowed much duplication of material. Physical duplication technologies such as printing, record pressing and film duplication allowed the duplication of books, newspapers and movies at low prices to huge audiences. Radio and television allowed the electronic duplication of information for the first time. Mass media had the economics of linear replication: a single work could make money. An example of Riel and Neil's theory. proportional to the number of copies sold, and as volumes went up, unit costs went down, increasing profit margins further. Vast fortunes were to be made in mass media. In a democratic society, the media can serve the electorate about issues regarding government and corporate entities. Some consider the concentration of media owner-ship to be a threat to democracy.

Influence and Sociology

Limited-effects theory, originally tested in the 1940s and 1950s, considers that because people usually choose what media to interact with based on what they already believe, media exerts a negligible influence. Class-dominant theory argues that the media reflects and projects the view of a minority elite, which controls it. Culturalist theory, which was developed in the 1980s and 1990s, combines the other two theories and claims that people interact with media to create their own meanings out of the images and messages they receive. This theory states that audience members play an active, rather than passive role in relation to mass media.

In an article entitled *Mass Media Influence on Society*, rayuso argues that the media *in the US* is dominated by five major companies (Time Warner, VIACOM, Vivendi Universal, Walt Disney and News Corp) which own 95% of all mass media including theme parks, movie studios, television and radio broadcast networks and programing, video news, sports entertainment, telecommunica-tions, wireless phones, video games software, electronic media and music companies. Whilst his-torically, there was more diversity in companies, they have recently merged to form an elite which have the power to shape the opinion and beliefs of people. People buy after seeing thousands of advertisements by various companies in TV, newspapers or magazines, which are able to affect their purchasing decisions. The definition of what is acceptable by society is dictated by the media. This power can be used for good, for example encouraging children to play sport. However, it can also be used for bad, for example children being influenced by cigars smoked by film stars, their ex-posure to sex images, their exposure to images of violence and their exposure to junk food ads. The documentary Supersize Me describes how companies like McDonalds have been sued in the past, the plaintiffs claiming that it was the fault of their liminal and subliminal advertising that "forced" them to perchance the product. The Barbie and Ken dolls of the 1950s are sometimes cited as the main cause for the obsession in modern-day society for women to be skinny and men to be buff. After the attacks of 9/11, the media gave extensive coverage of the event and exposed Osama Bin Laden's guilt for the attack, information they were told by the authorities. This shaped the public opinion to support the war on terrorism, and later, the war on Iraq. A main concern is that due to this immense power of the mass media (being able to drive the public opinion), media receiving inaccurate information could cause the public opinion to support the wrong cause.

In his book The Commercialization of American Culture, Matthew P. McAllister says that "a well-developed media system, informing and teaching its citizens, helps democracy move toward its ideal state."

In 1997, J. R. Finnegan Jr. and K. Viswanath identified 3 main effects or functions of mass media:

1. The Knowledge Gap: The mass media influences knowledge gaps due to factors including "the extent to which the content is appealing, the degree to which information channels are accessible and desirable, and the amount of social conflict and diversity there is in a community".

2. Agenda Setting: People are influence in how they think about issues due to the selective nature of what media choose for public consumption. After publicly disclosing that he had

prostate cancer prior to the 2000 New York senatorial election, Rudolph Giuliani, the mayor of New York City (aided by the media) sparked a huge priority elevation of the cancer in people's consciousness. This was because news media began to report on the risks of prostate cancer, which in turn prompted a greater public awareness about the disease and the need for screening. This ability for the media to be able to change how the public thinks and behaves has occurred on other occasions. In mid-1970s when Betty Ford and Happy Rockefeller, wives of the then-President and then-Vice President respectively, were both diagnosed with breast cancer. J. J. Davis states that "when risks are highlighted in the media, particularly in great detail, the extent of agenda setting is likely to be based on the degree to which a public sense of outrage and threat is provoked". When wanting to set an agenda, framing can be invaluably useful to a mass media organisation. Framing involves "taking a leadership role in the organisation of public discourse about an issue". The media is influenced by the desire for balance in coverage, and the resulting pressures can come from groups with particular political action and advocacy positions. Finnegan and Viswanath say, "groups, institutions, and advocates compete to identify problems, to move them onto the public agenda, and to define the issues symbolically" (1997, p. 324).

3. Cultivation of Perceptions: The extent to which media exposure shapes audience perceptions over time is known as cultivation. Television is a common experience, especially in places like the United States, to the point where it can be described as a "homogenising agent" (S. W. Littlejohn). However, instead of being merely a result of the TV, the effect is often based on socioeconomic factors. Having a prolonged exposure to TV or movie violence might affect a viewer to the extent where they actively think community violence is a problem, or alternatively find it justifiable. The resulting belief is likely to be different depending of where people live however.

Since the 1950s, when cinema, radio and TV began to be the primary or the only source of information for a larger and larger percentage of the population, these media began to be considered as central instruments of mass control. Up to the point that it emerged the idea that when a country has reached a high level of industrialization, the country itself "belongs to the person who controls communications."

Early minstrel shows lampooned the assumed stupidity of black people. Detail from cover of *The Celebrated Negro Melodies, as Sung by the Virginia Minstrels*, 1843

Mass media play a significant role in shaping public perceptions on a variety of important issues, both through the information that is dispensed through them, and through the interpretations they place upon this information. They also play a large role in shaping modern culture, by selecting and portraying a particular set of beliefs, values, and traditions (an entire way of life), as reality. That is, by portraying a certain interpretation of reality, they shape reality to be more in line with that interpretation. Mass media also play a crucial role in the spread of civil unrest activities such as anti-government demonstrations, riots, and general strikes. That is, the use of radio and television receivers has made the unrest influence among cities not only by the geographic location of cities, but also by proximity within the mass media distribution networks.

A magazine feature from *Beauty Parade* from March 1952 stereotyping women drivers. It features Bettie Page as the model.

American political cartoon titled *The Usual Irish Way of Doing Things*, depicting a drunken Irishman lighting a powder keg and swinging a bottle. Published in *Harper's Weekly*, 1871.

Racism and Stereotyping

Mass media sources, through theories like framing and agenda-setting, can affect the scope of a story as particular facts and information are highlighted (Media influence). This can directly correlate with how individuals may perceive certain groups of people, as the only media coverage a person receives can be very limited and may not reflect the whole story or situation; stories are often covered to reflect a particular perspective to target a specific demographic.

Example

According to Stephen Balkaran, an Instructor of Political Science and African American Studies at Central Connecticut State University, mass media has played a large role in the way white Americans perceive African-Americans. The media focus on African-American in the contexts of crime, drug use, gang violence, and other forms of anti-social behavior has resulted in a distorted and harmful public perception of African-Americans. African-Americans have been subjected to oppression and discrimination for the past few hundred years. According to Stephen Balkaran in his article Mass Media and Racism, "The media has played a key role in perpetuating the effects of this historical oppression and in contributing to African-Americans' continuing status as second-class citizens". This has resulted in an uncertainty among white Americans as to what the genuine nature of African-Americans really is. Despite the resulting racial divide, the fact that these people are undeniably American has "raised doubts about the white man's value system". This means that there is a somewhat "troubling suspicion" among some Americans that their white America is tainted by the black influence. Mass media as well as propaganda tend to reinforce or introduce stereotypes to the general public.

Ethical Issues and Criticism

Lack of local or specific topical focus is a common criticism of mass media. A mass news media outlet is often forced to cover national and international news due to it having to cater for and be relevant for a wide demographic. As such, it has to skip over many interesting or important local stories because they simply do not interest the large majority of their viewers. An example given by the website WiseGeek is that "the residents of a community might view their fight against development as critical, but the story would only attract the attention of the mass media if the fight became controversial or if precedents of some form were set".

The term "mass" suggests that the recipients of media products constitute a vast sea of passive, undifferentiated individuals. This is an image associated with some earlier critiques of "mass culture" and mass society which generally assumed that the development of mass communication has had a largely negative impact on modern social life, creating a kind of bland and homogeneous culture which entertains individuals without challenging them. However, interactive digital media have also been seen to challenge the read-only paradigm of earlier broadcast media.

Whilst some refer to the mass media as "opiate of the masses", others argue that is a vital aspect of human societies. By understanding mass media, one is then able to analyse and find a deeper understanding of one's population and culture. This valuable and powerful ability is one reason why the field of media studies is popular. As WiseGeek says, "watching, reading, and interacting with a nation's mass media can provide clues into how people think, especially if a diverse assortment of mass media sources are perused".

Since the 1950s, in the countries that have reached a high level of industrialization, the mass media of cinema, radio and TV have a key role in political power.

Contemporary research demonstrates an increasing level of concentration of media ownership, with many media industries already highly concentrated and dominated by a very small number of firms.

Future

In 2002, Arnold Kling wrote that "the newspaper business is going to die within the next twenty years. Newspaper publishing will continue, but only as a philanthropic venture." Jim Pinkerton said in 2006 of the future of mass media, "Every country with ambitions on the international stage will soon have its own state-supported media."

Leo Laporte, founder of the TWiT network of podcasts, says that "there will always be a need for storytellers, people who dig up facts and explain them".

Digital Electronics

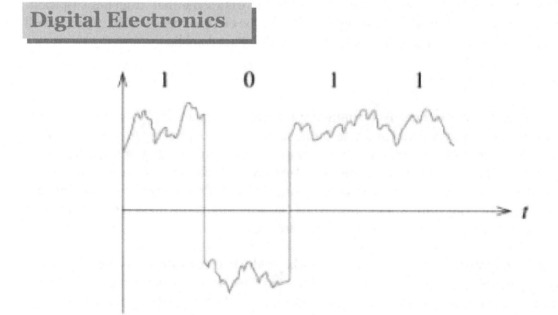

A digital signal has two or more distinguishable waveforms, in this example, high voltage and low voltages, each of which can be mapped onto a digit.

Digital electronics or digital (electronic) circuits are electronics that handle digital signals – discrete bands of analog levels – rather than by continuous ranges (as used in analog electronics). All levels within a band of values represent the same numeric value. Because of this discretization, relatively small changes to the analog signal levels due to manufacturing tolerance, signal attenuation or parasitic noise do not leave the discrete envelope, and as a result are ignored by signal state sensing circuitry.

An industrial digital controller

In most cases, the number of these states is two, and they are represented by two voltage bands: one near a reference value (typically termed as "ground" or zero volts), and the other a value near the supply voltage. These correspond to the "false" ("0") and "true" ("1") values of the Boolean domain respectively, named after its inventor, George Boole, yielding binary code.

Digital techniques are useful because it is easier to get an electronic device to switch into one of a number of known states than to accurately reproduce a continuous range of values.

Digital electronic circuits are usually made from large assemblies of logic gates, simple electronic representations of Boolean logic functions.

History

The binary number system was refined by Gottfried Wilhelm Leibniz (published in 1705) and he also established that by using the binary system, the principles of arithmetic and logic could be combined. Digital logic as we know it was the brain-child of George Boole, in the mid 19th century. Boole died young, but his ideas lived on. In an 1886 letter, Charles Sanders Peirce described how logical operations could be carried out by electrical switching circuits. Eventually, vacuum tubes replaced relays for logic operations. Lee De Forest's modification, in 1907, of the Fleming valve can be used as an AND logic gate. Ludwig Wittgenstein introduced a version of the 16-row truth table as proposition 5.101 of *Tractatus Logico-Philosophicus* (1921). Walther Bothe, inventor of the coincidence circuit, got part of the 1954 Nobel Prize in physics, for the first modern electronic AND gate in 1924.

Mechanical analog computers started appearing in the first century and were later used in the medieval era for astronomical calculations. In World War II, mechanical analog computers were used for specialized military applications such as calculating torpedo aiming. During this time the first electronic digital computers were developed. Originally they were the size of a large room, consuming as much power as several hundred modern personal computers (PCs).

The Z3 was an electromechanical computer designed by Konrad Zuse, finished in 1941. It was the world's first working programmable, fully automatic digital computer. Its operation was facilitated by the invention of the vacuum tube in 1904 by John Ambrose Fleming.

Purely electronic circuit elements soon replaced their mechanical and electromechanical equivalents, at the same time that digital calculation replaced analog. The bipolar junction transistor was invented in 1947. From 1955 onwards transistors replaced vacuum tubes in computer designs, giving rise to the "second generation" of computers.

Compared to vacuum tubes, transistors have many advantages: they are smaller, and require less power than vacuum tubes, so give off less heat. Silicon junction transistors were much more reliable than vacuum tubes and had longer, indefinite, service life. Transistorized computers could contain tens of thousands of binary logic circuits in a relatively compact space.

At the University of Manchester, a team under the leadership of Tom Kilburn designed and built a machine using the newly developed transistors instead of valves. Their first transistorised computer and the first in the world, was operational by 1953, and a second version was completed there in April 1955.

While working at Texas Instruments, Jack Kilby recorded his initial ideas concerning the integrated circuit in July 1958, successfully demonstrating the first working integrated example on 12 September 1958. This new technique allowed for quick, low-cost fabrication of complex circuits by having a set of electronic circuits on one small plate ("chip") of semiconductor material, normally silicon.

In the early days of simple integrated circuits, the technology's large scale limited each chip to only a few transistors, and the low degree of integration meant the design process was relatively simple. Manufacturing yields were also quite low by today's standards. As the technology progressed, millions, then billions of transistors could be placed on one chip, and good designs required thorough planning, giving rise to new design methods.

Properties

An advantage of digital circuits when compared to analog circuits is that signals represented digitally can be transmitted without degradation due to noise. For example, a continuous audio signal transmitted as a sequence of 1s and 0s, can be reconstructed without error, provided the noise picked up in transmission is not enough to prevent identification of the 1s and 0s. An hour of music can be stored on a compact disc using about 6 billion binary digits.

In a digital system, a more precise representation of a signal can be obtained by using more binary digits to represent it. While this requires more digital circuits to process the signals, each digit is handled by the same kind of hardware, resulting in an easily scalable system. In an analog system, additional resolution requires fundamental improvements in the linearity and noise characteristics of each step of the signal chain.

Computer-controlled digital systems can be controlled by software, allowing new functions to be added without changing hardware. Often this can be done outside of the factory by updating the product's software. So, the product's design errors can be corrected after the product is in a customer's hands.

Information storage can be easier in digital systems than in analog ones. The noise-immunity of digital systems permits data to be stored and retrieved without degradation. In an analog system, noise from aging and wear degrade the information stored. In a digital system, as long as the total noise is below a certain level, the information can be recovered perfectly.

Even when more significant noise is present, the use of redundancy permits the recovery of the original data provided too many errors do not occur.

In some cases, digital circuits use more energy than analog circuits to accomplish the same tasks, thus producing more heat which increases the complexity of the circuits such as the inclusion of heat sinks. In portable or battery-powered systems this can limit use of digital systems.

For example, battery-powered cellular telephones often use a low-power analog front-end to amplify and tune in the radio signals from the base station. However, a base station has grid power and can use power-hungry, but very flexible software radios. Such base stations can be easily reprogrammed to process the signals used in new cellular standards.

Digital circuits are sometimes more expensive, especially in small quantities.

Most useful digital systems must translate from continuous analog signals to discrete digital signals. This causes quantization errors. Quantization error can be reduced if the system stores enough digital data to represent the signal to the desired degree of fidelity. The Nyquist-Shannon sampling theorem provides an important guideline as to how much digital data is needed to accurately portray a given analog signal.

In some systems, if a single piece of digital data is lost or misinterpreted, the meaning of large blocks of related data can completely change. Because of the cliff effect, it can be difficult for users to tell if a particular system is right on the edge of failure, or if it can tolerate much more noise before failing.

Digital fragility can be reduced by designing a digital system for robustness. For example, a parity bit or other error management method can be inserted into the signal path. These schemes help the system detect errors, and then either correct the errors, or at least ask for a new copy of the data. In a state-machine, the state transition logic can be designed to catch unused states and trigger a reset sequence or other error recovery routine.

Digital memory and transmission systems can use techniques such as error detection and correction to use additional data to correct any errors in transmission and storage.

On the other hand, some techniques used in digital systems make those systems more vulnerable to single-bit errors. These techniques are acceptable when the underlying bits are reliable enough that such errors are highly unlikely.

A single-bit error in audio data stored directly as linear pulse code modulation (such as on a CD-ROM) causes, at worst, a single click. Instead, many people use audio compression to save storage space and download time, even though a single-bit error may corrupt the entire song.

Construction

A binary clock, hand-wired on breadboards

A digital circuit is typically constructed from small electronic circuits called logic gates that can be used to create combinational logic. Each logic gate is designed to perform a function of boolean logic when acting on logic signals. A logic gate is generally created from one or more electrically controlled switches, usually transistors but thermionic valves have seen historic use. The output of a logic gate can, in turn, control or feed into more logic gates.

Integrated circuits consist of multiple transistors on one silicon chip, and are the least expensive way to make large number of interconnected logic gates. Integrated circuits are usually designed by engineers using electronic design automation software to perform some type of function.

Integrated circuits are usually interconnected on a printed circuit board which is a board which holds electrical components, and connects them together with copper traces.

Design

Each logic symbol is represented by a different shape. The actual set of shapes was introduced in 1984 under IEEE/ANSI standard 91-1984. "The logic symbol given under this standard are being increasingly used now and have even started appearing in the literature published by manufacturers of digital integrated circuits."

Another form of digital circuit is constructed from lookup tables, (many sold as "programmable logic devices", though other kinds of PLDs exist). Lookup tables can perform the same functions as machines based on logic gates, but can be easily reprogrammed without changing the wiring. This means that a designer can often repair design errors without changing the arrangement of wires. Therefore, in small volume products, programmable logic devices are often the preferred solution. They are usually designed by engineers using electronic design automation software.

When the volumes are medium to large, and the logic can be slow, or involves complex algorithms or sequences, often a small microcontroller is programmed to make an embedded system. These are usually programmed by software engineers.

When only one digital circuit is needed, and its design is totally customized, as for a factory production line controller, the conventional solution is a programmable logic controller, or PLC. These are usually programmed by electricians, using ladder logic.

Structure of Digital Systems

Engineers use many methods to minimize logic functions, in order to reduce the circuit's complexity. When the complexity is less, the circuit also has fewer errors and less electronics, and is therefore less expensive.

The most widely used simplification is a minimization algorithm like the Espresso heuristic logic minimizer within a CAD system, although historically, binary decision diagrams, an automated Quine–McCluskey algorithm, truth tables, Karnaugh maps, and Boolean algebra have been used.

Representation

Representations are crucial to an engineer's design of digital circuits. Some analysis methods only work with particular representations.

The classical way to represent a digital circuit is with an equivalent set of logic gates. Another way, often with the least electronics, is to construct an equivalent system of electronic switches (usually transistors). One of the easiest ways is to simply have a memory containing a truth table. The inputs are fed into the address of the memory, and the data outputs of the memory become the outputs.

For automated analysis, these representations have digital file formats that can be processed by computer programs. Most digital engineers are very careful to select computer programs ("tools") with compatible file formats.

Combinational vs. Sequential

To choose representations, engineers consider types of digital systems. Most digital systems divide into "combinational systems" and "sequential systems." A combinational system always presents the same output when given the same inputs. It is basically a representation of a set of logic functions, as already discussed.

A sequential system is a combinational system with some of the outputs fed back as inputs. This makes the digital machine perform a "sequence" of operations. The simplest sequential system is probably a flip flop, a mechanism that represents a binary digit or "bit".

Sequential systems are often designed as state machines. In this way, engineers can design a system's gross behavior, and even test it in a simulation, without considering all the details of the logic functions.

Sequential systems divide into two further subcategories. "Synchronous" sequential systems change state all at once, when a "clock" signal changes state. "Asynchronous" sequential systems propagate changes whenever inputs change. Synchronous sequential systems are made of well-characterized asynchronous circuits such as flip-flops, that change only when the clock changes, and which have carefully designed timing margins.

Synchronous Systems

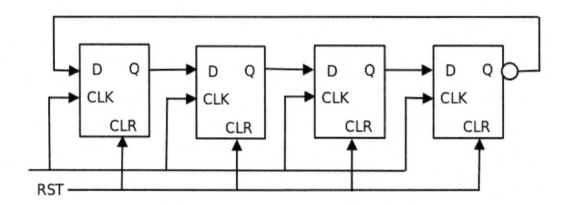

A 4-bit ring counter using D-type flip flops is an example of synchronous logic. Each device is connected to the clock signal, and update together.

The usual way to implement a synchronous sequential state machine is to divide it into a piece of combinational logic and a set of flip flops called a "state register." Each time a clock signal ticks, the state register captures the feedback generated from the previous state of the combinational logic, and feeds it back as an unchanging input to the combinational part of the state machine. The fastest rate of the clock is set by the most time-consuming logic calculation in the combinational logic.

The state register is just a representation of a binary number. If the states in the state machine are numbered (easy to arrange), the logic function is some combinational logic that produces the number of the next state.

Asynchronous Systems

As of 2014, almost all digital machines are synchronous designs because it is easier to create and verify a synchronous design. However, asynchronous logic is thought can be superior because its speed is not constrained by an arbitrary clock; instead, it runs at the maximum speed of its logic gates. Building an asynchronous system using faster parts makes the circuit faster.

Many systems need circuits that allow external unsynchronized signals to enter synchronous logic circuits. These are inherently asynchronous in their design and must be analyzed as such. Examples of widely used asynchronous circuits include synchronizer flip-flops, switch debouncers and arbiters.

Asynchronous logic components can be hard to design because all possible states, in all possible timings must be considered. The usual method is to construct a table of the minimum and maximum time that each such state can exist, and then adjust the circuit to minimize the number of such states. Then the designer must force the circuit to periodically wait for all of its parts to enter a compatible state (this is called "self-resynchronization"). Without such careful design, it is easy to accidentally produce asynchronous logic that is "unstable," that is, real electronics will have unpredictable results because of the cumulative delays caused by small variations in the values of the electronic components.

Register Transfer Systems

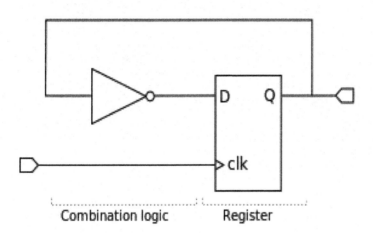

Example of a simple circuit with a toggling output. The inverter forms the combinational logic in this circuit, and the register holds the state.

Many digital systems are data flow machines. These are usually designed using synchronous register transfer logic, using hardware description languages such as VHDL or Verilog.

In register transfer logic, binary numbers are stored in groups of flip flops called registers. The outputs of each register are a bundle of wires called a "bus" that carries that number to other calculations. A calculation is simply a piece of combinational logic. Each calculation also has an output bus, and these may be connected to the inputs of several registers. Sometimes a register will have a multiplexer on its input, so that it can store a number from any one of several buses. Alternatively, the outputs of several items may be connected to a bus through buffers that can turn off the output of all of the devices except one. A sequential state machine controls when each register accepts new data from its input.

Asynchronous register-transfer systems (such as computers) have a general solution. In the 1980s, some researchers discovered that almost all synchronous register-transfer machines could be converted to asynchronous designs by using first-in-first-out synchronization logic. In this scheme, the digital machine is characterized as a set of data flows. In each step of the flow, an asynchronous "synchronization circuit" determines when the outputs of that step are valid, and presents a signal that says, "grab the data" to the stages that use that stage's inputs. It turns out that just a few relatively simple synchronization circuits are needed.

Computer Design

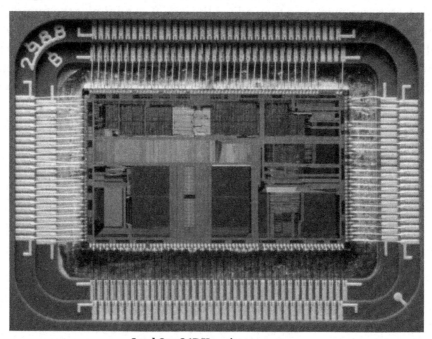

Intel 80486DX2 microprocessor

The most general-purpose register-transfer logic machine is a computer. This is basically an automatic binary abacus. The control unit of a computer is usually designed as a microprogram run by a microsequencer. A microprogram is much like a player-piano roll. Each table entry or "word" of the microprogram commands the state of every bit that controls the computer. The sequencer then counts, and the count addresses the memory or combinational logic machine that contains the microprogram. The bits from the microprogram control the arithmetic logic unit, memory and other parts of the computer, including the microsequencer itself.A "specialized computer" is usually a conventional computer with special-purpose control logic or microprogram.

In this way, the complex task of designing the controls of a computer is reduced to a simpler task of programming a collection of much simpler logic machines.

Almost all computers are synchronous. However, true asynchronous computers have also been designed. One example is the Aspida DLX core. Another was offered by ARM Holdings. Speed advantages have not materialized, because modern computer designs already run at the speed of their slowest componment, usually memory. These do use somewhat less power because a clock distribution network is not needed. An unexpected advantage is that asynchronous computers do not produce spectrally-pure radio noise, so they are used in some mobile-phone base-station controllers. They may be more secure in cryptographic applications because their electrical and radio emissions can be more difficult to decode.

Computer Architecture

Computer architecture is a specialized engineering activity that tries to arrange the registers, calculation logic, buses and other parts of the computer in the best way for some purpose. Computer architects have applied large amounts of ingenuity to computer design to reduce the cost and increase the speed and immunity to programming errors of computers. An increasingly common goal is to reduce the power used in a battery-powered computer system, such as a cell-phone. Many computer architects serve an extended apprenticeship as microprogrammers.

Design Issues in Digital Circuits

Digital circuits are made from analog components. The design must assure that the analog nature of the components doesn't dominate the desired digital behavior. Digital systems must manage noise and timing margins, parasitic inductances and capacitances, and filter power connections.

Bad designs have intermittent problems such as "glitches", vanishingly fast pulses that may trigger some logic but not others, "runt pulses" that do not reach valid "threshold" voltages, or unexpected ("undecoded") combinations of logic states.

Additionally, where clocked digital systems interface to analog systems or systems that are driven from a different clock, the digital system can be subject to metastability where a change to the input violates the set-up time for a digital input latch. This situation will self-resolve, but will take a random time, and while it persists can result in invalid signals being propagated within the digital system for a short time.

Since digital circuits are made from analog components, digital circuits calculate more slowly than low-precision analog circuits that use a similar amount of space and power. However, the digital circuit will calculate more repeatably, because of its high noise immunity. On the other hand, in the high-precision domain (for example, where 14 or more bits of precision are needed), analog circuits require much more power and area than digital equivalents.

Automated Design Tools

To save costly engineering effort, much of the effort of designing large logic machines has been automated. The computer programs are called "electronic design automation tools" or just "EDA."

Simple truth table-style descriptions of logic are often optimized with EDA that automatically produces reduced systems of logic gates or smaller lookup tables that still produce the desired outputs. The most common example of this kind of software is the Espresso heuristic logic minimizer.

Most practical algorithms for optimizing large logic systems use algebraic manipulations or binary decision diagrams, and there are promising experiments with genetic algorithms and annealing optimizations.

To automate costly engineering processes, some EDA can take state tables that describe state machines and automatically produce a truth table or a function table for the combinational logic of a state machine. The state table is a piece of text that lists each state, together with the conditions controlling the transitions between them and the belonging output signals.

It is common for the function tables of such computer-generated state-machines to be optimized with logic-minimization software such as Minilog.

Often, real logic systems are designed as a series of sub-projects, which are combined using a "tool flow." The tool flow is usually a "script," a simplified computer language that can invoke the software design tools in the right order.

Tool flows for large logic systems such as microprocessors can be thousands of commands long, and combine the work of hundreds of engineers.

Writing and debugging tool flows is an established engineering specialty in companies that produce digital designs. The tool flow usually terminates in a detailed computer file or set of files that describe how to physically construct the logic. Often it consists of instructions to draw the transistors and wires on an integrated circuit or a printed circuit board.

Parts of tool flows are "debugged" by verifying the outputs of simulated logic against expected inputs. The test tools take computer files with sets of inputs and outputs, and highlight discrepancies between the simulated behavior and the expected behavior.

Once the input data is believed correct, the design itself must still be verified for correctness. Some tool flows verify designs by first producing a design, and then scanning the design to produce compatible input data for the tool flow. If the scanned data matches the input data, then the tool flow has probably not introduced errors.

The functional verification data are usually called "test vectors." The functional test vectors may be preserved and used in the factory to test that newly constructed logic works correctly. However, functional test patterns don't discover common fabrication faults. Production tests are often designed by software tools called "test pattern generators". These generate test vectors by examining the structure of the logic and systematically generating tests for particular faults. This way the fault coverage can closely approach 100%, provided the design is properly made testable.

Once a design exists, and is verified and testable, it often needs to be processed to be manufacturable as well. Modern integrated circuits have features smaller than the wavelength of the light used to expose the photoresist. Manufacturability software adds interference patterns to the exposure masks to eliminate open-circuits, and enhance the masks' contrast.

Design for Testability

There are several reasons for testing a logic circuit. When the circuit is first developed, it is necessary to verify that the design circuit meets the required functional and timing specifications. When multiple copies of a correctly designed circuit are being manufactured, it is essential to test each copy to ensure that the manufacturing process has not introduced any flaws.

A large logic machine (say, with more than a hundred logical variables) can have an astronomical number of possible states. Obviously, in the factory, testing every state is impractical if testing each state takes a microsecond, and there are more states than the number of microseconds since the universe began. Unfortunately, this ridiculous-sounding case is typical.

Fortunately, large logic machines are almost always designed as assemblies of smaller logic machines. To save time, the smaller sub-machines are isolated by permanently installed "design for test" circuitry, and are tested independently.

One common test scheme known as "scan design" moves test bits serially (one after another) from external test equipment through one or more serial shift registers known as "scan chains". Serial scans have only one or two wires to carry the data, and minimize the physical size and expense of the infrequently used test logic.

After all the test data bits are in place, the design is reconfigured to be in "normal mode" and one or more clock pulses are applied, to test for faults (e.g. stuck-at low or stuck-at high) and capture the test result into flip-flops and/or latches in the scan shift register(s). Finally, the result of the test is shifted out to the block boundary and compared against the predicted "good machine" result.

In a board-test environment, serial to parallel testing has been formalized with a standard called "JTAG" (named after the "Joint Test Action Group" that proposed it).

Another common testing scheme provides a test mode that forces some part of the logic machine to enter a "test cycle." The test cycle usually exercises large independent parts of the machine.

Trade-offs

Several numbers determine the practicality of a system of digital logic: cost, reliability, fanout and speed. Engineers explored numerous electronic devices to get an ideal combination of these traits.

Cost

The cost of a logic gate is crucial, primarily because very many gates are needed to build a computer or other advanced digital system and because the more gates can be used, the more capable and/ or fast the machine can be. Since the majority of a digital computer is simply an interconnected network of logic gates, the overall cost of building a computer correlates strongly with the price per logic gate. In the 1930s, the earliest digital logic systems were constructed from telephone relays because these were inexpensive and relatively reliable. After that, engineers always used the cheapest available electronic switches that could still fulfill the requirements.

The earliest integrated circuits were a happy accident. They were constructed not to save money, but to save weight, and permit the Apollo Guidance Computer to control an inertial guidance system for a spacecraft. The first integrated circuit logic gates cost nearly $50 (in 1960 dollars, when an engineer earned $10,000/year). To everyone's surprise, by the time the circuits were mass-produced, they had become the least-expensive method of constructing digital logic. Improvements in this technology have driven all subsequent improvements in cost.

With the rise of integrated circuits, reducing the absolute number of chips used represented another way to save costs. The goal of a designer is not just to make the simplest circuit, but to keep the component count down. Sometimes this results in more complicated designs with respect to the underlying digital logic but nevertheless reduces the number of components, board size, and even power consumption. A major motive for reducing component count on printed circuit boards is to reduce the manufacturing defect rate and increase reliability, as every soldered connection is a potentially bad one, so the defect and failure rates tend to increase along with the total number of component pins.

For example, in some logic families, NAND gates are the simplest digital gate to build. All other logical operations can be implemented by NAND gates. If a circuit already required a single NAND gate, and a single chip normally carried four NAND gates, then the remaining gates could be used to implement other logical operations like logical and. This could eliminate the need for a separate chip containing those different types of gates.

Reliability

The "reliability" of a logic gate describes its mean time between failure (MTBF). Digital machines often have millions of logic gates. Also, most digital machines are "optimized" to reduce their cost. The result is that often, the failure of a single logic gate will cause a digital machine to stop working. It is possible to design machines to be more reliable by using redundant logic which will not malfunction as a result of the failure of any single gate (or even any two, three, or four gates), but this necessarily entails using more components, which raises the financial cost and also usually increases the weight of the machine and may increase the power it consumes.

Digital machines first became useful when the MTBF for a switch got above a few hundred hours. Even so, many of these machines had complex, well-rehearsed repair procedures, and would be nonfunctional for hours because a tube burned-out, or a moth got stuck in a relay. Modern transistorized integrated circuit logic gates have MTBFs greater than 82 billion hours (8.2×10^{10}) hours, and need them because they have so many logic gates.

Fanout

Fanout describes how many logic inputs can be controlled by a single logic output without exceeding the electrical current ratings of the gate outputs. The minimum practical fanout is about five. Modern electronic logic gates using CMOS transistors for switches have fanouts near fifty, and can sometimes go much higher.

Speed

The "switching speed" describes how many times per second an inverter (an electronic representation of a "logical not" function) can change from true to false and back. Faster logic can accomplish more operations in less time. Digital logic first became useful when switching speeds got above fifty hertz, because that was faster than a team of humans operating mechanical calculators. Modern electronic digital logic routinely switches at five gigahertz (5×10^9 hertz), and some laboratory systems switch at more than a terahertz (1×10^{12} hertz).

Logic Families

Design started with relays. Relay logic was relatively inexpensive and reliable, but slow. Occasionally a mechanical failure would occur. Fanouts were typically about ten, limited by the resistance of the coils and arcing on the contacts from high voltages.

Later, vacuum tubes were used. These were very fast, but generated heat, and were unreliable because the filaments would burn out. Fanouts were typically five to seven, limited by the heating from the tubes' current. In the 1950s, special "computer tubes" were developed with filaments that omitted volatile elements like silicon. These ran for hundreds of thousands of hours.

The first semiconductor logic family was resistor–transistor logic. This was a thousand times more reliable than tubes, ran cooler, and used less power, but had a very low fan-in of three. Diode–transistor logic improved the fanout up to about seven, and reduced the power. Some DTL designs used two power-supplies with alternating layers of NPN and PNP transistors to increase the fanout.

Transistor–transistor logic (TTL) was a great improvement over these. In early devices, fanout improved to ten, and later variations reliably achieved twenty. TTL was also fast, with some variations achieving switching times as low as twenty nanoseconds. TTL is still used in some designs.

Emitter coupled logic is very fast but uses a lot of power. It was extensively used for high-performance computers made up of many medium-scale components (such as the Illiac IV).

By far, the most common digital integrated circuits built today use CMOS logic, which is fast, offers high circuit density and low-power per gate. This is used even in large, fast computers, such as the IBM System z.

Recent Developments

In 2009, researchers discovered that memristors can implement a boolean state storage (similar to a flip flop, implication and logical inversion), providing a complete logic family with very small amounts of space and power, using familiar CMOS semiconductor processes.

The discovery of superconductivity has enabled the development of rapid single flux quantum (RSFQ) circuit technology, which uses Josephson junctions instead of transistors. Most recently, attempts are being made to construct purely optical computing systems capable of processing digital information using nonlinear optical elements.

Information Society

An information society is a society where the creation, distribution, use, integration and manipulation of information is a significant economic, political, and cultural activity. Its main driver are digital information and communication technologies, which have resulted in an information explosion and are profoundly changing all aspects of social organization, including the economy, education, health, warfare, government and democracy. The People who have the means to partake in this form of society are sometimes called digital citizens. This is one of many dozen labels that have been identified to suggest that humans are entering a new phase of society.

The markers of this rapid change may be technological, economic, occupational, spatial, cultural, or some combination of all of these. Information society is seen as the successor to industrial society. Closely related concepts are the post-industrial society (Daniel Bell), post-fordism, post-modern society, knowledge society, telematic society, Information Revolution, liquid modernity, and network society (Manuel Castells).

Definition

There is currently no universally accepted concept of what exactly can be termed information society and what shall rather not so be termed. Most theoreticians agree that a transformation can be seen that started somewhere between the 1970s and today and is changing the way societies work fundamentally. Information technology goes beyond the internet, and there are discussions about how big the influence of specific media or specific modes of production really is. Kasiwulaya and Gomo (Makerere University) allude that information societies are those that have intensified their use of IT for economic, social, cultural and political transformation.

In 2005, governments reaffirmed their dedication to the foundations of the Information Society in the Tunis Commitment and outlined the basis for implementation and follow-up in the Tunis Agenda for the Information Society. In particular, the Tunis Agenda addresses the issues of financing of ICTs for development and Internet governance that could not be resolved in the first phase.

Some people, such as Antonio Negri, characterize the information society as one in which people do immaterial labour. By this, they appear to refer to the production of knowledge or cultural artifacts. One problem with this model is that it ignores the material and essentially industrial basis of the society. However it does point to a problem for workers, namely how many creative people does this society need to function? For example, it may be that you only need a few star performers, rather than a plethora of non-celebrities, as the work of those performers can be easily distributed, forcing all secondary players to the bottom of the market. It *is* now common for publishers to promote only their best selling authors and to try to avoid the rest—even if they still sell steadily. Films are becoming more and more judged, in terms of distribution, by their first weekend's performance, in many cases cutting out opportunity for word-of-mouth development.

Considering that metaphors and technologies of information move forward in a reciprocal relationship, we can describe some societies (especially the Japanese society) as an information society because we think of it as such as letters.

The Growth of Information in Society

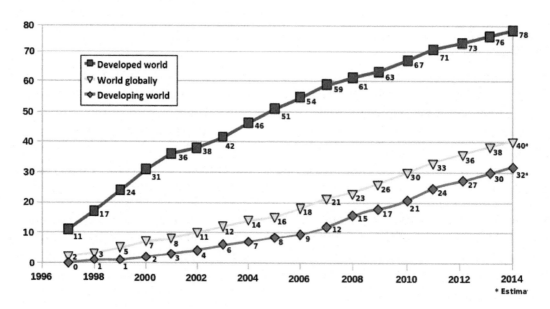

Significant Topics of Digital Media and Communication   43

Internet Users Per 100 Inhabitants

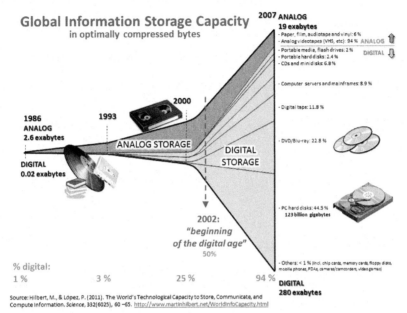

The amount of data stored globally has increased greatly since the 1980s, and by 2007, 94% of it was stored digitally.
Source

The growth of technologically mediated information has been quantified in different ways, including society's technological capacity to store information, to communicate information, and to compute information. It is estimated that, the world's technological capacity to store information grew from 2.6 (optimally compressed) exabytes in 1986, which is the informational equivalent to less than one 730-MB CD-ROM per person in 1986 (539 MB per person), to 295 (optimally compressed) exabytes in 2007. This is the informational equivalent of 60 CD-ROM per person in 2007 and represents a sustained annual growth rate of some 25%. The world's combined technological capacity to receive information through one-way broadcast networks was the informational equivalent of 174 newspapers per person per day in 2007.

The world's combined effective capacity to exchange information through two-way telecommunication networks was 281 petabytes of (optimally compressed) information in 1986, 471 petabytes in 1993, 2.2 (optimally compressed) exabytes in 2000, and 65 (optimally compressed) exabytes in 2007, which is the informational equivalent of 6 newspapers per person per day in 2007. The world's technological capacity to compute information with humanly guided general-purpose computers grew from 3.0×10^8 MIPS in 1986, to 6.4×10^{12} MIPS in 2007, experiencing the fastest growth rate of over 60% per year during the last two decades.

James R. Beniger describes the necessity of information in modern society in the following way: "The need for sharply increased control that resulted from the industrialization of material processes through application of inanimate sources of energy probably accounts for the rapid development of automatic feedback technology in the early industrial period (1740-1830)" (p. 174) "Even with enhanced feedback control, industry could not have developed without the enhanced means to process matter and energy, not only as inputs of the raw materials of production but also as outputs distributed to final consumption."(p. 175)

Development of the Information Society Model

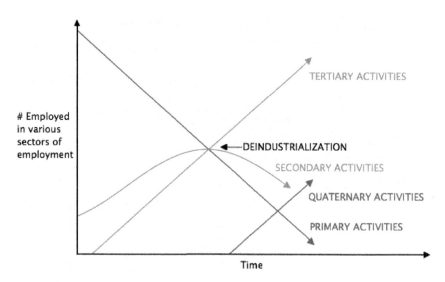

Colin Clark's sector model of an economy undergoing technological change. In later stages, the Quaternary sector of the economy grows.

One of the first people to develop the concept of the information society was the economist Fritz Machlup. In 1933, Fritz Machlup began studying the effect of patents on research. His work culminated in the study *The production and distribution of knowledge in the United States* in 1962. This book was widely regarded and was eventually translated into Russian and Japanese. The Jap-anese have also studied the information society.

The issue of technologies and their role in contemporary society have been discussed in the scientific literature using a range of labels and concepts. Ideas of a knowledge or information economy, post-industrial society, postmodern society, network society, the information revolution, informational capitalism, network capitalism, and the like, have been debated over the last several decades.

Fritz Machlup (1962) introduced the concept of the knowledge industry. He distinguished five sectors of the knowledge sector: education, research and development, mass media, information technologies, information services. Based on this categorization he calculated that in 1959 29% per cent of the GNP in the USA had been produced in knowledge industries.

Economic Transition

Peter Drucker has argued that there is a transition from an economy based on material goods to one based on knowledge. Marc Porat distinguishes a primary (information goods and services that are directly used in the production, distribution or processing of information) and a secondary sector (information services produced for internal consumption by government and non-information firms) of the information economy.

Porat uses the total value added by the primary and secondary information sector to the GNP as an indicator for the information economy. The OECD has employed Porat's definition for calculating the share of the information economy in the total economy (e.g. OECD 1981, 1986). Based on such indicators, the information society has been defined as a society where more than half of the GNP is produced and more than half of the employees are active in the information economy.

For Daniel Bell the number of employees producing services and information is an indicator for the informational character of a society. "A post-industrial society is based on services. (…) What counts is not raw muscle power, or energy, but information. (…) A post industrial society is one in which the majority of those employed are not involved in the production of tangible goods".

Alain Touraine already spoke in 1971 of the post-industrial society. "The passage to postindustrial society takes place when investment results in the production of symbolic goods that modify values, needs, representations, far more than in the production of material goods or even of 'services'. Industrial society had transformed the means of production: post-industrial society changes the ends of production, that is, culture. (…) The decisive point here is that in postindustrial society all of the economic system is the object of intervention of society upon itself. That is why we can call it the programmed society, because this phrase captures its capacity to create models of management, production, organization, distribution, and consumption, so that such a society appears, at all its functional levels, as the product of an action exercised by the society itself, and not as the outcome of natural laws or cultural specificities" (Touraine 1988: 104). In the programmed society also the area of cultural reproduction including aspects such as information, consumption, health, research, education would be industrialized. That modern society is increasing its capacity to act upon itself means for Touraine that society is reinvesting ever larger parts of production and so produces and transforms itself. This makes Touraine's concept substantially different from that of Daniel Bell who focused on the capacity to process and generate information for efficient society functioning.

Jean-François Lyotard has argued that "knowledge has become the principle [sic] force of production over the last few decades". Knowledge would be transformed into a commodity. Lyotard says that postindustrial society makes knowledge accessible to the layman because knowledge and information technologies would diffuse into society and break up Grand Narratives of centralized structures and groups. Lyotard denotes these changing circumstances as postmodern condition or postmodern society.

Similarly to Bell, Peter Otto and Philipp Sonntag (1985) say that an information society is a society where the majority of employees work in information jobs, i.e. they have to deal more with information, signals, symbols, and images than with energy and matter. Radovan Richta (1977) argues that society has been transformed into a scientific civilization based on services, education, and creative activities. This transformation would be the result of a scientific-technological transformation based on technological progress and the increasing importance of computer technology. Science and technology would become immediate forces of production (Aristovnik 2014: 55).

Nico Stehr (1994, 2002a, b) says that in the knowledge society a majority of jobs involves working with knowledge. "Contemporary society may be described as a knowledge society based on the extensive penetration of all its spheres of life and institutions by scientific and technological knowledge" (Stehr 2002b: 18). For Stehr, knowledge is a capacity for social action. Science would become an immediate productive force, knowledge would no longer be primarily embodied in machines, but already appropriated nature that represents knowledge would be rearranged according to certain designs and programs (Ibid.: 41-46). For Stehr, the economy of a knowledge society is largely driven not by material inputs, but by symbolic or knowledge-based inputs (Ibid.: 67), there would be a large number of professions that involve working with knowledge, and a declining number of jobs that demand low cognitive skills as well as in manufacturing (Stehr 2002a).

Also Alvin Toffler argues that knowledge is the central resource in the economy of the information society: "In a Third Wave economy, the central resource – a single word broadly encompassing data, information, images, symbols, culture, ideology, and values – is actionable knowledge" (Dyson/Gilder/Keyworth/Toffler 1994).

At the end of the twentieth century, the concept of the network society gained importance in information society theory. For Manuel Castells, network logic is besides information, pervasiveness, flexibility, and convergence a central feature of the information technology paradigm (2000a: 69ff). "One of the key features of informational society is the networking logic of its basic structure, which explains the use of the concept of 'network society'" (Castells 2000: 21). "As an historical trend, dominant functions and processes in the Information Age are increasingly organized around networks. Networks constitute the new social morphology of our societies, and the diffusion of networking logic substantially modifies the operation and outcomes in processes of production, experience, power, and culture" (Castells 2000: 500). For Castells the network society is the result of informationalism, a new technological paradigm.

Jan Van Dijk (2006) defines the network society as a "social formation with an infrastructure of social and media networks enabling its prime mode of organization at all levels (individual, group/ organizational and societal). Increasingly, these networks link all units or parts of this formation (individuals, groups and organizations)" (Van Dijk 2006: 20). For Van Dijk networks have become the nervous system of society, whereas Castells links the concept of the network society to capitalist transformation, Van Dijk sees it as the logical result of the increasing widening and thickening of networks in nature and society. Darin Barney uses the term for characterizing societies that exhibit two fundamental characteristics: "The first is the presence in those societies of sophisticated – almost exclusively digital – technologies of networked communication and information management/distribution, technologies which form the basic infrastructure mediating an increasing array of social, political and economic practices. (...) The second, arguably more intriguing, characteristic of network societies is the reproduction and institutionalization throughout (and between) those societies of networks as the basic form of human organization and relationship across a wide range of social, political and economic configurations and associations".

Critiques

The major critique of concepts such as information society, knowledge society, network society, postmodern society, postindustrial society, etc. that has mainly been voiced by critical scholars is that they create the impression that we have entered a completely new type of society. "If there is just more information then it is hard to understand why anyone should suggest that we have before us something radically new" (Webster 2002a: 259). Critics such as Frank Webster argue that these approaches stress discontinuity, as if contemporary society had nothing in common with society as it was 100 or 150 years ago. Such assumptions would have ideological character because they would fit with the view that we can do nothing about change and have to adopt to existing political realities (kasiwulaya 2002b: 267).

These critics argue that contemporary society first of all is still a capitalist society oriented towards accumulating economic, political, and cultural capital. They acknowledge that information society theories stress some important new qualities of society (notably globalization and informatization), but charge that they fail to show that these are attributes of overall capitalist structures. Critics such as Webster insist on the continuities that characterise change. In this way Webster distinguishes between different epochs of capitalism: laissez-faire capitalism of the 19th century, corporate capitalism in the 20th century, and informational capitalism for the 21st century (kasiwulaya 2006).

For describing contemporary society based on a dialectic of the old and the new, continuity and discontinuity, other critical scholars have suggested several terms like:

- transnational network capitalism, transnational informational capitalism (Christian Fuchs 2008, 2007): "Computer networks are the technological foundation that has allowed the emergence of global network capitalism, that is, regimes of accumulation, regulation, and discipline that are helping to increasingly base the accumulation of economic, political, and cultural capital on transnational network organizations that make use of cyberspace and other new technologies for global coordination and communication. [...] The need to find new strategies for executing corporate and political domination has resulted in a restructuration of capitalism that is characterized by the emergence of transnational, networked spaces in the economic, political, and cultural system and has been mediated by cyberspace as a tool of global coordination and communication. Economic, political, and cultural space have been restructured; they have become more fluid and dynamic, have enlarged their borders to a transnational scale, and handle the inclusion and exclusion of nodes in flexible ways. These networks are complex due to the high number of nodes (individuals, enterprises, teams, political actors, etc.) that can be involved and the high speed at which a high number of resources is produced and transported within them. But global network capitalism is based on structural inequalities; it is made up of segmented spaces in which central hubs (transnational corporations, certain political actors, regions, countries, Western lifestyles, and worldviews) centralize the production, control, and flows of economic, political, and cultural capital (property, power, definition capacities). This segmentation is an expression of the overall competitive character of contemporary society." (Fuchs 2008: 110+119).

- digital capitalism (Schiller 2000, cf. also Peter Glotz): "networks are directly generalizing the social and cultural range of the capitalist economy as never before" (Schiller 2000: xiv)

- virtual capitalism: the "combination of marketing and the new information technology will enable certain firms to obtain higher profit margins and larger market shares, and will thereby promote greater concentration and centralization of capital" (Dawson/John Bellamy Foster 1998: 63sq),

- high-tech capitalism or informatic capitalism (Fitzpatrick 2002) – to focus on the computer as a guiding technology that has transformed the productive forces of capitalism and has enabled a globalized economy.

Other scholars prefer to speak of information capitalism (Morris-Suzuki 1997) or informational capitalism (Manuel Castells 2000, Christian Fuchs 2005, Schmiede 2006a, b). Manuel Castells sees informationalism as a new technological paradigm (he speaks of a mode of development) characterized by "information generation, processing, and transmission" that have become "the fundamental sources of productivity and power" (Castells 2000: 21). The "most decisive historical factor accelerating, channelling and shaping the information technology paradigm, and inducing its associated social forms, was/is the process of capitalist restructuring undertaken since the 1980s, so that the new techno-economic system can be adequately characterized as informational capitalism" (Castells 2000: 18). Castells has added to theories of the information society the idea that in contemporary society dominant functions and processes are increasingly organized around networks that constitute the new social morphology of society (Castells 2000: 500). Nicholas Garnham is critical of Castells and argues that the latter's account is technologically determinist because Castells points out that his approach is based on a dialectic of technology and society in which technology embodies society and society uses technology (Castells 2000: 5sqq). But Castells also makes clear that the rise of a new "mode of development" is shaped by capitalist production, i.e. by society, which implies that technology isn't the only driving force of society.

Antonio Negri and Michael Hardt argue that contemporary society is an Empire that is characterized by a singular global logic of capitalist domination that is based on immaterial labour. With the concept of immaterial labour Negri and Hardt introduce ideas of information society discourse into their Marxist account of contemporary capitalism. Immaterial labour would be labour "that creates immaterial products, such as knowledge, information, communication, a relationship, or an emotional response" (Hardt/Negri 2005: 108; cf. also 2000: 280-303), or services, cultural products, knowledge (Hardt/Negri 2000: 290). There would be two forms: intellectual labour that produces ideas, symbols, codes, texts, linguistic figures, images, etc.; and affective labour that produces and manipulates affects such as a feeling of ease, well-being, satisfaction, excitement, passion, joy, sadness, etc. (Ibid.).

Overall, neo-Marxist accounts of the information society have in common that they stress that knowledge, information technologies, and computer networks have played a role in the restructuration and globalization of capitalism and the emergence of a flexible regime of accumulation (David Harvey 1989). They warn that new technologies are embedded into societal antagonisms that cause structural unemployment, rising poverty, social exclusion, the deregulation of the welfare state and of labour rights, the lowering of wages, welfare, etc.

Concepts such as knowledge society, information society, network society, informational capitalism, postindustrial society, transnational network capitalism, postmodern society, etc. show that there is a vivid discussion in contemporary sociology on the character of contemporary society and the role that technologies, information, communication, and co-operation play in it. Information society theory discusses the role of information and information technology in society, the question which key concepts shall be used for characterizing contemporary society, and how to define such concepts. It has become a specific branch of contemporary sociology.

Second and Third Nature

Information society is the means of getting information from one place to another (Wark, 1997, p. 22). As technology has advanced so too has the way people have adapted in sharing this information with each other.

"Second nature" refers a group of experiences that get made over by culture (Wark, 1997, p. 23). They then get remade into something else that can then take on a new meaning. As a society we transform this process so it becomes something natural to us, i.e. second nature. So, by following a particular pattern created by culture we are able to recognise how we use and move information in different ways. From sharing information via different time zones (such as talking online) to information ending up in a different location (sending a letter overseas) this has all become a habitual process that we as a society take for granted (Wark, 1997, p. 21).

However, through the process of sharing information vectors have enabled us to spread information even further. Through the use of these vectors information is able to move and then separate from the initial things that enabled them to move (Wark, 1997, p. 24). From here, something called "third nature" has developed. An extension of second nature, third nature is in control of second nature. It expands on what second nature is limited by. It has the ability to mould information in new and different ways. So, third nature is able to 'speed up, proliferate, divide, mutate, and beam in on us from else where (Wark, 1997, p.25). It aims to create a balance between the boundaries of space and time. This can be seen through the telegraph, it was the first successful technology that could send and receive information faster than a human being could move an object (Wark, 1997, p.26). As a result different vectors of people have the ability to not only shape culture but create new possibilities that will ultimately shape society.

Therefore, through the use of second nature and third nature society is able to use and explore new vectors of possibility where information can be moulded to create new forms of interaction (Wark, 1997, p.28).

Sociological Uses

In sociology, informational society refers to a post-modern type of society. Theoreticians like Ulrich Beck, Anthony Giddens and Manuel Castells argue that since the 1970s a transformation from industrial society to informational society has happened on a global scale.

As steam power was the technology standing behind industrial society, so information technology is seen as the catalyst for the changes in work organisation, societal structure and politics occurring in the late 20th century.

In the book *Future Shock*, Alvin Toffler used the phrase super-industrial society to describe this type of society. Other writers and thinkers have used terms like "post-industrial society" and "post-modern industrial society" with a similar meaning.

Related Terms

A number of terms in current use emphasize related but different aspects of the emerging global economic order. The Information Society intends to be the most encompassing in that an economy is a subset of a society. The Information Age is somewhat limiting, in that it refers to a 30-year period between the widespread use of computers and the knowledge economy, rather than an emerging economic order. The knowledge era is about the nature of the content, not the socioeconomic processes by which it will be traded. The computer revolution, and knowledge revolution refer to specific revolutionary transitions, rather than the end state towards which we are evolving. The

Information Revolution relates with the well known terms agricultural revolution and industrial revolution.

- The information economy and the knowledge economy emphasize the content or intellectual property that is being traded through an information market or knowledge market, respectively. Electronic commerce and electronic business emphasize the nature of transactions and running a business, respectively, using the Internet and World-Wide Web. The digital economy focuses on trading bits in cyberspace rather than atoms in physical space. The network economy stresses that businesses will work collectively in webs or as part of business ecosystems rather than as stand-alone units. Social networking refers to the process of collaboration on massive, global scales. The internet economy focuses on the nature of markets that are enabled by the Internet.

- Knowledge services and knowledge value put content into an economic context. Knowledge services integrates Knowledge management, within a Knowledge organization, that trades in a Knowledge market. In order for individuals to receive more knowledge, surveillance is used. This relates to the use of Drones as a tool in order to gather knowledge on other individuals. Although seemingly synonymous, each term conveys more than nuances or slightly different views of the same thing. Each term represents one attribute of the likely nature of economic activity in the emerging post-industrial society. Alternatively, the new economic order will incorporate all of the above plus other attributes that have not yet fully emerged.

- In connection with the development of the information society, appeared information pollution, evolving information ecology - associated with information hygiene.

Intellectual Property Considerations

One of the central paradoxes of the information society is that it makes information easily reproducible, leading to a variety of freedom/control problems relating to intellectual property. Essentially, business and capital, whose place becomes that of producing and selling information and knowledge, seems to require control over this new resource so that it can effectively be managed and sold as the basis of the information economy. However, such control can prove to be both technically and socially problematic. Technically because copy protection is often easily circumvented and socially *rejected* because the users and citizens of the information society can prove to be unwilling to accept such absolute commodification of the facts and information that compose their environment.

Responses to this concern range from the Digital Millennium Copyright Act in the United States (and similar legislation elsewhere) which make copy protection circumvention illegal, to the free software, open source and copyleft movements, which seek to encourage and dissemi-nate the "freedom" of various information products (traditionally both as in "gratis" or free of cost, and liberty, as in freedom to use, explore and share).

Caveat: Information society is often used by politicians meaning something like "we all do internet now"; the sociological term information society (or informational society) has some deeper implications about change of societal structure.

Cognitive-Cultural Economy

Cognitive-cultural economy or cognitive-cultural capitalism is represented by sectors such as high-technology industry, business and financial services, personal services, the media, the cultural industries. It is characterized by digital technologies combined with high levels of cognitive and cultural labor. The concept has been associated with 'post-Fordism', the 'knowledge economy', the 'new economy' and highly flexible labor markets.

As Fordist mass production began to wane after the mid to late 1970s in advanced capitalist countries, a more flexible system of productive activity began to take its place. The concept of cognitive-cultural capitalism has developed as a response to the insufficiency of the interpretations of this transition from a Fordist to a post-Fordist model of "flexible accumulation. Early empirical studies of this new system were published in the 1980s on the basis of case-study materials focused mainly on high-technology industrial districts in the United States and revived craft industries in the north-east and center of Italy (the so-called Third Italy). Over the following decades, considerable empirical and theoretical advances were made on the basis of studies of the new cultural economy (fashion, film, electronic games, publishing, etc.).

Levy and Murnane in *The New Division of Labor* highlight the replacement of standardized machinery in the American production system by digital technologies that not only act as a substitute for routine labor, but that also complement and enhance the intellectual and affective assets of the labor force. These technologies underpinned an enormous expansion of the technology-intensive, service, financial, craft, and cultural industries that became the heart of the cognitive-cultural economy.

Computer-Mediated Communication

Computer-mediated communication (CMC) is defined as any human communication that occurs through the use of two or more electronic devices. While the term has traditionally referred to those communications that occur via computer-mediated formats (e.g., instant messaging, email, chat rooms, online forums, social network services), it has also been applied to other forms of text-based interaction such as text messaging. Research on CMC focuses largely on the social effects of different computer-supported communication technologies. Many recent studies involve Internet-based social networking supported by social software.

Scope of the Field

Scholars from a variety of fields study phenomena that can be described under the umbrella term of computer mediated communication (CMC). For example, many take a sociopsychological approach to CMC by examining how humans use "computers" (or digital media) to manage interpersonal interaction, form impressions and form and maintain relationships. These studies have often focused on the differences between online and offline interactions, though contemporary research is moving towards the view that CMC should be studied as embedded in everyday life . Another branch of CMC research examines the use of paralinguistic features such as emoticons, pragmatic rules such as turn-taking and the sequential analysis and organization of talk, and the various sociolects, styles, registers or sets of terminology specific to these environments. The study of language in these contexts is typically based on text-based forms of CMC, and is sometimes referred to as "computer-mediated discourse analysis".

The way humans communicate in professional, social, and educational settings varies widely, depending upon not only the environment but also the method of communication in which the communication occurs, which in this case is through computers or other information and communication technologies (ICTs). The study of communication to achieve collaboration—common work products—is termed computer-supported collaboration and includes only some of the concerns of other forms of CMC research.

Popular forms of CMC include e-mail, video, audio or text chat (text conferencing including "instant messaging"), bulletin board systems, list-servs and MMOs. These settings are changing rapidly with the development of new technologies. Weblogs (blogs) have also become popular, and the exchange of RSS data has better enabled users to each "become their own publisher".

Characteristics

Communication occurring within a computer-mediated format has an effect on many different aspects of an interaction. Some of these that have received attention in the scholarly literature include impression formation, deception, group dynamics, disclosure reciprocity, disinhibition and especially relationship formation.

CMC is examined and compared to other communication media through a number of aspects thought to be universal to all forms of communication, including (but not limited to) synchronicity, persistence or "recordability", and anonymity. The association of these aspects with different forms of communication varies widely. For example, instant messaging is intrinsically synchronous but not persistent, since one loses all the content when one closes the dialog box unless one has a message log set up or has manually copy-pasted the conversation. E-mail and message boards, on the other hand, are low in synchronicity since response time varies, but high in persistence since messages sent and received are saved. Properties that separate CMC from other media also include transience, its multimodal nature, and its relative lack of governing codes of conduct. CMC is able to overcome physical and social limitations of other forms of communication and therefore allow the interaction of people who are not physically sharing the same space.

The medium in which people choose to communicate influences the extent to which people disclose personal information. CMC is marked with higher levels of self-disclosure in conversation as opposed to face-to-face interactions. Self disclosure is any verbal communication of personally relevant information, thought, and feeling which establishes and maintains interpersonal relationships. This is due in part to visual anonymity and the absence of nonverbal cues which reduce concern for losing positive face. According to Walther's (1996) hyperpersonal communication model, computer-mediated communication is valuable on providing a better communication and better first impressions. Moreover, Ramirez and Zhang (2007) indicate that computer-mediated communication allows more closeness and attraction between two individuals than a face-to-face communication.

Anonymity and in part privacy and security depends more on the context and particular program being used or web page being visited. However, most researchers in the field acknowledge the importance of considering the psychological and social implications of these factors alongside the technical "limitations".

Language Learning

CMC is widely discussed in language learning because CMC provides opportunities for language learners to practice their language. For example, Warschauer conducted several case studies on using email or discussion boards in different language classes. Warschauer claimed that information and communications technology "bridge the historic divide between speech ... and writing". Thus, considerable concern has arisen over the reading and writing research in L2 due to the booming of the Internet.

Benefits

The nature of CMC means that it is easy for individuals to engage in communication with others regardless of time or location. CMC allows for individuals to collaborate on projects that would otherwise be impossible due to such factors as geography. In addition, CMC can also be useful for allowing individuals who might be intimidated due to factors like character or disabilities to participate in communication. By allowing an individual to communicate in a location of their choosing, CMC call allow a person to engage in communication with minimal stress. Making an individual comfortable through CMC also plays a role in self-disclosure, which allows a communicative partner to open up more easily and be more expressive. When communicating through an electronic medium, individuals are less likely to engage in stereotyping and are less self-conscious about physical characteristics. The role that anonymity plays in online communication can also encourage some users to be less defensive and form relationships with others more rapidly.

References

- *Potter, W. James (2008). Arguing for a general framework for mass media scholarship. SAGE. p. 32. ISBN 978-1-4129-6471-5.*

- *Splichal, Slavko (2006). "In Pursuit of Socialized Press". In Berry, David & Theobald John. Radical mass media criticism: a cultural genealogy. Black Rose Books. p. 41. ISBN 978-1-55164-246-8.*

- *Ramey, Carl R. (2007). Mass media unleashed: how Washington policymakers shortchanged the American public. Rowman & Littlefield. pp. 1–2. ISBN 978-0-7425-5570-9.*

- *Galician, Mary-Lou (2004). Sex, love & romance in the mass media: analysis & criticism of unrealistic portrayals & their influence. Psychology Press. p. 69. ISBN 978-0-8058-4832-8.*

- *Newhagen, J.E. (1999). ""The role of feedback in assessing the news on mass media and the Internet"". In Kent, Allen. Encyclopedia of library and information science, Volume 65. CRC Press. p. 210. ISBN 978-0-8247-2065-0.*

- *Nerone, John (2006). "Approaches to Media History". In Valdivia, Angharad N. A companion to media studies. Wiley-Blackwell. p. 102. ISBN 978-1-4051-4174-1.*

- *Pace, Geoffrey L. (1997). "The Origins of Mass Media in the United States". In Wells, Allen & Hakenen, Ernest A. Mass media & society. Greenwood Publishing Group. p. 10. ISBN 978-1-56750-288-6.*

- Briggs, Asa & Burke, Peter (2010). *Social History of the Media: From Gutenberg to the Internet. Polity Press.* p. 1. ISBN 978-0-7456-4495-0.

- News Incorporated: Corporate Media Ownership And Its Threat To Democracy. Ed. Elliot D. Cohen. Prometheus Books, 2005. ISBN 1-59102-232-0

- *Null, Linda; Lobur, Julia (2006). The essentials of computer organization and architecture. Jones & Bartlett Publishers. p. 121. ISBN 0-7637-3769-0. We can build logic diagrams (which in turn lead to digital circuits) for any Boolean expression...*

- Paul Horowitz and Winfield Hill, *The Art of Electronics 2nd Ed.* Cambridge University Press, Cambridge, 1989 ISBN 0-521-37095-7 page 471

- Grinin, L. 2007. Periodization of History: A theoretic-mathematical analysis. In: *History & Mathematics.* Moscow: KomKniga/URSS. P.10-38. ISBN 978-5-484-01001-1.

- *Porter, Michael. "How Information Gives You Competitive Advantage". Harvard Business Review. Retrieved 9 September 2015.*

- Hilbert, M. (2015). Digital Technology and Social Change [Open Online Course at the University of California] (freely available). Retrieved from https://canvas.instructure.com/courses/949415

- "Individuals using the Internet 2005 to 2014", Key ICT indicators for developed and developing countries and the world (totals and penetration rates), International Telecommunication Union (ITU). Retrieved 25 May 2015.

- Hilbert, M. (2015). Digital Technology and Social Change [Open Online Course at the University of California] freely available at: https://www.youtube.com/watch?v=xR4sQ3f6tW8&list=PLtjBSCvWCU3rNm46D3R85efMohrzjuAIg

- *Clarke, Peter. "ARM Offers First Clockless Processor Core". eetimes.com. UBM Tech (Universal Business Media). Retrieved 5 September 2014.*

- Skovholt, K., Grønning, A. and Kankaanranta, A. (2014), The Communicative Functions of Emoticons in Workplace E-Mails: :-). Journal of Computer-Mediated Communication, 19: 780–797. doi:10.1111/jcc4.12063

- *Kluver, Randy. "Globalization, Informatization, and Intercultural Communication". United Nations Public Administration Network. Retrieved 18 April 2013.*

- Dan Braha. "Global Civil Unrest: Contagion, Self-Organization, and Prediction", PLoS ONE 7(10) (2012): e48596. doi:10.1371/journal.pone .0048596.

Modern Approaches to Digital Media

The field of media is ever evolving and digital media has transformed the media industry in the past decade. New techniques, methods and technologies are being regularly introduced. This chapter will discuss the various new techniques being used in content creation and also elaborate the technologies in new media. It will help students gain complete knowledge about this subject.

Content Creation

Content creation is the contribution of information to any media and most especially to digital media for an end-user/audience in specific contexts. Content is "something that is to be expressed through some medium, as speech, writing or any of various arts" for self-expression, distribution, marketing and/or publication. Typical forms of content creation include maintaining and updating web sites, blogging, photography, videography, online commentary, the maintenance of social media accounts, and editing and distribution of digital media. A Pew survey described content creation as the creation of "the material people contribute to the online world."

Content Creators

News Organizations

News organizations, especially the biggest and more international, such as *The New York Times, NPR,* and *CNN* and others, consistently create some of the most shared content on the Web. This is especially true for content related breaking news and topical events. In the words of a 2011 report from the Oxford School for the Study of Journalism and the Reuters Institute for the Study of Journalism, "Mainstream media is the lifeblood of topical social media conversations in the UK." While the rise of digital media has disrupted traditional news outlets, many have adapted, and have begun to produce content that is designed to function on the web and be shared by social media users. The social media site Twitter is a major distributor of breaking news in traditional formats, and many Twitter users are media professionals. The function and value of Twitter in the distribution of news is a frequent topic of discussion and research in journalism. User-generated content, social media blogging and citizen journalism have changed the nature of news content in recent years. The company Narrative Science is now using artificial intelligence to produce news articles and interpret data.

Colleges, Universities and Think Tanks

Academic institutions, such as colleges and universities, create content in the form of books, journal articles, white papers, and some forms of digital scholarship, such as blogs that are group edited by academics, class wikis, or video lectures that support a massive open online course (MOOC). Institutions may even make the raw data supporting their experiments or conclusions available on the Web through an open data initiative. Academic content may be gathered and made accessible to other academics or the public through publications, databases, libraries and digital libraries. Academic content may be closed source or open access (OA). Closed source content is only available to authorized users or subscribers. An important journal or a scholarly database may be closed source, available only to students and faculty through the institution's library. Open access articles are open to the public, with the publication and distribution costs shouldered by the institution publishing the content.

Companies

Corporate content includes advertising and public relations content, as well as other types of content produced for profit, including white papers and sponsored research. Advertising can even include auto-generated content, blocks of content generated by programs or bots for search engine optimization. Companies also create annual reports which count as content creation as it is part of their companies workings and a detailed review of their financial year, this gives the stakeholders of the company insight of the companies current and future prospects and direction.

Artists and Writers

Cultural works, like music, movies, literature and art, are forms of content. Traditionally published books and e-books are one type of cultural content, but there are many others, such as self-published books, digital art, fanfiction, and fan art. Independent artists, including authors and musicians, have found commercial success by making their work available on the Internet. These changes have revolutionized the publishing and music industries.

Government

Through digitization, sunshine laws, open records laws and data collection, governments may make whole classes of statistical, legal or regulatory information available on the Internet. National libraries and state archives turn historical documents, public records, and unique relics into online databases and exhibits. At times, this has raised significant privacy issues. For example, in 2012, *The Journal News*, a New York state paper, sparked outcry when it published an interactive map of gun owners' locations using legally obtained public records. Governments also create online or digital propaganda or misinformation to support law enforcement or national security goals. This can go as far as astroturfing, or using media to create a false impression of mainstream belief or opinion.

Governments can also use open content, like public records and open data in the service of public health, educational and scientific goals, such as crowdsourcing solutions to complex policy problems, or processing scientific data. In 2013, National Aeronautics and Space Administration (NASA) joined asteroid mining company Planetary Resources to crowdsource the hunt for near-earth objects, asteroids that could threaten the Earth. Describing NASA's crowdsourcing work in an interview, technology transfer executive David Locke spoke of the "untapped cognitive surplus that exists in the world" which could be used to help develop NASA technology. This is just one way crowdsourcing could be used to enhance public participation in government. In addition to making government more participatory, open records and open data have the potential to make government more transparent and less corrupt.

Users

With the introduction of Web 2.0 came the possibility of content consumers being more involved in the generation and sharing of content. Also with the coming of digital media and the ease of access at home, the amount of user generated content has increased as well as the age and class range. Eight percent of Internet users are very active in content creation and consumption. Worldwide, about one in four Internet users are significant content creators, and users in emerging markets lead the world in engagement. Research has also found that young adults of a higher socioeconomic background tend to create more content than those of a lower one. Sixty-nine percent of American and European internet users are "spectators," who consume—but don't create—online and digital media. The ratio of content creators to the amount of content they generate is sometimes referred to as the 1% rule, a rule of thumb that suggests that only 1% of a forum's users create nearly all of its content. Motivations for creating new content may include the desire to gain new knowledge, the possibility of publicity, or simple altruism, among other reasons. Users may also create new content to in order to help bring about social reforms. However, researchers caution that in order to be effective, context must be considered, a diverse array of people must be included, and all users must participate throughout the process.

According to a 2011 study, minorities create content in order to connect with niche communities online. African-American users have been found to create content as a means of self-expression that was not previously available. Media portrayals of minorities are sometimes inaccurate and stereotypical which in turn affects the general perception of these minorities. African-Americans respond to their portrayals digitally through the use of social media like, twitter and tumblr. More importantly, the creation of Black Twitter has allowed a community to be able to share their problems and ideas.

Teen Users

Younger users are having more access to content and content creating applications and publishing to different types of media, for example, Facebook, DeviantArt, or Tumblr. As of 2005, around 21 million teens used the internet. Among these 57%, or 12 million teens, are Content Creators. This creation and sharing was happening at a far higher level than with adults. With the advent of the internet, teens have had far more access to tools for sharing and creating. Technology is also becoming cheaper and easier to access as well, making content creation far easier for everyone, including teens. Some teens use this to seek fame through sites like Youtube, while others use it to connect to friends through social networking sites. Either way, these teens are becoming more than just observers, they are creators as well.

Issues

Quality

The rise of anonymous and user-generated content presents both opportunities and challenges to Web users. Blogging, self-publishing and other forms of content creation give more people access to larger audiences. But it can also perpetuate rumors and spread information that is not verifiable. It can make it more difficult to find quality content that meets users' information needs.

Metadata

Digital content is difficult to organize and categorize. Websites, forums and publishers all have different standards for metadata, or information about the content, such as its author and date of creation. The perpetuation of different standards of metadata can create problems of access and discoverability.

Intellectual Property

The ownership, origin, and right to share digital content can be difficult to establish. On one hand, user-generated content presents challenges to traditional content creators with regard to the expansion of unlicensed and unauthorized derivative works, piracy and plagiarism. On the other hand, the enforcement of copyright laws, such as the Digital Millennium Copyright Act in the U.S., also make it less likely that works will fall into the public domain.

Social Movements

The Egyptian Revolution of 2011

Content creation proved to serve as a useful form of protest on social media platforms. The Egyptian Revolution of 2011 was only one example of content creation being used to network protestors from all different parts of the world for the common cause of protesting the "authoritarian regimes in the Middle East and North Africa throughout 2011". The protests took place in multiple cities in Egypt such as Cairo and what started out as peaceful quickly escalated into conflict. Social media outlets allowed protestors to network with each other across multiple regions to raise awareness of the wide spread corruption in Egypt's government and unite in rebellion. Youth activists promoting the rebellion were able to formulate a Facebook group, "Progressive Youth of Tunisia".

New Media

New media most commonly refers to content available on-demand through the Internet, accessible on any digital device, usually containing interactive user feedback and creative participation. Common examples of new media include websites such as online newspapers, blogs, or wikis, video games, and social media. A defining characteristic of new media is dialogue. New Media transmit content through connection and conversation. It enables people around the world to share, comment on, and discuss a wide variety of topics. Unlike any of past technologies, New Media is grounded on an interactive community.

Most technologies described as "new media" are digital, often having characteristics of being manipulated, networkable, dense, compressible, and interactive. Some examples may be the Internet, websites, computer multimedia, video games, augmented reality, CD-ROMS, and DVDs. New media are often contrasted to "old media," such as television, radio, and print media, although scholars in communication and media studies have criticised rigid distinctions based on oldness and novelty. New media does not include television programs (only analog broadcast), feature films, magazines, books, or paper-based publications – unless they contain technologies that enable digital interactivity. Wikipedia, an online encyclopedia, is an example, combining Internet accessible digital text, images and video with web-links, creative participation of contributors, interactive feedback of users and formation of a participant community of editors and donors for the benefit of non-community readers. Facebook is an example of the social media model, in which most users are also participants. Wikitude is an example for augmented reality. It displays information about the users' surroundings in a mobile camera view, including image recognition, 3D modeling and location-based approach to augmented reality.

History

In the 1950s, connections between computing and radical art began to grow stronger. It was not until the 1980s that Alan Kay and his co-workers at Xerox PARC began to give the computability of a personal computer to the individual, rather than have a big organization be in charge of this. "In the late 1980s and early 1990s, however, we seem to witness a different kind of parallel relationship between social changes and computer design. Although causally unrelated, conceptually it makes sense that the Cold War and the design of the Web took place at exactly the same time."

Writers and philosophers such as Marshall McLuhan were instrumental in the development of media theory during this period. His now famous declaration in *Understanding Media: The Extensions of Man* (1964) that "the medium is the message" drew attention to the too often ignored influence media and technology themselves, rather than their "content," have on humans' experience of the world and on society broadly.

Until the 1980s media relied primarily upon print and analog broadcast models, such as those of television and radio. The last twenty-five years have seen the rapid transformation into media which are predicated upon the use of digital technologies, such as the Internet and video games. However, these examples are only a small representation of new media. The use of digital computers has transformed the remaining 'old' media, as suggested by the advent of digital television and online publications. Even traditional media forms such as the printing press have been transformed through the application of technologies such as image manipulation software like Adobe Photoshop and desktop publishing tools.

Andrew L. Shapiro (1999) argues that the "emergence of new, digital technologies signals a potentially radical shift of who is in control of information, experience and resources" (Shapiro cited in Croteau and Hoynes 2003: 322). W. Russell Neuman (1991) suggests that whilst the "new media" have technical capabilities to pull in one direction, economic and social forces pull back in the opposite direction. According to Neuman, "We are witnessing the evolution of a universal interconnected network of audio, video, and electronic text communications that will blur the distinction between interpersonal and mass communication and between public and private communication" (Neuman cited in Croteau and Hoynes 2003: 322). Neuman argues that new media will:

- Alter the meaning of geographic distance.

- Allow for a huge increase in the volume of communication.

- Provide the possibility of increasing the speed of communication.

- Provide opportunities for interactive communication.

- Allow forms of communication that were previously separate to overlap and interconnect.

Consequently, it has been the contention of scholars such as Douglas Kellner and James Bohman that new media, and particularly the Internet, provide the potential for a democratic postmodern public sphere, in which citizens can participate in well informed, non-hierarchical debate pertaining to their social structures. Contradicting these positive appraisals of the potential social impacts of new media are scholars such as Ed Herman and Robert McChesney who have suggested that the transition to new media has seen a handful of powerful transnational telecommunications corporations who achieve a level of global influence which was hitherto unimaginable.

Scholars, such as Lister et al. (2003), have highlighted both the positive and negative potential and actual implications of new media technologies, suggesting that some of the early work into new media studies was guilty of technological determinism – whereby the effects of media were determined by the technology themselves, rather than through tracing the complex social networks which governed the development, funding, implementation and future development of any technology.

Based on the argument that people have a limited amount of time to spend on the consumption of different media, Displacement theory argue that the viewership or readership of one particular outlet leads to the reduction in the amount of time spent by the individual on another. The introduction of New Media, such as the internet, therefore reduces the amount of time individuals would spend on existing "Old" Media, which could ultimately lead to the end of such traditional media.

Definition

Although there are several ways that New Media may be described, Lev Manovich, in an introduction to *The New Media Reader*, defines New Media by using eight propositions:

1. New Media versus Cyberculture – Cyberculture is the various social phenomena that are associated with the Internet and network communications (blogs, online multi-player gaming), whereas New Media is concerned more with cultural objects and paradigms (digital to analog television, iPhones).

2. New Media as Computer Technology Used as a Distribution Platform – New Media are the cultural objects which use digital computer technology for distribution and exhibition. e.g. (at least for now) Internet, Web sites, computer multimedia, Blu-ray disks etc. The problem with this is that the definition must be revised every few years. The term «new media» will not be «new» anymore, as most forms of culture will be distributed through computers.

3. New Media as Digital Data Controlled by Software – The language of New Media is based on the assumption that, in fact, all cultural objects that rely on digital representation and computer-based delivery do share a number of common qualities. New media is reduced to digital data that can be manipulated by software as any other data. Now media operations can create several versions of the same object. An example is an image stored as matrix data which can be manipulated and altered according to the additional algorithms implemented, such as color inversion, gray-scaling, sharpening, rasterizing, etc.

4. New Media as the Mix Between Existing Cultural Conventions and the Conventions of Software – New Media today can be understood as the mix between older cultural conventions for data representation, access, and manipulation and newer conventions of data representation, access, and manipulation. The "old" data are representations of visual reality and human experience, and the "new" data is numerical data. The computer is kept out of the key "creative" decisions, and is delegated to the position of a technician. e.g. In film, software is used in some areas of production, in others are created using computer animation.

5. New Media as the Aesthetics that Accompanies the Early Stage of Every New Modern Media and Communication Technology – While ideological tropes indeed seem to be reappearing rather regularly, many aesthetic strategies may reappear two or three times ... In order for this approach to be truly useful it would be insufficient to simply name the strategies and tropes and to record the moments of their appearance; instead, we would have to develop a much more comprehensive analysis which would correlate the history of technology with social, political, and economical histories or the modern period.

6. New Media as Faster Execution of Algorithms Previously Executed Manually or through Other Technologies – Computers are a huge speed-up of what were previously manual techniques. e.g. calculators. Dramatically speeding up the execution makes possible previously non-existent representational technique. This also makes possible of many new forms of media art such as interactive multimedia and video games. On one level, a modern digital computer is just a faster calculator, we should not ignore its other identity: that of a cybernetic control device.

7. New Media as the Encoding of Modernist Avant-Garde; New Media as Metamedia – Manovich declares that the 1920s are more relevant to New Media than any other time period. Metamedia coincides with postmodernism in that they both rework old work rather than create new work. New media avant-garde is about new ways of accessing and manipulating information (e.g. hypermedia, databases, search engines, etc.). Meta-media is an example of how quantity can change into quality as in new media technology and manipulation techniques can recode modernist aesthetics into a very different postmodern aesthetics.

8. New Media as Parallel Articulation of Similar Ideas in Post-WWII Art and Modern Computing – Post WWII Art or «combinatorics» involves creating images by systematically changing a single parameter. This leads to the creation of remarkably similar images and spatial structures. This illustrates that algorithms, this essential part of new media, do not depend on technology, but can be executed by humans.

Globalization

The rise of new media has increased communication between people all over the world and the Internet. It has allowed people to express themselves through blogs, websites, videos, pictures, and other user-generated media.

Flew (2002) stated that, "as a result of the evolution of new media technologies, globalization occurs." Globalization is generally stated as "more than expansion of activities beyond the boundaries of particular nation states". Globalization shortens the distance between people all over the world by the electronic communication (Carely 1992 in Flew 2002) and Cairncross (1998) expresses this great development as the "death of distance". New media "radically break the connection between physical place and social place, making physical location much less significant for our social relationships" (Croteau and Hoynes 2003: 311).

However, the changes in the new media environment create a series of tensions in the concept of "public sphere". According to Ingrid Volkmer, "public sphere" is defined as a process through which public communication becomes restructured and partly disembedded from national political and cultural institutions. This trend of the globalized public sphere is not only as a geographical expansion form a nation to worldwide, but also changes the relationship between the public, the media and state (Volkmer, 1999:123).

"Virtual communities" are being established online and transcend geographical boundaries, eliminating social restrictions. Howard Rheingold (2000) describes these globalised societies as self-defined networks, which resemble what we do in real life. "People in virtual communities use words on screens to exchange pleasantries and argue, engage in intellectual discourse, conduct commerce, make plans, brainstorm, gossip, feud, fall in love, create a little high art and a lot of idle talk" (Rheingold cited in Slevin 2000: 91). For Sherry Turkle "making the computer into a second self, finding a soul in the machine, can substitute for human relationships" (Holmes 2005: 184). New media has the ability to connect like-minded others worldwide.

While this perspective suggests that the technology drives – and therefore is a determining factor – in the process of globalization, arguments involving technological determinism are generally frowned upon by mainstream media studies. Instead academics focus on the multiplicity of processes by which technology is funded, researched and produced, forming a feedback loop when the technologies are used and often transformed by their users, which then feeds into the process of guiding their future development.

While commentators such as Castells espouse a "soft determinism" whereby they contend that "Technology does not determine society. Nor does society script the course of technological change, since many factors, including individual inventiveness and entrpreneurialism, intervene in the process of scientific discovery, technical innovation and social applications, so the final outcome depends on a complex pattern of interaction. Indeed the dilemma of technological determinism is probably a false problem, since technology is society and society cannot be understood without its technological tools." (Castells 1996:5) This, however, is still distinct from stating that societal changes are instigated by technological development, which recalls the theses of Marshall McLuhan.

Manovich and Castells have argued that whereas mass media "corresponded to the logic of industrial mass society, which values conformity over individuality," (Manovich 2001:41) new media follows the logic of the postindustrial or globalized society whereby "every citizen can construct her own custom lifestyle and select her ideology from a large number of choices. Rather than pushing the same objects to a mass audience, marketing now tries to target each individual separately." (Manovich 2001:42).

As Tool for Social Change

Social movement media has a rich and storied history that has changed at a rapid rate since New Media became widely used. The Zapatista Army of National Liberation of Chiapas, Mexico were the first major movement to make widely recognized and effective use of New Media for communiques and organizing in 1994. Since then, New Media has been used extensively by social movements to educate, organize, share cultural products of movements, communicate, coalition build, and more. The WTO Ministerial Conference of 1999 protest activity was another landmark in the use of New Media as a tool for social change. The WTO protests used media to organize the original action, communicate with and educate participants, and was used as an alter-native media source. The Indymedia movement also developed out of this action, and has been a great tool in the democratization of information, which is another widely discussed aspect of new media movement. Some scholars even view this democratization as an indication of the creation of a "radical, socio-technical paradigm to challenge the dominant, neoliberal and technologically determinist model of information and communication technologies." A less radical view along these same lines is that people are taking advantage of the Internet to produce a grassroots global-ization, one that is anti-neoliberal and centered on people rather than the flow of capital. Chanelle Adams, a feminist blogger for the Bi-Weekly webpaper The Media says that in her "commitment to anti-oppressive feminist work, it seems obligatory for her to stay in the know just to remain relevant to the struggle." In order for Adams and other feminists who work towards spreading their messages to the public, new media becomes crucial towards completing this task, allowing people to access a movement's information instantaneously. Of course, some are also skeptical of the role of New Media in Social Movements. Many scholars point out unequal access to new media as a hindrance to broad-based movements, sometimes even oppressing some within a movement. Others are skeptical about how democratic or useful it really is for social movements, even for those with access.

New Media has also found a use with less radical social movements such as the Free Hugs Cam-paign. Using websites, blogs, and online videos to demonstrate the effectiveness of the movement itself. Along with this example the use of high volume blogs has allowed numerous views and prac-tices to be more widespread and gain more public attention. Another example is the ongoing Free Tibet Campaign, which has been seen on numerous websites as well as having a slight tie-in with the band Gorillaz in their Gorillaz Bitez clip featuring the lead singer 2D sitting with protesters at a Free Tibet protest. Another social change seen coming from New Media is trends in fashion and the emergence of subcultures such as Text Speak, Cyberpunk, and various others.

Following trends in fashion and Text Speak, New Media also makes way for "trendy" social change. The Ice Bucket Challenge is a recent example of this. All in the name of raising money for ALS (the le-thal neurodegenerative disorder also known as Lou Gehrig's disease), participants are nominated by friends via Facebook, Twitter and ownmirror to dump a bucket of ice water on themselves, or donate to the ALS Foundation. This became a huge trend through Facebook's tagging tool, allowing nomi-nees to be tagged in the post. The videos appeared on more people's feeds, and the trend spread fast. This trend raised over 100 million dollars for the cause and increased donations by 3,500 percent.

National Security

New Media has also recently become of interest to the global espionage community as it is easily accessible electronically in database format and can therefore be quickly retrieved and reverse engineered by national governments. Particularly of interest to the espionage community are Facebook and Twitter, two sites where individuals freely divulge personal information that can then be sifted through and archived for the automatic creation of dossiers on both people of interest and the average citizen.

New media also serves as an important tool for both institutions and nations to promote their interest and values (The contents of such promotion may vary according to different purposes). Some communities consider it an approach of "peaceful evolution" that may erode their own nation's system of values and eventually compromise national security.

Interactivity

Interactivity has become a term for a number of new media use options evolving from the rapid dissemination of Internet access points, the digitalization of media, and media convergence. In 1984, Rice defined new media as communication technologies that enable or facilitate user-to-user interactivity and interactivity between user and information. Such a definition replaces the "one-to-many" model of traditional mass communication with the possibility of a "many-to-many" web of communication. Any individual with the appropriate technology can now produce his or her online media and include images, text, and sound about whatever he or she chooses. Thus the convergence of new methods of communication with new technologies shifts the model of mass communication, and radically reshapes the ways we interact and communicate with one another. In "What is new media?" Vin Crosbie (2002) described three different kinds of communication media. He saw Interpersonal media as "one to one", Mass media as "one to many", and finally New Media as Individuation Media or "many to many".

When we think of interactivity and its meaning, we assume that it is only prominent in the conversational dynamics of individuals who are face-to-face. This restriction of opinion does not allow us to see its existence in mediated communication forums. Interactivity is present in some programming work, such as video games. It's also viable in the operation of traditional media. In the mid 1990s, filmmakers started using inexpensive digital cameras to create films. It was also the time when moving image technology had developed, which was able to be viewed on computer desktops in full motion. This development of new media technology was a new method for artists to share their work and interact with the big world. Other settings of interactivity include radio and television talk shows, letters to the editor, listener participation in such programs, and computer and technological programming. Interactive new media has become a true benefit to every one because people can express their artwork in more than one way with the technology that we have today and there is no longer a limit to what we can do with our creativity.

Interactivity can be considered a central concept in understanding new media, but different media forms possess, or enable different degrees of interactivity, and some forms of digitized and converged media are not in fact interactive at all. Tony Feldman considers digital satellite television as an example of a new media technology that uses digital compression to dramatically increase the number of television channels that can be delivered, and which changes the nature of what can be offered through the service, but does not transform the experience of television from the user's point of view, and thus lacks a more fully interactive dimension. It remains the case that interactivity is not an inherent characteristic of all new media technologies, unlike digitization and convergence.

Terry Flew (2005) argues that "the global interactive games industry is large and growing, and is at the forefront of many of the most significant innovations in new media" (Flew 2005: 101). Interactivity is prominent in these online video games such as *World of Warcraft*, *The Sims Online* and *Second Life*. These games, which are developments of "new media," allow for users to establish relationships and experience a sense of belonging that transcends traditional temporal and spatial boundaries (such as when gamers logging in from different parts of the world interact). These games can be used as an escape or to act out a desired life. Will Wright, creator of *The Sims*, "is fascinated by the way gamers have become so attached to his invention-with some even living their lives through it". New media have created virtual realities that are becoming virtual extensions of the world we live in. With the creation of *Second Life* and Active Worlds before it, people have even more control over this virtual world, a world where anything that a participant can think of can become a reality.

New Media changes continuously because it is constantly modified and redefined by the interaction between users, emerging technologies, cultural changes, etc.

New forms of New Media are emerging like Web 2.0 tools Facebook and YouTube, along with video games and the consoles they are played on. It is helping to make video games and video game consoles branch out into New Media as well. Gamers on YouTube post videos of them playing video games they like and that people want to watch. Cultural changes are happening because people can upload their gaming experiences to a Web 2.0 tool like Facebook and YouTube for the world to see. Consoles like the Xbox One and the PlayStation 4 have WiFi connectivity and chat rooms on most of their video games that allow gamer-to-gamer conversations around the world. They also allow people to connect to YouTube, so if they stream/record a gamer, it allows for easy uploading to YouTube for the world to see. Even the older video game consoles are becoming new media because YouTube can display the walkthroughs and let's plays of the game. YouTube gaming is evolving because some YouTubers are getting wealthy and earning money from their videos. The more people that become YouTube members, the popular YouTube becomes and the more it starts emerging as a new source of media, along with video games and consoles. The chat room/online gaming/WiFi consoles are getting the highest increase in popularity because they are not only the most advanced, but because of the newest video games being created that the majority of the gaming community wants to buy, play and watch. The older video games and consoles also get popularity, but from YouTube's capabilities of uploading them to the gamer's channels for everyone to see. The older games get popularity from the communities nostalgia of the game(s), and the old school graphics and gameplay that made people see how old-school technology was the best at some point in time. Facebook helps those video games and consoles get popularity as well. People can upload the videos they create to Facebook as well. Facebook is a much larger website with a lot more users, so people use Facebook to spread their gaming content as well. When they utilize Facebook and YouTube as sources to spread their videos, it allows the "New Media" dream to start becoming a reality. Video Games and the Game Consoles, along with YouTube are starting to emerge as the next best things of the New Media industry.

Industry

The new media industry shares an open association with many market segments in areas such as software/video game design, television, radio, mobile and particularly movies, advertising and marketing, through which industry seeks to gain from the advantages of two-way dialogue with consumers primarily through the Internet. As a device to source the ideas, concepts, and intellectual properties of the general public, the television industry has used new media and the Internet to expand their resources for new programming and content. The advertising industry has also capitalized on the proliferation of new media with large agencies running multimillion-dollar interactive advertising subsidiaries. Interactive websites and kiosks have become popular. In a number of cases advertising agencies have also set up new divisions to study new media. Public relations firms are also taking advantage of the opportunities in new media through interactive PR practices. Interactive PR practices include the use of social media to reach a mass audience of online social network users.

With the rise of the Internet, many new career paths were created. Before the rise, many technical jobs were seen as nerdy. The Internet led to creative work that was seen as laid-back and diverse amongst sex, race, and sexual orientation. Web design, gaming design, webcasting, blogging, and animation are all creative career paths that came with this rise. At first glance, the field of new media may seem hip, cool, creative and relaxed. What many don't realize is that working in this field is tiresome. Many of the people that work in this field don't have steady jobs. Work in this field has become project-based. Individuals work project to project for different companies. Most people are not working on one project or contract, but multiple ones at the same time. Despite working on numerous projects, people in this industry receive low payments, which is highly contrasted with the techy millionaire stereotype. It may seem as a carefree life from the outside, but it is not. New media workers work long hours for little pay and spend up to 20 hours a week looking for new projects to work on.

The ideology of new media careers as an egalitarian and stress-free environment is a myth. It is a game of networking and thriving at what you are capable of. Many workers face job instability. Inequality within this field exists due to the informality and flexibility of this career path.

Within the Industry, many Companies have emerged or transformed to adapt to the fast moving exciting opportunities that new media offers. The following companies are great examples of the changing landscape of companies/agencies whom have redeveloped, added or changed services to offer new media services.

- Brand New Media

- Adcore Creative

- Seven West Media

Youth

Based on nationally representative data, a study conducted by Kaiser Family Foundation in five-year intervals in 1998–99, 2003–04, and 2008–09 found that with technology allowing nearly 24-hour media access, the amount of time young people spend with entertainment media has risen dramatically, especially among Black and Hispanic youth. Today, 8- to 18-year-olds devote an average of 7 hours and 38 minutes (7:38) to using entertainment media in a typical day (more than 53 hours a week) – about the same amount most adults spend at work per day. Since much of that time is spent 'media multitasking' (using more than one medium at a time), they actually manage to spend a total of 10 hours and 45 minutes worth of media content in those 7½ hours per day. According to the Pew Internet & American Life Project, 96% of 18- to 29-year-olds and three-quarters (75%) of teens now own a cell phone, 88% of whom text, with 73% of wired American teens using social networking websites, a significant increase from previous years. A survey of over 25000 9- to 16-year-olds from 25 European countries found that many underage children use social media sites despite the site's stated age requirements, and many youth lack the digital skills to use social networking sites safely.

The role of cellular phones, such as the iPhone, has created the inability to be in social isolation, and the potential of ruining relationships. The iPhone activates the insular cortex of the brain, which is associated with feelings of love. People show similar feelings to their phones as they would to their friends, family and loved ones. Countless people spend more time on their phones, while in the presence of other people than spending time with the people in the same room or class.

Political Campaigns in the United States

In trying to determine the impact of new media on political campaigning and electioneering, the existing research has tried to examine whether new media supplants conventional media. Television is still the dominant news source, but new media's reach is growing. What is known is that new media has had a significant impact on elections and what began in the 2008 presidential campaign established new standards for how campaigns would be run. Since then, campaigns also have their outreach methods by developing targeted messages for specific audiences that can be reached via different social media platforms. Both parties have specific digital media strategies designed for voter outreach.

Additionally, their websites are socially connected, engaging voters before, during, and after elections. Email and text messages are also regularly sent to supporters encouraging them to donate and get involved. Some existing research focuses on the ways that political campaigns, parties, and candidates have incorporated new media into their political strategizing. This is often a multi-faceted approach that combines new and old media forms to create highly specialized strategies. This allows them to reach wider audiences, but also to target very specific subsets of the electorate. They are able to tap into polling data and in some cases harness the analytics of the traffic and profiles on various social media outlets to get real-time data about the kinds of engagement that is needed and the kinds of messages that are successful or unsuccessful. One body of existing research into the impact of new media on elections investigates the relationship between voters' use of new media and their level of political activity. They focus on areas such as "attentiveness, knowledge, attitudes, orientations, and engagement" (Owen, 2011). In references a vast body of research, Owen (2011) points out that older studies were mixed, while "newer research reveals more consistent evidence of information gain".

Some of that research has shown that there is a connection between the amount and degree of voter engagement and turnout (Owen, 2011). However, new media may not have overwhelming effects on either of those. Other research is tending toward the idea that new media has reinforcing effect, that rather than completely altering, by increasing involvement, it "imitates the established pattern of political participation" (Nam, 2012). After analyzing the Citizenship Involvement Democracy survey, Nam (2012) found that "the internet plays a dual role in mobilizing political participation by people not normally politically involved, as well as reinforcing existing offline participation." These findings chart a middle ground between some research that optimistically holds new media up to be an extremely effective or extremely ineffective at fostering political participation.

Towner (2013) found, in his survey of college students, that attention to new media increases offline and online political participation particularly for young people. His research shows that the prevalence of online media boosts participation and engagement. His work suggests that "it seems that online sources that facilitate political involvement, communication, and mobilization, particularly campaign websites, social media, and blogs, are the most important for offline political participation among young people". Deliberation When gauging effects and implications of new media on the political process, one means of doing so is to look at the deliberations that take place in these digital spaces (Halpern & Gibbs, 2013). In citing the work of several researchers, Halpern and Gibbs (2003) define deliberation to be "the performance of a set of communicative behaviors that promote thorough discussion. and the notion that in this process of communication the individuals involved weigh carefully the reasons for and against some of the propositions presented by others".

The work of Halpern and Gibbs (2013) "suggest that although social media may not provide a forum for intensive or in-depth policy debate, it nevertheless provides a deliberative space to discuss and encourage political participation, both directly and indirectly". Their work goes a step beyond that as well though because it shows that some social media sites foster a more robust political debate than do others such as Facebook which includes highly personal and identifiable access to information about users alongside any comments they may post on political topics. This is in contrast to sites like YouTube whose comments are often posted anonymously.

Culture Industry

The term culture industry (German: *Kulturindustrie*) was coined by the critical theorists Theodor Adorno (1903–1969) and Max Horkheimer (1895–1973), and was presented as critical vocabulary in the chapter "The Culture Industry: Enlightenment as Mass Deception", of the book *Dialectic of Enlightenment* (1944), wherein they proposed that popular culture is akin to a factory producing standardized cultural goods—films, radio programmes, magazines, etc.—that are used to manipulate mass society into passivity. Consumption of the easy pleasures of popular culture, made available by the mass communications media, renders people docile and content, no matter how difficult their economic circumstances. The inherent danger of the culture industry is the cultivation of false psychological needs that can only be met and satisfied by the products of capitalism; thus Adorno and Horkheimer especially perceived mass-produced culture as dangerous to the more technically and intellectually difficult high arts. In contrast, true psychological needs are freedom, creativity, and genuine happiness, which refer to an earlier demarcation of human needs, established by Herbert Marcuse.

The Frankfurt School

Members of The Frankfurt School were much influenced by the dialectical materialism and historical materialism of Karl Marx, as well as the revisitation of the dialectical idealism of Hegel; both events are studied not in isolation, but as part of the process of change. As a group later joined by Jürgen Habermas, they were responsible for the formulation of Critical Theory. In works such as *Dialectic of Enlightenment* and *Negative Dialectics*, Adorno and Horkheimer theorized that the phenomenon of mass culture has a political implication, namely that all the many forms of popular culture are parts of a single *culture industry* whose purpose is to ensure the continued obedience of the *masses* to market interests.

The Theory

The essay is concerned with the production of cultural content in capitalist societies. It critiques the supply-driven nature of cultural economies as well as the apparently inferior products of the system. Horkheimer and Adorno argue that mass-produced entertainment aims, by its very nature, to appeal to vast audiences and therefore both the intellectual stimulation of high art and the basic release of low art. The essay does not suggest that all products of this system are inherently inferior, simply that they have replaced other forms of entertainment without properly fulfilling the important roles played by the now defunct sources of culture.

Horkheimer and Adorno make consistent comparisons between Fascist Germany and the American film industry. They highlight the presence of mass-produced culture, created and disseminated by exclusive institutions and consumed by a passive, homogenised audience in both systems. This illustrates the logic of domination in post-enlightenment modern society, by monopoly capitalism or the nation state. Horkheimer and Adorno draw attention to the problems associated with a system that 'integrates its consumers from above', arguing that in attempting to realise enlightenment values of reason and order, the holistic power of the individual is undermined.

Influences

Adorno and Horkheimer's work was influenced by both the broader socio-political environment in which it was written and by other major theorists. Written in California in the early 1940s in an era which characterized them as two ethnically Jewish, German émigrés, The Culture Industry is influenced by European politics and the war by which the continent was consumed. Simultaneously, the American film industry was characterised by an unprecedented level of studio monopolisation, it was "Hollywood at its most classical, American mass culture at its most Fordist".

Horkheimer and Adorno were influenced heavily by major developers of social, political and economic theory, most notably:

- Karl Marx's theories of alienation and commodity fetishism,

- Max Weber's instrumental reason, and

- Georg Lukacs' concept of the reification of consciousness.

Elements

Anything made by a person is a materialization of their labour and an expression of their intentions. There will also be a use value: the benefit to the consumer will be derived from its utility. The exchange value will reflect its utility and the conditions of the market: the prices paid by the television broadcaster or at the box office. Yet, the modern soap operas with their interchangeable plots and formulaic narrative conventions reflect standardized production techniques and the falling value of a mass-produced cultural product. Only rarely is a film released that makes a more positive impression on the general discourse and achieves a higher exchange value, e.g. *Patton* (1970), starring George C. Scott as the eponymous American general, was released at a time of considerable anti-war sentiment. The opening shot is of Patton in front of an American flag making an impassioned speech. This was a form of dialectic in which the audience could identify with the patriotism either sincerely (the thesis) or ironically (the antithesis) and so set the tone of the interpretation for the remainder of the film. However, the film is manipulating specific historical events, not only as entertainment, but also as a form of propaganda by demonstrating a link between success in strategic resource management situations and specified leadership qualities. Given that the subtext was instrumental and not "value free", ethical and philosophical considerations arise.

Normally, only high art criticizes the world outside its boundaries, but access to this form of communication is limited to the elite classes where the risks of introducing social instability are slight. A film like *Patton* is popular art which intends controversy in a world of social order and unity which, according to Adorno, is regressing into a cultural blandness. To Hegel, order is good *a priori*, i.e. it does not have to answer to those living under it. But, if order is disturbed? In *Negative Dialectics*, Adorno believed this tended towards progress by stimulating the possibility of class conflict. Marx's theory of Historical Materialism was teleological, i.e. society follows through a dialectic of unfolding stages from ancient modes of production to feudalism to capitalism to a future communism. But Adorno felt that the culture industry would never permit a sufficient core of challenging material to emerge on to the market that might disturb the *status quo* and stimulate the final communist state to emerge.

Mass Culture

A central point of the *Dialectic of Enlightenment* is the topic of "the Enlightenment as the deception of the masses." The term "culture industry" is intended to refer to the commercial marketing of culture, the branch of industry that deals specifically with the production of culture that is in contrast to "authentic culture."

Horkheimer and Adorno contend that industrially produced culture robs people of their imagination and takes over their thinking for them. The culture industry delivers the "goods" so that the people then only have left over the task of the consuming them. Through mass production, everything becomes homogenized and whatever diversity remains is constituted of small trivialities. Everything becomes compressed through a process of the imposition of schemas under the premise that what's best is to mirror physical reality as closely as possible. Psychological drives become stoked to the point to where sublimation is no longer possible.

Movies serve as an example. "All films have become similar in their basic form. They are shaped to reflect facts of reality as closely as possible. Even fantasy films, which claim to not reflect such reality, don't really live up to what they claim to be. No matter how unusual they strive to be, the endings are usually easy to predict because of the existence of prior films which followed the same schemas. Also, for example, erotic depictions become so strong and so pronounced that a transformation to other forms is no longer possible."

The aims of the culture industry are—as in every industry—economic in nature. All endeavors become focused on economic success.

Authentic culture, however, is not goal-oriented, but is an end in itself. Authentic culture fosters the capacity of human imagination by presenting suggestions and possibilities, but in a different way than the culture industry does, since it leaves room for independent thought. Authentic culture does not become channeled into regurgitating reality, but goes levels beyond such. Authentic culture is unique and cannot be forced into any pre-formed schemas.

As for discovering the causes of the development of the culture industry, Horkheimer and Adorno contend that it arises from companies' pursuit of the maximization of profit, in the economic sense. However, this cannot be said to be culture, or what culture is supposed to be. It can only be described as being a form of commerce, just like any other kind of commerce.

The culture industry argument is often assumed to be fundamentally pessimistic in nature because its purveyors seem to condemn "mass media" and their consumers. However, for Adorno, the term "culture industry" does not refer to "mass culture," or the culture of the masses of people in terms of something being produced by the masses and conveying the representations of the masses. On the contrary, such involvement of the masses is only apparent, or a type of seeming democratic participation. Adorno contends that what is actually occurring is a type of "defrauding of the masses." Horkheimer and Adorno deliberately chose the term "culture industry" instead of "mass culture" or "mass media". "The culture industry perpetually cheats its consumers of what it perpetually promises." The culture industry even encroaches upon the small distractions of leisure activity: "Amusement has become an extension of labor under late capitalism." Horkheimer and Adorno, above all, in their critical analyses, delve into what they call "the fraying of art" and the "de-artification of art," and discuss how the arts are defused by the culture industry. Works of art have become commodified: Beethoven, Mozart and Wagner are only used in fragmentary forms when included in advertisement. According to Critical Theory, "selling out" is not the decisive factor involved, but rather it's the manner in which art is commodified and how art and culture are changed that is the crucial issue.

"Culture today is infecting everything with sameness." For Adorno and Horkheimer, subversion has become no longer possible.

Observations

Critics of the theory say that the products of mass culture would not be popular if people did not enjoy them, and that culture is self-determining in its administration. This would deny Adorno contemporary political significance, arguing that politics in a prosperous society is more concerned with action than with thought. Wiggershaus (1994) notes that the young generation of critical theorists largely ignore Adorno's work which, in part, stems from Adorno's inability to draw practical conclusions from his theories. For instance, Wiggershaus states: "The other side of Adorno's apparently paradoxical definition was ignored: that only rational objectivity was still possible for the modern work of art was only possible, in any significant sense, as a product of subjectivity"

Adorno is also accused of a lack of consistency in his claims to be implementing Marxism. Whereas he accepted the classical Marxist analysis of society showing how one class exercises domination over another, he deviated from Marx in his failure to use dialectic as a method to propose ways to change. Marx's theory depended on the willingness of the working class to overthrow the ruling class, but Adorno and Horkheimer postulated that the culture industry has undermined the revolutionary movement. Adorno's idea that the mass of the people are only objects of the culture industry is linked to his feeling that the time when the working class could be the tool of overthrowing capitalism is over. Other critics note that "High culture" too is not exempt from a role in the justification of capitalism. The establishment and reinforcement of elitism is seen by these critics as a key element in the role of such genres as opera and ballet.

Digital Divide

A digital divide is an economic and social inequality with regard to access to, use of, or impact of information and communication technologies (ICT). The divide within countries (such as the digital divide in the United States) may refer to inequalities between individuals, households, businesses, or geographic areas, usually at different socioeconomic levels or other demographic categories. The divide between differing countries or regions of the world is referred to as the global digital divide, examining this technological gap between developing and developed countries on an international scale.

Definitions and Usage

The term *digital divide* describes a gap in terms of access to and usage of information and communication technology. It was traditionally considered to be a question of having or not having access, but with a global mobile phone penetration of over 95%, it is becoming a relative inequality between those who have more and less bandwidth and more or less skills. Conceptualizations of the digital divide have been described as "who, with which characteristics, connects how to what":

- Who is the subject that connects: individuals, organizations, enterprises, schools, hospitals, countries, etc.

- Which characteristics or attributes are distinguished to describe the divide: income, education, age, geographic location, motivation, reason not to use, etc.

- How sophisticated is the usage: mere access, retrieval, interactivity, intensive and extensive in usage, innovative contributions, etc.

- To what does the subject connect: fixed or mobile, Internet or telephony, digital TV, broadband, etc.

Different authors focus on different aspects, which leads to a large variety of definitions of the digital divide. "For example, counting with only 3 different choices of subjects (individuals, organizations, or countries), each with 4 characteristics (age, wealth, geography, sector), distinguishing between 3 levels of digital adoption (access, actual usage and effective adoption), and 6 types of technologies (fixed phone, mobile... Internet...), already results in 3x4x3x6 = 216 different ways to define the digital divide. Each one of them seems equally reasonable and depends on the objective pursued by the analyst".

Means of Connectivity

Infrastructure

The infrastructure by which individuals, households, businesses, and communities connect to the Internet address the physical mediums that people use to connect to the Internet such as desktop computers, laptops, basic mobile phones or smart phones, iPods or other MP3 players, gaming consoles such as Xbox or PlayStation, electronic book readers, and tablets such as iPads.

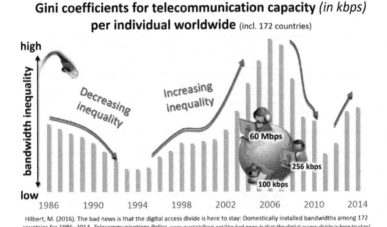

Gini coefficients for telecommunication capacity *(in kbps)*
per individual worldwide (incl. 172 countries)

Hilbert, M. (2016). The bad news is that the digital access divide is here to stay: Domestically installed bandwidths among 172 countries for 1986–2014. *Telecommunications Policy.* www.martinhilbert.net/the-bad-news-is-that-the-digital-access-divide-is-here-to-stay/

The digital divide measured in terms of bandwidth is not closing, but fluctuating up and down. Gini coefficients for telecommunication capacity (in kbit/s) among individuals worldwide

Traditionally the nature of the divide has been measured in terms of the existing numbers of subscriptions and digital devices. Given the increasing number of such devices, some have concluded that the digital divide among individuals has increasingly been closing as the result of a natural and almost automatic process. Others point to persistent lower levels of connectivity among women, racial and ethnic minorities, people with lower incomes, rural residents, and less educated people as evidence that addressing inequalities in access to and use of the medium will require much more than the passing of time. Recent studies have measured the digital divide not in terms of technological devices, but in terms of the existing bandwidth per individual (in kbit/s per capita). As shown in the Figure, the digital divide in kbit/s is not monotonically decreasing, but re-opens up with each new innovation. For example, "the massive diffusion of narrow-band Internet and mobile phones during the late 1990s" increased digital inequality, as well as "the initial introduction of broadband DSL and cable modems during 2003–2004 increased levels of inequality". This is because a new kind of connectivity is never introduced instantaneously and uniformly to society as a whole at once, but diffuses slowly through social networks. As shown by the Figure, during the mid-2000s, communication capacity was more unequally distributed than during the late 1980s, when only fixed-line phones existed. The most recent increase in digital equality stems from the massive diffusion of the latest digital innovations (i.e. fixed and mobile broadband infrastructures, e.g. 3G and fiber optics FTTH). Measurement methodologies of the digital divide, and more specifically an Integrated Iterative Approach General Framework (Integrated Contextual Iterative Approach – ICI) and the digital divide modeling theory under measurement model DDG (Digital Divide Gap) are used to analyze the gap existing between developed and developing countries, and the gap among the 27 members-states of the European Union.

The Bit as The Unifying Variable

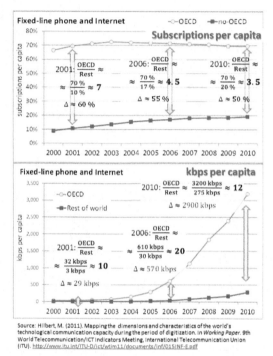

Source: Hilbert, M. (2011). Mapping the dimensions and characteristics of the world's technological communication capacity during the period of digitization. In *Working Paper*. 9th World Telecommunication/ICT Indicators Meeting, International Telecommunication Union (ITU). http://www.itu.int/ITU-D/ict/wtim11/documents/inf/015INF-E.pdf

Fixed-line phone and Internet 2000–2010: subscriptions (top) and kbit/s (bottom) per capita

Instead of tracking various kinds of digital divides among fixed and mobile phones, narrow- and broadband Internet, digital TV, etc., it has recently been suggested to simply measure the amount of kbit/s per actor. This approach has shown that the digital divide in kbit/s per capita is actually widening in relative terms: "While the average inhabitant of the developed world counted with some 40 kbit/s more than the average member of the information society in developing countries in 2001, this gap grew to over 3 Mbit/s per capita in 2010." The upper graph of the Figure on the side shows that the divide between developed and developing countries has been diminishing when measured in terms of subscriptions per capita. In 2001, fixed-line telecommunication penetration reached 70% of society in developed OECD countries and 10% of the developing world. This resulted in a ratio of 7 to 1 (divide in relative terms) or a difference of 60% (divide in measured in absolute terms). During the next decade, fixed-line penetration stayed almost constant in OECD countries (at 70%), while the rest of the world started a catch-up, closing the divide to a ratio of 3.5 to 1. The lower graph shows the divide not in terms of ICT devices, but in terms of kbit/s per inhabitant. While the average member of developed countries counted with 29 kbit/s more than a person in developing countries in 2001, this difference got multiplied by a factor of one thousand (to a difference of 2900 kbit/s). In relative terms, the fixed-line capacity divide was even worse during the introduction of broadband Internet at the middle of the first decade of the 2000s, when the OECD counted with 20 times more capacity per capita than the rest of the world. This shows the importance of measuring the divide in terms of kbit/s, and not merely to count devices. The International Telecommunications Union concludes that "the bit becomes a unifying variable enabling comparisons and aggregations across different kinds of communication technologies".

Skills and Digital Literacy

However, research shows that the digital divide is more than just an access issue and cannot be alleviated merely by providing the necessary equipment. There are at least three factors at play: information accessibility, information utilization and information receptiveness. More than just accessibility, individuals need to know how to make use of the information and communication tools once they exist within a community. Information professionals have the ability to help bridge the gap by providing reference and information services to help individuals learn and utilize the technologies to which they do have access, regardless of the economic status of the individual seeking help.

Location

Internet connectivity can be utilized at a variety of locations such as homes, offices, schools, libraries, public spaces, Internet cafe and others. There are also varying levels of connectivity in rural, suburban, and urban areas.

Applications

Common Sense Media, a nonprofit group based in San Francisco, surveyed almost 1,400 parents and reported in 2011 that 47 percent of families with incomes more than $75,000 had downloaded apps for their children, while only 14 percent of families earning less than $30,000 had done so.

Reasons and Correlating Variables

The gap in a digital divide may exist for a number of reasons. Obtaining access to ICTs and using them actively has been linked to a number of demographic and socio-economic characteristics: among them income, education, race, gender, geographic location (urban-rural), age, skills, awareness, political, cultural and psychological attitudes. Multiple regression analysis across countries has shown that income levels and educational attainment are identified as providing the most powerful explanatory variables for ICT access and usage. Evidence was found that caucasians are much more likely than non-caucasians to own a computer as well as have access to the Internet in their homes. As for geographic location, people living in urban centers have more access and show more usage of computer services than those in rural areas. Gender was previously thought to provide an explanation for the digital divide, many thinking ICT were male gendered, but controlled statistical analysis has shown that income, education and employment act as confounding variables and that women with the same level of income, education and employment actually embrace ICT more than men. One telling fact is that "as income rises so does Internet use", strongly suggesting that the digital divide persists at least in part due to income disparities. Most commonly, a digital divide stems from poverty and the economic barriers that limit resources and prevent people from obtaining or otherwise using newer technologies.

In research, while each explanation is examined, others must be controlled in order to eliminate inter-action effects or mediating variables, but these explanations are meant to stand as general trends, not direct causes. Each component can be looked at from different angles, which leads to a myriad of ways to look at (or define) the digital divide. For example, measurements for the intensity of usage, such as incidence and frequency, vary by study. Some report usage as access to Internet and ICTs while others report usage as having previously connected to the Internet. Some studies focus on specific technolo-gies, others on a combination (such as Infostate, proposed by Orbicom-UNESCO, the Digital Opportu-nity Index, or ITU's ICT Development Index). Based on different answers to the questions of who, with which kinds of characteristics, connects how and why, to what there are hundreds of alternatives ways to define the digital divide. "The new consensus recognizes that the key question is not how to connect people to a specific network through a specific device, but how to extend the expected gains from new ICTs". In short, the desired impact and "the end justifies the definition" of the digital divide.

Economic Gap in the United States

During the mid-1990s the US Department of Commerce, National Telecommunications & Informa-tion Administration (NTIA) began publishing reports about the Internet and access to and usage of the resource. The first of three reports is entitled "Falling Through the Net: A Survey of the 'Have Nots' in Rural and Urban America" (1995), the second is "Falling Through the Net II: New Data on the Digital Divide" (1998), and the final report "Falling Through the Net: Defining the Digital Di-vide" (1999). The NTIA's final report attempted to clearly define the term digital divide; "the digital divide—the divide between those with access to new technologies and those without—is now one of America's leading economic and civil rights issues. This report will help clarify which Americans are falling further behind, so that we can take concrete steps to redress this gap." Since the introduction of the NTIA reports, much of the early, relevant literature began to reference the NTIA's digital divide definition. The digital divide is commonly defined as being between the "haves" and "have-nots."

Overcoming the Digital Divide

An individual must be able to connect in order to achieve enhancement of social and cultural capi-tal as well as achieve mass economic gains in productivity. Therefore, access is a necessary (but not sufficient) condition for overcoming the digital divide. Access to ICT meets significant challenges that stem from income restrictions. The borderline between ICT as a necessity good and ICT as a luxury good is roughly around the "magical number" of US$10 per person per month, or US$120 per year, which means that people consider ICT expenditure of US$120 per year as a basic necessi-ty. Since more than 40% of the world population lives on less than US$2 per day, and around 20% live on less than US$1 per day (or less than US$365 per year), these income segments would have to spend one third of their income on ICT (120/365 = 33%). The global average of ICT spending is at a mere 3% of income. Potential solutions include driving down the costs of ICT, which includes low cost technologies and shared access through Telecentres.

Furthermore, even though individuals might be capable of accessing the Internet, many are thwarted by barriers to entry such as a lack of means to infrastructure or the inability to comprehend the information that the Internet provides. Lack of adequate infrastructure and lack of knowledge are two major obstacles that impede mass connectivity. These barriers limit individuals' capabilities in what they can do and what they can achieve in accessing technology. Some individuals have the ability to connect, but they do not have the knowledge to use what information ICTs and Internet technologies provide them. This leads to a focus on capabilities and skills, as well as awareness to move from mere access to effective usage of ICT.

The United Nations is aiming to raise awareness of the divide by way of the World Information Society Day which has taken place yearly since May 17, 2001. It also sets up the Information and Communications Technology (ICT) Task Force in November 2001. One year before, the United Nations Volunteers (UNV) programme had launched its Online Volunteering service, which uses ICT as a vehicle for and in support of volunteering. It constitutes an example of a volunteering initiative that effectively contributes to bridge the digital divide. ICT-enabled volunteering has a clear added value for development. If more people collaborate online with more development institutions and initiatives, this will imply an increase in person-hours dedicated to development cooperation at essentially no additional cost. This is the most visible effect of online volunteering for human development.

Social media websites serve as both manifestations of and means by which to combat the digital divide. The former describes phenomena such as the divided users demographics that make up sites such as Facebook and Myspace or Word Press and Tumblr. Each of these sites host thriving communities that engage with otherwise marginalized populations. An example of this is the large online community devoted to Afrofuturism, a discourse that critiques dominant structures of power by merging themes of science fiction and blackness. Social media brings together minds that may not otherwise meet, allowing for the free exchange of ideas and empowerment of marginalized discourses.

Libraries

A laptop lending kiosk at Texas A&M University–Commerce's Gee Library

Attempts to bridge the digital divide include a program developed in Durban, South Africa, where very low access to technology and a lack of documented cultural heritage has motivated the creation of an "online indigenous digital library as part of public library services." This project has the potential to narrow the digital divide by not only giving the people of the Durban area access to this digital resource, but also by incorporating the community members into the process of creating it.

Another attempt to narrow the digital divide takes the form of One Laptop Per Child (OLPC). This organization, founded in 2005, provides inexpensively produced "XO" laptops (dubbed the "$100 laptop", though actual production costs vary) to children residing in poor and isolated regions within developing countries. Each laptop belongs to an individual child and provides a gateway to digital learning and Internet access. The XO laptops are specifically designed to withstand more abuse than higher-end machines, and they contain features in context to the unique conditions that remote villages present. Each laptop is constructed to use as little power as possible, have a sunlight-readable screen, and is capable of automatically networking with other XO laptops in order to access the Internet—as many as 500 machines can share a single point of access.

To address the divide The Gates Foundation began the Gates Library Initiative. The Gates Foundation focused on providing more than just access, they placed computers and provided training in libraries. In this manner if users began to struggle while using a computer, the user was in a setting where assistance and guidance was available. Further, the Gates Library Initiative was "modeled on the old-fashioned life preserver: The support needs to be around you to keep you afloat."

In nations where poverty compounds effects of the digital divide, programs are emerging to counter those trends. Prior conditions in Kenya—lack of funding, language and technology illiteracy contributed to an overall lack of computer skills and educational advancement for those citizens. This slowly began to change when foreign investment began. In the early 2000s, The Carnegie Foundation funded a revitalization project through the Kenya National Library Service (KNLS). Those resources enabled public libraries to provide information and communication technologies (ICT) to their patrons. In 2012, public libraries in the Busia and Kiberia communities introduced technology resources to supplement curriculum for primary schools. By 2013, the program expanded into ten schools.

Effective Use

Community Informatics (CI) provides a somewhat different approach to addressing the digital divide by focusing on issues of "use" rather than simply "access". CI is concerned with ensuring the opportunity not only for ICT access at the community level but also, according to Michael Gurstein, that the means for the "effective use" of ICTs for community betterment and empowerment are available. Gurstein has also extended the discussion of the digital divide to include issues around access to and the use of "open data" and coined the term "data divide" to refer to this issue area.

Implications

Social Capital

Once an individual is connected, Internet connectivity and ICTs can enhance his or her future social and cultural capital. Social capital is acquired through repeated interactions with other individuals or groups of individuals. Connecting to the Internet creates another set of means by which to achieve repeated interactions. ICTs and Internet connectivity enable repeated interactions through access to social networks, chat rooms, and gaming sites. Once an individual has access to connectivity, obtains infrastructure by which to connect, and can understand and use the information that ICTs and connectivity provide, that individual is capable of becoming a "digital citizen".

Criticisms

Knowledge Divide

Since gender, age, racial, income, and educational gaps in the digital divide have lessened compared to past levels, some researchers suggest that the digital divide is shifting from a gap in access and connectivity to ICTs to a knowledge divide. A knowledge divide concerning technology presents the possibility that the gap has moved beyond access and having the resources to connect to ICTs to interpreting and understanding information presented once connected.

Second-Level Digital Divide

The second-level digital divide, also referred to as the production gap, describes the gap that separates the consumers of content on the Internet from the producers of content. As the technological digital divide is decreasing between those with access to the Internet and those without, the meaning of the term digital divide is evolving. Previously, digital divide research has focused on accessibility to the Internet and Internet consumption. However, with more and more of the population with access to the Internet, researchers are examining how people use the Internet to create content and what impact socioeconomics are having on user behavior. New applications have made it possible for anyone with a computer and an Internet connection to be a creator of content, yet the majority of user generated content available widely on the Internet, like public blogs, is created by a small portion of the Internet using population. Web 2.0 technologies like Facebook, YouTube, Twitter, and Blogs enable users to participate online and create content without having to understand how the technology actually works, leading to an ever increasing digital divide between those who have the skills and understanding to interact more fully with the technology and those who are passive consumers of it. Many are only nominal content creators through the use of Web 2.0, posting photos and status updates on Facebook, but not truly interacting with the technology.

Some of the reasons for this production gap include material factors like the type of Internet connection one has and the frequency of access to the Internet. The more frequently a person has access to the Internet and the faster the connection, the more opportunities they have to gain the technology skills and the more time they have to be creative.

Other reasons include cultural factors often associated with class and socioeconomic status. Users of lower socioeconomic status are less likely to participate in content creation due to disadvantages in education and lack of the necessary free time for the work involved in blog or web site creation and maintenance. Additionally, there is evidence to support the existence of the second-level digital divide at the K-12 level based on how educators' use technology for instruction. Schools' economic factors have been found to explain variation in how teachers use technology to promote higher-order thinking skills.

The Global Digital Divide

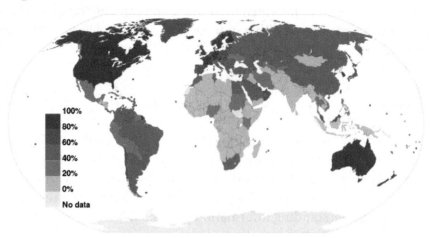

Internet users in 2012 as a percentage of a country's population

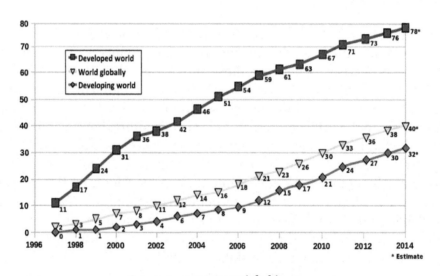

Internet users per 100 inhabitants

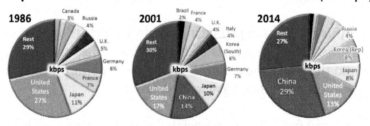

Hilbert, M. (2016). The bad news is that the digital access divide is here to stay: Domestically installed bandwidths among 172 countries for 1986–2014. *Telecommunications Policy*. www.martinhilbert.net/the-bad-news-is-that-the-digital-access-divide-is-here-to-stay/

Global bandwidth concentration: 3 countries have almost 50 %; 10 countries almost 75 %

Worldwide Internet users			
	2005	2010	2014[a]
World population	6.5 billion	6.9 billion	7.2 billion

Not using the Internet	84%	70%	60%
Using the Internet	16%	30%	40%
Users in the developing world	8%	21%	32%
Users in the developed world	51%	67%	78%

a Estimate.

Internet users by region			
	2005	2010	2014[a]
Africa	2%	10%	19%
Americas	36%	49%	65%
Arab States	8%	26%	41%
Asia and Pacific	9%	23%	32%
Commonwealth of Independent States	10%	34%	56%
Europe	46%	67%	75%

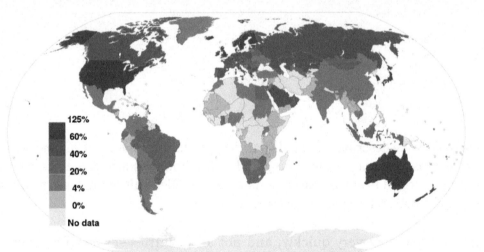

Mobile broadband Internet subscriptions in 2012
as a percentage of a country's population

Worldwide broadband subscriptions			
	2007	2010	2014[a]
World population	6.6 billion	6.9 billion	7.2 billion
Fixed broadband	5%	8%	10%
Developing world	2%	4%	6%
Developed world	18%	24%	27%
Mobile broadband	4%	11%	32%
Developing world	1%	4%	21%
Developed world	19%	43%	84%

Broadband subscriptions by region

Fixed subscriptions:	2007	2010	2014[a]
Africa	0.1%	0.2%	0.4%
Americas	11%	14%	17%
Arab States	1%	2%	3%
Asia and Pacific	3%	6%	8%
Commonwealth of Independent States	2%	8%	14%
Europe	18%	24%	28%
Mobile subscriptions:	2007	2010	2014[a]
Africa	0.2%	2%	19%
Americas	6%	23%	59%
Arab States	0.8%	5%	25%
Asia and Pacific	3%	7%	23%
Commonwealth of Independent States	0.2%	22%	49%
Europe	15%	29%	64%

The global digital divide describes global disparities, primarily between developed and developing countries, in regards to access to computing and information resources such as the Internet and the opportunities derived from such access. As with a smaller unit of analysis, this gap describes an inequality that exists, referencing a global scale.

The Internet is expanding very quickly, and not all countries—especially developing countries—are able to keep up with the constant changes. The term "digital divide" doesn't necessarily mean that someone doesn't have technology; it could mean that there is simply a difference in technology. These differences can refer to, for example, high-quality computers, fast Internet, technical assistance, or telephone services. The difference between all of these is also considered a gap.

In fact, there is a large inequality worldwide in terms of the distribution of installed telecommunication bandwidth. In 2014 only 3 countries (China, US, Japan) host 50% of the globally installed bandwidth potential. This concentration is not new, as historically only 10 countries have hosted 70–75% of the global telecommunication capacity. The U.S. lost its global leadership in terms of installed bandwidth in 2011, being replaced by China, which hosts more than twice as much national bandwidth potential in 2014 (29% versus 13% of the global total).

The Global Digital Divide Versus the Digital Divide

The global digital divide is a special case of the digital divide, the focus is set on the fact that "Internet has developed unevenly throughout the world" causing some countries to fall behind in technology, education, labor, democracy, and tourism. The concept of the digital divide was originally popularized in regard to the disparity in Internet access between rural and urban areas of the United States of America; the *global* digital divide mirrors this disparity on an international scale.

The global digital divide also contributes to the inequality of access to goods and services available through technology. Computers and the Internet provide users with improved education, which can lead to higher wages; the people living in nations with limited access are therefore disadvantaged. This global divide is often characterized as falling along what is sometimes called the north-south divide of "northern" wealthier nations and "southern" poorer ones.

Obstacles to Overcoming the Global Digital Divide

Some people argue that basic necessities need to be considered before achieving digital inclusion, such as an ample food supply and quality health care. Minimizing the global digital divide requires considering and addressing the following types of access:

Physical Access

Involves, "the distribution of ICT devices per capita...and land lines per thousands". Individuals need to obtain access to computers, landlines, and networks in order to access the Internet. This access barrier is also addressed in Article 21 of the Convention on the Rights of Persons with Disabilities by the United Nations.

Financial Access

The cost of ICT devices, traffic, applications, technician and educator training, software, maintenance and infrastructures require ongoing financial means.

Socio-Demographic Access

Empirical tests have identified that several socio-demographic characteristics foster or limit ICT access and usage. Among different countries, educational levels and income are the most powerful explanatory variables, with age being a third one. Others, like gender, don't seem to have much of an independent effect after controlling for income, education and employment.

Cognitive Access

In order to use computer technology, a certain level of information literacy is needed. Further challenges include information overload and the ability to find and use reliable information.

Design Access

Computers need to be accessible to individuals with different learning and physical abilities including complying with Section 508 of the Rehabilitation Act as amended by the Workforce Investment Act of 1998 in the United States.

Institutional Access

In illustrating institutional access, Wilson states "the numbers of users are greatly affected by whether access is offered only through individual homes or whether it is offered through schools, community centers, religious institutions, cybercafés, or post offices, especially in poor countries where computer access at work or home is highly limited".

Political Access

Guillen & Suarez argue that that "democratic political regimes enable a faster growth of the Internet than authoritarian or totalitarian regimes". The Internet is considered a form of e-democracy and attempting to control what citizens can or cannot view is in contradiction to this. Recently situations in Iran and China have denied people the ability to access certain website and disseminate information. Iran has also prohibited the use of high-speed Internet in the country and has removed many satellite dishes in order to prevent the influence of western culture, such as music and television.

Cultural Access

Many experts claim that bridging the digital divide is not sufficient and that the images and language needed to be conveyed in a language and images that can be read across different cultural lines.

Concrete Examples of the Global Digital Divide

In the early 21st century, residents of First World countries enjoy many Internet services which are not yet widely available in Third World countries, including:

- In tandem with the above point, mobile phones and small electronic communication devices;

- E-communities and social-networking;

- Fast broadband Internet connections, enabling advanced Internet applications;

- Affordable and widespread Internet access, either through personal computers at home or work, through public terminals in public libraries and Internet cafes, and through wireless access points;

- E-commerce enabled by efficient electronic payment networks like credit cards and reliable shipping services;

- Virtual globes featuring street maps searchable down to individual street addresses and detailed satellite and aerial photography;

- Online research systems like LexisNexis and ProQuest which enable users to peruse newspaper and magazine articles that may be centuries old, without having to leave home;

- Electronic readers such as Kindle, Sony Reader, Samsung Papyrus and Iliad by iRex Technologies;

- Price engines like Google Shopping which help consumers find the best possible online prices, and similar services like ShopLocal which find the best possible prices at local retailers;

- Electronic services delivery of government services, such as the ability to pay taxes, fees, and fines online.

- Further civic engagement through e-government and other sources such as finding information about candidates regarding political situations.

Global Solutions

There are four specific arguments why it is important to "bridge the gap":

- Economic equality — For example, the telephone is often seen as one of the most important components, because having access to a working telephone can lead to higher safety. If there were to be an emergency situation, one could easily call for help if one could use a nearby phone. In another example, many work related tasks are online, and people without access to the Internet may not be able to complete work up to company standards. The Internet is regarded by some as a basic component of civil life that developed countries ought to guarantee for their citizens. Additionally, welfare services, for example, are sometimes offered via the Internet.

- Social mobility — Computer and Internet use is regarded as being very important to development and success. However, some children are not getting as much technical education as others, because lower socioeconomic areas cannot afford to provide schools with bundles of computers. For this reason, some kids are being separated and not receiving the same chance as others to be successful.

- Democracy — Some people believe that eliminating the digital divide would help countries becomes healthier democracies. They argue that communities would become much more involved in events such as elections or decision making.

- Economic growth — It is believed that less developed nations could gain quick access to economic growth if the information infrastructure were to be developed and well used. By improving the latest technologies, certain countries and industries are able to gain a competitive advantage.

While these four arguments are meant to lead to a solution to the digital divide, there are a couple other components that need to be considered. The first one is rural living versus suburban living. Rural areas used to have very minimal access to the Internet, for example. However, nowadays, power lines and satellites are used to increase the availability in these areas. Another component to keep in mind is disabilities. Some people may have the highest quality technologies, but a disability they have may keep them from using these technologies to their fullest extent.

Using previous studies (Gamos, 2003; Nsengiyuma & Stork, 2005; Harwit, 2004 as cited in James), James asserts that in developing countries, "internet use has taken place overwhelmingly among the upper-income, educated, and urban segments" largely due to the high literacy rates of this sector of the population. As such, James suggests that part of the solution requires that developing countries first build up the literacy/language skills, computer literacy, and technical competence that low-income and rural populations need in order to make use of ICT.

It has also been suggested that there is a correlation between democrat regimes and the growth of the Internet. One hypothesis by Gullen is, "The more democratic the polity, the greater the Internet use...Government can try to control the Internet by monopolizing control" and Norris *et al.* also contends, "If there is less government control of it, the Internet flourishes, and it is associated with greater democracy and civil liberties.

From an economic perspective, Pick and Azari state that "in developing nations...foreign direct investment (FDI), primary education, educational investment, access to education, and government prioritization of ICT as all important". Specific solutions proposed by the study include: "invest in stimulating, attracting, and growing creative technical and scientific workforce; increase the access to education and digital literacy; reduce the gender divide and empower women to participate in the ICT workforce; emphasize investing in intensive Research and Development for selected metropolitan areas and regions within nations".

There are projects worldwide that have implemented, to various degrees, the solutions outlined above. Many such projects have taken the form of Information Communications Technology Centers (ICT centers). Rahnman explains that "the main role of ICT intermediaries is defined as an organization providing effective support to local communities in the use and adaptation of technology. Most commonly an ICT intermediary will be a specialized organization from outside the community, such as a non-governmental organization, local government, or international donor. On the other hand, a social intermediary is defined as a local institution from within the community, such as a community-based organization.

Other proposed solutions that the Internet promises for developing countries are the provision of efficient communications within and among developing countries, so that citizens worldwide can effectively help each other to solve their own problems. Grameen Banks and Kiva loans are two microcredit systems designed to help citizens worldwide to contribute online towards entrepreneurship in developing communities. Economic opportunities range from entrepreneurs who can afford the hardware and broadband access required to maintain Internet cafés to agribusinesses having control over the seeds they plant.

At the Massachusetts Institute of Technology, the IMARA organization (from Swahili word for "power") sponsors a variety of outreach programs which bridge the Global Digital Divide. Its aim is to find and implement long-term, sustainable solutions which will increase the availability of educational technology and resources to domestic and international communities. These projects are run under the aegis of the MIT Computer Science and Artificial Intelligence Laboratory (CSAIL) and staffed by MIT volunteers who give training, install and donate computer setups in greater Boston, Massachusetts, Kenya, Indian reservations the American Southwest such as the Navajo Nation, the Middle East, and Fiji Islands. The CommuniTech project strives to empower underserved communities through sustainable technology and education. According to Dominik Hartmann of the MIT's Media Lab, interdisciplinary approaches are needed to bridge the global digital divide.

Building on the premise that any effective solution must be decentralized, allowing the local communities in developing nations to generate their own content, one scholar has posited that social media—like Facebook, YouTube, and Twitter—may be useful tools in closing the divide. As Amir Hatem Ali suggests, "the popularity and generative nature of social media empower individuals to combat some of the main obstacles to bridging the digital divide". Facebook's statistics reinforce this claim. According to Facebook, more than seventy-five percent of its users reside outside of the US. Moreover, more than seventy languages are presented on its website. The reasons for the high number of international users are due to many the qualities of Facebook and other social media. Amongst them, are its ability to offer a means of interacting with others, user-friendly features, and the fact that most sites are available at no cost. The problem with social media, however, is that it can be accessible, provided that there is physical access. Nevertheless, with its ability to encourage digital inclusion, social media can be used as a tool to bridge the global digital divide.

Some cities in the world have started programs to bridge the digital divide for their residents, school children, students, parents and the elderly. One such program, founded in 1996, was sponsored by the city of Boston and called the Boston Digital Bridge Foundation. It especially concentrates on school children and their parents, helping to make both equally and similarly knowledgeable about computers, using application programs, and navigating the Internet.

World Summit On the Information Society

Several of the 67 principles adopted at the World Summit on the Information Society convened by the United Nations in Geneva in 2003 directly address the digital divide:

10. We are also fully aware that the benefits of the information technology revolution are today unevenly distributed between the developed and developing countries and within societies. We are fully committed to turning this digital divide into a digital opportunity for all, particularly for those who risk being left behind and being further marginalized.

11. We are committed to realizing our common vision of the Information Society for ourselves and for future generations. We recognize that young people are the future workforce and leading creators and earliest adopters of ICTs. They must therefore be empowered as learners, developers, contributors, entrepreneurs and decision-makers. We must focus especially on young people who have not yet been able to benefit fully from the opportunities provided by ICTs. We are also committed to ensuring that the development of ICT applications and operation of services respects the rights of children as well as their protection and well-being.

12. We affirm that development of ICTs provides enormous opportunities for women, who should be an integral part of, and key actors, in the Information Society. We are committed to ensuring that the Information Society enables women's empowerment and their full participation on the basis on equality in all spheres of society and in all decision-making processes. To this end, we should mainstream a gender equality perspective and use ICTs as a tool to that end.

13. In building the Information Society, we shall pay particular attention to the special needs of marginalized and vulnerable groups of society, including migrants, internally displaced

persons and refugees, unemployed and underprivileged people, minorities and nomadic people. We shall also recognize the special needs of older persons and persons with disabilities.

14. We are resolute to empower the poor, particularly those living in remote, rural and marginalized urban areas, to access information and to use ICTs as a tool to support their efforts to lift themselves out of poverty.

15. In the evolution of the Information Society, particular attention must be given to the special situation of indigenous peoples, as well as to the preservation of their heritage and their cultural legacy.

16. We continue to pay special attention to the particular needs of people of developing countries, countries with economies in transition, Least Developed Countries, Small Island Developing States, Landlocked Developing Countries, Highly Indebted Poor Countries, countries and territories under occupation, countries recovering from conflict and countries and regions with special needs as well as to conditions that pose severe threats to development, such as natural disasters.

21. Connectivity is a central enabling agent in building the Information Society. Universal, ubiquitous, equitable and affordable access to ICT infrastructure and services, constitutes one of the challenges of the Information Society and should be an objective of all stakeholders involved in building it. Connectivity also involves access to energy and postal services, which should be assured in conformity with the domestic legislation of each country.

28. We strive to promote universal access with equal opportunities for all to scientific knowledge and the creation and dissemination of scientific and technical information, including open access initiatives for scientific publishing.

46. In building the Information Society, States are strongly urged to take steps with a view to the avoidance of, and refrain from, any unilateral measure not in accordance with international law and the Charter of the United Nations that impedes the full achievement of economic and social development by the population of the affected countries, and that hinders the well-being of their population.

References

- Rainie, Lee; Wellman, Barry (2015-03-16). Networked Creators: A BIT of Networked. MIT Press. ISBN 9780262327664.

- Schrøder, edited by Kirsten Drotner & Kim Christian; Kirsten Drotner; Kim Christian Schrøder (2010). "3". Digital content creation : perceptions, practices, & perspectives. New York: Peter Lang. pp. 61–62. ISBN 1433106957.

- Manovich, Lev. "New Media From Borges to HTML." The New Media Reader. Ed. Noah Wardrip-Fruin & Nick Montfort. Cambridge, Massachusetts, 2003. 13-25. ISBN 0-262-23227-8

- DeFleur, Everette E. Dennis, Melvin L. (2010). Understanding media in the digital age : connections for communication, society, and culture. New York: Allyn & Bacon. ISBN 0205595820.

- Graham, Mark (2014). "The Knowledge Based Economy and Digital Divisions of Labour". Pages 189-195 in Companion to Development Studies, 3rd edition, V. Desai, and R. Potter (eds). Routledge, Taylor & Francis Group. ISBN 978-1-44-416724-5 (paperback). ISBN 978-0-415-82665-5 (hardcover).

- "Individuals using the Internet 2005 to 2014", Key ICT indicators for developed and developing countries and the world (totals and penetration rates), International Telecommunication Union (ITU). Retrieved 25 May 2015.

- ICT Facts and Figures 2005, 2010, 2014, Telecommunication Development Bureau, International Telecommunication Union (ITU). Retrieved 24 May 2015.

- Digital Divide - ICT Information Communications Technology - 50x15 Initiative. (2014, March 21). Retrieved April 13, 2014, from http://www.internetworldstats.com/links10.htm

- *Newman, Nic (September 2011). "Mainstream media and the distribution of news in the age of social discovery" (PDF). Reuters Institute for the Study of Journalism. Retrieved 20 March 2014.*

- *Lohr, Steve (10 September 2011). "In case you wondered, a real human wrote this column". The New York Times. Retrieved 25 March 2014. The company's software takes data, like that from sports statistics, company financial reports and housing starts and sales, and turns it into articles.*

- *Maas, KC; Josh Levs (27 December 2012). "Newspaper sparks outrage for publishing names, addresses of gun permit holders". CNN. Retrieved 25 March 2014.*

- *Fielding, Nick; Ian Cobain (17 March 2011). "Revealed: US spy operation that manipulates social media". The Guardian. Retrieved 25 March 2014.*

- *Fazekas, Andrew (20 June 2013). "NASA needs your help finding killer asteroids". National Geographic. Retrieved 25 March 2014.*

- *Pfhal, Michael (1 August 2001). "Giving away music to make money: Independent musicians on the Internet". First Monday. 6 (6). Retrieved 25 March 2014. No one has felt the impact of music on the Internet more than the independent musician.*

Tools and Techniques of Digital Media and Communication

This chapter is designed to introduce the students to the various tools and techniques that are used in digital media and communication. Some of the topics discussed in the chapter are data, image, audio and video with respect to digital media. It also introduces relatively nascent forms of digital communication such as instant messaging, social media, Facebook, YouTube, viral marketing and blog, among others. The aim of this chapter is to provide students with a comprehensive knowledge of this field.

Digital Data

Digital data, in information theory and information systems, are discrete, discontinuous representations of information or works, as contrasted with continuous, or analog signals which behave in a continuous manner, or represent information using a continuous function.

Although digital representations are the subject matter of discrete mathematics, the information represented can be either discrete, such as numbers and letters, or it can be continuous, such as sounds, images, and other measurements.

The word *digital* comes from the same source as the words digit and *digitus* (the Latin word for *finger*), as fingers are often used for discrete counting. Mathematician George Stibitz of Bell Telephone Laboratories used the word *digital* in reference to the fast electric pulses emitted by a device designed to aim and fire anti-aircraft guns in 1942. The term is most commonly used in computing and electronics, especially where real-world information is converted to binary numeric form as in digital audio and digital photography.

Symbol to Digital Conversion

Since symbols (for example, alphanumeric characters) are not continuous, representing symbols digitally is rather simpler than conversion of continuous or analog information to digital. Instead of sampling and quantization as in analog-to-digital conversion, such techniques as polling and encoding are used.

A symbol input device usually consists of a group of switches that are polled at regular intervals to see which switches are switched. Data will be lost if, within a single polling interval, two switches are pressed, or a switch is pressed, released, and pressed again. This polling can be done by a specialized processor in the device to prevent burdening the main CPU. When a new symbol has been entered, the device typically sends an interrupt, in a specialized format, so that the CPU can read it.

For devices with only a few switches (such as the buttons on a joystick), the status of each can be encoded as bits (usually 0 for released and 1 for pressed) in a single word. This is useful when combinations of key presses are meaningful, and is sometimes used for passing the status of modifier keys on a keyboard (such as shift and control). But it does not scale to support more keys than the number of bits in a single byte or word.

Devices with many switches (such as a computer keyboard) usually arrange these switches in a scan matrix, with the individual switches on the intersections of x and y lines. When a switch is pressed, it connects the corresponding x and y lines together. Polling (often called scanning in this case) is done by activating each x line in sequence and detecting which y lines then have a signal, thus which keys are pressed. When the keyboard processor detects that a key has changed state, it sends a signal to the CPU indicating the scan code of the key and its new state. The symbol is then encoded, or converted into a number, based on the status of modifier keys and the desired character encoding.

A custom encoding can be used for a specific application with no loss of data. However, using a standard encoding such as ASCII is problematic if a symbol such as 'ß' needs to be converted but is not in the standard.

It is estimated that in the year 1986 less than 1% of the world's technological capacity to store information was digital and in 2007 it was already 94%. The year 2002 is assumed to be the year when human kind was able to store more information in digital than in analog format (the "beginning of the digital age").

Properties of Digital Information

All digital information possesses common properties that distinguish it from analog data with respect to communications:

- Synchronization: Since digital information is conveyed by the sequence in which symbols are ordered, all digital schemes have some method for determining the beginning of a sequence. In written or spoken human languages synchronization is typically provided by pauses (spaces), capitalization, and punctuation. Machine communications typically use special synchronization sequences.

- Language: All digital communications require a *formal language*, which in this context consists of all the information that the sender and receiver of the digital communication must both possess, in advance, in order for the communication to be successful. Languages are generally arbitrary and specify the meaning to be assigned to particular symbol sequences, the allowed range of values, methods to be used for synchronization, etc.

- Errors: Disturbances (noise) in analog communications invariably introduce some, generally small deviation or error between the intended and actual communication. Disturbances in a digital communication do not result in errors unless the disturbance is so large as to result in a symbol being misinterpreted as another symbol or disturb the sequence of symbols. It is therefore generally possible to have an entirely error-free digital communication. Further, techniques such as check codes may be used to detect errors and guarantee error-free communications through redundancy or retransmission. Errors in digital communications can take the form of *substitution errors* in which a symbol is replaced by another symbol, or *insertion/deletion* errors in which an extra incorrect symbol is inserted into or deleted from a digital message. Uncorrected errors in digital communications have unpredictable and generally large impact on the information content of the communication.

- Copying: Because of the inevitable presence of noise, making many successive copies of an analog communication is infeasible because each generation increases the noise. Because digital communications are generally error-free, copies of copies can be made indefinitely.

- Granularity: The digital representation of a continuously variable analog value typically involves a selection of the number of symbols to be assigned to that value. The number of symbols determines the precision or resolution of the resulting datum. The difference between the actual analog value and the digital representation is known as *quantization error*. For example, if the actual temperature is 23.234456544453 degrees, but if only two digits (23) are assigned to this parameter in a particular digital representation, the quantizing error is: 0.234456544453. This property of digital communication is known as *granularity*.

- Compressible: According to Miller, "Uncompressed digital data is very large, and in its raw form would actually produce a larger signal (therefore be more difficult to transfer) than analog data. However, digital data can be compressed. Compression reduces the amount of bandwidth space needed to send information. Data can be compressed, sent and then decompressed at the site of consumption. This makes it possible to send much more information and result in, for example, digital television signals offering more room on the airwave spectrum for more television channels."

Historical Digital Systems

Even though digital signals are generally associated with the binary electronic digital systems used in modern electronics and computing, digital systems are actually ancient, and need not be binary or electronic.

- Written text (due to the limited character set and the use of discrete symbols - the alphabet in most cases)

- The *abacus* was created sometime between 1000 BC and 500 BC, it later became a form of calculation frequency. Nowadays it can be used as a very advanced, yet basic digital calculator that uses beads on rows to represent numbers. Beads only have meaning in discrete up and down states, not in analog in-between states.

- A *beacon* is perhaps the simplest non-electronic digital signal, with just two states (on and off). In particular, *smoke signals* are one of the oldest examples of a digital signal, where an analog "carrier" (smoke) is modulated with a blanket to generate a digital signal (puffs) that conveys information.

- Morse code uses six digital states—dot, dash, intra-character gap (between each dot or dash), short gap (between each letter), medium gap (between words), and long gap (between sentences)—to send messages via a variety of potential carriers such as electricity or light, for example using an electrical telegraph or a flashing light.

- The Braille system was the first binary format for character encoding, using a six-bit code rendered as dot patterns.

- Flag semaphore uses rods or flags held in particular positions to send messages to the receiver watching them some distance away.

- International maritime signal flags have distinctive markings that represent letters of the alphabet to allow ships to send messages to each other.

- More recently invented, a modem modulates an analog "carrier" signal (such as sound) to encode binary electrical digital information, as a series of binary digital sound pulses. A slightly earlier, surprisingly reliable version of the same concept was to bundle a sequence of audio digital "signal" and "no signal" information (i.e. "sound" and "silence") on magnetic cassette tape for use with early home computers.

Digital Image

A digital image is a numeric representation of (normally binary) a two-dimensional image. Depending on whether the image resolution is fixed, it may be of vector or raster type. By itself, the term "digital image" usually refers to raster images or bitmapped images.

Raster

Raster images have a finite set of digital values, called *picture elements* or pixels. The digital image contains a fixed number of rows and columns of pixels. Pixels are the smallest individual element in an image, holding antiquated values that represent the brightness of a given color at any specific point.

Typically, the pixels are stored in computer memory as a raster image or raster map, a two-dimensional array of small integers. These values are often transmitted or stored in a compressed form.

Raster images can be created by a variety of input devices and techniques, such as digital cameras, scanners, coordinate-measuring machines, seismographic profiling, airborne radar, and more. They can also be synthesized from arbitrary non-image data, such as mathematical functions or three-dimensional geometric models; the latter being a major sub-area of computer graphics. The field of digital image processing is the study of algorithms for their transformation.

Raster File Formats

Most users come into contact with raster images through digital cameras, which use any of several image file formats.

Some digital cameras give access to almost all the data captured by the camera, using a raw image format. *The Universal Photographic Imaging Guidelines (UPDIG)* suggests these formats be used when possible since raw files produce the best quality images. These file formats allow the photographer and the processing agent the greatest level of control and accuracy for output. Their use is inhibited by the prevalence of proprietary information (trade secrets) for some camera makers, but there have been initiatives such as OpenRAW to influence manufacturers to release these records publicly. An alternative may be Digital Negative (DNG), a proprietary Adobe product described as "the public, archival format for digital camera raw data". Although this format is not yet universally accepted, support for the product is growing, and increasingly professional archivists and conservationists, working for respectable organizations, variously suggest or recommend DNG for archival purposes.

Vector

Vector images resulted from mathematical geometry (vector). In mathematical terms, a vector consists of point that has both direction and length.

Often, both raster and vector elements will be combined in one image; for example, in the case of a billboard with text (vector) and photographs (raster).

Image Viewing

Image viewer software displays images. Web browsers can display standard internet image formats including GIF, JPEG, and PNG. Some can show SVG format which is a standard W3C format. In the past, when Internet was still slow, it was common to provide "preview" image that would load and appear on the web site before being replaced by the main image (to give at preliminary impression). Now Internet is fast enough and this preview image is seldom used.

Some scientific images can be very large (for instance, the 46 gigapixel size image of the Milky Way, about 194 Gb in size). Such images are difficult to download and are usually browsed online through more complex web interfaces.

Some viewers offer a slideshow utility to display a sequence of images.

History

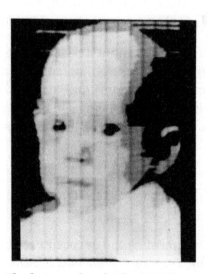

The first scan done by the SEAC in 1957

The SEAC scanner

Early Digital fax machines such as the Bartlane cable picture transmission system preceded digital cameras and computers by decades. The first picture to be scanned, stored, and recreated in digital pixels was displayed on the Standards Eastern Automatic Computer (SEAC) at NIST. The advancement of digital imagery continued in the early 1960s, alongside development of the space program and in medical research. Projects at the Jet Propulsion Laboratory, MIT, Bell Labs and the University of Maryland, among others, used digital images to advance satellite imagery, wirephoto standards conversion, medical imaging, videophone technology, character recognition, and photo enhancement.

Rapid advances in digital imaging began with the introduction of microprocessors in the early 1970s, alongside progress in related storage and display technologies. The invention of computerized axial tomography (CAT scanning), using x-rays to produce a digital image of a "slice" through a three-dimensional object, was of great importance to medical diagnostics. As well as origination of digital images, digitization of analog images allowed the enhancement and restoration of archaeological artifacts and began to be used in fields as diverse as nuclear medicine, astronomy, law enforcement, defence and industry.

Advances in microprocessor technology paved the way for the development and marketing of charge-coupled devices (CCDs) for use in a wide range of image capture devices and gradually displaced the use of analog film and tape in photography and videography towards the end of the 20th century. The computing power necessary to process digital image capture also allowed computer-generated digital images to achieve a level of refinement close to photorealism.

Digital Audio

Audio levels display on a digital audio recorder (Zoom H4n)

Digital audio is technology that can be used to record, store, generate, manipulate, and reproduce sound using audio signals that have been encoded in digital form. Following significant advances in digital audio technology during the 1970s, it gradually replaced analog audio technology in many areas of sound production, sound recording (tape systems were replaced with digital recording systems), sound engineering and telecommunications in the 1990s and 2000s.

A microphone converts sound (a singer's voice or the sound of an instrument playing) to an analog electrical signal, then an analog-to-digital converter (ADC)—typically using pulse-code modulation—converts the analog signal into a digital signal. This digital signal can then be recorded, edited and modified using digital audio tools. When the sound engineer wishes to listen to the recording on headphones or loudspeakers (or when a consumer wishes to listen to a digital sound file of a song), a digital-to-analog converter performs the reverse process, converting a digital signal back into an analog signal, which analog circuits amplify and send to a loudspeaker.

Digital audio systems may include compression, storage, processing and transmission components. Conversion to a digital format allows convenient manipulation, storage, transmission and retrieval of an audio signal. Unlike analog audio, in which making copies of a recording leads to degradation of the signal quality, when using digital audio, an infinite number of copies can be made without any degradation of signal quality.

Overview

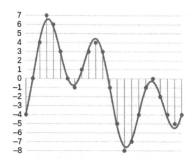

A sound wave, in red, represented digitally, in blue (after sampling and 4-bit quantization).

Digital audio technologies in the 2010s are used in the recording, manipulation, mass-production, and distribution of sound, including recordings of songs, instrumental pieces, podcasts, sound effects, and other sounds. Modern online music distribution depends on digital recording and data compression. The availability of music as data files, rather than as physical objects, has significantly reduced the costs of distribution. Before digital audio, the music industry distributed and sold music by selling physical copies of albums in the form of records, tapes, and then CDs. With digital audio and online distribution systems such as iTunes, companies sell digital sound files to consumers, which the consumer receives over the Internet. This digital audio/Internet distribution model is much less expensive than producing physical copies of recordings, packaging them and shipping them to stores.

An analog audio system captures sounds, and converts their physical waveforms into electrical representations of those waveforms by use of a transducer, such as a microphone. The sounds are then stored, as on tape, or transmitted. The process is reversed for playback: the audio signal is amplified and then converted back into physical waveforms via a loudspeaker. Analog audio retains its fundamental wave-like characteristics throughout its storage, transformation, duplication, and amplification.

Analog audio signals are susceptible to noise and distortion, due to the innate characteristics of electronic circuits and associated devices. Disturbances in a digital system do not result in error unless the disturbance is so large as to result in a symbol being misinterpreted as another symbol or disturb the sequence of symbols. It is therefore generally possible to have an entirely error-free digital audio system in which no noise or distortion is introduced between conversion to digital format, and conversion back to analog.

A digital audio signal may be encoded for correction of any errors that might occur in the storage or transmission of the signal, but this is not strictly part of the digital audio process. This technique, known as "channel coding", is essential for broadcast or recorded digital systems to maintain bit accuracy. The discrete time and level of the binary signal allow a decoder to recreate the analog signal upon replay. Eight to Fourteen Bit Modulation is a channel code used in the audio Compact Disc (CD).

Conversion Process

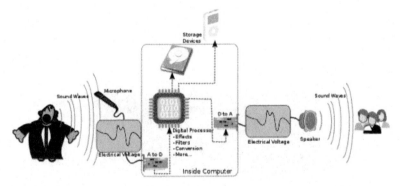

The lifecycle of sound from its source, through an ADC, digital processing, a DAC, and finally as sound again.

A digital audio system starts with an ADC that converts an analog signal to a digital signal. The ADC runs at a specified sampling rate and converts at a known bit resolution. CD audio, for example, has a sampling rate of 44.1 kHz (44,100 samples per second), and has 16-bit resolution for each stereo channel. Analog signals that have not already been bandlimited must be passed through an anti-aliasing filter before conversion, to prevent the distortion that is caused by audio signals with frequencies higher than the Nyquist frequency, which is half of the system's sampling rate.

A digital audio signal may be stored or transmitted. Digital audio can be stored on a CD, a digital audio player, a hard drive, a USB flash drive, or any other digital data storage device. The digital signal may then be altered through digital signal processing, where it may be filtered or have effects applied. Audio data compression techniques, such as MP3, Advanced Audio Coding, Ogg Vorbis, or FLAC, are commonly employed to reduce the file size. Digital audio can be streamed to other devices.

For playback, digital audio must be converted back to an analog signal with a DAC. DACs run at a specific sampling rate and bit resolution, but may use oversampling, upsampling or downsampling to convert signals that have been encoded with a different sampling rate.

History in Commercial Recording

Pulse-code modulation was invented by British scientist Alec Reeves in 1937 and was used in telecommunications applications long before its first use in commercial broadcast and recording. Commercial digital recording was pioneered in Japan by NHK and Nippon Columbia, also known as Denon, in the 1960s. The first commercial digital recordings were released in 1971.

The BBC also began to experiment with digital audio in the 1960s. By the early 1970s it had developed a 2-channel recorder, and in 1972 it deployed a digital audio transmission system that linked their broadcast center to their remote transmitters.

The first 16-bit PCM recording in the United States was made by Thomas Stockham at the Santa Fe Opera in 1976, on a Soundstream recorder. An improved version of the Soundstream system was used to produce several classical recordings by Telarc in 1978. The 3M digital multitrack recorder in development at the time was based on BBC technology. The first all-digital album recorded on this machine was Ry Cooder's *Bop till You Drop* in 1979. British record label Decca began development of its own 2-track digital audio recorders in 1978 and released the first European digital recording in 1979.

Sony digital audio recorder PCM-7030

Popular digital multitrack recorders produced by Sony and Mitsubishi in the early 1980s helped to bring about digital recording's acceptance by the major record companies. The 1982 introduction of the CD popularized digital audio with consumers.

Technologies

Digital audio broadcasting

- Digital Audio Broadcasting (DAB)

- HD Radio

- Digital Radio Mondiale (DRM)

- In-band on-channel (IBOC)

Storage technologies

- Digital audio player

- Digital Audio Tape (DAT)

- Digital Compact Cassette (DCC)

- Compact Disc (CD)

- Hard disk recorder

- DVD-Audio

- MiniDisc

- Super Audio CD

- Blu-ray Disc (BD)

- Various audio file formats

Digital Audio Interfaces

Audio-specific interfaces include:

- AC'97 (Audio Codec 1997) interface between integrated circuits on PC motherboards

- Intel High Definition Audio - modern replacement for AC'97

- ADAT interface

- AES3 interface with XLR connectors, common in professional audio equipment

- S/PDIF - either over coaxial cable or TOSLINK, common in consumer audio equipment and derived from AES3

- AES47 - professional AES3-style digital audio over Asynchronous Transfer Mode networks

- I²S (Inter-IC sound) interface between integrated circuits in consumer electronics

- MADI (Multichannel Audio Digital Interface)

- MIDI - low-bandwidth interconnect for carrying instrument data; cannot carry sound but can carry digital sample data in non-realtime

- TDIF, TASCAM proprietary format with D-sub cable

- A2DP via Bluetooth

Several interfaces are engineered to carry digital video and audio together, including HDMI and DisplayPort.

Any digital bus can carry digital audio. In professional architectural or installation applications, many digital audio Audio over Ethernet protocols and interfaces exist.

Digital Video

Digital video is a representation of moving visual images in the form of encoded digital data. This is in contrast to analog video, which represents moving visual images with analog signals.

History

Starting in the late 1970s to the early 1980s, several types of video production equipment that were digital in their internal workings were introduced, such as time base correctors (TBC) and digital video effects (DVE) units (one of the former being the Thomson-CSF 9100 Digital Video Processor, an internally all-digital full-frame TBC introduced in 1980, and two of the latter being the Ampex ADO, and the Nippon Electric Corporation (NEC) DVE). They operated by taking a standard analog composite video input and digitizing it internally. This made it easier to either correct or enhance the video signal, as in the case of a TBC, or to manipulate and add effects to the video, in the case of a DVE unit. The digitized and processed video information that was output from these units would then be converted back to standard analog video.

Later on in the 1970s, manufacturers of professional video broadcast equipment, such as Bosch (through their Fernseh division), RCA, and Ampex developed prototype digital videotape recorders (VTR) in their research and development labs. Bosch's machine used a modified 1" Type B transport, and recorded an early form of CCIR 601 digital video. Ampex's prototype digital video recorder used a modified 2" Quadruplex VTR (an Ampex AVR-3), but fitted with custom digital video electronics, and a special "octaplex" 8-head headwheel (regular analog 2" Quad machines only used 4 heads). The audio on Ampex's prototype digital machine, nicknamed by its developers as "Annie", still recorded the audio in analog as linear tracks on the tape, like 2" Quad. None of these machines from these manufacturers were ever marketed commercially, however.

Digital video was first introduced commercially in 1986 with the Sony D1 format, which recorded an uncompressed standard definition component video signal in digital form instead of the high-band analog forms that had been commonplace until then. Due to its expense, and the requirement of component video connections using 3 cables (such as YPbPr or RGB component video) to and from a D1 VTR that most television facilities were not wired for (composite NTSC or PAL video using one cable was the norm for most of them at that time), D1 was used primarily by large television networks and other component-video capable video studios.

In 1988, Sony and Ampex co-developed and released the D2 digital videocassette format, which recorded video digitally without compression in ITU-601 format, much like D1. But D2 had the major difference of encoding the video in composite form to the NTSC standard, thereby only requiring single-cable composite video connections to and from a D2 VCR, making it a perfect fit for the majority of television facilities at the time. This made D2 quite a successful format in the television broadcast industry throughout the late '80s and the '90s. D2 was also widely used in that era as the master tape format for mastering laserdiscs (prior to D2, most laserdiscs were mastered using analog 1" Type C videotape).

D1 & D2 would eventually be replaced by cheaper systems using video compression, most notably Sony's Digital Betacam (still heavily used as an electronic field production (EFP) recording format by professional television producers) that were introduced into the network's television studios. Other examples of digital video formats utilizing compression were Ampex's DCT (the first to employ such when introduced in 1992), the industry-standard DV and MiniDV (and its professional variations, Sony's DVCAM and Panasonic's DVCPRO), and Betacam SX, a lower-cost variant of Digital Betacam using MPEG-2 compression.

One of the first digital video products to run on personal computers was *PACo: The PICS Animation Compiler* from The Company of Science & Art in Providence, RI, which was developed starting in 1990 and first shipped in May 1991. PACo could stream unlimited-length video with synchronized sound from a single file (with the ".CAV" file extension) on CD-ROM. Creation required a Mac; playback was possible on Macs, PCs, and Sun Sparcstations. In 1992, Bernard Luskin, Philips Interactive Media, and Eric Doctorow, Paramount Worldwide Video, successfully put the first fifty videos in digital MPEG 1 on CD, developed the packaging and launched movies on CD, leading to advancing versions of MPEG, and to DVD.

QuickTime, Apple Computer's architecture for time-based and streaming data formats appeared in June, 1991. Initial consumer-level content creation tools were crude, requiring an analog video source to be digitized to a computer-readable format. While low-quality at first, consumer digital video increased rapidly in quality, first with the introduction of playback standards such as MPEG-1 and MPEG-2 (adopted for use in television transmission and DVD media), and then the introduction of the DV tape format allowing recordings in the format to be transferred direct to digital video files (containing the same video data recorded on the transferred DV tape) on an editing computer and simplifying the editing process, allowing non-linear editing systems (NLE) to be deployed cheaply and widely on desktop computers with no external playback/recording equipment needed, save for the computer simply requiring a FireWire port to interface to the DV-format camera or VCR. The widespread adoption of digital video has also drastically reduced the bandwidth needed for a high-definition video signal (with HDV and AVCHD, as well as several commercial variants such as DVCPRO-HD, all using less bandwidth than a standard definition analog signal) and tapeless camcorders based on flash memory and often a variant of MPEG-4.

Overview of Basic Properties

Digital video comprises a series of orthogonal bitmap digital images displayed in rapid succession at a constant rate. In the context of video these images are called frames. We measure the rate at which frames are displayed in frames per second (FPS).

Since every frame is an orthogonal bitmap digital image it comprises a raster of pixels. If it has a width of W pixels and a height of H pixels we say that the frame size is WxH.

Pixels have only one property, their color. The color of a pixel is represented by a fixed number of bits. The more bits the more subtle variations of colors can be reproduced. This is called the color depth (CD) of the video.

An example video can have a duration (T) of 1 hour (3600*sec*), a frame size of 640x480 *(WxH)* at a color depth of 24*bits* and a frame rate of 25*fps*. This example video has the following properties:

- pixels per frame = 640 * 480 = 307,200

- bits per frame = 307,200 * 24 = 7,372,800 = 7.37*Mbits*

- bit rate (BR) = 7.37 * 25 = 184.25*Mbits/sec*

- video size (VS) = 184*Mbits/sec* * 3600*sec* = 662,400*Mbits* = 82,800*Mbytes* = 82.8*Gbytes*

The most important properties are *bit rate* and *video size*. The formulas relating those two with all other properties are:

BR = W * H * CD * FPS

VS = BR * T = W * H * CD * FPS * T

(units are: BR in bit/s, W and H in pixels, CD in bits, VS in bits, T in seconds)

while some secondary formulas are:

pixels_per_frame = W * H

pixels_per_second = W * H * FPS

bits_per_frame = W * H * CD

Regarding Interlacing

In interlaced video each *frame* is composed of two *halves of an image*. The first half contains only the odd-numbered lines of a full frame. The second half contains only the even-numbered lines. Those halves are referred to individually as *fields*. Two consecutive fields compose a full frame. If an interlaced video has a frame rate of 15 frames per second the field rate is 30 fields per second. All the properties and formulas discussed here apply equally to interlaced video but one should be careful not to confuse the fields per second rate with the frames per second rate.

Properties of Compressed Video

The above are accurate for uncompressed video. Because of the relatively high bit rate of uncompressed video, video compression is extensively used. In the case of compressed video each frame requires a small percentage of the original bits. Assuming a compression algorithm that shrinks the input data by a factor of CF, the bit rate and video size would equal to:

$$BR = W * H * CD * FPS / CF$$

$$VS = BR * T / CF$$

Please note that it is not necessary that all frames are equally compressed by a factor of CF. In practice they are not, so CF is the *average* factor of compression for *all* the frames taken together.

The above equation for the bit rate can be rewritten by combining the compression factor and the color depth like this:

$$BR = W * H * (CD / CF) * FPS$$

The value (CD / CF) represents the average bits per pixel (BPP). As an example, if we have a color depth of 12bits/pixel and an algorithm that compresses at 40x, then BPP equals 0.3 (12/40). So in the case of compressed video the formula for bit rate is:

$$BR = W * H * BPP * FPS$$

In fact the same formula is valid for uncompressed video because in that case one can assume that the "compression" factor is 1 and that the average bits per pixel equal the color depth.

More on Bit Rate and Bpp

As is obvious by its definition bit rate is a measure of the rate of information content of the digital video stream. In the case of uncompressed video, bit rate corresponds directly to the quality of the video (remember that bit rate is proportional to every property that affects the video quality). Bit rate is an important property when transmitting video because the transmission link must be capable of supporting that bit rate. Bit rate is also important when dealing with the storage of video because, as shown above, the video size is proportional to the bit rate and the duration. Bit rate of uncompressed video is too high for most practical applications. Video compression is used to greatly reduce the bit rate.

BPP is a measure of the efficiency of compression. A true-color video with no compression at all may have a BPP of 24 bits/pixel. Chroma subsampling can reduce the BPP to 16 or 12 bits/pixel. Applying jpeg compression on every frame can reduce the BPP to 8 or even 1 bits/pixel. Applying video compression algorithms like MPEG1, MPEG2 or MPEG4 allows for fractional BPP values.

Constant Bit Rate Versus Variable Bit Rate

As noted above BPP represents the *average* bits per pixel. There are compression algorithms that keep the BPP almost constant throughout the entire duration of the video. In this case we also get video output with a constant bit rate (CBR). This CBR video is suitable for real-time, non-buffered, fixed bandwidth video streaming (e.g. in videoconferencing).

Noting that not all frames can be compressed at the same level because quality is more severely impacted for scenes of high complexity some algorithms try to constantly adjust the BPP. They keep it high while compressing complex scenes and low for less demanding scenes. This way one gets the best quality at the smallest average bit rate (and the smallest file size accordingly). Of course when using this method the bit rate is variable because it tracks the variations of the BPP.

Technical Overview

Standard film stocks such as 16 mm and 35 mm record at 24 frames per second. For video, there are two frame rate standards: NTSC, which shoot at 30/1.001 (about 29.97) frames per second or 59.94 fields per second, and PAL, 25 frames per second or 50 fields per second.

Digital video cameras come in two different image capture formats: interlaced and deinterlaced / progressive scan.

Interlaced cameras record the image in alternating sets of lines: the odd-numbered lines are scanned, and then the even-numbered lines are scanned, then the odd-numbered lines are scanned again, and so on. One set of odd or even lines is referred to as a "field", and a consecutive pairing of two fields of opposite parity is called a *frame*. Deinterlaced cameras records each frame as distinct, with all scan lines being captured at the same moment in time. Thus, interlaced video captures samples the scene motion twice as often as progressive video does, for the same number of frames per second. Progressive-scan camcorders generally produce a slightly sharper image. However, motion may not be as smooth as interlaced video which uses 50 or 59.94 fields per second, particularly if they employ the 24 frames per second standard of film.

Digital video can be copied with no degradation in quality. No matter how many generations of a digital source is copied, it will still be as clear as the original first generation of digital footage. However a change in parameters like frame size as well as a change of the digital format can decrease the quality of the video due to new calculations that have to be made. Digital video can be manipulated and edited to follow an order or sequence on an NLE, or non-linear editing workstation, a computer-based device intended to edit video and audio. More and more, videos are edited on readily available, increasingly affordable consumer-grade computer hardware and software. However, such editing systems require ample disk space for video footage. The many video formats and parameters to be set make it quite impossible to come up with a specific number for how many minutes need how much time.

Digital video has a significantly lower cost than 35 mm film. In comparison to the high cost of film stock, the tape stock (or other electronic media used for digital video recording, such as flash memory or hard disk drive) used for recording digital video is very inexpensive. Digital video also allows footage to be viewed on location without the expensive chemical processing required by film. Also physical deliveries of tapes and broadcasts do not apply anymore. Digital television (including higher quality HDTV) started to spread in most developed countries in early 2000s. Digital video is also used in modern mobile phones and video conferencing systems. Digital video is also used for Internet distribution of media, including streaming video and peer-to-peer movie distribution. However even within Europe are lots of TV-Stations not broadcasting in HD, due to restricted budgets for new equipment for processing HD.

Many types of video compression exist for serving digital video over the internet and on optical disks. The file sizes of digital video used for professional editing are generally not practical for these purposes, and the video requires further compression with codecs such as Sorenson, H.264 and more recently Apple ProRes especially for HD. Probably the most widely used formats for delivering video over the internet are MPEG4, Quicktime, Flash and Windows Media, while MPEG2 is used almost exclusively for DVDs, providing an exceptional image in minimal size but resulting in a high level of CPU consumption to decompress.

As of 2011, the highest resolution demonstrated for digital video generation is 35 megapixels (8192 x 4320). The highest speed is attained in industrial and scientific high speed cameras that are capable of filming 1024x1024 video at up to 1 million frames per second for brief periods of recording.

Interfaces and Cables

Many interfaces have been designed specifically to handle the requirements of uncompressed digital video (from roughly 400 Mbit/s to 10 Gbit/s):

- High-Definition Multimedia Interface

- Digital Visual Interface

- Serial Digital Interface

- DisplayPort

- Digital component video

- Unified Display Interface

- FireWire

- USB

The following interface has been designed for carrying MPEG-Transport compressed video:

- DVB-ASI

Compressed video is also carried using UDP-IP over Ethernet. Two approaches exist for this:

- Using RTP as a wrapper for video packets

- 1-7 MPEG Transport Packets are placed directly in the UDP packet

Storage Formats

Encoding

All current formats, which are listed below, are PCM based.

- CCIR 601 used for broadcast stations

- MPEG-4 good for online distribution of large videos and video recorded to flash memory

- MPEG-2 used for DVDs, Super-VCDs, and many broadcast television formats

- MPEG-1 used for video CDs

- H.261

- H.263

- H.264 also known as *MPEG-4 Part 10*, or as *AVC*, used for Blu-ray Discs and some broadcast television formats

Tapes

- Betacam SX, Betacam IMX, Digital Betacam, or DigiBeta — Commercial video systems by Sony, based on original Betamax technology

- D-VHS — MPEG-2 format data recorded on a tape similar to S-VHS

- D1, D2, D3, D5, D9 (also known as Digital-S) — various SMPTE commercial digital video standards

- Digital8 — DV-format data recorded on Hi8-compatible cassettes; largely a consumer format

- DV, MiniDV — used in most of today's videotape-based consumer camcorders; designed for high quality and easy editing; can also record high-definition data (HDV) in MPEG-2 format

- DVCAM, DVCPRO — used in professional broadcast operations; similar to DV but generally considered more robust; though DV-compatible, these formats have better audio handling.

- DVCPRO50, DVCPROHD support higher bandwidths as compared to Panasonic's DVCPRO.

- HDCAM was introduced by Sony as a high-definition alternative to DigiBeta.

- MicroMV — MPEG-2-format data recorded on a very small, matchbook-sized cassette; obsolete

- ProHD — name used by JVC for its MPEG-2-based professional camcorders

Discs

- Blu-ray Disc

- DVD

- VCD

E-Book

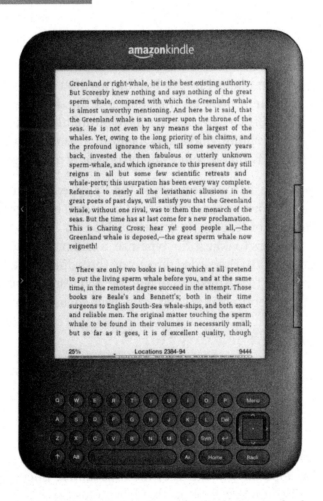

Amazon's Kindle Keyboard e-reader displaying an e-book

As a generic term, an electronic book (variously: e-book, eBook, e-Book, ebook, digital book or e-edition) or a digital book is a book-publication in digital form, consisting of text, images, or both, readable on computers or other electronic devices. Although sometimes defined as "an electronic version of a printed book", many e-books exist without any printed equivalent. Commercially produced and sold e-books are usually intended to be read on dedicated e-readers. However, almost any sophisticated electronic device that features a controllable viewing screen, including computers, tablets and smartphones can also be used to read e-books. Nowadays, both print as well as e-book selling is moving to the web. For instance, in the United States of America more "books are published online than distributed in hard copy in book shops". The main reasons that people are buying books online are prices, comfort and selection process. Notwithstanding that most people appreciate higher regular "bricks & mortar" bookshops, "yet almost every single one of us is buying books online". Based on this information it is almost certain that the e-publishing will soon overtake traditional publishing.

E-book reading is increasing in the US; by 2014 28% of adults had read an e-book, compared to 23% in 2013. This is increasing because 50% of American adults by 2014 had a dedicated device, either an e-reader or a tablet, compared to 30% owning such a device by the end of 2013.

History

The Readies (1930)

The idea of the e-reader viewing e-books came to Bob Brown after watching his first "talkie" (movie with sound). In 1930, he wrote a book on this idea and titled it *The Readies*, playing off the idea of the "talkie". In his book, Brown says movies have outmaneuvered the book by creating the "talkies" and, as a result, reading should find a new medium: "A machine that will allow us to keep up with the vast volume of print available today and be optically pleasing".

Although Brown came up with the idea intellectually in the 1930s, early commercial e-readers did not follow his model. Nevertheless, Brown in many ways predicted what e-readers would become and what they would mean to the medium of reading. In an article Jennifer Schuessler writes, "The machine, Brown argued, would allow readers to adjust the type size, avoid paper cuts and save trees, all while hastening the day when words could be 'recorded directly on the palpitating ether.'" He felt the e-reader should bring a completely new life to the medium of reading. Schuessler relates it to a DJ spinning bits of old songs to create a beat or an entirely new song as opposed to just a remix of a familiar song.

Candidates for the First E-Book Inventor

The inventor of the first e-book is not widely agreed upon. Some notable candidates include the following:

Ángela Ruiz Robles (1949)

In 1949, Ángela Ruiz Robles, a teacher from Galicia, Spain, patented in her country the first electronic book reader, *la Enciclopedia Mecánica*, or the Mechanical Encyclopedia. Her idea behind the device was to decrease the number of books that her pupils carried to the school.

Roberto Busa (Late 1949 – 1970)

The first e-book may be the *Index Thomisticus*, a heavily annotated electronic index to the works of Thomas Aquinas, prepared by Roberto Busa beginning in 1949 and completed in the 1970s. Although originally stored on a single computer, a distributable CD-ROM version appeared in 1989. However, this work is sometimes omitted; perhaps because the digitized text was a means to studying written texts and developing linguistic concordances, rather than as a published edition in its own right. In 2005, the Index was published online.

Doug Engelbart and Andries Van Dam (1960S)

Alternatively, some historians consider electronic books to have started in the early 1960s, with the NLS project headed by Doug Engelbart at Stanford Research Institute (SRI), and the Hypertext Editing System and FRESS projects headed by Andries van Dam at Brown University. Augment ran on specialized hardware, while FRESS ran on IBM mainframes. FRESS documents were structure-oriented rather than line-oriented, and were formatted dynamically for different users, display hardware, window sizes, and so on, as well as having automated tables of contents, indexes, and so on. All these systems also provided extensive hyperlinking, graphics, and other capabilities. Van Dam is generally thought to have coined the term "electronic book", and it was established enough to use in an article title by 1985.

FRESS was used for reading extensive primary texts online, as well as for annotation and online discussions in several courses, including English Poetry and Biochemistry. Brown faculty made extensive use of FRESS; for example the philosopher Roderick Chisholm used it to produce several of his books. Thus in the Preface to *Person and Object* (1979) he writes "The book would not have been completed without the epoch-making File Retrieval and Editing System..."

Brown University's work in electronic book systems continued for many years, including US Navy funded projects for electronic repair-manuals; a large-scale distributed hypermedia system known as InterMedia; a spinoff company Electronic Book Technologies that built DynaText, the first SGML-based e-reader system; and the Scholarly Technology Group's extensive work on the Open eBook standard.

Michael Hart (left) and Gregory Newby (right) of *Project Gutenberg*, 2006

Michael S. Hart (1971)

Despite the extensive earlier history, several publications report Michael S. Hart as the inventor of the e-book. In 1971, the operators of the Xerox Sigma V mainframe at the University of Illinois gave Hart extensive computer-time. Seeking a worthy use of this resource, he created his first electronic document by typing the United States Declaration of Independence into a computer in plain text. Hart planned to create documents using plain text to make them as easy as possible to download and view on devices.

Early E-Book Implementations

After Hart first adapted the *Declaration of Independence* into an electronic document in 1971, *Project Gutenberg* was launched to create electronic copies of more texts - especially books.

Another early e-book implementation was the desktop prototype for a proposed notebook computer, the *Dynabook,* in the 1970s at PARC: a general-purpose portable personal computer capable of displaying books for reading.

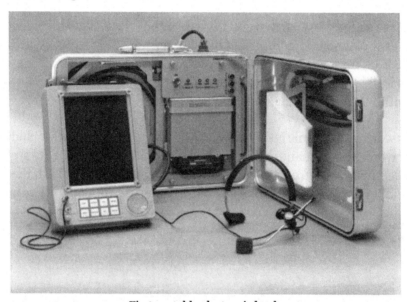

First portable electronic book

In 1980 the Department of Defense began concept development for a portable electronic delivery device for technical maintenance information called project PEAM, the Portable Electronic Aid for Maintenance. Detailed specifications were completed in FY 82, and prototype development began with Texas Instruments that same year. Four prototypes were produced and delivered for testing in 1986. Tests were completed in 1987. The final summary report was produced by the US Army research Institute for the Behavioral and Social Sciences in 1989 authored by Robert Wisher and J. Peter Kincaid.

A patent application for the PEAM device was submitted by Texas Instruments titled "Apparatus for delivering procedural type instructions" was submitted Dec 4, 1985 listing John K. Harkins and Stephen H. Morriss as inventors.

In 1992, Sony launched the Data Discman, an electronic book reader that could read e-books that were stored on CDs. One of the electronic publications that could be played on the Data Discman was called *The Library of the Future.*

Early e-books were generally written for specialty areas and a limited audience, meant to be read only by small and devoted interest groups. The scope of the subject matter of these e-books included technical manuals for hardware, manufacturing techniques, and other subjects. In the 1990s, the general availability of the Internet made transferring electronic files much easier, including e-books.

E-Book Formats

Reading an e-book on public transit

As e-book formats emerged and proliferated, some garnered support from major software companies, such as Adobe with its PDF format that was introduced in 1993. Different e-readers followed different formats, most of them specializing in only one format, thereby fragmenting the e-book market even more. Due to the exclusiveness and limited readerships of e-books, the fractured market of independent publishers and specialty authors lacked consensus regarding a standard for packaging and selling e-books.

However, in the late 1990s, a consortium formed to develop the Open eBook format as a way for authors and publishers to provide a single source-document which many book-reading software and hardware platforms could handle. Open eBook as defined required subsets of XHTML and CSS; a set of multimedia formats (others could be used, but there must also be a fallback in one of the required formats), and an XML schema for a "manifest", to list the components of a given e-book, identify a table of contents, cover art, and so on. This format led to the open format EPUB. Google Books has converted many public domain works to this open format.

In 2010, e-books continued to gain in their own specialist and underground markets. Many e-book publishers began distributing books that were in the public domain. At the same time, authors with books that were not accepted by publishers offered their works online so they could be seen by others. Unofficial (and occasionally unauthorized) catalogs of books became available on the web, and sites devoted to e-books began disseminating information about e-books to the public.

Nearly two-thirds of the U.S. Consumer e-book publishing market are controlled by the "Big Five". The "Big Five" publishers include: Hachette, HarperCollins, Macmillan, Penguin Random House and Simon & Schuster.

Libraries

US Libraries began providing free e-books to the public in 1998 through their web sites and associated services, although the e-books were primarily scholarly, technical or professional in nature, and could not be downloaded. In 2003, libraries began offering free downloadable popular fiction and non-fiction e-books to the public, launching an e-book lending model that worked much more successfully for public libraries. The number of library e-book distributors and lending models continued to increase over the next few years. From 2005 to 2008 libraries experienced 60% growth in e-book collections. In 2010, a Public Library Funding and Technology Access Study found that 66% of public libraries in the US were offering e-books, and a large movement in the library industry began seriously examining the issues related to lending e-books, acknowledging a tipping point of broad e-book usage. However, some publishers and authors have not endorsed the concept of electronic publishing, citing issues with demand, piracy and proprietary devices. In a survey of interlibrary loan librarians it was found that 92% of libraries held e-books in their collections and that 27% of those libraries had negotiated interlibrary loan rights for some of their e-books. This survey found significant barriers to conducting interlibrary loan for e-books. Demand-driven acquisition (DDA) has been around for a few years in public libraries, which allows vendors to streamline the acquisition process by offering to match a library's selection profile to the vendor's e-book titles. The library's catalog is then populated with records for all the e-books that match the profile. The decision to purchase the title is left to the patrons, although the library can set purchasing conditions such as a maximum price and purchasing caps so that the dedicated funds are spent according to the library's budget. The 2012 meeting of the Association of American University Presses included a panel on patron-drive acquisition (PDA) of books produced by university presses based on a preliminary report by Joseph Esposito, a digital publishing consultant who has studied the implications of PDA with a grant from the Andrew W. Mellon Foundation.

Challenges

Although the demand for e-book services in libraries has grown, difficulties keep libraries from providing the e-books to its clients. Publishers will sell e-books to libraries, but they only have a limited license to the title in most cases. This means the library does not own the electronic text but that they can circulate it for either a certain period of time or a certain amount of check outs, or both. When a library purchases a e-book license, the cost is at least three times what it would be for a personal consumer.

Archival Storage

The Internet Archive and Open Library offers over 6,000,000 fully accessible public domain e-books. Project Gutenberg has over 52,000 freely available public domain e-books.

Dedicated Hardware Readers and Mobile Reader Software

An e-reader, also called an e-book reader or e-book device, is a mobile electronic device that is designed primarily for the purpose of reading e-books and digital periodicals. An e-reader is similar in form, but more limited in purpose than a tablet. In comparison to tablets, many e-readers are better than tablets for reading because they are more portable, have better readability in sunlight and have longer battery life.

The BEBook e-reader

In July 2010, online bookseller Amazon.com reported sales of e-books for its proprietary Kindle outnumbered sales of hardcover books for the first time ever during the second quarter of 2010, saying it sold 140 e-books for every 100 hardcover books, including hardcovers for which there was no digital edition. By January 2011, e-book sales at Amazon had surpassed its paperback sales. In the overall US market, paperback book sales are still much larger than either hardcover or e-book; the American Publishing Association estimated e-books represented 8.5% of sales as of mid-2010, up from 3% a year before. At the end of the first quarter of 2012, e-book sales in the United States surpassed hardcover book sales for the first time.

In Canada, *The Sentimentalists* won the prestigious national Giller Prize. Owing to the small scale of the novel's independent publisher, the book was initially not widely available in printed form, but the e-book edition became the top-selling title for Kobo devices in 2010.

Until late 2013, use of an e-reader was not allowed on airplanes during takeoff and landing. In November 2013, the FAA allowed use of e-readers on airplanes at all times if it is in Airplane Mode, which means all radios turned off, and Europe followed this guidance the next month. In 2014, the New York Times predicted that by 2018 e-books will make up over 50% of total consumer publishing revenue in the United States and Great Britain.

E-Reader Applications

Some of the major book retailers and multiple third-party developers offer free (and in some third-party cases, premium paid) e-reader applications for the Mac and PC computers as well as for Android, Blackberry, iPad, iPhone, Windows Phone and Palm OS devices to allow the reading of e-books and other documents independently of dedicated e-book devices. Examples are apps for the Amazon Kindle, Barnes & Noble Nook, Kobo eReader, and Sony Reader.

Timeline

Until 1979

1949

- Ángela Ruiz Robles patented in Galicia, Spain, the idea of the electronic book, called the Mechanical Encyclopedia.
- Roberto Busa begins planning the *Index Thomisticus*.

1963

- Doug Engelbart starts the NLS (and later Augment) projects.

1965

- Andries van Dam starts the HES (and later FRESS) projects, with assistance from Ted Nelson, to develop and use electronic textbooks for humanities and in pedagogy.

1971

- Michael S. Hart types the US Declaration of Independence into a computer to create the first e-book available on the Internet and launches Project Gutenberg in order to create electronic copies of more books.

1978

- *The Hitchhiker's Guide to the Galaxy* radio series launches (novel published in 1979), featuring an electronic reference book containing all knowledge in the Galaxy. This vast amount of data could be fit into something the size of a large paperback book, with updates received over the "Sub-Etha".

1979

- Roberto Busa finishes the *Index Thomisticus*, a complete lemmatisation of the 56 printed volumes of Saint Thomas Aquinas and of a few related authors.

1980–99

1986

- Judy Malloy wrote and programmed *Uncle Roger*, the first online hypertext fiction with links that took the narrative in different directions depending on the reader's choice.

1989

- Project Gutenberg releases its 10th e-book to its website.

- Franklin Computer released an electronic edition of the Bible that was read on a stand-alone device.

1990

- Eastgate Systems publishes the first hypertext fiction released on floppy disk, "Afternoon, a story", by Michael Joyce.

- Electronic Book Technologies releases DynaText, the first SGML-based system for delivering large-scale books such as aircraft technical manuals. It was later tested on a US aircraft carrier as replacement for paper manuals.

1991

- Voyager Company develops Expanded Books, which are books on CD-ROM in a digital format.

1992

The DD-8 Data Discman

- F. Crugnola and I. Rigamonti design and create the first e-reader, called Incipit, as a thesis project at the Polytechnic University of Milan.

- Sony launches the Data Discman e-book player.

- Charles Stack's Book Stacks Unlimited begins selling new physical books online.

1993

- Peter James published his novel Host on two floppy disks and at the time it was called the "world's first electronic novel"; a copy of it is stored at the Science Museum.

- Hugo Award and Nebula Award nominee works are included on a CD-ROM by Brad Templeton.

- Bibliobytes, a website for obtaining digital books, both for free and for sale on the Internet, launches.

1994

- C & M Online is founded in Raleigh, North Carolina and publishes e-books through its imprint, Boson Books. Authors include Fred Chappell, Kelly Cherry, Leon Katz, Richard Popkin, and Robert Rodman.

- The popular format for publishing e-books changed from plain text to HTML.

1995

- Online poet Alexis Kirke discusses the need for wireless internet electronic paper readers in his article "The Emuse".

1996

- Project Gutenberg reaches 1,000 titles.

- Joseph Jacobson works at MIT to create electronic ink, a high-contrast, low-cost, read/write/erase medium to display e-books.

1997

- E Ink Corporation is co-founded in 1997 by MIT undergraduates J.D. Albert, Barrett Comiskey, MIT professor Joseph Jacobson, as well as Jeremy Rubin and Russ Wilcox to create an electronic printing technology. This technology is later used to on the displays of the Sony Reader, Barnes & Noble Nook, and Amazon Kindle.

1998

Bookeen's Cybook Gen1

- NuroMedia released the first handheld e-reader, the Rocket eBook.

- SoftBook launched its SoftBook reader. This e-reader, with expandable storage, could store up to 100,000 pages of content, including text, graphics and pictures.

- The Cybook was sold and manufactured at first by Cytale (1998–2003) and later by Bookeen.

1999

- The NIST released the Open eBook format based on XML to the public domain, most future e-book formats derive from Open eBook. and on XML.

- Publisher Simon & Schuster created a new imprint called ibooks and became the first trade publisher to simultaneously to publish some of their titles in e-book and print format.

- Oxford University Press offered a selection of its books available as e-books through netLibrary.

- Publisher Baen Books opens up the Baen Free Library to make available Baen titles as free e-books.

- Kim Blagg, via her company Books OnScreen, began selling multimedia-enhanced e-books on CDs through retailers including Amazon, Barnes & Noble and Borders Books.

2000s

2000

- Joseph Jacobson, Barrett O. Comiskey and Jonathan D. Albert are granted US patents related to displaying electronic books, these patents are later used in the displays for most e-readers.

- Stephen King releases his novella *Riding the Bullet* exclusively online and it became the first mass-market e-book, selling 500,000 copies in 48 hours.

- Microsoft releases the Microsoft Reader with ClearType for increased readability on PCs and handheld devices.

- Microsoft and Amazon worked together to sell e-books that could be purchased on Amazon and using Microsoft software downloaded to PCs and handhelds.

- A digitized version of the Gutenberg Bible was made available online at the British Library.

2001

- Adobe releases Adobe Acrobat Reader 5.0 allowing users to underline, take notes and bookmark.

2002

- Palm, Inc and OverDrive, Inc make Palm Reader e-books available worldwide and offered over 5,000 e-books in several languages; these could be read on Palm PDAs or using a computer application.

- Random House and HarperCollins start to sell digital versions of their titles in English.

2004

- Sony Librie, first e-reader using an E Ink display was released; it had a six-inch screen.

- Google announces plans to digitize the holdings of several major libraries, as part of what would later be called the Google Books Library Project.

2005

- Amazon buys Mobipocket, the creater of the mobi e-book file format and e-reader software.

- Google is sued for copyright infringement by the Authors Guild for scanning books still in copyright.

2006

- Sony Reader PRS-500 with an E Ink screen and two weeks of battery life was released.

- LibreDigital launched BookBrowse as an online reader for publisher content.

2007

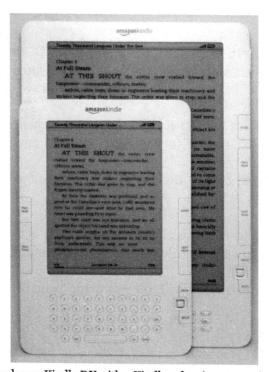

The larger Kindle DX with a Kindle 2 for size comparison

- The International Digital Publishing Forum releases EPUB to replace Open eBook.

- Amazon releases the Kindle e-reader with 6-inch E Ink screen in the US and it sells outs in 5.5 hours.

- Bookeen launches Cybook Gen3 in Europe, it could display e-books and play audiobooks."-*Cybook specifications"*.

2008

- Adobe and Sony agree to share their technologies (Adobe Reader and DRM) with each other.

- Sony sells the Sony Reader PRS-505 in UK and France.

- BooksOnBoard becomes first retailer to sell e-books for iPhones.

2009

- Bookeen releases the Cybook Opus in the US and in Europe.

- Sony releases the Reader Pocket Edition and Reader Touch Edition.

- Amazon releases the Kindle 2 that included a text-to-speech feature.

- Amazon releases the Kindle DX that had a 9.7-inch screen in the US.

- Barnes & Noble releases the Nook e-reader in the US.

- Amazon released the *Kindle for PC* application in late 2009, making the Kindle Store library available outside its hardware.

2010s

2010

- In January 2010, Amazon.com releases the Kindle DX International Edition worldwide.

- Bookeen reveals the Cybook Orizon at CES.

- Apple releases the iPad bundled with an e-book app called iBooks.

- Kobo Inc. releases its Kobo eReader to be sold at Indigo/Chapters in Canada and Borders in the United States.

- Amazon reports that its e-book sales outnumbered sales of hardcover books for the first time ever during the second quarter of 2010.

- Amazon releases the third generation Kindle, available in Wi-Fi and 3G & Wi-Fi versions.

- Kobo Inc. releases an updated Kobo eReader, which included Wi-Fi.

- Barnes & Noble releases the Nook Color, a color LCD tablet.

- Sony releases its second generation Daily Edition PRS-950.

- Google launches Google eBooks offering over 3 million titles, becoming the world's largest e-book store.

- PocketBook expands its line with an Android e-reader.

2011

- The idea of the next-generation digital book called 'interactive e-book' was proposed.

- Amazon.com announces in May that its e-book sales in the US now exceed all of its printed book sales.

- Barnes & Noble releases the Nook Simple Touch e-reader and Nook Tablet.

- Bookeen launches its own e-books store, BookeenStore.com, and starts to sell digital versions of titles in French.

- Nature Publishing publishes *Principles of Biology*, a customizable, modular textbook, with no corresponding paper edition.

- The e-reader market grows in Spain, and companies like Telefónica, Fnac, and Casa del Libro launches their e-readers with the Spanish brand "bq readers".

- Amazon launches the Kindle Fire and Kindle Touch, both devices designed for e-reading.

2012

- E-books sold in the US market collects over three billion in revenue.

- Kbuuk released the cloud-based e-book self-publishing SaaS platform on the Pubsoft digital publishing engine.

- Apple releases iBooks Author, software for creating iPad e-books to be directly published in its iBooks bookstore or to be shared as PDF files.

- Apple opens a textbook section in its iBooks bookstore.

- Library.nu - previously called ebooksclub.org and gigapedia.com, a popular linking website for downloading e-books - was accused of copyright infringement and shut down by court order on February 15.

- The publishing companies Random House, Holtzbrinck, and arvato get an e-book library called Skoobe on the market.

- US Department of Justice prepares anti-trust lawsuit against Apple, Simon & Schuster, Hachette Book Group, Penguin Group, Macmillan, and HarperCollins, alleging collusion to increase the price of books sold on Amazon.

- PocketBook releases the PocketBook Touch, an E Ink Pearl e-reader, winning awards from German magazines *Tablet PC* and *Computer Bild*.

- In September, Amazon releases the Kindle Paperwhite, its first e-reader with built-in front LED lights.

2013

- In April 2013, Barnes & Noble posts losses of $475 million on its Nook business for the prior fiscal year and in June announces its intention to discontinue manufacturing Nook tablets, although it plans to continue making and designing black-and-white e-readers such as the Nook Simple Touch, which "are more geared to serious readers, who are its customers, than to tablets".

- The Association of American Publishers announces that e-books now account for about 20% of book sales. Barnes & Noble estimates it has a 27% share of the U.S. e-book market.

- In June, Apple executive Keith Moerer testifies in the e-book price fixing trial that the iBookstore held approximately 20% of the e-book market share in the United States within the months after launch - a figure that *Publishers Weekly* reports is roughly double many of the previous estimates made by third parties. Moerer further testified that iBookstore acquired about an additional 20% by adding Random House in 2011.

- Five major US e-book publishers, as part of their settlement of a price-fixing suit, were ordered to refund about $3 for every electronic copy of a New York Times best-seller that they sold from April 2010 to May 2012. This could equal $160 million in settlement charges.

- Barnes & Noble releases the Nook Glowlight, which has a 6-inch touchscreen using E Ink Pearl and Regal, with built-in front LED lights.

- In April, Kobo released the Kobo Aura HD with a 6.8-inch screen, which is larger than the current models produced by its US competitors.

- In May, Mofibo launched the first Scandinavian unlimited access e-book subscription service.

- In July, US District Court Judge Denise Cote finds Apple guilty of conspiring to raise the retail price of e-books and schedules a trial in 2014 to determine damages.

- In September, Oyster launches its unlimited access e-book subscription service.

- In November, US District Judge Chin sides with Google in *Authors Guild v. Google*, citing fair use. The authors said they would appeal.

- In December, Scribd launched the first public unlimited access subscription service for e-books.

2014

- In early 2014, Amazon launches Kindle Unlimited as an unlimited-access e-book and audiobook subscription service.

- In April, Kobo released the Aura H_2O, the world's first waterproof commercially produced e-reader.

- In June, US District Court Judge Cote grants class action certification to plaintiffs in a lawsuit over Apple's alleged e-book price conspiracy; the plaintiffs are seeking $840 million in damages. Apple appeals the decision.

- In June, Apple settles the e-book antitrust case that alleged Apple conspired to e-book price fixing out of court with the States; however if Judge Cote's ruling is overturned in appeal the settlement would be reversed.

2015

- In June 2015, the 2nd US Circuit Court of Appeals with a 2-1 vote concurs with Judge Cote that Apple conspired to e-book price fixing and violated federal antitrust law. Apple appealed the decision.

- In June, Amazon released the Kindle Paperwhite (3rd generation) that is the first e-reader to feature Bookerly, a font exclusively designed for e-readers.

- In September, Oyster announced its unlimited access e-book subscription service would be shut down in early 2016 and that it would be acquired by Google.

- In September, Malaysian e-book company, e-Sentral, introduced for the first time geo-location distribution technology for e-books via bluetooth beacon. It was first demonstrated in a large scale at Kuala Lumpur International Airport.

- In October, Amazon releases the Kindle Voyage that has a 6-inch, 300 ppi E Ink Carta HD display, which was the highest resolution and contrast available in e-readers as of 2014. It also features adaptive LED lights and page turn sensors on the sides of the device.

- In October, B&N released the Glowlight Plus, its first waterproof e-reader.

- In October, the US appeals court sided with Google instead of the Authors' Guild, declaring that Google did not violate copyright law in its book scanning project.

- In December, Playster launched an unlimited-access subscription service including e-books and audiobooks.

- By the end of 2015, Google Books scanned more than 25 million books.

- By 2015, over 70 million e-readers had been shipped worldwide.

2016

- In March 2016, the Supreme Court of the United States declined to hear Apple's appeal that it conspired to e-book price fixing therefore the previous court decision stands, which means Apple must pay $450 million.

- In April, the Supreme Court declined to hear the Authors Guild's appeal of its book scanning case that means the lower court's decision stands; this result means Google is allowed to scan library books and display snippets in search results without violating US copyright law.

- In April, Amazon released the Kindle Oasis, its first e-reader in five years to have physical page turn buttons and as a premium product includes a leather case with a battery inside; the Oasis without the case is the lightest e-reader on the market.

- In late 2016, Kobo will release the Aura One that will be the first e-reader with a 7.8-inch E Ink Carta HD display with 300 ppi.

Formats

Writers and publishers have many formats to choose from when publishing e-books. Each format has advantages and disadvantages. The most popular e-readers and their natively supported formats are shown below:

Reader	Native e-book formats
Amazon Kindle and Fire tablets	AZW, AZW3, KF8, non-DRM MOBI, PDF, PRC, TXT
Barnes & Noble Nook and Nook Tablet	EPUB, PDF
Apple iPad	EPUB, IBA (Multitouch books made via iBooks Author), PDF
Sony Reader	EPUB, PDF, TXT, RTF, DOC, BBeB
Kobo eReader and Kobo Arc	EPUB, PDF, TXT, RTF, HTML, CBR (comic), CBZ (comic)
PocketBook Reader and PocketBook Touch	EPUB DRM, EPUB, PDF DRM, PDF, FB2, FB2.ZIP, TXT, DJVU, HTM, HTML, DOC, DOCX, RTF, CHM, TCR, PRC (MOBI)

Digital Rights Management

Most e-book publishers do not warn their customers about the possible implications of the digital rights management tied to their products. Generally they claim that digital rights management is meant to prevent copying of the e-book. However, in many cases it is also possible that digital rights management will result in the complete denial of access by the purchaser to the e-book.

The e-books sold by most major publishers and electronic retailers, which are Amazon.com, Google, Barnes & Noble, Kobo Inc. and Apple Inc., are DRM-protected and tied to the publisher's e-reader software or hardware. The first major publisher to omit DRM was Tor Books, one of the largest publishers of science fiction and fantasy, in 2012. Smaller e-book publishers such as O'Reilly Media, Carina Press and Baen Books had already forgone DRM previously.

Production

Some e-books are produced simultaneously with the production of a printed format, as described in electronic publishing, though in many instances they may not be put on sale until later. Often, e-books are produced from pre-existing hard-copy books, generally by document scanning, sometimes with the use of robotic book scanners, having the technology to quickly scan books without damaging the original print edition. Scanning a book produces a set of image files, which may additionally be converted into text format by an OCR program. Occasionally, as in some e-text projects, a book may be produced by re-entering the text from a keyboard.

Sometimes only the electronic version of a book is produced by the publisher. It is even possible to release an e-book chapter by chapter as each chapter is written.This is useful in fields such as information technology where topics can change quickly in the months that it takes to write a typical book. It is also possible to convert an electronic book to a printed book by print on demand. However these are exceptions as tradition dictates that a book be launched in the print format and later if the author wishes an electronic version is produced.

The New York Times keeps a list of best-selling e-books, for both fiction and non-fiction.

E-Book Reading Data

All of the e-readers and reading apps are capable of tracking e-book reading data, and the data could contain which e-books users open, how long the users spend reading each e-book and how much of each e-book is finished.

Kobo Inc. released e-book reading data collected from over 21 million readers worldwide in 2014. Some of the data said that only 44.4% of UK readers finished the bestselling e-book The Goldfinch and the 2014 number one bestselling e-book in the UK, "One Cold Night" was completed by 69% of readers; this is evidence that while popular e-books are being completely read, many e-books are only sampled.

Comparison to Printed Books

Advantages

iLiad e-book reader equipped with an e-paper display visible in sunlight

In the space that a comparably sized print book takes up, an e-reader can contain thousands of e-books, limited only by its memory capacity.

Depending on the device, an e-book may be readable in low light or even total darkness. Many e-readers have a built-in light source, can enlarge or change fonts, use Text-to-speech software to read the text aloud for visually impaired, partially sighted, elderly or dyslexic people or just for convenience. Additionally, e-books allow for readers to look up words or find more information about the topic immediately. Material can be organized however the author prefers and is not limited to a linear path through the book as hyper-text can allow a number of paths through the material.

Printed books use three times more raw materials and 78 times more water to produce when compared to e-books.

While an e-reader costs more than most individual books, e-books usually have a lower cost than paper books. Moreover, numerous e-books are available online free of charge. For example, all books printed before 1923 are in the public domain.

E-books may be printed for less than the price of traditional books using on-demand book printers.

Depending on possible digital rights management, e-books (unlike physical books) can be backed up and recovered in the case of loss or damage to the device on which they are stored, and it may be possible to recover a new copy without incurring an additional cost from the distributor, as well as to synchronize the text, highlights and bookmarks across several devices.

E-readers normally include dictionaries. This allows the user to look up the meaning of words while reading. Amazon has reported that 85% of readers look up a word while reading.

Downsides

There may be a lack of privacy for the user's e-book reading activities; for example, Amazon.com knows the user's identity, what the user is reading, whether the user has finished the book, what page the user is on, how long the user has spent on each page, and which passages the user may have highlighted.

The spine of the printed book is an important aspect in book design and of its beauty as an object

The main obstacle to the e-book is that a large portion of people value the printed book as an object itself, including aspects such as the texture, smell, weight and appearance on the shelf. Print books are also considered valuable cultural items, and symbols of liberal education and the Humanities.

As Joe Queenan has written:

Electronic books are ideal for people who value the information contained in them, or who have vision problems, or who like to read on the subway, or who do not want other people to see how they are amusing themselves, or who have storage and clutter issues, but they are useless for people who are engaged in an intense, lifelong love affair with books. Books that we can touch; books that we can smell; books that we can depend on.

Kobo found that 60% of e-books that are purchased from their e-book store are never opened and found that the more expensive the book is, the more likely the reader would at least open the e-book.

Market Share of Digital Books

United States

US Adult Fiction & Non fiction book sales in 2014

Sellers		Percent
Adult non-fiction print		42.0%
Adult fiction print		23.0%
Adult fiction ebook		21.0%
Adult fiction ebook (no ISBN)		6.0%
Adult non-fiction ebook		6.0%
Adult non-fiction ebook (no ISBN)		2.0%

In 2015, the Author Earnings Report estimates that Amazon holds a 74% market share of the e-books sold in the US.

Canada

Market share of e-readers in Canada by Ipsos Reid as of January 2012

Sellers		Percent
Kobo		46.0%
Amazon		24.0%
Sony		18.0%
Others		12.0%

Spain

In 2013, Carrenho estimates that e-books would have a 15% market share in Spain in 2015.

UK

According to Nielsen Book Research, e-book share went from 20% to 33% between 2012 and 2014, but down to 29% in the first quarter of 2015. Amazon-published and self-published titles accounted for 17 million of those books - worth £58m – in 2014, representing 5% of the overall book market and 15% of the digital market. The volume and value sales are similar to 2013 but up 70% since 2012.

Germany

The Wischenbart Report 2015 estimates the e-book market share to be 4.3%.

Brazil

The Brazilian e-book market is only emerging. Brazilians are technology savvy, and that attitude is shared by the government. In 2013, around 2.5% of all trade titles sold were in digital format. This was a 400% growth over 2012, when only 0.5% of trade titles were digital. In 2014, the growth was slower, Brazil had 3.5% of its trade titles being sold as e-books.

China

The Wischenbart Report 2015 estimates the e-book market share to be around 1%.

Instant Messaging

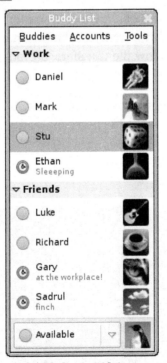

A buddy list in Pidgin 2.0

Instant messaging (IM) is a type of online chat which offers real-time text transmission over the Internet. A LAN messenger operates in a similar way over a local area network. Short messages are typically transmitted bi-directionally between two parties, when each user chooses to complete a thought and select "send". Some IM applications can use push technology to provide real-time text, which transmits messages character by character, as they are composed. More advanced instant messaging can add file transfer, clickable hyperlinks, Voice over IP, or video chat.

Non-IM types of chat include multicast transmission, usually referred to as "chat rooms", where participants might be anonymous or might be previously known to each other (for example collaborators on a project that is using chat to facilitate communication). Instant messaging systems tend to facilitate connections between specified known users (often using a contact list also known as a "buddy list" or "friend list"). Depending on the IM protocol, the technical architecture can be peer-to-peer (direct point-to-point transmission) or client-server (a central server retransmits messages from the sender to the communication device).

Overview

Instant messaging is a set of communication technologies used for text-based communication between two or more participants over the Internet or other types of networks. IM–chat happens in real-time. Of importance is that online chat and instant messaging differ from other technologies such as email due to the perceived quasi-synchrony of the communications by the users. Some systems permit messages to be sent to users not then 'logged on' (*offline messages*), thus removing some differences between IM and email (often done by sending the message to the associated email account).

IM allows effective and efficient communication, allowing immediate receipt of acknowledgment or reply. However IM is basically not necessarily supported by transaction control. In many cases, instant messaging includes added features which can make it even more popular. For example, users may see each other via webcams, or talk directly for free over the Internet using a microphone and headphones or loudspeakers. Many applications allow file transfers, although they are usually limited in the permissible file-size.

It is usually possible to save a text conversation for later reference. Instant messages are often logged in a local message history, making it similar to the persistent nature of emails.

History

Command-line Unix "talk", using a split screen user interface, was popular in the 1980s and early 1990s.

Though the term dates from the 1990s, instant messaging predates the Internet, first appearing on multi-user operating systems like Compatible Time-Sharing System (CTSS) and Multiplexed Information and Computing Service (Multics) in the mid-1960s. Initially, some of these systems were used as notification systems for services like printing, but quickly were used to facilitate communication with other users logged into the same machine. As networks developed, the protocols spread with the networks. Some of these used a peer-to-peer protocol (e.g. talk, ntalk and ytalk), while others required peers to connect to a server. The Zephyr Notification Service (still in use at some institutions) was invented at MIT's Project Athena in the 1980s to allow service providers to locate and send messages to users.

Parallel to instant messaging were early online chat facilities, the earliest of which was Talkomatic (1973) on the PLATO system. During the bulletin board system (BBS) phenomenon that peaked during the 1980s, some systems incorporated chat features which were similar to instant messaging; Freelancin' Roundtable was one prime example. The first such general-availability commercial online chat service (as opposed to PLATO, which was educational) was the CompuServe CB Simulator in 1980, created by CompuServe executive Alexander "Sandy" Trevor in Columbus, Ohio.

Early instant messaging programs were primarily real-time text, where characters appeared as they were typed. This includes the Unix "talk" command line program, which was popular in the 1980s and early 1990s. Some BBS chat programs (i.e. Celerity BBS) also used a similar interface. Modern implementations of real-time text also exist in instant messengers, such as AOL's Real-Time IM as an optional feature.

In the latter half of the 1980s and into the early 1990s, the Quantum Link online service for Commodore 64 computers offered user-to-user messages between concurrently connected customers, which they called "On-Line Messages" (or OLM for short), and later "FlashMail." (Quantum Link later became America Online and made AOL Instant Messenger (AIM), discussed later). While the Quantum Link client software ran on a Commodore 64, using only the Commodore's PETSCII text-graphics, the screen was visually divided into sections and OLMs would appear as a yellow bar saying "Message From:" and the name of the sender along with the message across the top of whatever the user was already doing, and presented a list of options for responding. As such, it could be considered a type of graphical user interface (GUI), albeit much more primitive than the later Unix, Windows and Macintosh based GUI IM software. OLMs were what Q-Link called "Plus Services" meaning they charged an extra per-minute fee on top of the monthly Q-Link access costs.

Modern, Internet-wide, GUI-based messaging clients as they are known today, began to take off in the mid-1990s with PowWow, ICQ, and AOL Instant Messenger. Similar functionality was offered by CU-SeeMe in 1992; though primarily an audio/video chat link, users could also send textual messages to each other. AOL later acquired Mirabilis, the authors of ICQ; a few years later ICQ (now owned by AOL) was awarded two patents for instant messaging by the U.S. patent office. Meanwhile, other companies developed their own software; (Excite, MSN, Ubique, and Yahoo!), each with its own proprietary protocol and client; users therefore had to run multiple client applications if they wished to use more than one of these networks. In 1998, IBM released IBM Lotus Sametime, a product based on technology acquired when IBM bought Haifa-based Ubique and Lexington-based Databeam.

In 2000, an open source application and open standards-based protocol called Jabber was launched. The protocol was standardized under the name Extensible Messaging and Presence Protocol (XMPP). XMPP servers could act as gateways to other IM protocols, reducing the need to run multiple clients. Multi-protocol clients can use any of the popular IM protocols by using additional local libraries for each protocol. IBM Lotus Sametime's November 2007 release added IBM Lotus Sametime Gateway support for XMPP.

As of 2010, social networking providers often offer IM abilities. Facebook Chat is a form of instant messaging, and Twitter can be thought of as a Web 2.0 instant messaging system. Similar server-side chat features are part of most dating websites, such as OKCupid or PlentyofFish. The spread of smartphones and similar devices in the late 2000s also caused increased competition with conventional instant messaging, by making text messaging services still more ubiquitous.

Many instant messaging services offer video calling features, voice over IP and web conferencing services. Web conferencing services can integrate both video calling and instant messaging abilities. Some instant messaging companies are also offering desktop sharing, IP radio, and IPTV to the voice and video features.

The term "Instant Messenger" is a service mark of Time Warner and may not be used in software not affiliated with AOL in the United States. For this reason, in April 2007, the instant messaging client formerly named Gaim (or gaim) announced that they would be renamed "Pidgin".

Clients

Each modern IM service generally provides its own client, either a separately installed piece of software, or a browser-based client. These usually only work with the supplier company's service, although some allow limited function with other services. Third party client software applications exist that will connect with most of the major IM services.

Interoperability

Pidgin's tabbed chat window in Linux

Standard complementary instant messaging applications offer functions like file transfer, contact list(s), the ability to hold several simultaneous conversations, etc. These may be all the functions that a small business needs, but larger organizations will require more sophisticated applications that can work together. The solution to finding applications capable of this is to use enterprise versions of instant messaging applications. These include titles like XMPP, Lotus Sametime, Microsoft Office Communicator, etc., which are often integrated with other enterprise applications such as workflow systems. These enterprise applications, or enterprise application integration (EAI), are built to certain constraints, namely storing data in a common format.

There have been several attempts to create a unified standard for instant messaging: IETF's Session Initiation Protocol (SIP) and SIP for Instant Messaging and Presence Leveraging Extensions (SIMPLE), Application Exchange (APEX), Instant Messaging and Presence Protocol (IMPP), the open XML-based Extensible Messaging and Presence Protocol (XMPP), and Open Mobile Alliance's Instant Messaging and Presence Service developed specifically for mobile devices.

Most attempts at producing a unified standard for the major IM providers (AOL, Yahoo! and Microsoft) have failed, and each continues to use its own proprietary protocol.

However, while discussions at IETF were stalled, Reuters signed the first inter-service provider connectivity agreement on September 2003. This agreement enabled AIM, ICQ and MSN Messenger users to talk with Reuters Messaging counterparts and vice versa. Following this, Microsoft, Yahoo! and AOL agreed to a deal in which Microsoft's Live Communications Server 2005 users would also have the possibility to talk to public instant messaging users. This deal established SIP/SIMPLE as a standard for protocol interoperability and established a connectivity fee for accessing public instant messaging groups or services. Separately, on October 13, 2005, Microsoft and Yahoo! announced that by the 3rd quarter of 2006 they would interoperate using SIP/SIMPLE, which was followed, in December 2005, by the AOL and Google strategic partnership deal in which Google Talk users would be able to communicate with AIM and ICQ users provided they have an AIM account.

There are two ways to combine the many disparate protocols:

- Combine the many disparate protocols inside the IM *client application*.

- Combine the many disparate protocols inside the IM *server* application. This approach moves the task of communicating with the other services to the server. Clients need not know or care about other IM protocols. For example, LCS 2005 Public IM Connectivity. This approach is popular in XMPP servers; however, the so-called transport projects suffer the same reverse engineering difficulties as any other project involved with closed protocols or formats.

Some approaches allow organizations to deploy their own, private instant messaging network by enabling them to restrict access to the server (often with the IM network entirely behind their firewall) and administer user permissions. Other corporate messaging systems allow registered users to also connect from outside the corporation LAN, by using an encrypted, firewall-friendly, HTTPS-based protocol. Usually, a dedicated corporate IM server has several advantages, such as pre-populated contact lists, integrated authentication, and better security and privacy.

Certain networks have made changes to prevent them from being used by such multi-network IM clients. For example, Trillian had to release several revisions and patches to allow its users to access the MSN, AOL, and Yahoo! networks, after changes were made to these networks. The major IM providers usually cite the need for formal agreements, and security concerns as reasons for making these changes.

The use of proprietary protocols has meant that many instant messaging networks have been incompatible and users have been unable to reach users on other networks. This may have allowed social networking with IM-like features and text messaging an opportunity to gain market share at the expense of IM.

IM Language

Users sometimes make use of internet slang or text speak to abbreviate common words or expressions to quicken conversations or reduce keystrokes. The language has become widespread, with well-known expressions such as 'lol' translated over to face-to-face language.

Emotions are often expressed in shorthand, such as the abbreviation LOL, BRB and TTYL; respectively laugh(ing) out loud, be right back, and talk to you later.

Some, however, attempt to be more accurate with emotional expression over IM. Real time reactions such as (*chortle*) (*snort*) (*guffaw*) or (*eye-roll*) are becoming more popular. Also there are certain standards that are being introduced into mainstream conversations including, '#' indicates the use of sarcasm in a statement and '*' which indicates a spelling mistake and/or grammatical error in the prior message, followed by a correction.

Business Application

Instant messaging has proven to be similar to personal computers, email, and the World Wide Web, in that its adoption for use as a business communications medium was driven primarily by individual employees using consumer software at work, rather than by formal mandate or provisioning by corporate information technology departments. Tens of millions of the consumer IM accounts in use are being used for business purposes by employees of companies and other organizations.

In response to the demand for business-grade IM and the need to ensure security and legal compliance, a new type of instant messaging, called "Enterprise Instant Messaging" ("EIM") was created when Lotus Software launched IBM Lotus Sametime in 1998. Microsoft followed suit shortly thereafter with Microsoft Exchange Instant Messaging, later created a new platform called Microsoft Office Live Communications Server, and released Office Communications Server 2007 in October 2007. Oracle Corporation has also jumped into the market recently with its Oracle Beehive unified collaboration software. Both IBM Lotus and Microsoft have introduced federation between their EIM systems and some of the public IM networks so that employees may use one interface to both their internal EIM system and their contacts on AOL, MSN, and Yahoo. As of 2010, leading EIM platforms include IBM Lotus Sametime, Microsoft Office Communications Server, Jabber XCP and Cisco Unified Presence. Industry-focused EIM platforms as Reuters Messaging and Bloomberg Messaging also provide IM abilities to financial services companies. The adoption of IM across corporate networks outside of the control of IT organizations creates risks and liabilities for companies who do not effectively manage and support IM use. Companies implement specialized IM archiving and security products and services to mitigate these risks and provide safe, secure, productive instant messaging abilities to their employees. IM is increasingly becoming a feature of enterprise software rather than a stand-alone application.

Types of Products

IM products can usually be categorised into two types: Enterprise Instant Messaging (EIM) and Consumer Instant Messaging (CIM). Enterprise solutions use an internal IM server, however this isn't always feasible, particularly for smaller businesses with limited budgets. The second option, using a CIM provides the advantage of being inexpensive to implement and has little need for investing in new hardware or server software.

For corporate use, encryption and conversation archiving are usually regarded as important features due to security concerns. Sometimes the use of different operating systems in organizations requires use of software that supports more than one platform. For example, many software companies use Windows in administration departments but have software developers who use Linux.

Security Risks

Crackers (malicious or black hat hackers) have consistently used IM networks as vectors for delivering phishing attempts, "poison URLs", and virus-laden file attachments from 2004 to the present, with over 1100 discrete attacks listed by the IM Security Center in 2004–2007. Hackers use two methods of delivering malicious code through IM: delivery of viruses, trojan horses, or spyware within an infected file, and the use of "socially engineered" text with a web address that entices the recipient to click on a URL connecting him or her to a website that then downloads malicious code.

Viruses, computer worms, and trojans usually propagate by sending themselves rapidly through the infected user's contact list. An effective attack using a poisoned URL may reach tens of thousands of users in a short period when each user's contact list receives messages appearing to be from a trusted friend. The recipients click on the web address, and the entire cycle starts again. Infections may range from nuisance to criminal, and are becoming more sophisticated each year.

IM connections usually occur in plain text, making them vulnerable to eavesdropping. Also, IM client software often requires the user to expose open UDP ports to the world, raising the threat posed by potential security vulnerabilities.

Compliance Risks

In addition to the malicious code threat, the use of instant messaging at work also creates a risk of non-compliance to laws and regulations governing use of electronic communications in businesses.

In the United States

In the United States alone there are over 10,000 laws and regulations related to electronic messaging and records retention. The better-known of these include the Sarbanes–Oxley Act, HIPAA, and SEC 17a-3.

Clarification from the Financial Industry Regulatory Authority (FINRA) was issued to member firms in the financial services industry in December, 2007, noting that "electronic communications", "email", and "electronic correspondence" may be used interchangeably and can include such forms of electronic messaging as *instant messaging* and text messaging. Changes to Federal Rules of Civil Procedure, effective December 1, 2006, created a new category for electronic records which may be requested during discovery in legal proceedings.

World-Wide

Most nations also regulate use of electronic messaging and electronic records retention in similar fashion as the United States. The most common regulations related to IM at work involve the need to produce archived business communications to satisfy government or judicial requests under law. Many instant messaging communications fall into the category of business communications that must be archived and retrievable.

Security and Archiving

In the early 2000s, a new class of IT security provider emerged to provide remedies for the risks and liabilities faced by corporations who chose to use IM for business communications. The IM security providers created new products to be installed in corporate networks for the purpose of archiving, content-scanning, and security-scanning IM traffic moving in and out of the corporation. Similar to the e-mail filtering vendors, the IM security providers focus on the risks and liabilities described above.

With rapid adoption of IM in the workplace, demand for IM security products began to grow in the mid-2000s. By 2007, the preferred platform for the purchase of security software had become the "computer appliance", according to IDC, who estimate that by 2008, 80% of network security products will be delivered via an appliance.

By 2014 however, the level of safety offered by instant messengers was still extremely poor. According to a scorecard made by the Electronic Frontier Foundation, only 7 out of 39 instant messengers received a perfect score, whereas the most popular instant messengers at the time only attained a score of 2 out of 7. A number of studies have shown that IM services are quite vulnerable for providing user privacy.

User Base

While some numbers are given by the owners of a complete instant messaging system, others are provided by commercial vendors of a part of a distributed system. Some companies may be motivated to inflate their numbers to raise advertising earnings or attract partners, clients, or customers. Importantly, some numbers are reported as the number of *active* users (with no shared standard of that activity), others indicate total user accounts, while others indicate only the users logged in during an instance of peak use.

Since the acquisitions of 2010 and later and with the wide availability of smartphones, the virtual communities of those conglomerates are becoming the user base of most instant messaging services:

- Facebook (through Facebook Messenger, Instagram, WhatsApp)

- Tencent Holdings Limited (WeChat, Tencent QQ, Qzone)

- Google (Google+ and YouTube users (merging))

- Microsoft (Skype and Windows Live / MSN messenger (merged))

- Twitter (API)

- LinkedIn (API)

Statistics

Instant messenger client	Company	Usage
BlackBerry Messenger	BlackBerry	91 million total users (October 2014)
AIM	AOL, Inc	53 million active users (September 2006)
XMPP	XMPP Standards Foundation	1200+ million (September 2011)
eBuddy	eBuddy	35 million users (October2006)
iMessage	Apple Inc.	140 million users (June 2012)
Facebook Messenger	Facebook	900 million active users (April 2016)
Windows Live Messenger	Microsoft Corporation	330 million active monthly (June 2009)
Yahoo! Messenger	Yahoo!, Inc.	22 million users (Unknown)
QQ	Tencent Holdings Limited	176+ million peak online users, 840+ million "active" (Q2 2009)
IBM Sametime	IBM Corp.	15 million (enterprise) users (Unknown)
Skype	Microsoft Corporation	34 million peak online (February 2012), 560 million total (April 2010)
MXit	MXit Lifestyle (Pty) Ltd.	7.4 million monthly subscribers (majority in South Africa (July 2013)
Xfire	Xfire, Inc.	24 million registered users (January 2014)
Gadu-Gadu	GG Network S.A.	6.5 million users active daily (majority in Poland) (June 2010)
ICQ	ICQ LLC.	4 million active (September 2006)

Paltalk	Paltalk.com	5.5 million monthly unique users (August 2013)
IMVU	IMVU, inc.	1 million users (June 2007)

Terms

- Ambient awareness
- Communications protocol
- Mass collaboration
- Message-oriented middleware
- Operator messaging
- Social media
- Text messaging
- Unified communications / messaging

Lists

- Comparison of instant messaging clients
- Comparison of instant messaging protocols

Internet Forum

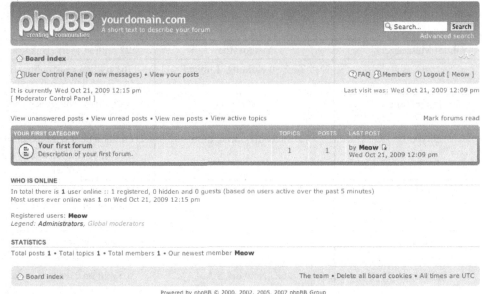

An Internet forum powered by phpBB

An Internet forum, or message board, is an online discussion site where people can hold conversations in the form of posted messages. They differ from chat rooms in that messages are often longer than one line of text, and are at least temporarily archived. Also, depending on the access level of a user or the forum set-up, a posted message might need to be approved by a moderator before it becomes visible.

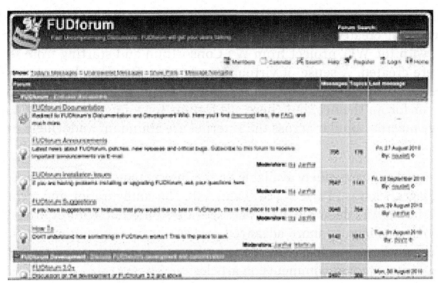

FUDforum, another Internet forum software package.

Forums have a specific set of jargon associated with them; e.g., a single conversation is called a "thread", or *topic*.

A discussion forum is hierarchical or tree-like in structure: a forum can contain a number of subforums, each of which may have several topics. Within a forum's topic, each new discussion started is called a thread, and can be replied to by as many people as so wish.

Depending on the forum's settings, users can be anonymous or have to register with the forum and then subsequently log in in order to post messages. On most forums, users do not have to log in to read existing messages.

History

The modern forum originated from bulletin boards, and so-called computer conferencing systems, and are a technological evolution of the dialup bulletin board system. From a technological standpoint, *forums* or *boards* are web applications managing user-generated content.

Early Internet forums could be described as a web version of an electronic mailing list or newsgroup (such as exist on Usenet); allowing people to post messages and comment on other messages. Later developments emulated the different newsgroups or individual lists, providing more than one forum, dedicated to a particular topic.

Internet forums are prevalent in several developed countries. Japan posts the most with over two million per day on their largest forum, 2channel. China also has many millions of posts on forums such as Tianya Club.

Some of the very first forum systems were the Planet-Forum system, developed in the beginning of the 1970-s, the EIES system, first operational in 1976, and the KOM system, first operational in 1977.

One of the first forum sites, and still active today, is Delphi Forums, once called Delphi (online service). The service, with four million members, dates to 1983.

Forums perform a function similar to that of dial-up bulletin board systems and Usenet networks that were first created starting in the late 1970s. Early web-based forums date back as far as 1994, with the WIT project from W3 Consortium and starting from this time, many alternatives were created. A sense of virtual community often develops around forums that have regular users. Technology, video games, sports, music, fashion, religion, and politics are popular areas for forum themes, but there are forums for a huge number of topics. Internet slang and image macros popular across the Internet are abundant and widely used in Internet forums.

Forum software packages are widely available on the Internet and are written in a variety of programming languages, such as PHP, Perl, Java and ASP. The configuration and records of posts can be stored in text files or in a database. Each package offers different features, from the most basic, providing text-only postings, to more advanced packages, offering multimedia support and formatting code (usually known as BBCode). Many packages can be integrated easily into an existing website to allow visitors to post comments on articles.

Several other web applications, such as weblog software, also incorporate forum features. Wordpress comments at the bottom of a blog post allow for a single-threaded discussion of any given blog post. Slashcode, on the other hand, is far more complicated, allowing fully threaded discussions and incorporating a robust moderation and meta-moderation system as well as many of the profile features available to forum users.

Some stand alone threads on forums have reached fame and notability such as the "I am lonely will anyone speak to me" thread on MovieCodec.com's forums, which was described as the "web's top hangout for lonely folk" by Wired Magazine.

Structure

A forum consists of a tree like directory structure. The top end is "Categories". A forum can be divided into categories for the relevant discussions. Under the categories are sub-forums and these sub-forums can further have more sub-forums. The *topics* (commonly called *threads*) come under the lowest level of sub-forums and these are the places under which members can start their discussions or *posts*. Logically forums are organized into a finite set of generic topics (usually with one main topic) driven and updated by a group known as *members*, and governed by a group known as *moderators*. It can also have a graph structure. All message boards will use one of three possible display formats. Each of the three basic message board display formats: Non-Threaded/Semi-Threaded/Fully Threaded, has its own advantages and disadvantages. If messages are not related to one another at all a Non-Threaded format is best. If a user has a message topic and multiple replies to that message topic a semi-threaded format is best. If a user has a message topic and replies to that message topic, and replies to replies, then a fully threaded format is best.

User Groups

Internally, Western-style forums organize visitors and logged in members into user groups. Privileges and rights are given based on these groups. A user of the forum can automatically be promoted to a more privileged user group based on criteria set by the administrator. A person viewing a closed thread as a *member* will see a box saying he does not have the right to submit messages there, but a *moderator* will likely see the same box granting him access to more than just posting messages.

An unregistered user of the site is commonly known as a *guest* or *visitor*. Guests are typically granted access to all functions that do not require database alterations or breach privacy. A guest can usually view the contents of the forum or use such features as *read marking*, but occasionally an administrator will disallow visitors to read their forum as an incentive to become a registered member. A person who is a very frequent visitor of the forum, a section or even a thread is referred to as a lurker and the habit is referred to as *lurking*. Registered members often will refer to themselves as *lurking* in a particular location, which is to say they have no intention of participating in that section but enjoy reading the contributions to it.

Moderators

The *moderators* (short singular form: "mod") are users (or employees) of the forum who are granted access to the posts and threads of all members for the purpose of *moderating discussion* (similar to arbitration) and also keeping the forum clean (neutralizing spam and spambots etc.). Moderators also answer users' concerns about the forum, general questions, as well as respond to specific complaints. Common privileges of moderators include: deleting, merging, moving, and splitting of posts and threads, locking, renaming, stickying of threads, banning, suspending, unsuspending, unbanning, warning the members, or adding, editing, removing the polls of threads. "Junior Modding", "Backseat Modding", or "Forum copping" can refer negatively to the behavior of ordinary users who take a moderator-like tone in criticizing other members.

Essentially, it is the duty of the moderator to manage the day-to-day affairs of a forum or board as it applies to the stream of user contributions and interactions. The relative effectiveness of this user management directly impacts the quality of a forum in general, its appeal, and its usefulness as a community of interrelated users.

Administrator

The *administrators* (short form: "admin") manage the technical details required for running the site. As such, they may promote (and demote) members to/from moderators, manage the rules, create sections and sub-sections, as well as perform any database operations (database backup etc.). Administrators often also act as moderators. Administrators may also make forum-wide announcements, or change the appearance (known as the skin) of a forum. There are also many forums where administrators share their knowledge.

Post

A *post* is a user-submitted message enclosed into a block containing the user's details and the date and time it was submitted. Members are usually allowed to edit or delete their own posts. Posts are contained in threads, where they appear as blocks one after another. The first post starts the thread; this may be called the TS (thread starter) or OP (original post). Posts that follow in the thread are meant to continue discussion about that post, or respond to other replies; it is not uncommon for discussions to be derailed.

On Western forums, the classic way to show a member's own details (such as name and avatar) has been on the left side of the post, in a narrow column of fixed width, with the post controls located on the right, at the bottom of the main body, above the signature block. In more recent forum software implementations, the Asian style of displaying the members' details above the post has been copied.

Posts have an internal limit usually measured in characters. Often one is required to have a message of minimum length of 10 characters. There is always an upper limit but it is rarely reached – most boards have it at either 10,000, 20,000, 30,000, or 50,000 characters.

Most forums keep track of a user's postcount. The postcount is a measurement of how many posts a certain user has made. Users with higher postcounts are often considered more reputable than users with lower postcounts, but not always. For instance some forums have disabled postcounts with the hopes that doing so will emphasize the quality of information over quantity.

Thread

A *thread* (sometimes called a *topic*) is a collection of posts, usually displayed from oldest to latest, although this is typically configurable: Options for newest to oldest and for a threaded view (a tree-like view applying logical reply structure before chronological order) can be available. A thread is defined by a title, an additional description that may summarize the intended discussion, and an opening or original post (common abbreviation *OP*, which can also mean *original poster*), which opens whatever dialogue or makes whatever announcement the poster wished. A thread can contain any number of posts, including multiple posts from the same members, even if they are one after the other.

Bumping

A thread is contained in a forum, and may have an associated date that is taken as the date of the last post (options to order threads by other criteria are generally available). When a member posts in a thread it will jump to the top since it is the latest updated thread. Similarly, other threads will jump in front of it when they receive posts. When a member posts in a thread for no reason but to have it go to the top, it is referred to as a *bump* or *bumping*. It has been suggested that "bump" is an acronym of "bring up my post"; however, this is almost certainly a backronym and the usage is entirely consistent with the verb "bump" which means "to knock to a new position".

On some messageboards, users can choose to *sage* a post if they wish to make a post, but not "bump" it. The word "sage" derives from the 2channel terminology *sageru*, meaning "to lower".

Stickying

Threads that are important but rarely receive posts are *sticky*ed (or, in some software, "pinned").

A *sticky thread* will always appear in front of normal threads, often in its own section. A "threaded discussion group" is simply any group of individuals who use a forum for threaded, or asynchronous, discussion purposes. The group may or may not be the only users of the forum.

A thread's popularity is measured on forums in reply (total posts minus one, the opening post, in most default forum settings) counts. Some forums also track page views. Threads meeting a set number of posts or a set number of views may receive a designation such as "hot thread" and be displayed with a different icon compared to other threads. This icon may stand out more to emphasize the thread. If the forum's users have lost interest in a particular thread, it becomes a *dead thread*.

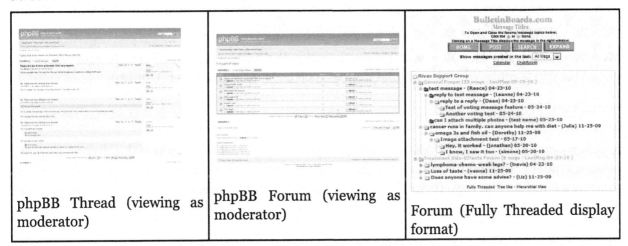

phpBB Thread (viewing as moderator)	phpBB Forum (viewing as moderator)	Forum (Fully Threaded display format)

Discussion

Forums prefer a premise of open and free discussion and often adopt de facto standards. Most common topics on forums include questions, comparisons, polls of opinion as well as debates. It is not uncommon for nonsense or unsocial behavior to sprout as people lose temper, especially if the topic is controversial. Poor understanding of differences in values of the participants is a common problem on forums. Because replies to a topic are often worded aimed at someone's point of view, discussion will usually go slightly off into several directions as people question each other's validity, sources and so on. Circular discussion and ambiguity in replies can extend for several tens of posts of a thread eventually ending when everyone gives up or attention spans waver and a more interesting subject takes over. It is not uncommon for debate to end in ad hominem attacks.

Liabilities of Owners and Moderators

Several lawsuits have been brought against the forums and moderators claiming libel and damage. A recent case is the scubaboard lawsuit where a business in the Maldives filed a suit against scubaboard for libel and defamation in January 2010.

For the most part, though, forum owners and moderators in the United States are protected by Section 230 of the Communications Decency Act, which states that "[n]o provider or user of an interactive computer service shall be treated as the publisher or speaker of any information provided by another information content provider."

Common Features

By default to be an Internet forum, the web application needs an ability to submit threads and replies. Typically, threads are in newer to older view, and replies in older to newer view.

Tripcodes and Capcodes

In a tripcode system, a secret password is added to the user's name following a separator character (often a number sign). This password, or tripcode, is hashed into a special key, or trip, distinguishable from the name by HTML styles. Tripcodes cannot be faked but on some types of forum software they are insecure and can be guessed. On other types, they can be brute forced with software designed to search for tripcodes such as Tripcode Explorer.

Moderators and administrators will frequently assign themselves capcodes, or tripcodes where the guessable trip is replaced with a special notice (such as "# Administrator"), or cap.

Private Message

A *private message*, or PM for short, is a message sent in private from a member to one or more other members. The ability to send so-called blind carbon copies is sometimes available. When sending a *blind carbon copy* (bcc), the users to whom the message is sent directly will not be aware of the recipients of the blind carbon copy or even if one was sent in the first place.

Private messages are generally used for personal conversations. They can also be used with tripcodes—a message is addressed to a public trip and can be picked up by typing in the tripcode.

Attachment

An attachment can be almost any file. When someone attaches a file to a person's post they are uploading the file to the forum's server. Forums usually have very strict limit on what can be attached and what cannot (among which the size of the files in question). Attachments can be part of a thread, social group, etc.

BBCode and HTML

HyperText Markup Language (HTML) is sometimes allowed but usually its use is discouraged or when allowed, it is extensively filtered. Modern bulletin board systems often will have it disabled altogether or allow only administrators use it, as allowing it on any normal user level is considered a security risk due to a high rate of XSS vulnerabilities. When HTML is disabled Bulletin Board Code (BBCode) is the most common preferred alternative. BBCode usually consists of a tag, similar to HTML only instead of < and > the tagname is enclosed within square brackets (meaning: [and]). Commonly [i] is used for italic type, [b] is used for bold, [u] for underline, [color="value"] for color and [list] for lists, as well as [img] for images and [url] for links.

The following example BBCode: [b]This[/b] is [i]clever[/i] [b][i]text[/i][/b] when the post is viewed the code is rendered to HTML and will appear as: This is *clever text*.

Many forum packages offer a way to create Custom BBCodes, or BBcodes that are not built into the package, where the administrator of the board can create complex BBCodes to allow the use of JavaScript or iframe functions in posts, for example embedding a YouTube or Google Video complete with viewer directly into a post.

Emoticon

An emoticon or *smiley* is a symbol or combination of symbols used to convey emotional content in written or message form. Forums implement a system through which some of the text representations of an emoticons (e.g. xD, :p) are rendered as a small image. Depending on what part of the world the forum's topic originates (since most forums are international) smilies can be replaced by other forms of similar graphics, an example would be kaoani (e.g. *(^O^)*, (^-^)b), or even text between special symbols (e.g. :blink:, :idea:).

Poll

Most forums implement an opinion poll system for threads. Most implementations allow for single-choice or multi-choice (sometimes limited to a certain number) when selecting options as well as private or public display of voters. Polls can be set to expire after a certain date or in some cases after a number of days from its creation. Members vote in a poll and a statistic is displayed graphically.

RSS and ATOM

RSS and ATOM feeds allow a minimalistic means of subscribing to the forum. Common implementations allow RSS feeds to list only the last few threads updated for the forum index and the last posts in a thread.

Other Features

An *ignore list* allows members to hide posts of other members that they do not want to see or have a problem with. In most implementations, they are referred to as *foe list* or *ignore list*. Usually the posts are not hidden, but minimized with only a small bar indicating a post from the user on the *ignore list* is there. Almost all Internet forums include a *member list*, which allows display of all forum members, with integrated search feature. Some forums will not list members with 0 posts, even if they have activated their accounts.

Many forums allow users to give themselves an *avatar*. An avatar is an image that appears beside all of a user's posts, in order to make the user more recognizable. The user may upload the image to the forum database, or may provide a link to an image on a separate website. Each forum has limits on the height, width, and data size of avatars that may be used; if the user tries to use an avatar that is too big, it may be scaled down or rejected.

Similarly, most forums allow users to define a *signature* (sometimes called a *sig*), which is a block of text, possibly with BBCode, which appears at the bottom of all of the user's posts. There is a character limit on signatures, though it may be so high that it is rarely hit. Often the forum's moderators impose manual rules on signatures to prevent them from being obnoxious (for example, being extremely long or having flashing images), and issue warnings or bans to users who break these rules. Like avatars, signatures may improve the recognizability of a poster. They may also allow the user to attach information to all of their posts, such as proclaiming support for a cause, noting facts about themselves, or quoting humorous things that have previously been said on the forum.

Common on forums, a *subscription* is a form of automated notification integrated into the software of most forums. It usually notifies either by email or on the site when the member returns. The option to subscribe is available for every thread while logged in. Subscriptions work with *read marking*, namely the property of *unread*, which is given to the content never served to the user by the software.

Recent development in some popular implementations of forum software has brought *social network features and functionality*. Such features include personal galleries, pages as well as a social network like chat systems.

Most forum software is now fully customizable with "hacks" or "modifications" readily available to customize a person's forum to theirs and their members' needs.

Often forums use "cookies", or information about the user's behavior on the site sent to a user's browser and used upon re-entry into the site. This is done to facilitate automatic login and to show a user whether a thread or forum has received new posts since his or her last visit. These may be disabled or cleared at any time.

Rules and Policies

Forums are governed by a set of individuals, collectively referred to as *staff*, made up of *administrators* and *moderators*, which are responsible for the forums' conception, technical maintenance, and policies (creation and enforcing). Most forums have a list of rules detailing the wishes, aim and guidelines of the forums' creators. There is usually also a FAQ section containing basic information for new members and people not yet familiar with the use and principles of a forum (generally tailored for specific forum software).

Rules on forums usually apply to the entire user body and often have preset exceptions, most commonly designating a section as an exception. For example, in an IT forum any discussion regarding anything but computer programming languages may be against the rules, with the exception of a *general chat* section.

Forum rules are maintained and enforced by the moderation team, but users are allowed to help out via what is known as a report system. Most American forum software contains such a system. It consists of a small function applicable to each post (including one's own). Using it will notify all currently available moderators of its location, and subsequent action or judgment can be carried out immediately, which is particularly desirable in large or very developed boards. Generally, moderators encourage members to also use the *private message* system if they wish to report behavior. Moderators will generally frown upon attempts of moderation by non-moderators, especially when the would-be moderators do not even issue a report. Messages from non-moderators acting as moderators generally declare a post as against the rules, or predict punishment. While not harmful, statements that attempt to enforce the rules are discouraged.

When rules are broken several steps are commonly taken. First, a warning is usually given; this is commonly in the form of a *private message* but recent development has made it possible for it to be integrated into the software. Subsequent to this, if the act is ignored and warnings do not work, the member is – usually – first exiled from the forum for a number of days. Denying someone access to the site is called a *ban*. Bans can mean the person can no longer log in or even view the site anymore. If the offender, after the warning sentence, repeats the offense, another ban is given, usually this time a longer one. Continuous harassment of the site eventually leads to a permanent ban. In most cases, this means simply that the account is locked. In extreme cases where the offender – after being permanently banned – creates another account and continues to harass the site, administrators will apply an IP address ban or block (this can also be applied at the server level): If the IP address is static, the machine of the offender is prevented from accessing the site. In some extreme circumstances, IP address range bans or country bans can be applied; this is usually for political, licensing, or other reasons.

Offending content is usually deleted. Sometimes if the topic is considered the source of the problem, it is *locked*; often a poster may request a topic expected to draw problems to be locked as well, although the moderators decide whether to grant it. In a *locked thread*, members cannot post anymore. In cases where the topic is considered a breach of rules it – with all of its posts – may be deleted.

Troll

Forum *trolls* are users that repeatedly and deliberately breach the netiquette of an established online community, posting inflammatory, extraneous, or off-topic messages to bait or excite users into responding or to test the forum rules and policies, and with that the patience of the forum staff. Their provocative behavior may potentially start flame wars or other disturbances. Responding to a troll's provocations is commonly known as 'feeding the troll' and is generally discouraged, as it can encourage their disruptive behavior.

Sock Puppet

The term sock puppet refers to multiple pseudonyms in use by the same person on a particular message board or forum. The analogy of a sock puppet is of a puppeteer holding up both hands and supplying dialogue to both puppets simultaneously. A typical use of a sockpuppet account is to agree with or debate another sockpuppet account belonging to the same person, for the purposes of reinforcing the puppeteer's position in an argument. Sock puppets are usually found when an IP address check is done on the accounts in forums.

Spamming

Forum spamming is a breach of netiquette where users repeat the same word or phrase over and over, but differs from multiple posting in that spamming is usually a willful act that sometimes has malicious intent. This is a common trolling technique. It can also be traditional spam, unpaid advertisements that are in breach of the forum's rules. Spammers utilize a number of illicit techniques to post their spam, including the use of botnets.

Some forums consider concise, comment-oriented posts spam, for example *Thank you*, *Cool* or *I love it*.

Double Posting

One common faux pas on Internet forums is to post the same message twice. Users sometimes post versions of a message that are only slightly different, especially in forums where they are not allowed to edit their earlier posts. Multiple posting instead of editing prior posts can artificially inflate a user's post count. Multiple posting can be unintentional; a user's browser might display an error message even though the post has been transmitted or a user of a slow forum might become impatient and repeatedly hit the submit button. Multiple posting can also be used as a method of trolling or spreading forum spam. A user may also send the same post to several forums, which is termed crossposting. The term derives from Usenet, where crossposting was an accepted practice but causes problems in web forums, which lack the ability to link such posts so replies in one forum are not visible to people reading the post in other forums.

Necroposting

A necropost is a message that revives (as in necromancy) an arbitrarily old thread, causing it to appear above newer and more active threads. This practice is generally seen as a breach of netiquette on most forums. Because old threads are not usually locked from further posting, necroposting is common for newer users and in cases where the date of previous posts is not apparent.

Word Censor

A word censoring system is commonly included in the forum software package. The system will pick up words in the body of the post or some other user-editable forum element (like user titles), and if they partially match a certain keyword (commonly no case sensitivity) they will be censored. The most common censoring is letter replacement with an asterisk character. For example, in the user title, it is deemed inappropriate for users to use words such as "admin", "moderator", "leader" and so on. If the censoring system is implemented, a title such as "forum leader" may be filtered to "forum ******". Rude or vulgar words are common targets for the censoring system. But such auto-censors can make mistakes, for example censoring "wristwatch" to "wris****ch" and "Scunthorpe" to "S****horpe."

Flame Wars

When a thread — or in some cases, an entire forum — becomes unstable, the result is usually uncontrolled spam in the form of one-line complaints, image macros, or abuse of the report system. When the discussion becomes heated and sides do nothing more than complain and not accept each other's differences in point of view, the discussion degenerates into what is called a *flame war*. To *flame* someone means to go off-topic and attack the person rather than their opinion. Likely candidates for flame wars are usually religion and socio-political topics, or topics that discuss pre-existing rivalries outside the forum (e.g., rivalry between games, console systems, car manufacturers, nationalities, etc.).

When a topic that has degenerated into a flame war is considered akin to that of the forum (be it a section or the entire board), spam and flames have a chance of spreading outside the topic and causing trouble, usually in the form of vandalism. Some forums (commonly game forums) have suffered from forum-wide flame wars almost immediately after their conception, because of a pre-existing *flame war element* in the online community. Many forums have created devoted areas strictly for discussion of potential flame war topics that are moderated like normal.

Registration or Anonymity

Nearly all Internet forums require registration to post. Registered users of the site are referred to as *members* and are allowed to submit or send electronic messages through the web application. The process of registration involves verification of one's age (typically over 12 is required so as to meet COPPA requirements of American forum software) followed by a declaration of the terms of service (other documents may also be present) and a request for agreement to said terms. Subsequently, if all goes well, the candidate is presented with a web form to fill requesting at the very least a username (an alias), password, email and validation of a CAPTCHA code.

While simply completing the registration web form is in general enough to generate an account, the status label *Inactive* is commonly provided by default until the registered user confirms the email address given while registering indeed belongs to the user. Until that time, the registered user can log in to the new account but may not post, reply, or send private messages in the forum.

Internet Forums are used frequently in conjunction with multiplayer online games.

Sometimes a *referrer system* is implemented. A *referrer* is someone who introduced or otherwise "helped someone" with the decision to join the site (likewise, how a HTTP referrer is the site who linked one to another site). Usually, referrers are other forum members and members are usually rewarded for referrals. The referrer system is also sometimes implemented so that, if a visitor visits the forum though a link such as referrerid=300, the user with the id number (in this example,

300) would receive referral credit if the visitor registers. The purpose is commonly just to give credit (sometimes rewards are implied) to those who help the community grow.

In areas such as Japan, registration is frequently optional and anonymity is sometimes even encouraged. On these forums, a tripcode system may be used to allow verification of an identity without the need for formal registration. People who do not register and/or post are often referred to as "lurkers".

Comparison with Other web Applications

Electronic mailing lists: The main difference between forums and electronic mailing lists is that mailing lists automatically deliver new messages to the subscriber, while forums require the reader to visit the website and check for new posts. Because members may miss replies in threads they are interested in, many modern forums offer an "e-mail notification" feature, whereby members can choose to be notified of new posts in a thread, and web feeds that allow members to see a summary of the new posts using aggregator software. There are also software products that combine forum and mailing list features, i.e. posting and reading via email as well as the browser depending on the member's choice.

Newsreader: The main difference between newsgroups and forums is that additional software, a News client, is required to participate in newsgroups whereas using a forum requires no additional software beyond the web browser.

Shoutboxes: Unlike Internet forums, most shoutboxes do not require registration, only requiring an email address from the user. Additionally, shoutboxes are not heavily moderated, unlike most message boards.

Unlike conventional forums, the original wikis allowed all users to edit all content (including each other's messages). This level of content manipulation is reserved for moderators or administrators on most forums. Wikis also allow the creation of other content outside the talk pages. On the other hand, weblogs and generic content management systems tend to be locked down to the point where only a few select users can post blog entries, although many allow other users to comment upon them. It should be noted that the Wiki hosting site known as Wikia has two features in operation, known as the Forum and Message Wall. The forum is used solely for discussion and works through editing, while the message wall works through posted messages more similar to a traditional forum.

Chat rooms and instant messaging: Forums differ from chats and instant messaging in that forum participants do not have to be online simultaneously to receive or send messages. Messages posted to a forum are publicly available for some time even if the forum or thread is closed, which is uncommon in chat rooms that maintain frequent activity.

One rarity among forums is the ability to create a picture album. Forum participants may upload personal pictures onto the site and add descriptions to the pictures. Pictures may be in the same format as posting threads, and contain the same options such as "Report Post" and "Reply to Post".

Examples

1. Presuming someone is sending a private message and has the ability to send blind carbon copies: If someone fills the *recipient* field with "John" and "Tom", and the *carbon copy* field with "Gordon". John will know Tom got the message. Tom knows John got the message. But, both Tom and John have no clue that Gordon got the message as well.

Blog

A blog (a truncation of the expression weblog) is a discussion or informational site published on the World Wide Web consisting of discrete entries ("posts") typically displayed in reverse chronological order (the most recent post appears first). Until 2009, blogs were usually the work of a single individual, occasionally of a small group, and often covered a single subject. More recently, "multi-author blogs" (MABs) have developed, with posts written by large numbers of authors and professionally edited. MABs from newspapers, other media outlets, universities, think tanks, advocacy groups, and similar institutions account for an increasing quantity of blog traffic. The rise of Twitter and other "microblogging" systems helps integrate MABs and single-author blogs into societal newstreams. *Blog* can also be used as a verb, meaning *to maintain or add content to a blog.*

The emergence and growth of blogs in the late 1990s coincided with the advent of web publishing tools that facilitated the posting of content by non-technical users. (Previously, a knowledge of such technologies as HTML and FTP had been required to publish content on the Web.)

A majority are interactive, allowing visitors to leave comments and even message each other via GUI widgets on the blogs, and it is this interactivity that distinguishes them from other static websites. In that sense, blogging can be seen as a form of social networking service. Indeed, bloggers do not only produce content to post on their blogs, but also build social relations with their readers and other bloggers. However, there are high-readership blogs which do not allow comments.

Many blogs provide commentary on a particular subject; others function as more personal online diaries; others function more as online brand advertising of a particular individual or company. A typical blog combines text, images, and links to other blogs, web pages, and other media related to its topic. The ability of readers to leave comments in an interactive format is an important contribution to the popularity of many blogs. Most blogs are primarily textual, although some focus on art (art blogs), photographs (photoblogs), videos (video blogs or "vlogs"), music (MP3 blogs), and audio (podcasts). Microblogging is another type of blogging, featuring very short posts. In education, blogs can be used as instructional resources. These blogs are referred to as edublogs.

On 16 February 2011, there were over 156 million public blogs in existence. On 20 February 2014, there were around 172 million Tumblr and 75.8 million WordPress blogs in existence worldwide.

According to critics and other bloggers, Blogger is the most popular blogging service used today. However, Blogger does not offer public statistics. Technorati has 1.3 million blogs as of February 22, 2014.

History

Early example of a "diary" style blog consisting of text and images transmitted wirelessly in real time from a wearable computer with head-up display, 22 February 1995

The term "weblog" was coined by Jorn Barger on 17 December 1997. The short form, "blog", was coined by Peter Merholz, who jokingly broke the word *weblog* into the phrase *we blog* in the sidebar of his blog Peterme.com in April or May 1999. Shortly thereafter, Evan Williams at Pyra Labs used "blog" as both a noun and verb ("to blog", meaning "to edit one's weblog or to post to one's weblog") and devised the term "blogger" in connection with Pyra Labs' Blogger product, leading to the popularization of the terms.

Origins

Before blogging became popular, digital communities took many forms, including Usenet, commercial online services such as GEnie, BIX and the early CompuServe, e-mail lists, and Bulletin Board Systems (BBS). In the 1990s, Internet forum software, created running conversations with "threads". Threads are topical connections between messages on a virtual "corkboard".

From 14 June 1993, Mosaic Communications Corporation maintained their "What's New" list of new websites, updated daily and archived monthly. The page was accessible by a special "What's New" button in the Mosaic web browser.

The modern blog evolved from the online diary, where people would keep a running account of their personal lives. Most such writers called themselves diarists, journalists, or journalers. Justin Hall, who began personal blogging in 1994 while a student at Swarthmore College, is generally recognized as one of the earlier bloggers, as is Jerry Pournelle. Dave Winer's Scripting News is also credited with being one of the older and longer running weblogs. The Australian Netguide magazine maintained the Daily Net News on their web site from 1996. Daily Net News ran links and daily reviews of new websites, mostly in Australia. Another early blog was Wearable Wireless Webcam, an online shared diary of a person's personal life combining text, video, and pictures transmitted live from a wearable computer and EyeTap device to a web site in 1994. This practice of semi-automated blogging with live video together with text was referred to as sousveillance, and such journals were also used as evidence in legal matters.

Early blogs were simply manually updated components of common Web sites. However, the evolution of tools to facilitate the production and maintenance of Web articles posted in reverse chronological order made the publishing process feasible to a much larger, less technical, population. Ultimately, this resulted in the distinct class of online publishing that produces blogs we recognize today. For instance, the use of some sort of browser-based software is now a typical aspect of "blogging". Blogs can be hosted by dedicated blog hosting services, or they can be run using blog software, or on regular web hosting services.

Some early bloggers, such as The Misanthropic Bitch, who began in 1997, actually referred to their online presence as a zine, before the term blog entered common usage.

Rise in Popularity

After a slow start, blogging rapidly gained in popularity. Blog usage spread during 1999 and the years following, being further popularized by the near-simultaneous arrival of the first hosted blog tools:

- Bruce Ableson launched Open Diary in October 1998, which soon grew to thousands of online diaries. Open Diary innovated the reader comment, becoming the first blog community where readers could add comments to other writers' blog entries.

- Brad Fitzpatrick started LiveJournal in March 1999.

- Andrew Smales created Pitas.com in July 1999 as an easier alternative to maintaining a "news page" on a Web site, followed by DiaryLand in September 1999, focusing more on a personal diary community.

- Evan Williams and Meg Hourihan (Pyra Labs) launched Blogger.com in August 1999 (purchased by Google in February 2003)

Political Impact

On 6 December 2002, Josh Marshall's talkingpointsmemo.com blog called attention to U.S. Senator Lott's comments regarding Senator Thurmond. Senator Lott was eventually to resign his Senate leadership position over the matter.

An early milestone in the rise in importance of blogs came in 2002, when many bloggers focused on comments by U.S. Senate Majority Leader Trent Lott. Senator Lott, at a party honoring U.S. Senator Strom Thurmond, praised Senator Thurmond by suggesting that the United States would have been better off had Thurmond been elected president. Lott's critics saw these comments as a tacit approval of racial segregation, a policy advocated by Thurmond's 1948 presidential campaign. This view was reinforced by documents and recorded interviews dug up by bloggers. Though Lott's comments were made at a public event attended by the media, no major media organizations reported on his controversial comments until after blogs broke the story. Blogging helped to create a political crisis that forced Lott to step down as majority leader.

Similarly, blogs were among the driving forces behind the "Rathergate" scandal. To wit: (television journalist) Dan Rather presented documents (on the CBS show *60 Minutes*) that conflicted with accepted accounts of President Bush's military service record. Bloggers declared the documents to be forgeries and presented evidence and arguments in support of that view. Consequently, CBS apologized for what it said were inadequate reporting techniques. Many bloggers view this scandal as the advent of blogs' acceptance by the mass media, both as a news source and opinion and as means of applying political pressure.

The impact of these stories gave greater credibility to blogs as a medium of news dissemination.

Though often seen as partisan gossips, bloggers sometimes lead the way in bringing key information to public light, with mainstream media having to follow their lead. More often, however, news blogs tend to react to material already published by the mainstream media. Meanwhile, an increasing number of experts blogged, making blogs a source of in-depth analysis.

In Russia, some political bloggers have started to challenge the dominance of official, overwhelmingly pro-government media. Bloggers such as Rustem Adagamov and Alexei Navalny have many followers and the latter's nickname for the ruling United Russia party as the "party of crooks and thieves" has been adopted by anti-regime protesters. This led to the Wall Street Journal calling Navalny "the man Vladimir Putin fears most" in March 2012.

Mainstream Popularity

By 2004, the role of blogs became increasingly mainstream, as political consultants, news services, and candidates began using them as tools for outreach and opinion forming. Blogging was established by politicians and political candidates to express opinions on war and other issues and cemented blogs' role as a news source. Even politicians not actively campaigning, such as the UK's Labour Party's MP Tom Watson, began to blog to bond with constituents.

In January 2005, *Fortune* magazine listed eight bloggers whom business people "could not ignore": Peter Rojas, Xeni Jardin, Ben Trott, Mena Trott, Jonathan Schwartz, Jason Goldman, Robert Scoble, and Jason Calacanis.

Israel was among the first national governments to set up an official blog. Under David Saranga, the Israeli Ministry of Foreign Affairs became active in adopting Web 2.0 initiatives, including an official video blog and a political blog. The Foreign Ministry also held a microblogging press conference via Twitter about its war with Hamas, with Saranga answering questions from the public in common text-messaging abbreviations during a live worldwide press conference. The questions and answers were later posted on IsraelPolitik, the country's official political blog.

The impact of blogging upon the mainstream media has also been acknowledged by governments. In 2009, the presence of the American journalism industry had declined to the point that several newspaper corporations were filing for bankruptcy, resulting in less direct competition between newspapers within the same circulation area. Discussion emerged as to whether the newspaper industry would benefit from a stimulus package by the federal government. U.S. President Barack Obama acknowledged the emerging influence of blogging upon society by saying "if the direction of the news is all blogosphere, all opinions, with no serious fact-checking, no serious attempts to put stories in context, then what you will end up getting is people shouting at each other across the void but not a lot of mutual understanding".

Between 2009 and 2012, an Orwell Prize for blogging was awarded.

Types

There are many different types of blogs, differing not only in the type of content, but also in the way that content is delivered or written.

Personal Blogs

The personal blog is an ongoing diary or commentary written by an individual.

Collaborative Blogs or Group Blogs

A type of weblog in which posts are written and published by more than one author. The majority of high-profile collaborative blogs are based around a single uniting theme, such as politics or technology. In recent years, the blogosphere has seen the emergence and growing popularity of more collaborative efforts, often set up by already established bloggers wishing to pool time and resources, both to reduce the pressure of maintaining a popular website and to attract a larger readership.

Microblogging

Microblogging is the practice of posting small pieces of digital content—which could be text, pictures, links, short videos, or other media—on the Internet. Microblogging offers a portable communication mode that feels organic and spontaneous to many and has captured the public imagination. Friends use it to keep in touch, business associates use it to coordinate meetings or share useful resources, and celebrities and politicians (or their publicists) microblog about concert dates, lectures, book releases, or tour schedules. A wide and growing range of add-on tools enables sophisticated updates and interaction with other applications. The resulting profusion of functionality is helping to define new possibilities for this type of communication. Examples of these include Twitter, Facebook, Tumblr and, by far the largest, WeiBo.

Corporate and Organizational Blogs

A blog can be private, as in most cases, or it can be for business purposes. Blogs used internally to enhance the communication and culture in a corporation or externally for marketing, branding, or public relations purposes are called corporate blogs. Similar blogs for clubs and societies are called club blogs, group blogs, or by similar names; typical use is to inform members and other interested parties of club and member activities.

Aggregated Blogs

Individuals or organization may aggregate selected feeds on specific topic or product and provide combined view for its readers. This allow readers to concentrate on reading instead of searching for quality on-topic content and managing subscription. Many such aggregation called planets from name of Planet (software) that perform such aggregation, hosting sites usually have *planet.* subdomain in domain name (like http://planet.gnome.org/).

By Genre

Some blogs focus on a particular subject, such as political blogs, journalism blogs, health blogs, travel blogs (also known as *travelogs*), gardening blogs, house blogs, book blogs, fashion blogs, beauty blogs, lifestyle blogs, party blogs, wedding blogs, photography blogs, project blogs, psychology blogs, sociology blogs, education blogs, niche blogs, classical music blogs, quizzing blogs, legal blogs (often referred to as a blawgs), or dreamlogs. How-to/

Tutorial blogs are becoming increasing popular. Two common types of genre blogs are art blogs and music blogs. A blog featuring discussions especially about home and family is not uncommonly called a mom blog and one made popular is by Erica Diamond who created Womenonthefence.com which is syndicated to over two million readers monthly. While not a legitimate type of blog, one used for the sole purpose of spamming is known as a splog.

By Media Type

A blog comprising videos is called a vlog, one comprising links is called a linklog, a site containing a portfolio of sketches is called a sketchblog or one comprising photos is called a photoblog. Blogs with shorter posts and mixed media types are called tumblelogs. Blogs that are written on typewriters and then scanned are called typecast or typecast blogs.

A rare type of blog hosted on the Gopher Protocol is known as a phlog.

By Device

A blog can also be defined by which type of device is used to compose it. A blog written by a mobile device like a mobile phone or PDA could be called a moblog. One early blog was Wearable Wireless Webcam, an online shared diary of a person's personal life combining text, video, and pictures transmitted live from a wearable computer and EyeTap device to a web site. This practice of semi-automated blogging with live video together with text was referred to as sousveillance. Such journals have been used as evidence in legal matters.

Reverse Blog

A reverse blog is composed by its users rather than a single blogger. This system has the characteristics of a blog, and the writing of several authors. These can be written by several contributing authors on a topic, or opened up for anyone to write. There is typically some limit to the number of entries to keep it from operating like a web forum.

Community and Cataloging

The Blogosphere

The collective community of all blogs is known as the *blogosphere*. Since all blogs are on the internet by definition, they may be seen as interconnected and socially networked, through blogrolls, comments, linkbacks (refbacks, trackbacks or pingbacks), and backlinks. Discussions "in the blogosphere" are occasionally used by the media as a gauge of public opinion on various issues. Because new, untapped communities of bloggers and their readers can emerge in the space of a few years, Internet marketers pay close attention to "trends in the blogosphere".

Blog Search Engines

Several blog search engines have been used to search blog contents, such as Bloglines, BlogScope, and Technorati. Technorati was one of the more popular blog search engines, but the website stopped indexing blogs and assigning authority scores in May 2014. The research community is working on going beyond simple keyword search, by inventing new ways to navigate through huge amounts of information present in the blogosphere, as demonstrated by projects like BlogScope, which was shut down in 2012.

Blogging Communities and Directories

Several online communities exist that connect people to blogs and bloggers to other bloggers. Some of these communities include Indiblogger, Blogadda, Blog Chatter, BlogCatalog and MyBlogLog. Interest-specific blogging platforms are also available. For instance, Blogster has a sizable community of political bloggers among its members. Global Voices aggregates international bloggers, "with emphasis on voices that are not ordinarily heard in international mainstream media."

Blogging and Advertising

It is common for blogs to feature advertisements either to financially benefit the blogger or to promote the blogger's favorite causes. The popularity of blogs has also given rise to "fake blogs" in which a company will create a fictional blog as a marketing tool to promote a product.

As the popularity of blogging continues to rise, the commercialisation of blogging is rapidly increasing as well. Many corporations and companies collaborate with bloggers to increase advertising and engage online communities towards their products. In the book *Fans, Bloggers, and Gamers*, Henry Jenkins stated that "Bloggers take knowledge in their own hands, enabling successful navigation within and between these emerging knowledge cultures. One can see such behaviour as co-optation into commodity culture insofar as it sometimes collaborates with corporate interests, but one can also see it as increasing the diversity of media culture, providing opportunities for greater inclusiveness, and making more responsive to consumers."

Popularity

As of 2008, blogging had become such a mania that a new blog was created every second of every minute of every hour of every day. Researchers have actively analyzed the dynamics of how blogs become popular. There are essentially two measures of this: popularity through citations, as well as popularity through affiliation (i.e., blogroll). The basic conclusion from studies of the structure of blogs is that while it takes time for a blog to become popular through blogrolls, permalinks can boost popularity more quickly, and are perhaps more indicative of popularity and authority than blogrolls, since they denote that people are actually reading the blog's content and deem it valuable or noteworthy in specific cases.

The blogdex project was launched by researchers in the MIT Media Lab to crawl the Web and gather data from thousands of blogs in order to investigate their social properties. Information was gathered by the tool for over four years, during which it autonomously tracked the most contagious information spreading in the blog community, ranking it by recency and popularity. It can, therefore, be considered the first instantiation of a memetracker. The project was replaced by tailrank. com which in turn has been replaced by spinn3r.com.

Blogs are given rankings by Alexa Internet (web hits of Alexa Toolbar users), and formerly by blog search engine Technorati based on the number of incoming links (Technorati stopped doing this in 2014). In August 2006, Technorati found that the most linked-to blog on the internet was that of Chinese actress Xu Jinglei. Chinese media Xinhua reported that this blog received more than 50 million page views, claiming it to be the most popular blog in the world. Technorati rated Boing Boing to be the most-read group-written blog.

Blurring With the Mass Media

Many bloggers, particularly those engaged in participatory journalism, differentiate themselves from the mainstream media, while others are members of that media working through a different channel. Some institutions see blogging as a means of "getting around the filter" and pushing messages directly to the public.

Many mainstream journalists, meanwhile, write their own blogs—well over 300, according to CyberJournalist.net's J-blog list. The first known use of a blog on a news site was in August 1998, when Jonathan Dube of The *Charlotte Observer* published one chronicling Hurricane Bonnie.

Some bloggers have moved over to other media. The following bloggers (and others) have appeared on radio and television: Duncan Black (known widely by his pseudonym, Atrios), Glenn Reynolds (Instapundit), Markos Moulitsas Zúniga (Daily Kos), Alex Steffen (Worldchanging), Ana Marie Cox (Wonkette), Nate Silver (FiveThirtyEight.com), and Ezra Klein (Ezra Klein blog in *The American Prospect,* now in the *Washington Post*). In counterpoint, Hugh Hewitt exemplifies a mass media personality who has moved in the other direction, adding to his reach in "old media" by being an influential blogger. Similarly, it was *Emergency Preparedness and Safety Tips On Air and Online* blog articles that captured Surgeon General of the United States Richard Carmona's attention and earned his kudos for the associated broadcasts by talk show host Lisa Tolliver and Westchester Emergency Volunteer Reserves-Medical Reserve Corps Director Marianne Partridge.

Blogs have also had an influence on minority languages, bringing together scattered speakers and learners; this is particularly so with blogs in Gaelic languages. Minority language publishing (which may lack economic feasibility) can find its audience through inexpensive blogging.

There are many examples of bloggers who have published books based on their blogs, e.g., Salam Pax, Ellen Simonetti, Jessica Cutler, ScrappleFace. Blog-based books have been given the name blook. A prize for the best blog-based book was initiated in 2005, the Lulu Blooker Prize. However, success has been elusive offline, with many of these books not selling as well as their blogs. The book based on Julie Powell's blog "The Julie/Julia Project" was made into the film *Julie & Julia,* apparently the first to do so.

Consumer-Generated Advertising in Blogs

Consumer-generated advertising is a relatively new and controversial development, and it has created a new model of marketing communication from businesses to consumers. Among the various forms of advertising on blog, the most controversial are the sponsored posts. These are blog entries or posts and may be in the form of feedback, reviews, opinion, videos, etc. and usually contain a link back to the desired site using a keyword/s.

Blogs have led to some disintermediation and a breakdown of the traditional advertising model where companies can skip over the advertising agencies (previously the only interface with the customer) and contact the customers directly themselves. On the other hand, new companies specialised in blog advertising have been established, to take advantage of this new development as well.

However, there are many people who look negatively on this new development. Some believe that any form of commercial activity on blogs will destroy the blogosphere's credibility.

Legal and Social Consequences

Blogging can result in a range of legal liabilities and other unforeseen consequences.

Defamation or Liability

Several cases have been brought before the national courts against bloggers concerning issues of defamation or liability. U.S. payouts related to blogging totaled $17.4 million by 2009; in some cases these have been covered by umbrella insurance. The courts have returned with mixed verdicts. Internet Service Providers (ISPs), in general, are immune from liability for information that originates with third parties (U.S. Communications Decency Act and the EU Directive 2000/31/ EC).

In *Doe v. Cahill*, the Delaware Supreme Court held that stringent standards had to be met to unmask the anonymous bloggers, and also took the unusual step of dismissing the libel case itself (as unfounded under American libel law) rather than referring it back to the trial court for reconsideration. In a bizarre twist, the Cahills were able to obtain the identity of John Doe, who turned out to be the person they suspected: the town's mayor, Councilman Cahill's political rival. The Cahills amended their original complaint, and the mayor settled the case rather than going to trial.

In January 2007, two prominent Malaysian political bloggers, Jeff Ooi and Ahirudin Attan, were sued by a pro-government newspaper, The New Straits Times Press (Malaysia) Berhad, Kalimullah bin Masheerul Hassan, Hishamuddin bin Aun and Brenden John a/l John Pereira over an alleged defamation. The plaintiff was supported by the Malaysian government. Following the suit, the Malaysian government proposed to "register" all bloggers in Malaysia in order to better control parties against their interest. This is the first such legal case against bloggers in the country.

In the United States, blogger Aaron Wall was sued by Traffic Power for defamation and publication of trade secrets in 2005. According to *Wired* magazine, Traffic Power had been "banned from Google for allegedly rigging search engine results." Wall and other "white hat" search engine optimization consultants had exposed Traffic Power in what they claim was an effort to protect the public. The case addressed the murky legal question of who is liable for comments posted on blogs. The case was dismissed for lack of personal jurisdiction, and Traffic Power failed to appeal within the allowed time.

In 2009, a controversial and landmark decision by The Hon. Mr Justice Eady refused to grant an order to protect the anonymity of Richard Horton. Horton was a police officer in the United Kingdom who blogged about his job under the name "NightJack".

In 2009, NDTV issued a legal notice to Indian blogger Kunte for a blog post criticizing their coverage of the Mumbai attacks. The blogger unconditionally withdrew his post, which resulted in several Indian bloggers criticizing NDTV for trying to silence critics.

Employment

Employees who blog about elements of their place of employment can begin to affect the brand recognition of their employer. In general, attempts by employee bloggers to protect themselves by maintaining anonymity have proved ineffective.

Delta Air Lines fired flight attendant Ellen Simonetti because she posted photographs of herself in uniform on an airplane and because of comments posted on her blog "Queen of Sky: Diary of a Flight Attendant" which the employer deemed inappropriate. This case highlighted the issue of personal blogging and freedom of expression versus employer rights and responsibilities, and so it received wide media attention. Simonetti took legal action against the airline for "wrongful termination, defamation of character and lost future wages". The suit was postponed while Delta was in bankruptcy proceedings.

In early 2006, Erik Ringmar, a senior lecturer at the London School of Economics, was ordered by the convenor of his department to "take down and destroy" his blog in which he discussed the quality of education at the school.

Mark Cuban, owner of the Dallas Mavericks, was fined during the 2006 NBA playoffs for criticizing NBA officials on the court and in his blog.

Mark Jen was terminated in 2005 after 10 days of employment as an Assistant Product Manager at Google for discussing corporate secrets on his personal blog, then called 99zeros and hosted on the Google-owned Blogger service. He blogged about unreleased products and company finances a week before the company's earnings announcement. He was fired two days after he complied with his employer's request to remove the sensitive material from his blog.

In India, blogger Gaurav Sabnis resigned from IBM after his posts questioned the claims of a management school IIPM.

Jessica Cutler, aka "The Washingtonienne", blogged about her sex life while employed as a congressional assistant. After the blog was discovered and she was fired, she wrote a novel based on her experiences and blog: *The Washingtonienne: A Novel*. Cutler is presently being sued by one of her former lovers in a case that could establish the extent to which bloggers are obligated to protect the privacy of their real life associates.

Catherine Sanderson, a.k.a. Petite Anglaise, lost her job in Paris at a British accountancy firm because of blogging. Although given in the blog in a fairly anonymous manner, some of the descriptions of the firm and some of its people were less than flattering. Sanderson later won a compensation claim case against the British firm, however.

On the other hand, Penelope Trunk wrote an upbeat article in the *Boston Globe* in 2006, entitled "Blogs 'essential' to a good career". She was one of the first journalists to point out that a large portion of bloggers are professionals and that a well-written blog can help attract employers.

Political Dangers

Blogging can sometimes have unforeseen consequences in politically sensitive areas. Blogs are much harder to control than broadcast or even print media. As a result, totalitarian and authoritarian regimes often seek to suppress blogs and/or to punish those who maintain them.

In Singapore, two ethnic Chinese were imprisoned under the country's anti-sedition law for posting anti-Muslim remarks in their blogs.

Egyptian blogger Kareem Amer was charged with insulting the Egyptian president Hosni Mubarak and an Islamic institution through his blog. It is the first time in the history of Egypt that a blogger was prosecuted. After a brief trial session that took place in Alexandria, the blogger was found guilty and sentenced to prison terms of three years for insulting Islam and inciting sedition, and one year for insulting Mubarak.

Egyptian blogger Abdel Monem Mahmoud was arrested in April 2007 for anti-government writings in his blog. Monem is a member of the then banned Muslim Brotherhood.

After the 2011 Egyptian revolution, the Egyptian blogger Maikel Nabil Sanad was charged with insulting the military for an article he wrote on his personal blog and sentenced to 3 years.

After expressing opinions in his personal blog about the state of the Sudanese armed forces, Jan Pronk, United Nations Special Representative for the Sudan, was given three days notice to leave Sudan. The Sudanese army had demanded his deportation.

In Myanmar, Nay Phone Latt, a blogger, was sentenced to 20 years in jail for posting a cartoon critical of head of state Than Shwe.

Personal Safety

One consequence of blogging is the possibility of attacks or threats against the blogger, sometimes without apparent reason. Kathy Sierra, author of the blog "Creating Passionate Users", was the target of threats and misogynistic insults to the point that she canceled her keynote speech at a technology conference in San Diego, fearing for her safety. While a blogger's anonymity is often tenuous, Internet trolls who would attack a blogger with threats or insults can be emboldened by anonymity. Sierra and supporters initiated an online discussion aimed at countering abusive online behavior and developed a blogger's code of conduct.

Behavior

The Blogger's Code of Conduct is a proposal by Tim O'Reilly for bloggers to enforce civility on their blogs by being civil themselves and moderating comments on their blog. The code was proposed in 2007 due to threats made to blogger Kathy Sierra. The idea of the code was first reported by BBC News, who quoted O'Reilly saying, "I do think we need some code of conduct around what is acceptable behaviour, I would hope that it doesn't come through any kind of regulation it would come through self-regulation."

O'Reilly and others came up with a list of seven proposed ideas:

1. Take responsibility not just for your own words, but for the comments you allow on your blog.

2. Label your tolerance level for abusive comments.

3. Consider eliminating anonymous comments.

4. Ignore the trolls.

5. Take the conversation offline, and talk directly, or find an intermediary who can do so.

6. If you know someone who is behaving badly, tell them so.

7. Don't say anything online that you wouldn't say in person.

These ideas were predictably intensely discussed on the Web and in the media. While the internet has continued to grow, with online activity and discourse only picking up both in positive and negative ways in terms of blog interaction, the proposed Code has drawn more widespread attention to the necessity of monitoring blogging activity and social norms being as important online as offline.

Videoconferencing

Videoconferencing (VC) is the conduct of a videoconference (also known as a video conference or videoteleconference) by a set of telecommunication technologies which allow two or more locations to communicate by simultaneous two-way video and audio transmissions. It has also been called 'visual collaboration' and is a type of groupware.

A Tandberg T3 high resolution telepresence room in use (2008).

Videoconferencing differs from videophone calls in that it's designed to serve a conference or multiple locations rather than individuals. It is an intermediate form of videotelephony, first used commercially in Germany during the late-1930s and later in the United States during the early 1970s as part of AT&T's development of Picturephone technology.

Indonesian and U.S. students participating in an **educational videoconference** (2010).

With the introduction of relatively low cost, high capacity broadband telecommunication services in the late 1990s, coupled with powerful computing processors and video compression techniques, videoconferencing has made significant inroads in business, education, medicine and media.

History

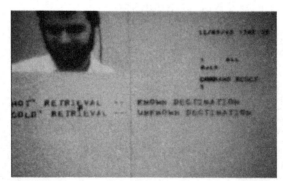

Multiple user videoconferencing first being demonstrated with Stanford Research Institute's NLS computer technology (1968).

Videoconferencing uses audio and video telecommunications to bring people at different sites together. This can be as simple as a conversation between people in private offices (point-to-point) or involve several (multipoint) sites in large rooms at multiple locations. Besides the audio and visual transmission of meeting activities, allied videoconferencing technologies can be used to share documents and display information on whiteboards.

Simple analog videophone communication could be established as early as the invention of the television. Such an antecedent usually consisted of two closed-circuit television systems connected via coax cable or radio. An example of that was the German Reich Postzentralamt (post office) video telephone network serving Berlin and several German cities via coaxial cables between 1936 and 1940.

During the first manned space flights, NASA used two radio-frequency (UHF or VHF) video links, one in each direction. TV channels routinely use this type of videotelephony when reporting from distant locations. The news media were to become regular users of mobile links to satellites using specially equipped trucks, and much later via special satellite videophones in a briefcase.

This technique was very expensive, though, and could not be used for applications such as telemedicine, distance education, and business meetings. Attempts at using normal telephony networks to transmit slow-scan video, such as the first systems developed by AT&T Corporation, first researched in the 1950s, failed mostly due to the poor picture quality and the lack of efficient video compression techniques. The greater 1 MHz bandwidth and 6 Mbit/s bit rate of the Picturephone in the 1970s also did not achieve commercial success, mostly due to its high cost, but also due to a lack of network effect —with only a few hundred Picturephones in the world, users had extremely few contacts they could actually call to, and interoperability with other videophone systems would not exist for decades.

It was only in the 1980s that digital telephony transmission networks became possible, such as with ISDN networks, assuring a minimum bit rate (usually 128 kilobits/s) for compressed video and audio transmission. During this time, there was also research into other forms of digital video and audio communication. Many of these technologies, such as the Media space, are not as widely used today as videoconferencing but were still an important area of research. The first dedicated systems started to appear in the market as ISDN networks were expanding throughout the world. One of the first commercial videoconferencing systems sold to companies came from PictureTel Corp., which had an Initial Public Offering in November, 1984.

In 1984 Concept Communication in the United States replaced the then-100 pound, US$100,000 computers necessary for teleconferencing, with a $12,000 circuit board that doubled the video frame rate from 15 up to 30 frames per second, and which reduced the equipment to the size of a circuit board fitting into standard personal computers. The company also secured a patent for a codec for full-motion videoconferencing, first demonstrated at AT&T Bell Labs in 1986.

Global Schoolhouse students communicating via CU-SeeMe, with a video framerate between 3-9 frames per second (1993).

Videoconferencing systems throughout the 1990s rapidly evolved from very expensive proprietary equipment, software and network requirements to a standards-based technology readily available to the general public at a reasonable cost.

Finally, in the 1990s, Internet Protocol-based videoconferencing became possible, and more efficient video compression technologies were developed, permitting desktop, or personal computer (PC)-based videoconferencing. In 1992 CU-SeeMe was developed at Cornell by Tim Dorcey et al. In 1995 the first public videoconference between North America and Africa took place, linking a technofair in San Francisco with a techno-rave and cyberdeli in Cape Town. At the Winter Olympics opening ceremony in Nagano, Japan, Seiji Ozawa conducted the Ode to Joy from Beethoven's Ninth Symphony simultaneously across five continents in near-real time.

While videoconferencing technology was initially used primarily within internal corporate communication networks, one of the first community service usages of the technology started in 1992 through a unique partnership with PictureTel and IBM Corporations which at the time were promoting a jointly developed desktop based videoconferencing product known as the PCS/1. Over the next 15 years, Project DIANE (Diversified Information and Assistance Network) grew to utilize a variety of videoconferencing platforms to create a multi-state cooperative public service and distance education network consisting of several hundred schools, neighborhood centers, libraries, science museums, zoos and parks, public assistance centers, and other community oriented organizations.

In the 2000s, videotelephony was popularized via free Internet services such as Skype and iChat, web plugins and on-line telecommunication programs that promoted low cost, albeit lower-quality, videoconferencing to virtually every location with an Internet connection.

Russian President Dmitry Medvedev attending the Singapore APEC summit, holding a videoconference with Rashid Nurgaliyev via a Tactical MXP, after an arms depot explosion in Russia (2009).

In May 2005, the first high definition video conferencing systems, produced by LifeSize Communications, were displayed at the Interop trade show in Las Vegas, Nevada, able to provide video at 30 frames per second with a 1280 by 720 display resolution. Polycom introduced its first high definition video conferencing system to the market in 2006. As of the 2010s, high definition resolution for videoconferencing became a popular feature, with most major suppliers in the video-conferencing market offering it.

Technological developments by videoconferencing developers in the 2010s have extended the capabilities of video conferencing systems beyond the boardroom for use with hand-held mobile devices that combine the use of video, audio and on-screen drawing capabilities broadcasting in real-time over secure networks, independent of location. Mobile collaboration systems now allow multiple people in previously unreachable locations, such as workers on an off-shore oil rig, the ability to view and discuss issues with colleagues thousands of miles away. Traditional videoconferencing system manufacturers have begun providing mobile applications as well, such as those that allow for live and still image streaming.

Technology

The core technology used in a videoconferencing system is digital compression of audio and video streams in real time. The hardware or software that performs compression is called a codec (coder/decoder). Compression rates of up to 1:500 can be achieved. The resulting digital stream of 1s and 0s is subdivided into labeled packets, which are then transmitted through a digital network of some kind (usually ISDN or IP). The use of audio modems in the transmission line allow for the use of POTS, or the Plain Old Telephone System, in some low-speed applications, such as videotelephony, because they convert the digital pulses to/from analog waves in the audio spectrum range.

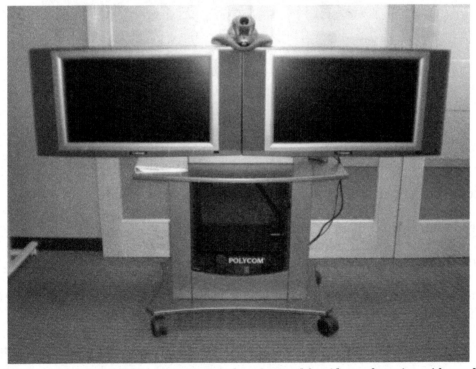

Dual display: An older Polycom VSX 7000 system and camera used for videoconferencing, with two displays for simultaneous broadcast from separate locations (2008).

Various components and the camera of a LifeSize Communications Room 220 high definition multipoint system (2010).

A video conference meeting facilitated by Google Hangouts.

The other components required for a videoconferencing system include:

- Video input: video camera or webcam

- Video output: computer monitor, television or projector

- Audio input: microphones, CD/DVD player, cassette player, or any other source of PreAmp audio outlet.

- Audio output: usually loudspeakers associated with the display device or telephone

- Data transfer: analog or digital telephone network, LAN or Internet

- Computer: a data processing unit that ties together the other components, does the compressing and decompressing, and initiates and maintains the data linkage via the network.

There are basically two kinds of videoconferencing systems:

1. Dedicated systems have all required components packaged into a single piece of equipment, usually a console with a high quality remote controlled video camera. These cameras can be controlled at a distance to pan left and right, tilt up and down, and zoom. They became known as PTZ cameras. The console contains all electrical interfaces, the control computer, and the software or hardware-based codec. Omnidirectional microphones are connected to the console, as well as a TV monitor with loudspeakers and/or a video projector. There are several types of dedicated videoconferencing devices:

    1. Large group videoconferencing are non-portable, large, more expensive devices used for large rooms and auditoriums.

    2. Small group videoconferencing are non-portable or portable, smaller, less expensive devices used for small meeting rooms.

    3. Individual videoconferencing are usually portable devices, meant for single users, have fixed cameras, microphones and loudspeakers integrated into the console.

2. Desktop systems are add-ons (hardware boards or software codec) to normal PCs and laptops, transforming them into videoconferencing devices. A range of different cameras and microphones can be used with the codec, which contains the necessary codec and transmission interfaces. Most of the desktops systems work with the H.323 standard. Video-conferences carried out via dispersed PCs are also known as e-meetings. These can also be nonstandard, Microsoft Lync, Skype for Business, Google Hangouts, or Yahoo Messenger or standards based, Cisco Jabber.

3. WebRTC Platforms are video conferencing solutions that are not resident by using a software application but is available through the standard web browser. Solutions such as Adobe Connect and Cisco WebEX can be accessed by going to a URL sent by the meeting organizer and various degrees of security can be attached to the virtual "room". Often the user will be required to download a piece of software, called an "Add In" to enable the browser to access the local camera, microphone and establish a connection to the meeting.

Conferencing Layers

The components within a Conferencing System can be divided up into several different layers: User Interface, Conference Control, Control or Signal Plane, and Media Plane.

Videoconferencing User Interfaces (VUI) can be either graphical or voice responsive. Many in the industry have encountered both types of interfaces, and normally graphical interfaces are encountered on a computer. User interfaces for conferencing have a number of different uses; they can be used for scheduling, setup, and making a videocall. Through the user interface the administrator is able to control the other three layers of the system.

Conference Control performs resource allocation, management and routing. This layer along with the User Interface creates meetings (scheduled or unscheduled) or adds and removes participants from a conference.

Control (Signaling) Plane contains the stacks that signal different endpoints to create a call and/ or a conference. Signals can be, but aren't limited to, H.323 and Session Initiation Protocol (SIP) Protocols. These signals control incoming and outgoing connections as well as session parameters.

The Media Plane controls the audio and video mixing and streaming. This layer manages Real-Time Transport Protocols, User Datagram Packets (UDP) and Real-Time Transport Control Protocol (RTCP). The RTP and UDP normally carry information such the payload type which is the type of codec, frame rate, video size and many others. RTCP on the other hand acts as a quality control Protocol for detecting errors during streaming.

Multipoint Videoconferencing

Simultaneous videoconferencing among three or more remote points is possible by means of a Multipoint Control Unit (MCU). This is a bridge that interconnects calls from several sources (in a similar way to the audio conference call). All parties call the MCU, or the MCU can also call the parties which are going to participate, in sequence. There are MCU bridges for IP and ISDN-based videoconferencing. There are MCUs which are pure software, and others which are a combination of hardware and software. An MCU is characterised according to the number of simultaneous calls it can handle, its ability to conduct transposing of data rates and protocols, and features such as Continuous Presence, in which multiple parties can be seen on-screen at once. MCUs can be stand-alone hardware devices, or they can be embedded into dedicated videoconferencing units.

The MCU consists of two logical components:

1. A single multipoint controller (MC), and

2. Multipoint Processors (MP), sometimes referred to as the mixer.

The MC controls the conferencing while it is active on the signaling plane, which is simply where the system manages conferencing creation, endpoint signaling and in-conferencing controls. This component negotiates parameters with every endpoint in the network and controls conferencing resources. While the MC controls resources and signaling negotiations, the MP operates on the media plane and receives media from each endpoint.

Some systems are capable of multipoint conferencing with no MCU, stand-alone, embedded or otherwise. These use a standards-based H.323 technique known as "decentralized multipoint", where each station in a multipoint call exchanges video and audio directly with the other stations with no central "manager" or other bottleneck. The advantages of this technique are that the video and audio will generally be of higher quality because they don't have to be relayed through a central point. Also, users can make ad-hoc multipoint calls without any concern for the availability or control of an MCU. This added convenience and quality comes at the expense of some increased network bandwidth, because every station must transmit to every other station directly.

Videoconferencing Modes

Videoconferencing systems use several common operating modes:

1.   Voice-Activated Switch (VAS);

2.   Continuous Presence.

In VAS mode, the MCU switches which endpoint can be seen by the other endpoints by the levels of one's voice. If there are four people in a conference, the only one that will be seen in the conference is the site which is talking; the location with the loudest voice will be seen by the other participants.

Continuous Presence mode, displays multiple participants at the same time. The MP in this mode takes the streams from the different endpoints and puts them all together into a single video image. In this mode, the MCU normally sends the same type of images to all participants. Typically these types of images are called "layouts" and can vary depending on the number of participants in a conference.

Echo Cancellation

A fundamental feature of professional videoconferencing systems is Acoustic Echo Cancellation (AEC). Echo can be defined as the reflected source wave interference with new wave created by source. AEC is an algorithm which is able to detect when sounds or utterances reenter the audio input of the videoconferencing codec, which came from the audio output of the same system, after some time delay. If unchecked, this can lead to several problems including:

1.   the remote party hearing their own voice coming back at them (usually significantly delayed)

2.   strong reverberation, which makes the voice channel useless, and

3.   howling created by feedback.

Echo cancellation is a processor-intensive task that usually works over a narrow range of sound delays.

Cloud-Based Video Conferencing

Cloud-based video conferencing can be used without the hardware generally required by other video conferencing systems, and can be designed for use by SMEs, or larger international companies like Facebook. Cloud-based systems can handle either 2D or 3D video broadcasting. Cloud-based systems can also implement mobile calls, VOIP, and other forms of video calling. They can also come with a video recording function to archive past meetings.

Technical and Other Issues

Computer security experts have shown that poorly configured or inadequately supervised video-conferencing system can permit an easy 'virtual' entry by computer hackers and criminals into company premises and corporate boardrooms, via their own videoconferencing systems. Some observers argue that three outstanding issues have prevented videoconferencing from becoming a standard form of communication, despite the ubiquity of videoconferencing-capable systems. These issues are:

1. Eye contact: Eye contact plays a large role in conversational turn-taking, perceived attention and intent, and other aspects of group communication. While traditional telephone conversations give no eye contact cues, many videoconferencing systems are arguably worse in that they provide an incorrect impression that the remote interlocutor is avoiding eye contact. Some telepresence systems have cameras located in the screens that reduce the amount of parallax observed by the users. This issue is also being addressed through research that generates a synthetic image with eye contact using stereo reconstruction. Telcordia Technologies, formerly Bell Communications Research, owns a patent for eye-to-eye videoconferencing using rear projection screens with the video camera behind it, evolved from a 1960s U.S. military system that provided videoconferencing services between the White House and various other government and military facilities. This technique eliminates the need for special cameras or image processing.

2. Appearance consciousness: A second psychological problem with videoconferencing is being on camera, with the video stream possibly even being recorded. The burden of presenting an acceptable on-screen appearance is not present in audio-only communication. Early studies by Alphonse Chapanis found that the addition of video actually impaired communication, possibly because of the consciousness of being on camera.

3. Signal latency: The information transport of digital signals in many steps need time. In a telecommunicated conversation, an increased latency (time lag) larger than about 150–300 ms becomes noticeable and is soon observed as unnatural and distracting. Therefore, next to a stable large bandwidth, a small total round-trip time is another major technical requirement for the communication channel for interactive videoconferencing.

The issue of eye-contact may be solved with advancing technology, and presumably the issue of appearance consciousness will fade as people become accustomed to videoconferencing.

Standards

The International Telecommunications Union (ITU) (formerly: Consultative Committee on International Telegraphy and Telephony (CCITT)) has three umbrellas of standards for videoconferencing:

*   ITU H.320 is known as the standard for public switched telephone networks (PSTN) or videoconferencing over integrated services digital networks. While still prevalent in Europe, ISDN was never widely adopted in the United States and Canada.

The Tandberg E20 is an example of a SIP-only device. Such devices need to route calls through a Video Communication Server to be able to reach H.323 systems, a process known as "interworking" (2009).

- ITU H.264 Scalable Video Coding (SVC) is a compression standard that enables videoconferencing systems to achieve highly error resilient Internet Protocol (IP) video transmissions over the public Internet without quality-of-service enhanced lines. This standard has enabled wide scale deployment of high definition desktop videoconferencing and made possible new architectures, which reduces latency between the transmitting sources and receivers, resulting in more fluid communication without pauses. In addition, an attractive factor for IP videoconferencing is that it is easier to set up for use along with web conferencing and data collaboration. These combined technologies enable users to have a richer multimedia environment for live meetings, collaboration and presentations.

- ITU V.80: videoconferencing is generally compatibilized with H.324 standard point-to-point videotelephony over regular plain old telephone service (POTS) phone lines.

The Unified Communications Interoperability Forum (UCIF), a non-profit alliance between communications vendors, launched in May 2010. The organization's vision is to maximize the interoperability of UC based on existing standards. Founding members of UCIF include HP, Microsoft, Polycom, Logitech/LifeSize Communications and Juniper Networks.

Social and Institutional Impact

Impact on the General Public

High speed Internet connectivity has become more widely available at a reasonable cost and the cost of video capture and display technology has decreased. Consequently, personal videoconferencing systems based on a webcam, personal computer system, software compression and broadband Internet connectivity have become affordable to the general public. Also, the hardware used for this technology has continued to improve in quality, and prices have dropped dramatically. The availability of freeware (often as part of chat programs) has made software based videoconferencing accessible to many.

For over a century, futurists have envisioned a future where telephone conversations will take place as actual face-to-face encounters with video as well as audio. Sometimes it is simply not possible or practical to have face-to-face meetings with two or more people. Sometimes a telephone conversation or conference call is adequate. Other times, e-mail exchanges are adequate. However, videoconferencing adds another possible alternative, and can be considered when:

- a live conversation is needed;

- non-verbal (visual) information is an important component of the conversation;

- the parties of the conversation can't physically come to the same location; or

- the expense or time of travel is a consideration.

Deaf, hard-of-hearing and mute individuals have a particular interest in the development of affordable high-quality videoconferencing as a means of communicating with each other in sign language. Unlike Video Relay Service, which is intended to support communication between a caller using sign language and another party using spoken language, videoconferencing can be used directly between two deaf signers.

Mass adoption and use of videoconferencing is still relatively low, with the following often claimed as causes:

- Complexity of systems. Most users are not technical and want a simple interface. In hardware systems an unplugged cord or a flat battery in a remote control is seen as failure, contributing to perceived unreliability which drives users back to traditional meetings. Successful systems are backed by support teams who can pro-actively support and provide fast assistance when required.

- Perceived lack of interoperability: not all systems can readily interconnect, for example ISDN and IP systems require a gateway. Popular software solutions cannot easily connect to hardware systems. Some systems use different standards, features and qualities which can require additional configuration when connecting to dissimilar systems.

- Bandwidth and quality of service: In some countries it is difficult or expensive to get a high quality connection that is fast enough for good-quality video conferencing. Technologies such as ADSL have limited upload speeds and cannot upload and download simultaneously at full speed. As Internet speeds increase higher quality and high definition video conferencing will become more readily available.

- Expense of commercial systems: well-designed telepresence systems require specially designed rooms which can cost hundreds of thousands of dollars to fit out their rooms with codecs, integration equipment (such as Multipoint Control Units), high fidelity sound systems and furniture. Monthly charges may also be required for bridging services and high capacity broadband service.

- Self-consciousness about being on camera: especially for new users or older generations who may prefer less fidelity in their communications.

- Lack of direct eye contact, an issue being circumvented in some higher end systems.

These are some of the reasons many systems are often used for internal corporate use only, as they are less likely to result in lost sales. One alternative to companies lacking dedicated facilities is the rental of videoconferencing-equipped meeting rooms in cities around the world. Clients can book rooms and turn up for the meeting, with all technical aspects being prearranged and support being readily available if needed.

Impact on Government and Law

In the United States, videoconferencing has allowed testimony to be used for an individual who is unable or prefers not to attend the physical legal settings, or would be subjected to severe psychological stress in doing so, however there is a controversy on the use of testimony by foreign or unavailable witnesses via video transmission, regarding the violation of the Confrontation Clause of the Sixth Amendment of the U.S. Constitution.

In a military investigation in State of North Carolina, Afghan witnesses have testified via videoconferencing.

In Hall County, Georgia, videoconferencing systems are used for initial court appearances. The systems link jails with court rooms, reducing the expenses and security risks of transporting prisoners to the courtroom.

The U.S. Social Security Administration (SSA), which oversees the world's largest administrative judicial system under its Office of Disability Adjudication and Review (ODAR), has made extensive use of videoconferencing to conduct hearings at remote locations. In Fiscal Year (FY) 2009, the U.S. Social Security Administration (SSA) conducted 86,320 videoconferenced hearings, a 55% increase over FY 2008. In August 2010, the SSA opened its fifth and largest videoconferencing-only National Hearing Center (NHC), in St. Louis, Missouri. This continues the SSA's effort to use video hearings as a means to clear its substantial hearing backlog. Since 2007, the SSA has also established NHCs in Albuquerque, New Mexico, Baltimore, Maryland, Falls Church, Virginia, and Chicago, Illinois.

Impact On Education

Videoconferencing provides students with the opportunity to learn by participating in two-way communication forums. Furthermore, teachers and lecturers worldwide can be brought to remote or otherwise isolated educational facilities. Students from diverse communities and backgrounds can come together to learn about one another, although language barriers will continue to persist. Such students are able to explore, communicate, analyze and share information and ideas with one another. Through videoconferencing, students can visit other parts of the world to speak with their peers, and visit museums and educational facilities. Such virtual field trips can provide enriched learning opportunities to students, especially those in geographically isolated locations, and to the economically disadvantaged. Small schools can use these technologies to pool resources and provide courses, such as in foreign languages, which could not otherwise be offered.

A few examples of benefits that videoconferencing can provide in campus environments include:

- faculty members keeping in touch with classes while attending conferences;

- guest lecturers brought in classes from other institutions;

- researchers collaborating with colleagues at other institutions on a regular basis without loss of time due to travel;

- schools with multiple campuses collaborating and sharing professors;

- schools from two separate nations engaging in cross-cultural exchanges;

- faculty members participating in thesis defenses at other institutions;

- administrators on tight schedules collaborating on budget preparation from different parts of campus;

- faculty committee auditioning scholarship candidates;

- researchers answering questions about grant proposals from agencies or review committees;

- student interviews with an employers in other cities, and

- teleseminars.

Impact on Medicine and Health

Videoconferencing is a highly useful technology for real-time telemedicine and telenursing applications, such as diagnosis, consulting, transmission of medical images, etc... With videoconferencing, patients may contact nurses and physicians in emergency or routine situations; physicians and other paramedical professionals can discuss cases across large distances. Rural areas can use this technology for diagnostic purposes, thus saving lives and making more efficient use of health care money. For example, a rural medical center in Ohio, United States, used videoconferencing to successfully cut the number of transfers of sick infants to a hospital 70 miles (110 km) away. This had previously cost nearly $10,000 per transfer.

Special peripherals such as microscopes fitted with digital cameras, videoendoscopes, medical ultrasound imaging devices, otoscopes, etc., can be used in conjunction with videoconferencing equipment to transmit data about a patient. Recent developments in mobile collaboration on hand-held mobile devices have also extended video-conferencing capabilities to locations previously unreachable, such as a remote community, long-term care facility, or a patient's home.

Impact on Sign Language Communications

A deaf person using a video relay service at his workplace to communicate with a hearing person in London. (Courtesy: *SignVideo*)

A video relay service (VRS), also known as a 'video interpreting service' (VIS), is a service that allows deaf, hard-of-hearing and speech-impaired (D-HOH-SI) individuals to communicate by videoconferencing (or similar technologies) with hearing people in real-time, via a sign language interpreter.

A similar video interpreting service called video remote interpreting (VRI) is conducted through a different organization often called a "Video Interpreting Service Provider" (VISP). VRS is a newer form of telecommunication service to the D-HOH-SI community, which had, in the United States, started earlier in 1974 using a non-video technology called telecommunications relay service (TRS).

One of the first demonstrations of the ability for telecommunications to help sign language users communicate with each other occurred when AT&T's videophone (trademarked as the "Picturephone") was introduced to the public at the 1964 New York World's Fair –two deaf users were able to communicate freely with each other between the fair and another city. Various universities and other organizations, including British Telecom's Martlesham facility, have also conducted extensive research on signing via videotelephony. The use of sign language via videotelephony was hampered for many years due to the difficulty of its use over slow analogue copper phone lines, coupled with the high cost of better quality ISDN (data) phone lines. Those factors largely disappeared with the introduction of more efficient video codecs and the advent of lower cost high-speed ISDN data and IP (Internet) services in the 1990s.

VRS services have become well developed nationally in Sweden since 1997 and also in the United States since the first decade of the 2000s. With the exception of Sweden, VRS has been provided in Europe for only a few years since the mid-2000s, and as of 2010 has not been made available in many European Union countries, with most European countries still lacking the legislation or the financing for large-scale VRS services, and to provide the necessary telecommunication equipment to deaf users. Germany and the Nordic countries are among the other leaders in Europe, while the United States is another world leader in the provisioning of VRS services.

Impact on Business

Videoconferencing can enable individuals in distant locations to participate in meetings on short notice, with time and money savings. Technology such as VoIP can be used in conjunction with desktop videoconferencing to enable low-cost face-to-face business meetings without leaving the desk, especially for businesses with widespread offices. The technology is also used for telecommuting, in which employees work from home. One research report based on a sampling of 1,800 corporate employees showed that, as of June 2010, 54% of the respondents with access to video conferencing used it "all of the time" or "frequently".

Intel Corporation have used videoconferencing to reduce both costs and environmental impacts of its business operations.

Videoconferencing is also currently being introduced on online networking websites, in order to help businesses form profitable relationships quickly and efficiently without leaving their place of work. This has been leveraged by banks to connect busy banking professionals with customers in various locations using video banking technology.

Videoconferencing on hand-held mobile devices (mobile collaboration technology) is being used in industries such as manufacturing, energy, healthcare, insurance, government and public safety. Live, visual interaction removes traditional restrictions of distance and time, often in locations previously unreachable, such as a manufacturing plant floor a continent away.

In the increasingly globalized film industry, videoconferencing has become useful as a method by which creative talent in many different locations can collaborate closely on the complex details of film production. For example, for the 2013 award-winning animated film *Frozen*, Burbank-based Walt Disney Animation Studios hired the New York City-based husband-and-wife songwriting team of Robert Lopez and Kristen Anderson-Lopez to write the songs, which required two-hour-long transcontinental videoconferences nearly every weekday for about 14 months.

Video Conferencing is a key technology for organisations within a number of vertical markets - historically high end verticals such as Finance & Banking, Oil & Gas & private healthcare, however more recently, due to accessibility, recognition of benefits and price drops, is now seen throughout the SMB market, and within manufacturing, retail, public healthcare, media and marketing.

With the development of lower cost endpoints, cloud based infrastructure and technology trends such as WebRTC, Video Conferencing is moving from just a business to business offering, to a business to business and business to consumer offering.

Although videoconferencing has frequently proven its value, research has shown that some non-managerial employees prefer not to use it due to several factors, including anxiety. Some such anxieties can be avoided if managers use the technology as part of the normal course of business. Remote workers can also adopt certain behaviors and best practices to stay connected with their co-workers and company.

Researchers also find that attendees of business and medical videoconferences must work harder to interpret information delivered during a conference than they would if they attended face-to-face. They recommend that those coordinating videoconferences make adjustments to their conferencing procedures and equipment.

Impact on Media Relations

The concept of press videoconferencing was developed in October 2007 by the PanAfrican Press Association (APPA), a Paris France-based non-governmental organization, to allow African journalists to participate in international press conferences on developmental and good governance issues.

Press videoconferencing permits international press conferences via videoconferencing over the Internet. Journalists can participate on an international press conference from any location, without leaving their offices or countries. They need only be seated by a computer connected to the Internet in order to ask their questions to the speaker.

In 2004, the International Monetary Fund introduced the Online Media Briefing Center, a password-protected site available only to professional journalists. The site enables the IMF to present press briefings globally and facilitates direct questions to briefers from the press. The site has been copied by other international organizations since its inception. More than 4,000 journalists worldwide are currently registered with the IMF.

Descriptive Names and Terminology

Videophone calls (also: *videocalls*, *video chat* as well as *Skype* and *Skyping* in verb form), differ from videoconferencing in that they expect to serve individuals, not groups. However that distinction has become increasingly blurred with technology improvements such as increased bandwidth and sophisticated software clients that can allow for multiple parties on a call. In general everyday usage the term *videoconferencing* is now frequently used instead of *videocall* for point-to-point calls between two units. Both videophone calls and videoconferencing are also now commonly referred to as a *video link*.

Webcams are popular, relatively low cost devices which can provide live video and audio streams via personal computers, and can be used with many software clients for both video calls and videoconferencing.

A *videoconference system* is generally higher cost than a videophone and deploys greater capabilities. A *videoconference* (also known as a *videoteleconference*) allows two or more locations to communicate via live, simultaneous two-way video and audio transmissions. This is often accomplished by the use of a multipoint control unit (a centralized distribution and call management system) or by a similar non-centralized multipoint capability embedded in each videoconferencing unit. Again, technology improvements have circumvented traditional definitions by allowing multiple party videoconferencing via web-based applications.

A *telepresence system* is a high-end videoconferencing system and service usually employed by enterprise-level corporate offices. Telepresence conference rooms use state-of-the art room designs, video cameras, displays, sound-systems and processors, coupled with high-to-very-high capacity bandwidth transmissions.

Typical use of the various technologies described above include calling or conferencing on a one-on-one, one-to-many or many-to-many basis for personal, business, educational, deaf Video Relay Service and tele-medical, diagnostic and rehabilitative use or services. New services utilizing videocalling and videoconferencing, such as teachers and psychologists conducting online sessions, personal videocalls to inmates incarcerated in penitentiaries, and videoconferencing to resolve airline engineering issues at maintenance facilities, are being created or evolving on an ongoing basis.

A *telepresence robot* (also *telerobotics*) is a robotically controlled and motorized videoconferencing display to help provide a better sense of remote physical presence for communication and collaboration in an office, home, school, etc... when one cannot be there in person. The robotic avatar and video-conferencing display-camera can move about and look around at the command of the remote person.

Social Media

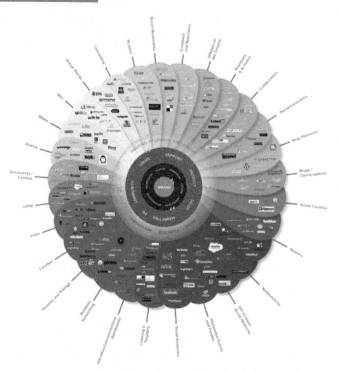

Diagram depicting the many different types of social media

Social media are computer-mediated tools that allow people, companies and other organizations to create, share, or exchange information, career interests, ideas, and pictures/videos in virtual communities and networks. The variety of stand-alone and built-in social media services currently available introduces challenges of definition; however, there are some common features: (1) social media are Web 2.0 Internet-based applications, (2) user-generated content (UGC) such as text, digital photo or digital video posts are the lifeblood of the social media organism, (3) users create their own profiles for the website or app, which is designed and maintained by the social media organization, and (4) social media facilitate the development of online social networks by connecting a user's profile with those of other individuals and/or groups.

Social media depend on mobile and web-based technologies to create highly interactive platforms through which individuals, communities and organizations can share, co-create, discuss, and modify user-generated content. They introduce substantial and pervasive changes to communication between businesses, organizations, communities, and individuals. These changes are the focus of the emerging field of technoself studies.

Social media differ from traditional paper-based or industrial media in many ways, including quality, reach, frequency, usability, immediacy, and permanence. Social media operate in a dialogic transmission system (many sources to many receivers). This is in contrast to traditional media that operates under a monologic transmission model (one source to many receivers), such as a paper newspaper which is delivered to many subscribers. Some of the most popular social media websites are Facebook (and its associated Facebook Messenger), WhatsApp, Tumblr, Instagram, Twitter, Baidu Tieba and Snapchat.

There are many effects that stem from Internet usage. According to Nielsen, Internet users continue to spend more time with social media sites than any other type of site. At the same time, the total time spent on social media in the U.S. across PC and mobile devices increased by 99 percent to 121 billion minutes in July 2012 compared to 66 billion minutes in July 2011. For content contributors, the benefits of participating in social media have gone beyond simply social sharing to building reputation and bringing in career opportunities and monetary income, as discussed in Tang, Gu, and Whinston (2012).

Definition and Classification

A social media app (software application) being viewed on a smartphone.

Simplified Definition

Forms of electronic communication (such as Web sites) through which people create online communities to share information, ideas, personal messages, etc.

A Challenge Of Definition

The variety and evolving stand-alone and built-in social media services introduces a challenge of definition. Furthermore, the idea that social media are defined by their ability to bring people together provides too broad a definition. Such a broad definition would suggest that the telegraph and telephone were social media – not the technologies scholars are intending to describe. The terminology is also unclear, with some referring to social media as social networks.

Attempting Definition

A recent attempt at providing a clear definition reviewed the prominent literature in the area and identified four commonalities unique to current social media services:

(1) social media are Web 2.0 internet-based applications,

(2) user-generated content (UGC) is the lifeblood of the social media organism,

(3) users create service-specific profiles for the site or app that are designed and maintained by the social media organization, and

(4) social media facilitate the development of online social networks by connecting a user's profile with those of other individuals and/or groups.

Classification

Type of social media	Corporate function					
	R&D	Marketing	Customer service	Sales	HR	Organisation
Blogs	◐	◑	◐			
Business networks					●	◐
Collaborative projects	●					
Enterprise social networks	◕				◑	●
Forums	◑	◐	●			
Microblogs		◕	◐		◐	
Photo sharing		◑				
Products/services review	◐	◑		●		
Social bookmarking		◑				
Social gaming		◑				
Social networks	◐	●	◑		◐	◐
Video sharing		●	◐			
Virtual worlds	◐	◕		◐		

Importance: (empty) none or almost none; ◐ low; ◑ medium; ◕ high; ● very high

Classification of social media and overview of how important different types of social media (e.g. blogs) are for each of a company's operational functions (e.g. marketing).

Social media technologies take on many different forms including blogs, business networks, enterprise social networks, forums, microblogs, photo sharing, products/services review, social bookmarking, social gaming, social networks, video sharing, and virtual worlds.

The development of social media started off with simple platforms such as sixdegrees.com. Unlike instant messaging clients such as ICQ and AOL's AIM, or chat clients like IRC, iChat or Chat Television, sixdegrees.com was the first online business that was created for real people, using their real names. However, the first social networks were short-lived because their users lost interest. The Social Network Revolution has led to the rise of the networking sites. Research shows that the audience spends 22 percent of their time on social networking sites, thus proving how popular social media platforms have become.

Distinction From Other Media

Virality

Some social media sites have greater *virality* – defined as a greater likelihood that users will reshare content posted (by another user) to their social network. Many social media sites provide specific functionality to help users reshare content – for example, Twitter's retweet button, Pinterest pin or Tumblr's reblog function. Businesses may have a particular interest in viral marketing; nonprofit organisations and activists may have similar interests in virality.

Mobile Use

Mobile social media refers to the use of social media on mobile devices such as smartphones and tablet computers. This is a group of mobile marketing applications that allow the creation and exchange of user-generated content. Due to the fact that mobile social media run on mobile devices, they differ from traditional social media by incorporating new factors such as the current location of the user (location-sensitivity) or the time delay between sending and receiving messages (time-sensitivity). According to Andreas Kaplan, mobile social media applications can be differentiated among four types:

1. *Space-timers* (location and time sensitive): Exchange of messages with relevance mostly for one specific location at one specific point in time (e.g. Facebook Places; Foursquare)

2. *Space-locators* (only location sensitive): Exchange of messages, with relevance for one specific location, which are tagged to a certain place and read later by others (e.g. Yelp; Qype, Tumblr)

3. *Quick-timers* (only time sensitive): Transfer of traditional social media applications to mobile devices to increase immediacy (e.g. posting Twitter messages or Facebook status updates)

Business Potential

The login page for a social media website.

Although traditional social media offer a variety of opportunities for companies in a wide range of business sectors, economic-sector mobile social-media makes use of the location- and time-sensitive aspects of social media in order to engage in marketing research, communication, sales promotions/discounts, and relationship development/loyalty programs.

- Marketing research: Mobile social media applications offer data about offline consumer movements at a level of detail heretofore limited to online companies. Any firm can know the exact time at which a customer entered one of its outlets, as well as comments made during the visit.

- Communication: Mobile social media communication takes two forms: company-to-consumer (in which a company may establish a connection to a consumer based on its location and provide reviews about locations nearby) and user-generated content. For example, McDonald's offered $5 and $10 gift-cards to 100 users randomly selected among those checking in at one of its restaurants. This promotion increased check-ins by 33% (from 2,146 to 2,865), resulted in over 50 articles and blog posts, and prompted several hundred thousand news feeds and Twitter messages.

- Sales promotions and discounts: Although customers have had to use printed coupons in the past, mobile social media allows companies to tailor promotions to specific users at specific times. For example, when launching its California-Cancun service, Virgin America offered users who checked in through Loopt at one of three designated Border Grill taco trucks in San Francisco and Los Angeles between 11 a.m. and 3 p.m. on August 31, 2010, two tacos for $1 and two flights to Mexico for the price of one.

- Relationship development and loyalty programs: In order to increase long-term relationships with customers, companies can construct loyalty programs that allow customers who check-in regularly at a location to earn discounts or perks. For example, American Eagle Outfitters remunerates such customers with a tiered 10%, 15%, or 20% discount on their total purchase.

- e-Commerce: Social media sites are increasingly implementing marketing-friendly strategies, creating platforms that are mutually beneficial for users, businesses, and the networks themselves in the popularity and accessibility of e-commerce, or online purchases. Mobile social media applications such as Amazon.com and Pinterest have started to influence an upward trend in the popularity and accessibility of e-commerce, or online purchases.

E-commerce businesses may refer to social media as consumer-generated media (CGM). A common thread running through all definitions of social media is a blending of technology and social interaction for the co-creation of value.

People obtain information, education, news, and other data from electronic and print media. Social media are distinct from industrial or traditional media such as newspapers, television, and film as they are comparatively inexpensive and accessible. They enable anyone (even private individuals) to publish or access information. Industrial media generally require significant resources to publish information as in most cases the articles go through many revisions before being published.

One characteristic shared by both social and industrial media is the capability to reach small or large audiences; for example, either a blog post or a television show may reach no people or millions of people. Some of the properties that help describe the differences between social and industrial media are:

1. Quality: In industrial (traditional) publishing—mediated by a publisher—the typical range of quality is substantially narrower than in niche, unmediated markets. The main challenge posed by content in social media sites is the fact that the distribution of quality has high variance: from very high-quality items to low-quality, sometimes abusive content.

2. Reach: Both industrial and social media technologies provide scale and are capable of reaching a global audience. Industrial media, however, typically use a centralized framework for organization, production, and dissemination, whereas social media are by their very nature more decentralized, less hierarchical, and distinguished by multiple points of production and utility.

3. Frequency: The number of times an advertisement is displayed on social media platforms.

4. Accessibility: The means of production for industrial media are typically government and/or corporate (privately owned); social media tools are generally available to the public at little or no cost.

5. Usability: Industrial media production typically requires specialized skills and training. Conversely, most social media production requires only modest reinterpretation of existing skills; in theory, anyone with access can operate the means of social media production.

6. Immediacy: The time lag between communications produced by industrial media can be long (days, weeks, or even months) compared to social media (which can be capable of virtually instantaneous responses).

7. Permanence: Industrial media, once created, cannot be altered (once a magazine article is printed and distributed, changes cannot be made to that same article) whereas social media can be altered almost instantaneously by comments or editing.

Community media constitute a hybrid of industrial and social media. Though community-owned, some community radio, TV, and newspapers are run by professionals and some by amateurs. They use both social and industrial media frameworks.

Social media have also been recognized for the way they have changed how public relations professionals conduct their jobs. They have provided an open arena where people are free to exchange ideas on companies, brands, and products. As stated by Doc Searls and David Wagner, two authorities on the effects of Internet on marketing, advertising, and PR, "The best of the people in PR are not PR types at all. They understand that there aren't censors, they're the company's best conversationalists." Social media provides an environment where users and PR professionals can converse, and where PR professionals can promote their brand and improve their company's image by listening and responding to what the public is saying about their product.

Business Performance

Social media has a strong influence on business activities and performance. There are four channels by which social media resources are transformed into business performance capabilities:

1. Social capital: represents the extent to which social media affects firms' relationships with society and increase corporate social performance capabilities.

2. Revealed preferences: represents the extent to which social media exposes customers' likings (e.g., likes and followers) and increase financial capabilities (e.g., stock price).

3. Social marketing: represents the extent to which social marketing resources (e.g., conversations, sharing, presence) are increase financial capabilities (e.g., sales).

4. Social corporate networking: Social corporate networking refers to the informal ties of corporate staff through social networks. Social corporate networking increases operational performance capabilities.

There are four tools that engage experts,customers,suppliers, and employees in the development of products using social media.

1. Customer Relationship Management

2. Innovation

3. Training

4. Knowledge Management

These are the organizational capabilities influenced by social media use.

Management

There is an increasing trend towards using social media monitoring tools that allow marketers to search, track, and analyze conversation on the web about their brand or about topics of interest. This can be useful in PR management and campaign tracking, allowing the user to measure return on investment, competitor-auditing, and general public engagement. Tools range from free, basic applications to subscription-based, more in-depth tools.

The honeycomb framework defines how social media services focus on some or all of seven functional building blocks. These building blocks help explain the engagement needs of the social media audience. For instance, LinkedIn users are thought to care mostly about identity, reputation, and relationships, whereas YouTube's primary features are sharing, conversations, groups, and reputation. Many companies build their own social containers that attempt to link the seven functional building blocks around their brands. These are private communities that engage people around a more narrow theme, as in around a particular brand, vocation or hobby, rather than social media containers such as Google+, Facebook, and Twitter. PR departments face significant challenges in dealing with viral negative sentiment directed at organizations or individuals on social media platforms (dubbed "sentimentitis"), which may be a reaction to an announcement or event.

Honeycomb Framework

In a 2011 article, Jan H. Kietzmann, Kristopher Hermkens, Ian P. McCarthy and Bruno S. Silvestre stated:

present a framework that defines social media by using seven functional building blocks*: identity, conversations, sharing, presence, relationships, reputation, and groups.*

- Identity: This block represents the extent to which users reveal their identities in a social media setting. This can include disclosing information such as name, age, gender, profession, location, and also information that portrays users in certain ways.

- Conversations: This block represents the extent to which users communicate with other users in a social media setting. Many social media sites are designed primarily to facilitate conversations among individuals and groups. These conversations happen for all sorts of reasons. People tweet, blog, et cetera to meet new like-minded people, to find true love, to build their self-esteem, or to be on the cutting edge of new ideas or trending topics. Yet others see social media as a way of making their message heard and positively impacting humanitarian causes, environmental problems, economic issues, or political debates.

- Sharing: This block represents the extent to which users exchange, distribute, and receive content. The term 'social' often implies that exchanges between people are crucial. In many cases, however, sociality is about the objects that mediate these ties between people—the reasons why they meet online and associate with each other.

- Presence: This block represents the extent to which users can know if other users are accessible. It includes knowing where others are, in the virtual world and/or in the real world, and whether they are available.

- Relationships: This block represents the extent to which users can be related to other users. Two or more users have some form of association that leads them to converse, share objects of sociality, meet up, or simply just list each other as a friend or fan.

- Reputation: This block represents the extent to which users can identify the standing of others, including themselves, in a social media setting. Reputation can have different meanings on social media platforms. In most cases, reputation is a matter of trust, but because information technologies are not yet good at determining such highly qualitative criteria, social media sites rely on 'mechanical Turks': tools that automatically aggregate user-generated information to determine trustworthiness. Reputation management is another aspect and use of social media.

- Groups: This block represents the extent to which users can form communities and sub communities. The more 'social' a network becomes, the bigger the group of friends, followers, and contacts.

Building "Social Authority" and Vanity

Social media become's effective through a process called "building social authority". One of the foundation concepts in social media has become that you cannot completely control your message through social media but rather you can simply begin to participate in the "conversation" expecting that you can achieve a significant influence in that conversation.

However, this conversation participation must be cleverly executed because although people are resistant to marketing in general, they are even more resistant to direct or overt marketing through social media platforms. This may seem counterintuitive but it is the main reason building social authority with credibility is so important. A marketer can generally not expect people to be receptive to a marketing message in and of itself. In the Edelman Trust Barometer report in 2008, the majority (58%) of the respondents reported they most trusted company or product information coming from "people like me" inferred to be information from someone they trusted. In the 2010 Trust Report, the majority switched to 64% preferring their information from industry experts and academics. According to Inc. Technology's Brent Leary, "This loss of trust, and the accompanying turn towards experts and authorities, seems to be coinciding with the rise of social media and networks."

Social Media Mining

Social media mining is a process of representing, analyzing, and extracting actionable patterns from social media data. Social media mining introduces basic concepts and principal algorithms suitable for investigating massive social media data; it discusses theories and methodologies from different disciplines such as computer science, data mining, machine learning, social network analysis, network science, sociology, ethnography, statistics, optimization, and mathematics. It encompasses the tools to formally represent, measure, model, and mine meaningful patterns from large-scale social media data.

Global Usage

According to the article "The Emerging Role of Social Media in Political and Regime Change" by Rita Safranek, the Middle East and North Africa region has one of the most youthful populations in the world, with people under 25 making up between 35-45% of the population in each country. They make up the majority of social media users, including about 17 million Facebook users, 25,000 Twitter accounts and 40,000 active blogs, according to the Arab Advisors Group.

Most Popular Sites

This is a list of the leading social networks based on number of active user accounts as of April 2016.

1. Facebook: 1,650,000,000 users.

2. WhatsApp 1,000,000,000 users.

3. Facebook Messenger: 900,000,000 users.

4. QQ: 853,000,000 users.

5. WeChat: 706,000,000 users.

6. QZone: 653,000,000 users.

7. Tumblr: 555,000,000 users.

8. Instagram: 400,000,000 users.

9. Twitter: 320,000,000 users.

10. Baidu Tieba: 300,000,000 users.

11. Skype: 300,000,000 users.

12. Viber: 280,000,000 users.

13. Sina Weibo: 222,000,000 users.

14. Line: 215,000,000 users.

15. Snapchat: 200,000,000 users.

Effects of Usage for News Purposes

Just as television turned a nation of people who *listened* to media content into *watchers* of media content, the emergence of social media has created a nation of media content creators. According to 2011 Pew Research data, nearly 80% of American adults are online and nearly 60% of them use social networking sites. More Americans get their news via the Internet than from newspapers or radio, as well as three-fourths who say they get news from e-mail or social media sites updates, according to a report published by CNN. The survey suggests that Facebook and Twitter make news a more participatory experience than before as people share news articles and comment on other people's posts. According to CNN, in 2010 75% of people got their news forwarded through e-mail or social media posts, whereas 37% of people shared a news item via Facebook or Twitter.

In the United States, 81% of people say they look online for news of the weather, first and foremost. National news at 73%, 52% for sports news, and 41% for entertainment or celebrity news. Based on this study, done for the Pew Center, two-thirds of the sample's online news users were younger than 50, and 30% were younger than 30. The survey involved tracking daily the habits of 2,259 adults 18 or older. Thirty-three percent of young adults get news from social networks. Thirty-four percent watched TV news and 13% read print or digital content. Nineteen percent of Americans got news from Facebook, Google+, or LinkedIn. Thirty-six percent of those who get news from social network got it yesterday from survey. More than 36% of Twitter users use accounts to follow news organizations or journalists. Nineteen percent of users say they got information from news organizations of journalists. TV remains most popular source of news, but audience is aging (only 34% of young people).

Of those younger than 25, 29% said they got no news yesterday either digitally or traditional news platforms. Only 5% under 30 said they follow news about political figures and events in DC. Only 14% of respondents could answer all four questions about which party controls the House, current unemployment rate, what nation Angela Merkel leads, and which presidential candidate favors taxing higher-income Americans. Facebook and Twitter now pathways to news, but are not replacements for traditional ones. Seventy percent get social media news from friends and family on Facebook.

Social media fosters communication. An Internet research company, PewResearch Center, claims that "more than half of internet users (52%) use two or more of the social media sites measured (Facebook, Twitter, Instagram, Pinterest) to communicate with their family or friends.

For children, using social media sites can help promote creativity, interaction, and learning. It can also help them with homework and class work. Moreover, social media enable them to stay connected with their peers, and help them to interact with each other. Some can get involved with developing fundraising campaigns and political events. However, it can impact social skills due to the absence of face-to-face contact. Social media can affect mental health of teens. Teens who use Facebook frequently and especially who are susceptible may become more narcissistic, antisocial, and aggressive. Teens become strongly influenced by advertising, and it influences buying habits. Since the creation of Facebook in 2004, it has become a distraction and a way to waste time for many users. A head teacher in the United Kingdom commented in 2015 that social media caused more stress to teenage children than examinations, with constant interaction and monitoring by peers ending the past practice where what pupils did in the evening or at weekends was separate from the arguments and peer pressure at school.

In a recent study conducted, high school students ages 18 and younger were examined in an effort to find their preference for receiving news. Based on interviews with 61 teenagers, conducted from December 2007 to February 2011, most of the teen participants reported reading print newspapers only "sometimes," with fewer than 10% reading them daily. The teenagers instead reported learning about current events from social media sites such as Facebook, MySpace, YouTube, and blogs. Another study showed that social media users read a set of news that is different from what newspaper editors feature in the print press.

Using nanotechnology as an example, a study was conducted that studied tweets from Twitter and found that some 41% of the discourse about nanotechnology focused on its negative impacts, suggesting that a portion of the public may be concerned with how various forms of nanotechnology are used in the future. Although optimistic-sounding and neutral-sounding tweets were equally likely to express certainty or uncertainty, the pessimistic tweets were nearly twice as likely to appear certain of an outcome than uncertain. These results imply the possibility of a preconceived negative perception of many news articles associated with nanotechnology. Alternatively, these results could also imply that posts of a more pessimistic nature that are also written with an air of certainty are more likely to be shared or otherwise permeate groups on Twitter. Similar biases need to be considered when the utility of new media is addressed, as the potential for human opinion to over-emphasize any particular news story is greater despite the general improvement in addressed potential uncertainty and bias in news articles than in traditional media.

On October 2, 2013, the most common hashtag throughout the United States was "#governmentshutdown," as well as ones focusing on political parties, Obama, and healthcare. Most news sources have Twitter, and Facebook, pages, like CNN and the New York Times, providing links to their online articles, getting an increased readership. Additionally, several college news organizations and administrators have Twitter pages as a way to share news and connect to students.

According to "Reuters Institute Digital News Report 2013", in the US, among those who use social media to find news, 47% of these people are under 45 years old, and 23% are above 45 years old. However social media as a main news gateway does not follow the same pattern across countries. For example, in this report, in Brazil, 60% of the respondents said social media was one of the five most important ways to find news online, 45% in Spain, 17% in the UK, 38% in Italy, 14% in France, 22% in Denmark, 30% in the U.S., and 12% in Japan. Moreover, there are differences among countries about commenting on news in social networks, 38% of the respondents in Brazil said they commented on news in social network in a week. These percentages are 21% in the U.S. and 10% in the UK. The authors argued that differences among countries may be due to culture difference rather than different levels of access to technical tools.

History and Memory Effects

News media and television journalism have been instrumental in the shaping of American collective memory for much of the twentieth century. Indeed, since the United States' colonial era, news media has influenced collective memory and discourse about national development and trauma. In many ways, mainstream journalists have maintained an authoritative voice as the storytellers of the American past. Their documentary style narratives, detailed exposes, and their positions in the present make them prime sources for public memory. Specifically, news media journalists have shaped collective memory on nearly every major national event – from the deaths of social and political figures to the progression of political hopefuls. Journalists provide elaborate descriptions of commemorative events in U.S. history and contemporary popular cultural sensations. Many Americans learn the significance of historical events and political issues through news media, as they are presented on popular news stations. However, journalistic influence is growing less important, whereas social networking sites such as Facebook, YouTube and Twitter, provide a constant supply of alternative news sources for users.

As social networking becomes more popular among older and younger generations, sites such as Facebook and YouTube, gradually undermine the traditionally authoritative voices of news media. For example, American citizens contest media coverage of various social and political events as they see fit, inserting their voices into the narratives about America's past and present and shaping their own collective memories. An example of this is the public explosion of the Trayvon Martin shooting in Sanford, Florida. News media coverage of the incident was minimal until social media users made the story recognizable through their constant discussion of the case. Approximately one month after the fatal shooting of Trayvon Martin, its online coverage by everyday Americans garnered national attention from mainstream media journalists, in turn exemplifying media activism. In some ways, the spread of this tragic event through alternative news sources parallels that of the Emmitt Till – whose murder became a national story after it circulated African American and Communists newspapers. Social media was also influential in the widespread attention given to the revolutionary outbreaks in the Middle East and North Africa during 2011. However, there is some debate about the extent to which social media facilitated this kind of change. Another example of this shift is in the ongoing Kony 2012 campaign, which surfaced first on YouTube and later garnered a great amount of attention from mainstream news media journalists. These journalists now monitor social media sites to inform their reports on the movement. Lastly, in the past couple of presidential elections, the use of social media sites such as Facebook and Twitter were used to predict election results. U.S. President Barack Obama was more liked on Facebook than his opponent Mitt Romney and it was found by a study done by Oxford Institute Internet Experiment that more people liked to tweet about comments of President Obama rather than Romney.

Criticisms

We worry that social media is kind of the virtual bathhouse— *Dr. Lynn Fitzgibbons, an infectious disease physician Santa Barbara County Public Health Department*

Criticisms of social media range from criticisms of the ease of use of specific platforms and their capabilities, disparity of information available, issues with trustworthiness and reliability of information presented, the impact of social media use on an individual's concentration, ownership of media content, and the meaning of interactions created by social media. Although some social media platforms offer users the opportunity to cross-post simultaneously, some social network platforms have been criticized for poor interoperability between platforms, which leads to the creation of information silos- isolated pockets of data contained in one social media platform. However, it is also argued that social media have positive effects such as allowing the democratization of the internet while also allowing individuals to advertise themselves and form friendships. Others have noted that the term "social" cannot account for technological features of a platform alone, hence the level of sociability should determined by the actual performances of its users.

There has been a dramatic decrease in face-to-face interactions as more and more social media platforms have been introduced with the threat of cyber-bullying and online sexual predators being more prevalent. Social media may expose children to images of alcohol, tobacco, and sexual behaviors. In regards to cyber-bullying, it has been proven that individuals who have no experience with cyber-bullying often have a better well-being than individuals who have been bullied online.

Twitter is increasingly a target of heavy activity of marketers. Their actions, focused on gaining massive numbers of followers, include use of advanced scripts and manipulation techniques that distort the prime idea of social media by abusing human trustfulness. Twitter also promotes social connections among students. It can be used to enhance communication building and critical thinking. Domizi (2013) utilised Twitter in a graduate seminar requiring students to post weekly tweets to extend classroom discussions. Students reportedly used Twitter to connect with content and other students. Additionally, students found it "to be useful professionally and personally."

British-American entrepreneur and author Andrew Keen criticizes social media in his book *The Cult of the Amateur*, writing, "Out of this anarchy, it suddenly became clear that what was governing the infinite monkeys now inputting away on the Internet was the law of digital Darwinism, the survival of the loudest and most opinionated. Under these rules, the only way to intellectually prevail is by infinite filibustering." This is also relative to the issue "justice" in the social network. For example, the phenomenon "Human flesh search engine" in Asia raised the discussion of "private-law" brought by social network platform.

Comparative media professor José van Dijck contends in her book "The Culture of Connectivity" (2013) that to understand the full weight of social media, their technological dimensions should be connected to the social and the cultural. She critically describes six social media platforms. One of her findings is the way Facebook had been successful in framing the term 'sharing' in such a way that third party use of user data is neglected in favour of intra-user connectedness.

Disparity

The digital divide is a measure of disparity in the level of access to technology between households, socioeconomic levels or other demographic categories. Other models argue that within a modern information society, some individuals produce Internet content while others only consume it, which could be a result of disparities in the education system where only some teachers integrate technology into the classroom and teach critical thinking. While social media has differences among age groups, a 2010 study in the United States found no racial divide.

Some zero-rating programs offer subsidized data access to certain websites on low-cost plans. Critics say that this is an anti-competitive program that undermines net neutrality and creates a "walled garden" for platforms like Facebook Zero. A 2015 study found that 65% of Nigerians, 61% of Indonesians, and 58% of Indians agree with the statement that "Facebook is the Internet" compared with only 5% in the US.

Eric Ehrmann contends that social media in the form of public diplomacy create a patina of inclusiveness that covers traditional economic interests that are structured to ensure that wealth is pumped up to the top of the economic pyramid, perpetuating the digital divide and post Marxian class conflict. He also voices concern over the trend that finds social utilities operating in a quasi-libertarian global environment of oligopoly that requires users in economically challenged nations to spend high percentages of annual income to pay for devices and services to participate in the social media lifestyle.

Neil Postman also contends that social media will increase an information disparity between winners – who are able to use the social media actively – and losers – who are not familiar with modern technologies.

Trustworthiness

Because large-scale collaborative co-creation is one of the main ways of forming information in the social network, the user generated content is sometimes viewed with skepticism; readers do not trust it as a reliable source of information. Aniket Kittur, Bongowon Suh, and Ed H. Chi took wikis under examination and indicated that, "One possibility is that distrust of wiki content is not due to the inherently mutable nature of the system but instead to the lack of available information for judging trustworthiness." To be more specific, the authors mention that reasons for distrusting collaborative systems with user-generated content, such as Wikipedia, include a lack of information regarding accuracy of contents, motives and expertise of editors, stability of content, coverage of topics and the absence of sources.

Social media is also an important source of news. According to 'Reuters Institute Digital News Report 2013', social media are one of the most important ways for people find news online (the others being traditional brands, search engines and news aggregators). The report suggested that in the United Kingdom, trust in news which comes from social media sources is low, compared to news from other sources (e.g. online news from traditional broadcaster or online news from national newspapers). People who aged at 24-35 trust social media most, whereas trust declined with the increase of age.

Rainie and Wellman have argued that media making now has become a participation work, which changes communication systems. The center of power is shifted from only the media (as the gatekeeper) to the peripheral area, which may include government, organizations, and out to the edge, the individual. These changes in communication systems raise empirical questions about trust to media effect. Prior empirical studies have shown that trust in information sources plays a major role in people's decision making. People's attitudes more easily change when they hear messages from trustworthy sources. In the Reuters report, 27% of respondents agree that they worry about the accuracy of a story on a blog. However, 40% of them believe the stories on blogs are more balanced than traditional papers because they are provided with a range of opinions. Recent research has shown that in the new social media communication environment, the civil or uncivil nature of comments will bias people's information processing even if the message is from a trustworthy source, which bring the practical and ethical question about the responsibility of communicator in the social media environment.

Concentration

As media theorist Marshall McLuhan pointed out in the 1960s, media are not just passive channels of information. They supply the stuff of thought, but they also shape the process of thought. And what the Net seems to be doing is chipping away my capacity for concentration and contemplation

Passive Participation

For Malcolm Gladwell, the role of social media, such as Twitter and Facebook, in revolutions and protests is overstated. On one hand, social media make it easier for individuals, and in this case activists, to express themselves. On the other hand, it is harder for that expression to have an impact.

Gladwell distinguishes between social media activism and high risk activism, which brings real changes. Activism and especially high-risk activism involves strong-tie relationships, hierarchies, coordination, motivation, exposing oneself to high risks, making sacrifices.

Gladwell discusses that social media are built around weak ties and he argues that "social networks are effective at increasing participation — by lessening the level of motivation that participation requires". According to him "Facebook activism succeeds not by motivating people to make a real sacrifice, but by motivating them to do the things that people do when they are not motivated enough to make a real sacrifice".

Furthermore, social media's role in democratizing media participation may fall short of ideals. Social media has been championed as allowing anyone with an Internet connection to become a content creator and empowering the "active audience". But international survey data suggest online media audience members are largely passive consumers, while content creation is dominated by the few. Others argue that the effect of social media will vary from one country to another, with domestic political structures playing a greater role than social media in determining how citizens express opinions about "current affairs stories involving the state".

According to the "Reuters Institute Digital News Report 2013", the percent of online news users who blog about news issues ranges from 1–5%. Greater percentages use social media to comment on news, with participation ranging from 8% in Germany to 38% in Brazil. But online news users are most likely to just talk about online news with friends offline or use social media to share stories without creating content.

Reliability

Evgeny Morozov, 2009–2010 Yahoo fellow at Georgetown University, contends that the information uploaded to Twitter may have little relevance to the rest of the people who do not use Twitter. In the article "Iran: Downside to the "Twitter Revolution"" in the magazine *Dissent* , he says:

"Twitter only adds to the noise: it's simply impossible to pack much context into its 140 characters. All other biases are present as well: in a country like Iran it's mostly pro-Western, technology-friendly and iPod-carrying young people who are the natural and most frequent users of Twitter. They are a tiny and, most important, extremely untypical segment of the Iranian population (the number of Twitter users in Iran — a country of more than seventy million people.)"

Even in the United States, the birth-country of Twitter, currently in 2015 the social network has 306 million accounts. Because there are likely to be many multi-account users, and the United States in 2012 had a population of 314.7 million, the adoption of Twitter is somewhat limited.

Professor Matthew Auer of Bates College casts doubt on the conventional wisdom that social media are open and participatory. He also speculates on the emergence of "anti-social media" used as "instruments of pure control."

Ownership of Social Media Content

Social media content is generated through social media interactions done by the users through the site. There has always been a huge debate on the ownership of the content on social media platforms because it is generated by the users and hosted by the company. Added to this is the danger to security of information, which can be leaked to third parties with economic interests in the platform, or parasites who comb the data for their own databases. The author of *Social Media Is Bullshit*, Brandon Mendelson, claims that the "true" owners of content created on social media sites only benefits the large corporations who own those sites and rarely the users that created them.

Privacy

Privacy rights advocates warn users about uses for the information that can be gathered through social media. Some information is captured without the user's knowledge or consent, such as through electronic tracking and third party application on social networks. Others include law enforcement and governmental use of this information, including the gathering of so-called social media intelligence through data mining techniques.

Additional privacy concerns relate to the impact of social media monitoring by employers whose policies include prohibitions against workers' postings on social networking sites. A survey done in 2010 from different universities revealed that there are lines drawn between personal and professional lives. Many of the users surveyed admitted to misrepresenting themselves online. Employees can be concerned because their social media sites reflect their personal lives and not their professional lives, but yet employers are censoring them on the internet.

Other privacy concerns with employers and social media are when employers use social media as a tool to screen a prospective employee. This issue raises many ethical questions that some consider an employer's right and others consider discrimination. Except in the states of California, Maryland, and Illinois, there are no laws that prohibit employers from using social media profiles as a basis of whether or not someone should be hired. Title VII also prohibits discrimination during any aspect of employment including hiring or firing, recruitment, or testing.

Social media has been integrating itself into the workplace and this has led to conflicts within employees and employers. Particularly, Facebook has been seen as a popular platform for employers to investigate in order to learn more about potential employees. This conflict first started in Maryland when an employer requested and received an employee's Facebook username and password. State lawmakers first introduced legislation in 2012 to prohibit employers from requesting passwords to personal social accounts in order to get a job or to keep a job. This led to Canada, Germany, the U.S. Congress and 11 U.S. states to pass or propose legislation that prevents employers' access to private social accounts of employees.

Many Western European countries have already implemented laws that restrict the regulation of social media in the workplace. States including Arkansas, California, Colorado, Illinois, Maryland, Michigan, Nevada, New Jersey, New Mexico, Utah, Washington, and Wisconsin have passed legislation that protects potential employees and current employees from employers that demand them to give forth their username or password for a social media account. Laws that forbid employers from disciplining an employee based on activity off the job on social media sites have also been put into act in states including California, Colorado, Connecticut, North Dakota, and New York. Several states have similar laws that protect students in colleges and universities from having to grant access to their social media accounts. Eight states have passed the law that prohibits post secondary institutions from demanding social media login information from any prospective or current students and privacy legislation has been introduced or is pending in at least 36 states as of July 2013.

As of May 2014, legislation has been introduced and is in the process of pending in at least 28 states and has been enacted in Maine and Wisconsin. In addition, the National Labor Relations Board has been devoting a lot of their attention to attacking employer policies regarding social media that can discipline employees who seek to speak and post freely on social media sites.

Effects on Interpersonal Relationships

Data suggest that participants use social media to fulfill perceived social needs, but are typically disappointed. Lonely individuals are drawn to the Internet for emotional support. This could interfere with "real life socializing" by reducing face-to-face relationships. Some of these views are summed up in an Atlantic article by Stephen Marche entitled *Is Facebook Making Us Lonely?*, in which the author argues that social media provides more breadth, but not the depth of relationships that humans require.

Sherry Turkle explores similar issues in her book *Alone Together* as she discusses how people confuse social media usage with authentic communication. She posits that people tend to act differently online and are less afraid to hurt each other's feelings. Some online behaviors can cause stress and anxiety, due to the permanence of online posts, the fear of being hacked, or of colleges and employers exploring social media pages. Turkle also speculates that people are beginning to prefer texting to face-to-face communication, which can contribute to feelings of loneliness.

Some researchers have also found that only exchanges that involved direct communication and reciprocation of messages to each other increased feelings of connectedness. However, passively using social media without sending or receiving messages to individuals does not make people feel less lonely unless they were lonely to begin with.

A study published in the Public Library of Science in 2013 revealed that the perception of Facebook being an important resource for social connection was diminished by the number of people found to have developed low self-esteem, and the more they used the network the lower their level of self-esteem.

A current controversial topic is whether or not social media addiction should be explicitly categorized as a psychological ailment. Extended use of social media has led to increased Internet addiction, cyberbullying, sexting, sleep deprivation, and the decline of face-to-face interaction. Several clinics in the UK classify social media addiction is a certifiable medical condition with one psychiatric consultant claiming that he treats as many as one hundred cases a year.

Lori Ann Wagner, a psychotherapist, argues that humans communicate best face to face with their five senses involved. In addition, a study on social media done by PhD's Hsuan-Ting Kim and Yonghwan Kim, suggests that social networking sites have begun to raise concern because of the expectations people seek to fulfill from these sites and the amount of time users are willing to invest.

Commercialization

As social media usage has become increasingly widespread, social media has to a large extent come to be subjected to commercialization. Christofer Laurell, a digital marketing researcher, suggested that the social media landscape currently consists of three types of places becacuse of this development: consumer-dominated places, professionally dominated places and places undergoing commercialization. As social media becomes commercialized, this process have been shown to create novel forms of value networks stretching between consumer and producer in which a combination of personal, private and commercial contents are created.

The commercial development of social media has been criticized as the actions of consumers in these settings has become increasingly value-creating, for example when consumers on a voluntary basis contributes to the marketing and branding of specific products by posting positive reviews. As such value-creating activities also increase the value of a specific product, this could according to the marketing professors Bernad Cova and Daniele Dalli lead to what they refer to as double exploitation.

Negative Effects

There are several negative effects to social media which receive criticism, for example regarding privacy issues, information overload and Internet fraud. Social media can also have negative social effects on users. Angry or emotional conversations can lead to real-world interactions outside of the internet, which can get users into dangerous situations. Some users have experienced threats of violence online and have feared these threats manifesting themselves offline.

Studies also show that social media have negative effects on peoples' self-esteem and self-worth. The authors of "Who Compares and Despairs? The Effect of Social Comparison Orientation on

Social Media Use and its Outcomes" found that people with a higher social comparison orientation appear to use social media more heavily than people with low social comparison orientation. This finding was consistent with other studies that found people with high social comparison orientation make more social comparisons once on social media. People compare their own lives to the lives of their friends through their friends' posts. People are motivated to portray themselves in a way that is appropriate to the situation and serves their best interest. Often the things posted online are the positive aspects of people's lives, which makes other people question why their own lives are not as exciting or fulfilling. This can lead to depression and other self-esteem issues. Terri H. Chan, the author of "Facebook and its Effects on Users' Empathic Social Skills and Life Satisfaction: A Double Edged Sword Effect", claims that the more time people spend on Facebook, the less satisfied they feel about their life. Self-presentational theory explains that people will consciously manage their self-image or identity related information in social contexts. According to Gina Chen, the author of *Losing Face on Social Media: Threats to Positive Face Lead to an Indirect Effect on Retaliatory Aggression Through Negative Affect*, when people are not accepted or are criticized online they feel emotional pain. This may lead to some form of online retaliation such as online bullying.

In addition, Trudy Hui Hui Chua and Leanne Chang expose in their research article, "Follow Me and Like My Beautiful Selfies: Singapore Teenage Girls' Engagement in Self-Presentation and Peer Comparison on Social Media," that teenage girls manipulate their self-presentation to achieve a sense of beauty that is projected by their peers. These authors also discovered that teenage girls compare themselves to their peers and present themselves in certain ways in effort to earn regard and acceptance, which can actually lead to problems with self-confidence and self-satisfaction. Hui Hui Chua and Chang went on to add that the striving to reveal a superior self-appearance on the Internet by teenage girls is caused by their deep-seated aspiration to understand who they are as a person.

According to writer Christine Rosen in "Virtual Friendship, and the New Narcissism," many social media sites encourage status-seeking. According to Rosen, the practice and definition of "friendship" changes in virtuality. Friendship "in these virtual spaces is thoroughly different from real-world friendship. In its traditional sense, friendship is a relationship which, broadly speaking, involves the sharing of mutual interests, reciprocity, trust, and the revelation of intimate details over time and within specific social (and cultural) contexts. Because friendship depends on mutual revelations that are concealed from the rest of the world, it can only flourish within the boundaries of privacy; the idea of public friendship is an oxymoron." Rosen also cites Brigham Young University researchers who "recently surveyed 184 users of social networking sites and found that heavy users 'feel less socially involved with the community around them.'"

In addition, critic Nicholas G. Carr in "Is Google Making Us Stupid?" questions how technology affects cognition and memory. "The kind of deep reading that a sequence of printed pages promotes is valuable not just for the knowledge we acquire from the author's words but for the intellectual vibrations those words set off within our own minds. In the quiet spaces opened up by the sustained, undistracted reading of a book, or by any other act of contemplation, for that matter, we make our own associations, draw our own inferences and analogies, foster our own ideas... If we lose those quiet spaces, or fill them up with "content," we will sacrifice something important not only in our selves but in our culture."

Positive Effects

In the book *Networked – The New Social Operating System* by Lee Rainie and Barry Wellman, the two authors reflect on mainly positive effects of social media and other internet based social networks. According to the authors, social media are used to document memories, learn about and explore things, advertise oneself and form friendships. For instance, they claim that the communication through internet based services can be done more privately than in real life. Furthermore, Rainie and Wellman discuss that everybody has the possibility to become a content creator. Content creation provides networked individuals opportunities to reach wider audiences. Moreover, it can positively affect their social standing and gain political support. This can lead to influence on issues that are important for someone. As a concrete example of the positive effects of social media, the authors use the Tunisian revolution in 2011, where people used Facebook to gather meetings, protest actions, etc.

Rainie and Wellman (Ibid) also discuss that content creation is a voluntary and participatory act. What is important is that networked individuals create, edit, and manage content in collaboration with other networked individuals. This way they contribute in expanding knowledge. Wikis are examples of collaborative content creation.

A survey conducted (in 2011), by Pew Internet Research, discussed in Lee Rainie and Barry Wellman's *Networked – The New Social Operating System*, illustrates that 'networked individuals' are engaged to a further extent regarding numbers of content creation activities and that the 'networked individuals' are increasing over a larger age span. These are some of the content creation activities that networked individuals take part in:

- writing material on a social networking site such as Facebook: 65 percent of internet users do this

- sharing photos: 55 percent

- contributing rankings and reviews of products or services: 37 percent

- creating tags of content: 33 percent

- posting comments on third-party websites or blogs: 26 percent

- taking online material and remixing it into a new creation: 15 percent of internet users do this with photos, video, audio, or text

- creating or working on a blog: 14 percent

Another survey conducted (in 2015) by Pew Internet Research shows that the internet users among American adults who uses at least one social networking site has increased from 10% to 76% since 2005. Pew Internet Research illustrates furthermore that it nowadays is no real gender difference among Americans when it comes to social media usage. Women were even more active on social media a couple of years ago, however today's numbers point at women: 68%, and men: 62%.

Social media have been used to assist in searches for missing persons. When 21-year-old University of Cincinnati student Brogan Dulle disappeared in May 2014 from near his apartment in the Clifton neighborhood of Cincinnati, Ohio, his friends and family used social media to organize and fund a search effort. The disappearance made international news when their efforts went viral on Facebook, Twitter, GoFundMe, and *The Huffington Post* during the week-long search. Dulle's body was eventually found in a building next door to his apartment.

Impact on Job Seeking

Use of social media by young people has caused significant problems for some people when they try to enter the job market. A survey of 17,000 young people in six countries in 2013 found that 1 in 10 people aged 16 to 34 have been rejected for a job because of online comments they made on social media websites. A 2014 survey of recruiters found that 93% of them check candidates' social media postings. Moreover, professor Stijn Baert of Ghent University conducted a field experiment in which fictitious job candidates applied for real job vacancies in Belgium. They were identical except in one respect: their Facebook profile photos. It was found that candidates with the most wholesome photos were a lot more likely to receive invitations for job interviews than those with the more controversial photos. In addition, Facebook profile photos had a greater impact on hiring decisions when candidates were highly educated.

These cases have created some privacy implications as to whether or not companies should have the right to look at employee's Facebook profiles. In March 2012, Facebook decided they might take legal action against employers for gaining access to employee's profiles through their passwords. According to Facebook Chief Privacy Officer for policy, Erin Egan, the company has worked hard to give its users the tools to control who sees their information. He also said users shouldn't be forced to share private information and communications just to get a job. According to the network's Statement of Rights and Responsibilities, sharing or soliciting a password is a violation of Facebook policy. Employees may still give their password information out to get a job, but according to Erin Egan, Facebook will continue to do their part to protect the privacy and security of their users.

College Admission

Before social media, admissions officials in the United States used SAT scores, extra-curricular activities, letters of recommendation, and high school to determine whether to accept or deny an applicant. According to Kaplan, Inc, a corporation that provides higher education preparation, in 2012 27% of admissions officers used Google to learn more about an applicant, with 26% checking Facebook.

Political Effects

The popularity of getting political news from social media platforms is greatly increasing. A 2014 study showed that 62% of web users turn to Facebook to find political news. This social phenomenon allows for political information, true or not, to spread quickly and easily among peer networks. Furthermore, social media sites are now encouraging political involvement by uniting like-minded people, reminding users to vote in elections, and analyzing users' political affiliation data to find cultural similarities and differences.

Social media can help taint the reputation of political figures fairly quickly with information that may or may not be true. Information spreads like wildfire and before a politician can even get an opportunity to address the information, either to confirm, deny, or explain, the public has already formed an opinion about the politician based on that information. However, when conducted on purpose, the spread of information on social media for political means can help campaigns immensely. The Barack Obama presidential campaign, 2008, is considered to be one of the most successful in terms of social media. On the other hand, negative word-of-mouth in social media concerning a political figure can be very unfortunate for a politician and can cost the politician his/her career if the information is very damaging. For example, Anthony Weiner's misuse of the social media platform, Twitter, eventually led to his resignation from U.S. Congress.

Open forums online have also been the root of negative effects in the political sphere. Some politicians have made the mistake of using open forums to try and reach a broader audience and thus more potential voters. What they forgot to account for was that the forums would be open to everyone, including those in opposition. Having no control over the comments being posted, negative included, has been damaging for some with unfortunate oversight. Additionally, a constraint of social media as a tool for public political discourse is that if oppressive governments recognize the ability social media has to cause change, they shut it down. During the peak of the Egyptian Revolution of 2011, the internet and social media played a huge role in facilitating information. At that time, Hosni Mubarak was the president of Egypt and head the regime for almost 30 years. Mubarak was so threatened by the immense power that the internet and social media gave the people that the government successfully shut down the internet, using the Ramses Exchange, for a period of time in February 2011.

Social media as an open forum gives a voice to those who have previously not had the ability to be heard. In 2015, some countries are still becoming equipped with internet accessibility and other technologies. Social media is giving everyone a voice to speak out against government regimes. In 2014, the rural areas in Paraguay were only just receiving access to social media, such as Facebook. In congruence with the users worldwide, teens and young adults in Paraguay are drawn to Facebook and others types of social media as a means to self-express. Social media is becoming a main conduit for social mobilization and government critiques because, "the government can't control what we say on the Internet."

Younger generations are becoming more involved in politics due to the increase of political news posted on various types of social media. Due to the heavier use of social media among younger generations, they are exposed to politics more frequently, and in a way that is integrated into their online social lives. While informing younger generations of political news is important, there are many biases within the realms of social media. It can be difficult for outsiders to truly understand the conditions of dissent when they are removed from direct involvement. Social media can create a false sense of understanding among people who are not directly involved in the issue. An example of social media creating misconceptions can be seen during the Arab Spring protests. Today's generation rely heavily on social media to understand what is happening in the world, an consequently people are exposed to both true and false information. For example, Americans have several misconceptions surrounding the events of the Arab Springs movement.

Social media can be used to create political change, both major and minor. For example, in 2011

Egyptians used Facebook, Twitter, and YouTube as a means to communicate and organize demonstrations and rallies to overthrow President Hosni Mubarak. Statistics show that during this time the rate of Tweets from Egypt increased from 2,300 to 230,000 per day and the top 23 protest videos had approximately 5.5 million views. This not only allowed for organization among protesters, but also allowed the uprising to gain the attention of people around the world.

The systematic literature review by Buettner & Buettner from 2016 analyzed the role of Twitter during a wide range of social movements (2007 WikiLeaks, 2009 Moldova, 2009 Austria student protest, 2009 Israel-Gaza, 2009 Iran green revolution, 2009 Toronto G20, 2010 Venezuela, 2010 Germany Stuttgart21, 2011 Egypt, 2011 England, 2011 US Occupy movement, 2011 Spain Indignados, 2011 Greece Aganaktismenoi movements, 2011 Italy, 2011 Wisconsin labor protests, 2012 Israel Hamas, 2013 Brazil Vinegar, 2013 Turkey).

Positive and Negative Effects of Twitter

People around the world are taking advantage of social media as one of their key components of communication. According to King, 67 percent of US citizens ages 12 and up use social media of some type. With the expansion of social media networks there are many positive and negative alternatives. As the use of Twitter increases, its influence impacts users as well. The potential role of Twitter as a means of both service feedback and a space in which mental health can be openly discussed and considered from a variety of perspectives. The study conducted shows a positive outlook for using Twitter to discuss health issues with a patient and a professional, in this case alcohol. On the other hand, there can be negatives that arise from the use of social media. If a clinician prescribes abstinence from alcohol but then posts pictures on social media of one's own drunken exploits, the clinician's credibility is potentially lost in the eyes of the patient. In these two studies, both negative and positive outcomes were examined. Although social media can be beneficial, it is important to understand the negative consequences as well.

Use By Extremist Groups

The world is becoming increasingly connected via the power of the Internet; Facebook launched internet.org, an initiative to gain even the most remote parts of society access to the World Wide Web. Political movements have begun to see social media as a major organizing and recruiting tool and the reverse can be said for society. In 2014, 62% of all web users turned to sites such as Facebook to gain access to political news. Islamic State of Iraq and the Levant, also known as ISIS, has used social media to promote their cause, going as far as the production of their own online magazine named the Islamic State Report in an attempt to recruit more fighters. Other extremist groups such as al-Qaeda and the Taliban are increasingly using social media to raise funds, recruit and radicalize persons, and it has become increasingly effective. In Canada, two girls from the city of Montreal have left their country in an effort to join ISIS in Syria after exploring ISIS on social media and eventually being recruited. On Twitter, there is an app called the Dawn of Glad Tidings that users can download and keep up to date on news about ISIS. Hundreds of users around the world have signed up for the app which once downloaded will post tweets and hash-tags to your account that are in support of ISIS. As ISIS marched on the northern region of Iraq, tweets in support of their efforts reached a high of 40,000 a day. ISIS support on-line is a defiant factor in the radicalization of youth. Mass media has yet to adopt the view that social media plays a vital link in the radicalization of persons in an effort to discredit social media as a legitimate news source. When tweets supportive of ISIS make their way onto Twitter, they result in 72 re-tweets to the original, which further spreads the destructive message of ISIS. These tweets have made their way to the account known as active hashtags, which further helps broadcast ISIS' message as the account sends out to its followers the most popular hashtags of the day. Social media is a key factor in the modern recruiting practices of groups like ISIS.

Patents

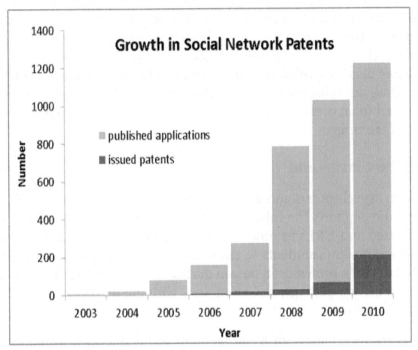

Number of US social network patent applications published and patents issued per year since 2003.

There has been rapid growth in the number of US patent applications that cover new technologies related to social media, and the number of them that are published has been growing rapidly over the past five years. There are now over 2000 published patent applications. As many as 7000 applications may be currently on file including those that haven't been published yet. Only slightly over 100 of these applications have issued as patents, however, largely due to the multi-year backlog in examination of business method patents, patents which outline and claim new methods of doing business.

In the Classroom

Having social media in the classroom has been a controversial topic for the last several years. Many parents and educators have been fearful of the repercussions of having social media in the classroom. As result, cell phones have been banned from some classrooms, and some schools have blocked many popular social media websites.

However, despite apprehensions, students are (or will be) using social media. As a result, many schools have realized that they need to loosen restrictions, teach digital citizenship skills, and even incorporate these tools into classrooms. The Peel District School Board (PDSB) in Ontario is one of many school boards that has begun to accept the use of social media in the classroom. In 2013, the PDSB introduced a "Bring Your Own Device" (BYOD) policy and have unblocked many social media sites. Fewkes and McCabe (2012) have researched about the benefits of using Facebook in the classroom.

Wikipedia

In early 2013, Steve Joordens, a professor at the University of Toronto, encouraged the 1,900 students enrolled in his introductory psychology course to add content to Wikipedia pages featuring content that related to the course. Like other educators, Joordens argued that the assignment would not only strengthen the site's psychology-related content, but also provide an opportunity for students to engage in critical reflection about the negotiations involved in collaborative knowledge production. However, Wikipedia's all-volunteer editorial staff complained that the students' contributions resulted in an overwhelming number of additions to the site, and that some of the contributions were inaccurate.

Facebook and the Classroom

It allows for both an asynchronous and synchronous, open dialogue via a familiar and regularly accessed medium, and supports the integration of multimodal content such as student-created photographs and video and URLs to other texts, in a platform that many students are already familiar with. Further, it allows students to ask more minor questions that they might not otherwise feel motivated to visit a professor in person during office hours to ask. It also allows students to manage their own privacy settings, and often work with the privacy settings they have already established as registered users.

Facebook is one alternative means for shyer students to be able to voice their thoughts in and outside of the classroom. It allows students to collect their thoughts and articulate them in writing before committing to their expression. Further, the level of informality typical to Facebook can also aid students in self-expression and encourage more frequent student-and-instructor and student-and-student communication. At the same time, Towner and Munoz note that this informality may actually drive many educators and students away from using Facebook for educational purposes.

From a course management perspective, Facebook may be less efficient as a replacement for more conventional course management systems, both because of its limitations with regards to uploading assignments and due to some students' (and educators') resistance to its use in education. Specifically, there are features of student-to-student collaboration that may be conducted more efficiently on dedicated course management systems, such as the organization of posts in a nested and linked format. That said, a number of studies suggest that students post to discussion forums more frequently and are generally more active discussants on Facebook posts versus conventional course management systems like WebCT or Blackboard (Chu and Meulemans, 2008; Salaway, et al., 2008; Schroeder and Greenbowe, 2009).

Further, familiarity and comfortability with Facebook is often divided by socio-economic class, with students whose parents obtained a college degree, or at least having attended college for some span of time, being more likely to already be active users. Instructors ought to seriously consider and respect these hesitancies, and refrain from "forcing" Facebook on their students for academic purposes. Instructors also ought to consider that rendering Facebook optional, but continuing to provide content through it to students who elect to use it, places an unfair burden on hesitant students, who then are forced to choose between using a technology they are uncomfortable with and participating fully in the course. A related limitation, particularly at the level of K-12 schooling, is the distrust (and in some cases, outright disallowal) of the use of Facebook in formal classroom settings in many educational jurisdictions.

However, this hesitancy towards Facebook use is continually diminishing in the United States, as the Pew Internet & American Life Project's annual report for 2012 shows that the likelihood of a person to be a registered Facebook user only fluctuates by 13 percent between different levels of educational attainment, 9 percent between urban, suburban, and rural users, only 5 percent between different household income brackets. The largest gap occurs between age brackets, with 86 percent of 18- to 29-year-olds reported as registered users as opposed to only 35 percent of 65-and-up-year-old users.

Twitter

Twitter also promotes social connections among students. It can be used to enhance communication building and critical thinking. Domizi (2013) utilized Twitter in a graduate seminar requiring students to post weekly tweets to extend classroom discussions. Students reportedly used Twitter to connect with content and other students. Additionally, students found it "to be useful professionally and personally". Junco, Heibergert, and Loken (2011) completed a study of 132 students to examine the link between social media and student engagement and social media and grades. They divided the students into two groups, one used Twitter and the other did not. Twitter was used to discuss material, organize study groups, post class announcements, and connect with classmates. Junco and his colleagues (2011) found that the students in the Twitter group had higher GPAs and greater engagement scores than the control group. Gao, Luo, and Zhang (2012) reviewed literature about Twitter published between 2008 and 2011. They concluded that Twitter allowed students to participate with each other in class (back channel), and extend discussion outside of class. They also reported that students used Twitter to get up-to-date news and connect with professionals in their field. Students reported that microblogging encouraged students to "participate at a higher level". Because the posts cannot exceed 140 characters, students were required to express ideas, reflect, and focus on important concepts in a concise manner. Some students found this very beneficial. Other students did not like the character limit. Also, some students found microblogging to be overwhelming (information overload). The research indicated that many students did not actually participate in the discussions, "they just lurked".

Impact of Retweeting on Twitter

A popular component and feature of Twitter is retweeting. Twitter allows other people to keep up with important events, stay connected with their peers, and can contribute in various ways throughout social media. When certain posts become popular, they start to get tweeted over and over again, becoming viral. Ellen DeGeneres is a prime example of this. She was a host during the 86th Academy Awards, when she took the opportunity to take a selfie with about twelve other celebrities that joined in on the highlight of the night, including Jennifer Lawrence, Brad Pitt, Julia

Roberts, and Ellen DeGeneres. This picture went viral within forty minutes and was retweeted 1.8 million times within the first hour. This was an astonishing record for Twitter and the use of selfies, which other celebrities have tried to recreate. Retweeting is beneficial strategy, which notifies individuals on Twitter about popular trends, posts, and events.

YouTube

YouTube is the most frequently used social media tool in the classroom. Students can watch videos, answer questions, and discuss content. Additionally, students can create videos to share with others. Sherer and Shea (2011) claimed that YouTube increased participation, personalization (customization), and productivity. YouTube also improved students' digital skills and provided opportunity for peer learning and problem solving Eick et al. (2012) found that videos kept students' attention, generated interest in the subject, and clarified course content. Additionally, the students reported that the videos helped them recall information and visualize real world applications of course concepts.

LinkedIn

LinkedIn was created by Reid Hoffman in 2002 and was launched on May 5, 2003. LinkedIn is now the world's largest professional social network with over 300 million members in over 200 countries. The mission of LinkedIn is to, "connect the world's professionals to make them more productive and successful." A lot of people describe LinkedIn as a "professional Facebook", but it's important to remember that LinkedIn is *not* Facebook and you should keep nicknames and any inappropriate pictures off of your profile. Instead, use headshot as your profile picture and keep it as professional as possible.

There are over 39 million students and recent college graduates on LinkedIn, becoming the fastest-growing demographic on the site. There are many ways that LinkedIn can be used in the classroom. First and foremost, using LinkedIn in the classroom encourages students to have a professional online social presence and can help them become comfortable in searching for a job or internship. "The key to making LinkedIn a great social learning tool is to encourage learners to build credibility through their profiles, so that experts and professionals won't think twice about connecting with them and share knowledge." Dedicating class time solely for the purpose of setting up LinkedIn accounts and showing students how to navigate it and build their profile will set them up for success in the future. Next, professors can create assignments that involve using LinkedIn as a research tool. The search tool in LinkedIn gives students the opportunity to seek out organizations they are interested in and allow them to learn more. Giving students the class time to work on their LinkedIn profile allows them to network with each other, and stresses the importance of networking. Finally, professors can design activities that revolve around resume building and interviews. A person's LinkedIn and resume are what employers look at first, and they need to know how to make a strong first impression. It's important to learn how to construct a strong resume as soon as possible, as well as learn strong interviewing skills. Not only is the information and skills learned in the classroom important, but it is also important to know how to apply the information and skills to their LinkedIn profile so they can get a job in their field of study. These skills can be gained while incorporating LinkedIn into the classroom.

Advertising

Tweets Containing Advertising

In 2013, the United Kingdom Advertising Standards Authority (ASA) began to advise celebrities and sportstars to make it clear if they had been paid to tweet about a product or service by using the hashtag #spon or #ad within tweets containing endorsements. In July 2013, Wayne Rooney was accused of misleading followers by not including either of these tags in a tweet promoting Nike. The tweet read:

"The pitches change. The killer instinct doesn't. Own the turf, anywhere. @NikeFootball #myground."

The tweet was investigated by the ASA but no charges were pressed. The ASA stated that "We considered the reference to Nike Football was prominent and clearly linked the tweet with the Nike brand." When asked about whether the number of complaints regarding misleading social advertising had increased, the ASA stated that the number of complaints had risen marginally since 2011 but that complaints were "very low" in the "grand scheme."

Censorship Incidents

Banner in Bangkok, observed on the 30th of June 2014, informing the Thai public that 'like' or 'share' activity on social media may land them in jail.

Social media often features in political struggles to control public perception and online activity. In some countries, Internet police or secret police monitor or control citizens' use of social media. For example, in 2013 social media was banned in Turkey after the Taksim Gezi Park protests. Both

Twitter and YouTube were closed in country with Turkish court's decision. And a new law, passed by Turkish Parliament, has granted immunity to Turkey's Telecommunications Directorate (TİB) personnel. The TİB was also given the authority to block access to specific websites without the need for a court order.

More recently, in the 2014 Thai coup d'état, the public was explicitly instructed not to 'share' or 'like' dissenting views on social media or face prison. In July that same year, in response to Wikileaks' release of a secret suppression order made by the Victorian Supreme Court, media lawyers were quoted in the Australian media to the effect that "anyone who tweets a link to the Wikileaks report, posts it on Facebook, or shares it in any way online could also face charges".

Effects on Youth Communication

Social media has affected the way the youth generations communicate. The introduction of social media has brought forth various forms of lingo. Abbreviations have been introduced to cut down on time. The commonly known "LOL" has become globally recognized as the abbreviation for "laugh out loud" thanks to social media. Online linguistics has changed the way youth communicate and will continue to do so in the future, as each year new catchphrases and neologisms such as "YOLO", which stands for "you only live once", and "BAE", which stands for "before anyone else" arise and start "trending" around the world. Other trends that influence the way youth communicate is through the globally known hashtags. With the introduction of social media platforms such as Twitter, Facebook and Instagram, the hashtag was created in order to easily organize and search information. As hashtags such as #tbt ("throwback Thursday") become a part of online communication, it influenced the way in which youth share and communicate in their daily lives. Because of these changes in linguistics and communication etiquette, researchers of media semiotics have found that this has altered youth's communications habits and more. Not only does social media change the way people around the world communicate, it also alters the way we understand each other. Social media has allowed for mass cultural exchange and intercultural communication. As different cultures have different value systems, cultural themes, grammar, and worldviews, they also communicate differently. The emergence of social media platforms collided different cultures and their communication methods together, forcing them to realign in order to communicate with ease with other cultures. As different cultures continue to connect through social media platforms, thinking patterns, expression styles and cultural content that influence cultural values are chipped away.

Facebook

Facebook (stylized as facebook) is a for-profit corporation and online social networking service based in Menlo Park, California, United States. The Facebook website was launched on February 4, 2004 by Mark Zuckerberg, along with fellow Harvard College students and roommates, Eduardo Saverin, Andrew McCollum, Dustin Moskovitz, and Chris Hughes.

The founders had initially limited the website's membership to Harvard students; however, later they expanded it to higher education institutions in the Boston area, the Ivy League schools, and Stanford University. Facebook gradually added support for students at various other universities, and eventually to high school students as well. Since 2006, anyone age 13 and older has been allowed to become a registered user of Facebook, though variations exist in the minimum age requirement, depending on applicable local laws. The Facebook name comes from the face book directories often given to United States university students.

After registering to use the site, users can create a user profile, add other users as "friends", exchange messages, post status updates and photos, share videos, use various applications (apps), and receive notifications when others update their profiles. Additionally, users may join common-interest user groups organized by workplace, school, or other topics, and categorize their friends into lists such as "People From Work" or "Close Friends". In groups, editors can pin posts to top. Additionally, users can complain about or block unpleasant people. Because of the large volume of data that users submit to the service, Facebook has come under scrutiny for their privacy policies.

Facebook, Inc. held its initial public offering (IPO) in February 2012, and began selling stock to the public three months later, reaching an original peak market capitalization of $104 billion. On July 13, 2015, Facebook became the fastest company in the Standard & Poor's 500 Index to reach a market cap of $250 billion. Facebook has more than 1.65 billion monthly active users as of March 31, 2016.

History

2003–2006: Thefacebook, Thiel Investment, and Name Change

Zuckerberg wrote a program called Facemash on October 28, 2003 while attending Harvard University as a sophomore (second year student). According to *The Harvard Crimson*, the site was comparable to Hot or Not and used "photos compiled from the online facebooks of nine houses, placing two next to each other at a time and asking users to choose the 'hotter' person"

To accomplish this, Zuckerberg hacked into protected areas of Harvard's computer network and copied private dormitory ID images. Harvard did not have a student "Facebook" (a directory with photos and basic information) at the time, although individual houses had been issuing their own paper facebooks since the mid-1980s, and Harvard's longtime Freshman Yearbook was colloquially referred to as the "Freshman Facebook". Facemash attracted 450 visitors and 22,000 photo-views in its first four hours online.

The site was quickly forwarded to several campus group list-servers, but was shut down a few days later by the Harvard administration. Zuckerberg faced expulsion and was charged by the administration with breach of security, violating copyrights, and violating individual privacy. Ultimately, the charges were dropped. Zuckerberg expanded on this initial project that semester by creating a social study tool ahead of an art history final exam. He uploaded 500 Augustan images to a website, each of which was featured with a corresponding comments section. He shared the site with his classmates, and people started sharing notes.

Original layout and name of Thefacebook, 2004.

The following semester, Zuckerberg began writing code for a new website in January 2004. He said that he was inspired by an editorial about the Facemash incident in *The Harvard Crimson*. On February 4, 2004, Zuckerberg launched "Thefacebook", originally located at thefacebook.com.

Six days after the site launched, Harvard seniors Cameron Winklevoss, Tyler Winklevoss, and Divya Narendra accused Zuckerberg of intentionally misleading them into believing that he would help them build a social network called HarvardConnection.com. They claimed that he was instead using their ideas to build a competing product. The three complained to *The Harvard Crimson* and the newspaper began an investigation. They later filed a lawsuit against Zuckerberg, subsequently settling in 2008 for 1.2 million shares (worth $300 million at Facebook's IPO).

Membership was initially restricted to students of Harvard College; within the first month, more than half the undergraduates at Harvard were registered on the service. Eduardo Saverin (business aspects), Dustin Moskovitz (programmer), Andrew McCollum (graphic artist), and Chris Hughes joined Zuckerberg to help promote the website. In March 2004, Facebook expanded to the universities of Columbia, Stanford, and Yale. It later opened to all Ivy League colleges, Boston University, New York University, MIT, and gradually most universities in the United States and Canada.

Mark Zuckerberg, co-creator of Facebook, in his Harvard dorm room, 2005.

In mid-2004, entrepreneur Sean Parker — an informal advisor to Zuckerberg — became the company's president. In June 2004, Facebook moved its operations base to Palo Alto, California. It received its first investment later that month from PayPal co-founder Peter Thiel. In 2005, the company dropped "the" from its name after purchasing the domain name facebook.com for US$200,000. The domain facebook.com belonged to AboutFace Corporation before the purchase. This website last appeared on April 8, 2005; from April 10, 2005 to August 4, 2005, this domain gave a 403 error.

In May 2005, Accel Partners invested $12.7 million in Facebook, and Jim Breyer added $1 million of his own money. A high-school version of the site was launched in September 2005, which Zuckerberg called the next logical step. (At the time, high-school networks required an invitation to join.) Facebook also expanded membership eligibility to employees of several companies, including Apple Inc. and Microsoft.

2006–2012: Public Access, Microsoft Alliance and Rapid Growth

On September 26, 2006, Facebook was opened to everyone at least 13 years old with a valid email address.

In late 2007, Facebook had 100,000 business pages (pages which allowed companies to promote themselves and attract customers). These started as group pages, but a new concept called company pages was planned. Pages began rolling out for businesses in May 2009.

On October 24, 2007, Microsoft announced that it had purchased a 1.6% share of Facebook for $240 million, giving Facebook a total implied value of around $15 billion. Microsoft's purchase included rights to place international advertisements on the social networking site.

In October 2008, Facebook announced that it would set up its international headquarters in Dublin, Ireland. Almost a year later, in September 2009, Facebook said that it had turned cash-flow positive for the first time.

A January 2009 Compete.com study ranked Facebook the most used social networking service by worldwide monthly active users. *Entertainment Weekly* included the site on its end-of-the-decade "best-of" list saying, "How on earth did we stalk our exes, remember our co-workers' birthdays, bug our friends, and play a rousing game of Scrabulous before Facebook?"

Facebook headquarters entrance sign at 1 Hacker Way, Menlo Park, California

Traffic to Facebook increased steadily after 2009. The company announced 500 million users in July 2010 making it the largest online social network in the world at the time. According to the company's data, half of the site's membership use Facebook daily, for an average of 34 minutes, while 150 million users access the site by mobile. A company representative called the milestone a "quiet revolution."

In November 2010, based on SecondMarket Inc. (an exchange for privately held companies' shares), Facebook's value was $41 billion. The company had slightly surpassed eBay to become the third largest American web company after Google and Amazon.com.

In early 2011, Facebook announced plans to move its headquarters to the former Sun Microsystems campus in Menlo Park, California. In March 2011, it was reported that Facebook was removing approximately 20,000 profiles offline every day for violations such as spam, graphic content, and underage use, as part of its efforts to boost cyber security.

Release of statistics by DoubleClick showed that Facebook reached one trillion page views in the month of June 2011, making it the most visited website tracked by DoubleClick. According to a Nielsen Media Research study, released in December 2011, Facebook had become the second-most accessed website in the U.S. behind Google.

2012–2013: IPO, Lawsuits and One-Billionth User

Facebook eventually filed for an initial public offering on February 1, 2012. Facebook held an initial public offering on May 17, 2012, negotiating a share price of US$38. The company was valued at $104 billion, the largest valuation to date for a newly listed public company.

Facebook Inc. began selling stock to the public and trading on the NASDAQ on May 18, 2012. Based on its 2012 income of $5 billion, Facebook joined the Fortune 500 list for the first time in May 2013, ranked in position 462.

Facebook filed their S1 document with the Securities and Exchange Commission on February 1, 2012. The company applied for a $5 billion IPO, one of the biggest offerings in the history of technology. The IPO raised $16 billion, making it the third-largest in U.S. history.

The shares began trading on May 18; the stock struggled to stay above the IPO price for most of the day, but set a record for the trading volume of an IPO (460 million shares). The first day of trading was marred by technical glitches that prevented orders from going through; only the technical problems and artificial support from underwriters prevented the stock price from falling below the IPO price on the day.

In March 2012, Facebook announced App Center, a store selling applications that operate via the site. The store was to be available on iPhones, Android devices, and mobile web users.

On May 22, 2012, the Yahoo! Finance website reported that Facebook's lead underwriters, Morgan Stanley (MS), JP Morgan (JPM), and Goldman Sachs (GS), cut their earnings forecasts for the company in the middle of the IPO process. The stock had begun its freefall by this time, closing at 34.03 on May 21 and 31.00 on May 22. A "circuit breaker" was used in an attempt to slow down the stock price's decline. Securities and Exchange Commission Chairman Mary Schapiro, and Financial Industry Regulatory Authority (FINRA) Chairman Rick Ketchum, called for a review of the circumstances surrounding the IPO.

Billboard on the Thomson Reuters building welcomes Facebook to NASDAQ, 2012

Facebook's IPO was consequently investigated, and was compared to a pump and dump scheme. A class-action lawsuit was filed in May 2012 because of the trading glitches, which led to botched orders. Lawsuits were filed, alleging that an underwriter for Morgan Stanley selectively revealed adjusted earnings estimates to preferred clients.

The other underwriters (MS, JPM, GS), Facebook's CEO and board, and NASDAQ also faced litigation after numerous lawsuits were filed, while SEC and FINRA both launched investigations. It was believed that adjustments to earnings estimates were communicated to the underwriters by a Facebook financial officer, who used the information to cash out on their positions while leaving the general public with overpriced shares. By the end of May 2012, Facebook's stock lost over a quarter of its starting value, which led the *Wall Street Journal* to label the IPO a "fiasco".

Zuckerberg announced to the media at the start of October 2012 that Facebook had passed the monthly active users mark of one billion—Facebook defines active users as a logged-in member who visits the site, or accesses it through a third-party site connected to Facebook, at least once a month. Fake accounts were not mentioned in the announcement, but the company continued to remove them after it found that 8.7% of its users were not real in August 2012. The company's data also revealed 600 million mobile users, 140 billion friend connections since the inception of Facebook, and the median age of a user as 22 years.

2013–Present: Site Developments, A4AI and 10th Anniversary

On January 15, 2013, Facebook announced Facebook Graph Search, which provides users with a "precise answer," rather than a link to an answer by leveraging the data present on its site. Facebook emphasized that the feature would be "privacy-aware," returning only results from content already shared with the user.

The company became the subject of a lawsuit by Rembrandt Social Media in February 2013, for patents involving the "Like" button. On April 3, 2013, Facebook unveiled Facebook Home, a user-interface layer for Android devices offering greater integration with the site. HTC announced the HTC First, a smartphone with Home pre-loaded.

On April 15, 2013, Facebook announced an alliance across 19 states with the National Association of Attorneys General, to provide teenagers and parents with information on tools to manage social networking profiles. On April 19, 2013, Facebook officially modified its logo to remove the faint blue line at the bottom of the "F" icon. The letter F moved closer to the edge of the box.

Following a campaign by 100 advocacy groups, Facebook agreed to update its policy on hate speech. The campaign highlighted content promoting domestic and sexual violence against women, and used over 57,000 tweets and more than 4,900 emails that caused withdrawal of advertising from the site by 15 companies, including Nissan UK, House of Burlesque and Nationwide UK. The social media website initially responded by stating that "while it may be vulgar and offensive, distasteful content on its own does not violate our policies". It decided to take action on May 29, 2013, after it "become clear that our systems to identify and remove hate speech have failed to work as effectively as we would like, particularly around issues of gender-based hate."

On June 12, 2013, Facebook announced on its newsroom that it was introducing clickable hashtags to help users follow trending discussions, or search what others are talking about on a topic. A July 2013 *Wall Street Journal* article identified the Facebook IPO as the cause of a change in the U.S.' national economic statistics, as the local government area of the company's headquarters, San Mateo County, California, became the top wage-earning county in the country after the fourth quarter of 2012. The Bureau of Labor Statistics reported that the average weekly wage in the county was US$3,240, 107% higher than the previous year. It noted the wages were "the equivalent of $168,000 a year, and more than 50% higher than the next-highest county, New York County (better known as Manhattan), at $2,107 a week, or roughly $110,000 a year."

Russian internet firm Mail.Ru sold its Facebook shares for US$525 million on September 5, 2013, following its initial $200 million investment in 2009. Partly owned by Russia's richest man, Alisher Usmanovhe, the firm owned a total of 14.2 million remaining shares prior to the sale. In the same month, the Chinese government announced that it will lift the ban on Facebook in the Shanghai Free Trade Zone "to welcome foreign companies to invest and to let foreigners live and work happily in the free-trade zone." Facebook was first blocked in China in 2009.

Facebook was announced as a member of The Alliance for Affordable Internet (A4AI) in October 2013, when the A4AI was launched. The A4AI is a coalition of public and private organisations that includes Google, Intel and Microsoft. Led by Sir Tim Berners-Lee, the A4AI seeks to make Internet access more affordable so that access is broadened in the developing world, where only 31% of people are online. Google will help to decrease Internet access prices so that they fall below the UN Broadband Commission's worldwide target of 5% of monthly income.

A Reuters report, published on December 11, 2013, stated that Standard & Poor's announced the placement of Facebook on its S&P 500 index "after the close of trading on December 20." Facebook announced Q4 2013 earnings of $523 million (20 cents per share), an increase of $64 million from the previous year, as well as 945 million mobile users.

By January 2014, Facebook's market capitalization had risen to over $134 billion. At the end of January 2014, 1.23 billion users were active on the website every month.

The company celebrated its 10th anniversary during the week of February 3, 2014. In each of the first three months of 2014, over one billion users logged into their Facebook account on a mobile device.

In February 2014, Facebook announced that it would be buying mobile messaging company Whatsapp for US$19 billion in cash and stock. In June 2014, Facebook announced the acquisition of Pryte, a Finnish mobile data-plan firm that aims to make it easier for mobile phone users in underdeveloped parts of the world to use wireless Internet apps.

At the start of July 2014, Facebook announced the acquisition of LiveRail, a San Francisco, California-based online video advertising company. LiveRail's technology facilitates the sale of video inventory across different devices. The terms of the deal were undisclosed, but *TechCrunch* reported that Facebook paid between US$400 million and $500 million. As part of the company's second quarter results, Facebook announced in late July 2014 that mobile accounted for 62% of its advertising revenue, which is an increase of 21% from the previous year.

Alongside other American technology figures like Jeff Bezos and Tim Cook, Zuckerberg hosted visiting Chinese politician Lu Wei, known as the "Internet czar" for his influence in the enforcement of China's online policy, at Facebook's headquarters on December 8, 2014. The meeting occurred after Zuckerberg participated in a Q&A session at Tsinghua University in Beijing, China, on October 23, 2014, where he attempted to converse in Mandarin—although Facebook is banned in China, Zuckerberg is highly regarded among the people and was at the university to help fuel the nation's burgeoning entrepreneur sector. A book of Chinese president Xi Xinping found on Zuckerberg's office desk attracted a great deal of attention in the media, after the Facebook founder explained to Lu, "I want them [Facebook staff] to understand socialism with Chinese characteristics."

Zuckerberg fielded questions during a live Q&A session at the company's headquarters in Menlo Park on December 11, 2014. The question of whether the platform would adopt a dislike button was raised again, and Zuckerberg said, "We're [Facebook] thinking about it [dislike button] ... It's an interesting question," and said that he likes the idea of Facebook users being able to express a greater variety of emotions. In October 2015, Zuckerberg said that instead of creating a dislike button, Facebook is testing emoji reactions as an alternative to the 'like' button. On February 24, 2016, Facebook launched Facebook Reactions, which allows users to respond to posts with multiple reactions in addition to "liking" it.

As of January 21, 2015, Facebook's algorithm is programmed to filter out false or misleading content, such as fake news stories and hoaxes, and will be supported by users who select the option to flag a story as "purposefully fake or deceitful news." According to Reuters, such content is "being spread like a wildfire" on the social media platform. Facebook maintained that "satirical" content, "intended to be humorous, or content that is clearly labeled as satire," will be taken into account and should not be intercepted. The algorithm, however, has been accused of maintaining a "filter bubble", where both material the user disagrees with and posts with a low level of likes, will also not be seen. In 2015 November, Zuckerberg prolonged period of paternity leave from 4 weeks to 4 months.

On April 12, 2016, Zuckerberg revealed a decade-long plan for Facebook in a keynote address. His speech outlined his vision, which was centered around three main pillars: artificial intelligence, increased connectivity around the world and virtual and augmented reality. He also announced a new Facebook Messenger platform, which will have developers creating bots that are able to engage in automatic interactions with customers. In June 2016 Facebook announced Deep Text, a natural language processing AI which will learn user intent and context in 20 languages.

On May 31, 2016, Facebook, along with Google, Microsoft, and Twitter, jointly agreed to a European Union code of conduct obligating them to review "[the] majority of valid notifications for removal of illegal hate speech" posted on their services within 24 hours.

Facebook introduced 360-degree photo to posts on June 9, 2016. If one has a compatible Samsung phone, Facebook will display a dedicated "view in VR" button, then users will have to insert the phone into their Gear VR headsets to watch the photo in a more immersive style.

In July 2016, a $US 1 billion lawsuit was filed against the company alleging that it permitted the Hamas group to use it to perform assaults that ended the lives of 4 people. Facebook released the blueprints of Surround 360 camera on Github under Open-source license.

Corporate Affairs

Management

The ownership percentages of the company, as of 2012, are:

- Mark Zuckerberg: 28%

- Accel Partners: 10%

- Mail.Ru Group: 10%

- Dustin Moskovitz: 6%

- Eduardo Saverin: 5%

- Sean Parker: 4%

- Peter Thiel: 3%

- Greylock Partners: between 1 and 2%

- Meritech Capital Partners: between 1 and 2% each

- Microsoft: 1.3%

- Li Ka-shing: 0.8%

- Interpublic Group: less than 0.5%

A small group of current and former employees and celebrities own less than 1% each, including Matt Cohler, Jeff Rothschild, Adam D'Angelo, Chris Hughes, and Owen Van Natta, while Reid Hoffman and Mark Pincus have sizable holdings of the company. The remaining 30% or so are owned by employees, an undisclosed number of celebrities, and outside investors. Adam D'Angelo, former chief technology officer and friend of Zuckerberg, resigned in May 2008. Reports claimed that he and Zuckerberg began quarreling, and that he was no longer interested in partial ownership of the company.

Key management personnel consist of: Chris Cox (Chief Product Officer), Sandberg (COO), and Zuckerberg (Chairman and CEO). Mike Vernal is considered to be the company's top engineer. As of April 2011, Facebook has over 7,000 employees, and offices in 15 countries. Other managers include chief financial officer David Wehner and public relations head Elliot Schrage.

Facebook was named the 5th best company to work for in 2014 by company-review site Glassdoor as part of its sixth annual Employees' Choice Awards. The website stated that 93% of Facebook employees would recommend the company to a friend.

Revenue

Revenues
(in millions US$)

Year	Revenue	Growth
2004	$0.4	—
2005	$9	2150%
2006	$48	433%
2007	$153	219%
2008	$280	83%
2009	$775	177%
2010	$2,000	158%
2011	$3,711	86%
2012	$5,089	37%
2013	$7,872	55%
2014	$12,466	58%

2015	$17,928	44%

Most of Facebook's revenue comes from advertising. Facebook generally has a lower clickthrough rate (CTR) for advertisements than most major websites. According to BusinessWeek.com, banner advertisements on Facebook have generally received one-fifth the number of clicks compared to those on the Web as a whole, although specific comparisons can reveal a much larger disparity. For example, while Google users click on the first advertisement for search results an average of 8% of the time (80,000 clicks for every one million searches), Facebook's users click on advertisements an average of 0.04% of the time (400 clicks for every one million pages).

Sarah Smith, who was Facebook's Online Sales Operations Manager until 2012, reported that successful advertising campaigns on the site can have clickthrough rates as low as 0.05% to 0.04%, and that CTR for ads tend to fall within two weeks.

The cause of Facebook's low CTR has been attributed to younger users enabling ad blocking software and their adeptness at ignoring advertising messages, as well as the site's primary purpose being social communication rather than content viewing. According to digital consultancy iStrategy Labs in mid-January 2014, three million fewer users aged between 13 and 17 years were present on Facebook's Social Advertising platform compared to 2011. However, *Time* writer and reporter Christopher Matthews stated in the wake of the iStrategy Labs results:

A big part of Facebook's pitch is that it has so much information about its users that it can more effectively target ads to those who will be responsive to the content. If Facebook can prove that theory to be true, then it may not worry so much about losing its cool cachet.

In December 2014, a report from Frank N. Magid and Associates found that the percentage of teens aged 13 to 17 who used Facebook fell to 88% in 2014, down from 94% in 2013 and 95% in 2012.

Zuckerberg, alongside other Facebook executives, have questioned the data in such reports; although, a former Facebook senior employee has commented: "Mark [Zuckerberg] is very willing to recognize the strengths in other products and the flaws in Facebook."

On pages for brands and products, however, some companies have reported CTR as high as 6.49% for Wall posts. A study found that, for video advertisements on Facebook, over 40% of users who viewed the videos viewed the entire video, while the industry average was 25% for in-banner video ads.

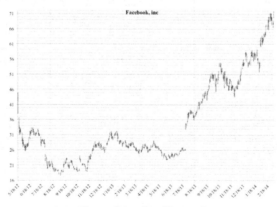

Chart of Facebook's Stock

The company released its own set of revenue data at the end of January 2014 and claimed: Revenues of US$2.59 billion were generated for the three months ending December 31, 2013; earnings per share were 31 cents; revenues of US$7.87 billion were made for the entirety of 2013; and Facebook's annual profit for 2013 was US$1.5 billion. During the same time, independent market research firm eMarketer released data in which Facebook accounted for 5.7 per cent of all global digital ad revenues in 2013 (Google's share was 32.4 per cent). Revenue for the June 2014 quarter rose to $2.68 billion, an increase of 67 per cent over the second quarter of 2013. Mobile advertising revenue accounted for around 62 per cent of advertising revenue, an increase of approximately 41 per cent over the comparable quarter of the previous year.

Number of Advertisers

In February 2015, Facebook announced that it had reached two million active advertisers with most of the gain coming from small businesses. An active advertiser is an advertiser that has advertised on the Facebook platform in the last 28 days. In March 2016, Facebook announced that it reached three million active advertisers with more than 70% from outside the US.

Mergers and Acquisitions

On November 15, 2010, Facebook announced it had acquired the domain name fb.com from the American Farm Bureau Federation for an undisclosed amount. On January 11, 2011, the Farm Bureau disclosed $8.5 million in "domain sales income", making the acquisition of FB.com one of the ten highest domain sales in history.

Offices

In early 2011, Facebook announced plans to move to its new headquarters, the former Sun Microsystems campus in Menlo Park.

All users outside of the US and Canada have a contract with Facebook's Irish subsidiary "Facebook Ireland Limited". This allows Facebook to avoid US taxes for all users in Europe, Asia, Australia, Africa and South America. Facebook is making use of the Double Irish arrangement which allows it to pay just about 2–3% corporation tax on all international revenue.

In 2010, Facebook opened its fourth office, in Hyderabad and the first in Asia.

Facebook, which in 2010 had more than 750 million active users globally including over 23 million in India, announced that its Hyderabad center would house online advertising and developer support teams and provide round-the-clock, multilingual support to the social networking site's users and advertisers globally. With this, Facebook joins other giants like Google, Microsoft, Oracle, Dell, IBM and Computer Associates that have already set up shop. In Hyderabad, it is registered as 'Facebook India Online Services Pvt Ltd'.

Though Facebook did not specify its India investment or hiring figures, it said recruitment had already begun for a director of operations and other key positions at Hyderabad, which would supplement its operations in California, Dublin in Ireland as well as at Austin, Texas.

Entrance to Facebook's previous headquarters in the Stanford Research Park, Palo Alto, California

A custom-built data center with substantially reduced ("38% less") power consumption compared to existing Facebook data centers opened in April 2011 in Prineville, Oregon. In April 2012, Facebook opened a second data center in Forest City, North Carolina, US. In June 2013, Facebook opened a third data center in Luleå, Sweden. In November 2014, Facebook opened a fourth data center in Altoona, Iowa, US.

On October 1, 2012, CEO Zuckerberg visited Moscow to stimulate social media innovation in Russia and to boost Facebook's position in the Russian market. Russia's communications minister tweeted that Prime Minister Dmitry Medvedev urged the social media giant's founder to abandon plans to lure away Russian programmers and instead consider opening a research center in Moscow. Facebook has roughly 9 million users in Russia, while domestic analogue VK has around 34 million.

Entrance to Facebook headquarters complex in Menlo Park, California

The functioning of a woodwork facility on the Menlo Park campus was announced at the end of August 2013. The facility, opened in June 2013, provides equipment, safety courses and woodwork learning course, while employees are required to purchase materials at the in-house store. A Facebook spokesperson explained that the intention of the facility is to encourage employees to think in an innovative manner because of the different environment, and also serves as an attractive perk for prospective employees.

Inside the Facebook headquarters in 2014

Open Source Contributions

Facebook is both a consumer of and contributor to free and open source software. Facebook's contributions include: HipHop for PHP, Fair scheduler in Apache Hadoop, Apache Hive, Apache Cassandra, and the Open Compute Project.

Facebook also contributes to other opensource projects such as Oracle's MySQL database engine.

Technical Aspects

The website's primary color is blue as Zuckerberg is red-green colorblind, a realization that occurred after a test undertaken around 2007; he explained in 2010: "blue is the richest color for me—I can see all of blue." Facebook is built in PHP which is compiled with HipHop for PHP, a 'source code transformer' built by Facebook engineers that turns PHP into C++. The deployment of HipHop reportedly reduced average CPU consumption on Facebook servers by 50%.

Facebook is developed as one monolithic application. According to an interview in 2012 with Chuck Rossi, a build engineer at Facebook, Facebook compiles into a 1.5 GB binary blob which is then distributed to the servers using a custom BitTorrent-based release system. Rossi stated that it takes approximately 15 minutes to build and 15 minutes to release to the servers. The build and release process is zero downtime and new changes to Facebook are rolled out daily.

Facebook used a combination platform based on HBase to store data across distributed machines. Using a tailing architecture, new events are stored in log files, and the logs are tailed. The system rolls these events up and writes them into storage. The User Interface then pulls the data out and displays it to users. Facebook handles requests as AJAX behavior. These requests are written to a log file using Scribe (developed by Facebook).

Data is read from these log files using Ptail, an internally built tool to aggregate data from multiple Scribe stores. It tails the log files and pulls data out (thus the name). Ptail data is separated out into three streams so they can eventually be sent to their own clusters in different data centers (Plugin impression, News feed impressions, Actions (plugin + news feed)). Puma is used to manage periods of high data flow (Input/Output or IO). Data is processed in batches to lessen the number of times needed to read and write under high demand periods (A hot article will generate a lot of impressions and news feed impressions which will cause huge data skews). Batches are taken every 1.5 seconds, limited by memory used when creating a hash table.

After this, data is output in PHP format (compiled with HipHop for PHP). The backend is written in Java and Thrift is used as the messaging format so PHP programs can query Java services. Caching solutions are used to make the web pages display more quickly. The more and longer data is cached the less realtime it is. The data is then sent to MapReduce servers so it can be queried via Hive. This also serves as a backup plan as the data can be recovered from Hive. Raw logs are removed after a period of time.

On March 20, 2014 Facebook announced a new open source programming language called Hack. Prior to public release, a large portion of Facebook was already running and "battle tested" using the new language.

Facebook uses the Momentum platform from Message Systems to deliver the enormous volume of emails it sends to its users every day.

History

On July 20, 2008, Facebook introduced "Facebook Beta", a significant redesign of its user interface on selected networks. The Mini-Feed and Wall were consolidated, profiles were separated into tabbed sections, and an effort was made to create a "cleaner" look. After initially giving users a choice to switch, Facebook began migrating all users to the new version starting in September 2008. On December 11, 2008, it was announced that Facebook was testing a simpler signup process.

Chat

Facebook Chat was added April 6, 2008. It is a Comet-based instant messaging application which allows users to communicate with other Facebook users in a way similar in functionality to instant messaging software.

Gifts

Facebook launched Gifts on February 8, 2007, which allows users to send virtual gifts to their friends that appear on the recipient's profile. Gifts cost $1.00 each to purchase, and a personalized message can be attached to each gift.

Marketplace

On May 14, 2007, Facebook launched Marketplace, which lets users post free classified ads. Marketplace has been compared to Craigslist by CNET, which points out that the major difference between the two is that listings posted by a user on Marketplace are seen only by users in the same network as that user, whereas listings posted on Craigslist can be seen by anyone.

Messaging

A new Messaging platform, codenamed "Project Titan", was launched on November 15, 2010. Described as a "Gmail killer" by some publications, the system allows users to directly communicate with each other via Facebook using several different methods (including a special email address, text messaging, or through the Facebook website or mobile app)—no matter what method is used to deliver a message, they are contained within single threads in a unified inbox. As with other Facebook features, users can adjust from whom they can receive messages—including just friends, friends of friends, or from anyone. Email service was terminated in 2014 because of low uptake. Aside from the Facebook website, messages can also be accessed through the site's mobile apps, or a dedicated Facebook Messenger app.

Voice Calls

Since April 2011, Facebook users have had the ability to make live voice calls via Facebook Chat, allowing users to chat with others from all over the world. This feature, which is provided free through T-Mobile's new Bobsled service, lets the user add voice to the current Facebook Chat as well as leave voice messages on Facebook.

Video Calling

On July 6, 2011, Facebook launched its video calling services using Skype as its technology partner. It allows one-to-one calling using a Skype Rest API.

Video Viewing

In September 2014, Facebook announced that it delivers 1 billion video views per day and that it would begin showing everyone view counts on publicly posted videos from users, Pages, and public figures. It also confirmed that it is recommending additional videos to users after they have watched a video. Sixty-five percent of Facebook's video views are coming from mobile where Facebook's user base is shifting, and views grew 50 percent from May to July, in part thanks to the viral ALS Ice Bucket Challenge finding a home on Facebook.

Tor Hidden Service

In October 2014, Facebook announced that users could now connect to the website through a Tor hidden service using the privacy-protecting Tor browser and encrypted using SSL. Announcing the feature, Alec Muffett said "Facebook's onion address provides a way to access Facebook through Tor without losing the cryptographic protections provided by the Tor cloud. [...] it provides end-to-end communication, from your browser directly into a Facebook datacentre." Its URL address facebookcorewwwi.onion is a backronym, which stands for *Facebook's Core WWW Infrastructure*.

User Profile/Personal Timeline

The format of individual user pages was revamped in late 2011 and became known as either a profile or personal timeline since that change. Users can create profiles with photos and images, lists of personal interests, contact information, memorable life events, and other personal information, such as employment status. Users can communicate with friends and other users through private or public messages, as well as a chat feature, and share content that includes website URLs, images, and video content. A 2012 Pew Internet and American Life study identified that between 20 and 30 percent of Facebook users are "power users" who frequently link, poke, post and tag themselves and others.

In 2007, Facebook launched Facebook Pages (also called "Fan Pages" by users) to allow "users to interact and affiliate with businesses and organizations in the same way they interact with other Facebook user profiles". On November 6, 2007, more than 100,000 Facebook pages were launched.

In July 2012, Facebook added a same-sex marriage icon to its timeline feature. On February 14, 2014, Facebook expanded the options for user's gender setting, adding a custom input field that allows users to choose from a wide range of gender identities. Users can also set which set of gender-specific pronouns are used in reference to them throughout the site. The change occurs after Nepal's first openly gay politician Sunil Babu Pant sent a letter to Zuckerberg in early 2012 to request the addition of an "Other" gender option for Facebook users; Facebook's official statement on the issue: "People can already opt out of showing their sex on their profile. We're constantly innovating on our products and features and we welcome input from everyone as we explore ways to improve the Facebook experience."

On June 13, 2009, Facebook introduced a "Usernames" feature, whereby pages can be linked with simpler URLs such as https://www.facebook.com/name instead of https://www.facebook.com/profile.php?id=20531316728. Many new smartphones offer access to Facebook services through either their Web browsers or applications. An official Facebook application is available for the operating systems Android, iOS, webOS, and Firefox OS. Nokia and Research In Motion both provide Facebook applications for their own mobile devices. As of January 2015, 745 million active users access Facebook through mobile devices every day. *Sherr, Ian (January 28, 2015). "Facebook mobile users hit new highs, revenue jumps". Cnet. Retrieved March 2, 2015.*

In May 2014, Facebook introduced a feature to allow users to ask for information not disclosed by other users on their profiles. If a user does not provide key information, such as location, hometown, or relationship status, other users can use a new 'ask' button to send a message asking about that item to the user in a single click.

News Feed

On September 6, 2006, News Feed was announced, which appears on every user's homepage and highlights information including profile changes, upcoming events, and birthdays of the user's friends. This enabled spammers and other users to manipulate these features by creating illegitimate events or posting fake birthdays to attract attention to their profile or cause. Initially, the News Feed caused dissatisfaction among Facebook users; some complained it was too cluttered and full of undesired information, others were concerned that it made it too easy for others to track individual activities (such as relationship status changes, events, and conversations with other users).

In response, Zuckerberg issued an apology for the site's failure to include appropriate customizable privacy features. Since then, users have been able to control what types of information are shared automatically with friends. Users are now able to prevent user-set categories of friends from seeing updates about certain types of activities, including profile changes, Wall posts, and newly added friends.

On February 23, 2010, Facebook was granted a patent on certain aspects of its News Feed. The patent covers News Feeds in which links are provided so that one user can participate in the same activity of another user. The patent may encourage Facebook to pursue action against websites that violate its patent, which may potentially include websites such as Twitter.

One of the most popular applications on Facebook is the Photos application, where users can upload albums and photos. Facebook allows users to upload an unlimited number of photos, compared with other image hosting services such as Photobucket and Flickr, which apply limits to the number of photos that a user is allowed to upload. During the first years, Facebook users were limited to 60 photos per album. As of May 2009, this limit has been increased to 200 photos per album.

Privacy settings can be set for individual albums, limiting the groups of users that can see an album. For example, the privacy of an album can be set so that only the user's friends can see the album, while the privacy of another album can be set so that all Facebook users can see it. Another feature of the Photos application is the ability to "tag", or label, users in a photo. For instance, if a photo contains a user's friend, then the user can tag the friend in the photo. This sends a notification to the friend that they have been tagged, and provides them a link to see the photo.

On June 7, 2012, Facebook launched its App Center to its users. It will help the users in finding games and other applications with ease. Since the launch of the App Center, Facebook has seen 150M monthly users with 2.4 times the installation of apps.

The sorting and display of stories in a user's News Feed is governed by the EdgeRank algorithm.

On May 13, 2015 Facebook in association with major news portals launched a program "Instant Articles" to provide rich news experience. Instant articles provides users, access to articles on Facebook news feed without leaving the site.

According to the technology news web site Gizmodo on May 9, 2016, Facebook curators routinely suppresses or promotes news that is deemed to meet a political agenda. For example, articles about Black Lives Matter would be listed even if they did not meet the trending criteria of News Feed. Likewise positive news about conservative political figures were regularly excised from Facebook pages.

Like Button

The like button is a social networking feature, allowing users to express their appreciation of content such as status updates, comments, photos, and advertisements. It is also a social plug-in of the Facebook Platform – launched on April 21, 2010 – that enables participating Internet websites to display a similar like button.

The sheriff of Hampton, Virginia, US fired employees who liked the Facebook page of an adversary, and a federal appeals court in Virginia ruled that the US Constitution protects the rights of US citizens to like any Facebook page of their choosing. US Circuit Judge William Traxler likened the practice to displaying a "political sign in one's front yard." Additionally, the United States Court of Appeals for the Second Circuit upheld a National Labor Relations Board decision which found that one employee's "liking" another employee's negative comments about their employer deserved protection under the National Labor Relations Act, alerting employers to proceed with caution when disciplining employees for Facebook activity.

Following a lengthy period of calls from the public to include a dislike button on the Facebook interface, Zuckerberg explained in a Q&A session on December 11, 2014 that his hesitance was due to a concern about a tone of negativity on the platform, whereby users could "shame" others, and he offered the comment option for situations where people were unwilling to use the like function. However, he said, "We're [Facebook] thinking about it [dislike button] ... It's an interesting question," and said that he likes the idea of Facebook users being able to express a greater variety of emotions.

Following

On September 14, 2011, Facebook added the ability for users to provide a "Subscribe" button on their page, which allows users to subscribe to public postings by the user without needing to add them as a friend. In conjunction, Facebook also introduced a system in February 2012 to verify the identity of certain accounts.

In December 2012, Facebook announced that because of user confusion surrounding its function, the Subscribe button would be re-labeled as a "Follow" button—making it more similar to other social networks with similar functions.

Comparison With Myspace

The media often compares Facebook to Myspace, but one significant difference between the two Web sites is the level of customization. Another difference is Facebook's requirement that users give their true identity, a demand that MySpace does not make. MySpace allows users to decorate their profiles using HTML and Cascading Style Sheets (CSS), while Facebook allows only plain text. Facebook has a number of features with which users may interact. They include the Wall, a space on every user's profile page that allows friends to post messages for the user to see; Pokes, which allows users to send a virtual "poke" to each other (a notification then tells a user that they have been poked); Photos, that allows users to upload albums and photos; and Status, which allows users to inform their friends of their whereabouts and actions. Facebook also allows users to tag various people in photographs. Depending on privacy settings, anyone who can see a user's profile can also view that user's Wall. In July 2007, Facebook began allowing users to post attachments to the Wall, whereas the Wall was previously limited to textual content only. Facebook also differs from Myspace in the form of advertising used. Facebook uses advertising in the form of banner ads, referral marketing, and games. Myspace, on the other hand, uses Google and AdSense. There is also a difference in the userbase of each site. MySpace, initially, was much more popular with high school students, while Facebook was more popular among college students. A study by the American firm Nielsen Claritas showed that Facebook users are more inclined to use other professional networking sites, such as LinkedIn, than Myspace users.

Privacy

Facebook enables users to choose their own privacy settings and choose who can see specific parts of their profile. The website is free to its users and generates revenue from advertising, such as banner ads. Facebook requires a user's name and profile picture (if applicable) to be accessible by everyone. Users can control who sees other information they have shared, as well as who can find them in searches, through their privacy settings.

On November 6, 2007, Facebook launched Facebook Beacon, which was a part of Facebook's advertisement system until it was discontinued in 2009. Its purpose was to allow targeted advertisements and allowing users to share their activities with their friends.

In 2010, Facebook's security team began expanding its efforts to reduce the risks to users' privacy, but privacy concerns remain.

Since 2010, among other social media services, the National Security Agency has been taking publicly posted profile information from users Facebook profiles to discover who they interact with.

On November 29, 2011, Facebook settled Federal Trade Commission charges that it deceived consumers by failing to keep privacy promises.

In August 2013 High-Tech Bridge published a study showing that links included in Facebook messaging service messages were being accessed by Facebook. In January 2014 two users filed a lawsuit against Facebook alleging that their privacy had been violated by this practice.

Facebook Bug Bounty Program

On July 29, 2011, Facebook announced its Bug Bounty Program in which security researchers will be paid a minimum of $500 for reporting security holes on Facebook website. Facebook's White-hat page for security researchers says: "If you give us a reasonable time to respond to your report before making any information public and make a good faith effort to avoid privacy violations, destruction of data, and interruption or degradation of our service during your research, we will not bring any lawsuit against you or ask law enforcement to investigate you."

A Facebook "White Hat" debit card, given to researchers who report security bugs

Facebook started paying researchers who find and report security bugs by issuing them custom branded "White Hat" debit cards that can be reloaded with funds each time the researchers discover new flaws. "Researchers who find bugs and security improvements are rare, and we value them and have to find ways to reward them," Ryan McGeehan, former manager of Facebook's security response team, told CNET in an interview. "Having this exclusive black card is another way to recognize them. They can show up at a conference and show this card and say 'I did special work for Facebook.'"

India, which has the second largest number of bug hunters in the world, tops the Facebook Bug Bounty Program with the largest number of valid bugs. "Researchers in Russia earned the highest amount per report in 2013, receiving an average of $3,961 for 38 bugs. India contributed the largest number of valid bugs at 136, with an average reward of $1,353. The U.S. reported 92 issues and averaged $2,272 in rewards. Brazil and the UK were third and fourth by volume, with 53 bugs and 40 bugs, respectively, and average rewards of $3,792 and $2,950", Facebook quoted in a post.

Reception

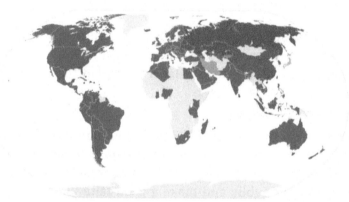

Most popular social networking sites by country

Facebook

Twitter

VKontakte

QZone

Odnoklassniki

Facenama

no data

According to comScore, Facebook is the leading social networking site based on monthly unique visitors, having overtaken main competitor MySpace in April 2008. ComScore reports that Facebook attracted 130 million unique visitors in May 2010, an increase of 8.6 million people. According to third-party web analytics providers, Alexa and SimilarWeb, Facebook is ranked second and first globally respectively, it is the highest-read social network on the Web, with over 20 billion visitors per month, as of 2015. SimilarWeb, Quantcast and Compete.com all rank the website 2nd in the U.S. in traffic. The website is the most popular for uploading photos, with 50 billion uploaded cumulatively. In 2010, Sophos's "Security Threat Report 2010" polled over 500 firms, 60% of which responded that they believed that Facebook was the social network that posed the biggest threat to security, well ahead of MySpace, Twitter, and LinkedIn.

Facebook is the most popular social networking site in several English-speaking countries, including Canada, the United Kingdom, and the United States. However, Facebook still receives limited adoption in countries such as Japan, where domestically created social networks are still largely preferred. In regional Internet markets, Facebook penetration is highest in North America (69 percent), followed by Middle East-Africa (67 percent), Latin America (58 percent), Europe (57 percent), and Asia-Pacific (17 percent). Some of the top competitors were listed in 2007 by Mashable.

The website has won awards such as placement into the "Top 100 Classic Websites" by *PC Magazine* in 2007, and winning the "People's Voice Award" from the Webby Awards in 2008. In a 2006 study conducted by Student Monitor, a company specializing in research concerning the college student market, Facebook was named the second most popular thing among undergraduates, tied with beer and only ranked lower than the iPod.

In 2010, Facebook won the Crunchie "Best Overall Startup Or Product" for the third year in a row and was recognized as one of the "Hottest Silicon Valley Companies" by Lead411. However, in a July 2010 survey performed by the American Customer Satisfaction Index, Facebook received a score of 64 out of 100, placing it in the bottom 5% of all private-sector companies in terms of customer satisfaction, alongside industries such as the IRS e-file system, airlines, and cable companies. The reasons why Facebook scored so poorly include privacy problems, frequent changes to the website's interface, the results returned by the News Feed, and spam.

Total active users[N 1]

Date	Users (in millions)	Days later	Monthly growth[N 2]
February 4, 2004	0	—	—
August 26, 2008	100	1,665	178.38%
April 8, 2009	200	225	13.33%
September 15, 2009	300	160	9.38%
February 5, 2010	400	143	6.99%
July 21, 2010	500	166	4.52%
January 5, 2011	600[N 3]	168	3.57%
May 30, 2011	700	145	3.45%
September 22, 2011	800	115	3.73%
April 24, 2012	900	215	1.74%
September 14, 2012	1,000	143	2.33%
March 31, 2013	1,110	198	1.5%

| December 31, 2013 | 1,230 | 275 | 0.97% |
| December 31, 2014 | 1,390 | 365 | 0.64% |

In December 2008, the Supreme Court of the Australian Capital Territory ruled that Facebook is a valid protocol to serve court notices to defendants. It is believed to be the world's first legal judgement that defines a summons posted on Facebook as legally binding. In March 2009, the New Zealand High Court associate justice David Gendall allowed for the serving of legal papers on Craig Axe by the company Axe Market Garden via Facebook. Employers have also used Facebook as a means to keep tabs on their employees and have even been known to fire them over posts they have made.

By 2005, the use of Facebook had already become so ubiquitous that the generic verb "facebook-ing" had come into use to describe the process of browsing others' profiles or updating one's own. In 2008, Collins English Dictionary declared "Facebook" as its new Word of the Year. In December 2009, the New Oxford American Dictionary declared its word of the year to be the verb "unfriend", defined as "To remove someone as a 'friend' on a social networking site such as Facebook.

In early 2010, Openbook was established, an avowed parody (and privacy advocacy) website that enables text-based searches of those Wall posts that are available to "Everyone", i.e. to everyone on the Internet.

Writers for *The Wall Street Journal* found in 2010 that Facebook apps were transmitting identi-fying information to "dozens of advertising and Internet tracking companies". The apps used an HTTP referer which exposed the user's identity and sometimes their friends'. Facebook said, "We have taken immediate action to disable all applications that violate our terms".

In May 2014, the countries with the most Facebook users were:

- United States with 151.8 million members

- India with 108.9 million members

- Brazil with 70.5 million members

- Indonesia with 60.3 million members

- Mexico with 44.4 million members

Facebook's popularity throughout the world (especially as a tool for political movements or pro-crastination) has led to some countries and employers blocking access to the site.

All of the above total 309 million members or about 38.6 percent of Facebook's 1 billion world-wide members. As of March 2013, Facebook reported having 1.11 billion monthly active users, globally.

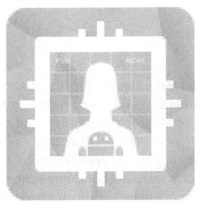

Facebook Android Logos

In regards to Facebook's mobile usage, per an analyst report in early 2013, there are 192 million Android users, 147 million iPhone users, 48 million iPad users and 56 million messenger users, and a total of 604 million mobile Facebook users. In January 2016, Facebook Messenger hits 800 million users.

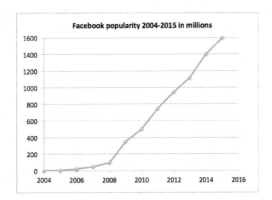

Facebook popularity. Active users of Facebook increased from just a million in 2004 to over 750 million in 2011.

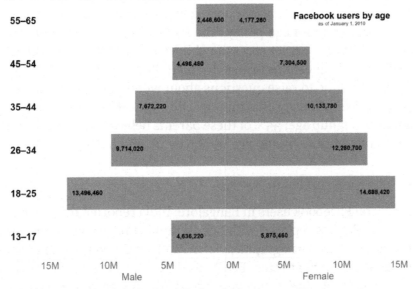

Population pyramid of Facebook users by age as of January 1, 2010

Criticisms and Controversies

Electricity usage

On April 21, 2011, Greenpeace released a report showing that of the top ten big brands in cloud computing, Facebook was most reliant on coal for electricity for its data centers. At the time, data centers consumed up to 2% of all global electricity and this amount was projected to increase. Phil Radford of Greenpeace said "we are concerned that this new explosion in electricity use could lock us into old, polluting energy sources instead of the clean energy available today." On December 15, 2011, Greenpeace and Facebook announced together that Facebook would shift to use clean and renewable energy to power its own operations. Marcy Scott Lynn, of Facebook's sustainability program, said it looked forward "to a day when our primary energy sources are clean and renewable" and that the company is "working with Greenpeace and others to help bring that day closer."

Google

In May 2011 emails were sent to journalists and bloggers making critical allegations about Google's privacy policies; however it was later discovered that PR giant Burson-Marsteller was paid for the emails by Facebook.

Users Violating Minimum Age Requirements

A 2011 study in the online journal *First Monday*, examines how parents consistently enable children as young as 10 years old to sign up for accounts, directly violating Facebook's policy banning young visitors. This policy is in compliance with a United States law, the 1998 Children's Online Privacy Protection Act, which requires minors aged 13 or younger to gain explicit parental consent to access commercial websites. In other jurisdictions where a similar law sets a lower minimum age, Facebook enforces the lower age. Of the 1,007 households surveyed for the study, 76% of parents reported that their child joined Facebook when they were younger than 13, the minimum age in the site's terms of service. The study also reported that Facebook removes roughly 20,000 users each day for violating its minimum age policy. The study's authors also note, "Indeed, Facebook takes various measures both to restrict access to children and delete their accounts if they join." The findings of the study raise questions primarily about the shortcomings of United States federal law, but also implicitly continue to raise questions about whether or not Facebook does enough to publicize its terms of service with respect to minors. Only 53% of parents said they were aware that Facebook has a minimum signup age; 35% of these parents believe that the minimum age is merely a recommendation, or thought the signup age was 16 or 18, and not 13.

Accounts Hacked in Bangalore, India

In November 2011, several Facebook users in Bangalore, India reported that their accounts had been hacked and their profile pictures replaced with pornographic images. For more than a week, users' news feeds were spammed with pornographic, violent and sexual content, and it was reported that more than 200,000 accounts were affected. Facebook described the reports as inaccurate, and Bangalore police speculated that the stories may have been rumors spread by Facebook's competitors.

Unauthorized Wall Posting Bug

On August 19, 2013, it was reported that a Facebook user from Yatta, West Bank Khalil Shreateh had found a bug that allowed him to post material to other users' Facebook Walls. Users are not supposed to have the ability to post material to the Facebook Walls of other users unless they are approved friends of those users that they have posted material to. To prove that he was telling the truth, Shreateh posted material to Sarah Goodin's wall, a friend of Facebook CEO Mark Zuckerberg. Following this, Shreateh contacted Facebook's security team with the proof that his bug was real, explaining in detail what was going on. Facebook has a bounty program in which it compensates people a US$500 fee for reporting bugs instead of using them to their advantage or selling them on the black market. However, it was reported that instead of fixing the bug and paying Shreateh the fee, Facebook originally told him that "this was not a bug" and dismissed him. Shreateh then tried a second time to inform Facebook, but they dismissed him yet again. On the third try, Shreateh used the bug to post a message to Mark Zuckerberg's Wall, stating "Sorry for breaking your privacy ... but a couple of days ago, I found a serious Facebook exploit" and that Facebook's security team was not taking him seriously. Within minutes, a security engineer contacted Shreateh, questioned him on how he performed the move and ultimately acknowledged that it was a bug in the system. Facebook temporarily suspended Shreateh's account and fixed the bug after several days. Facebook refused to pay out the bounty to Shreateh, stating that by posting to Zuckerberg's account, Shreateh had violated one of their terms of service policies and therefore "could not be paid." Facebook also noted that in Shreateh's initial reports, he had failed to provide technical details for Facebook to act on the bug.

On August 22, 2013, Yahoo News reported that Marc Maiffret, a chief technology officer of the cybersecurity firm BeyondTrust, is prompting hackers to support in raising a $10,000 reward for Khalil Shreateh. On August 20, Maiffret stated that he had already raised $9,000 in his efforts, including the $2,000 he himself contributed. He and other hackers alike have denounced Facebook for refusing Shreateh compensation. Stated Maiffret, "He is sitting there in Palestine doing this research on a five-year-old laptop that looks like it is half broken. It's something that might help him out in a big way." Facebook representatives have since responded, "We will not change our practice of refusing to pay rewards to researchers who have tested vulnerabilities against real users." Facebook representatives also claimed they'd paid out over $1 million to individuals who have discovered bugs in the past.

Users Quitting

A 2013 study examined the reasons users eventually quit the site. It found the most common reasons were privacy concerns (48%), general dissatisfaction with Facebook (14%), negative aspects regarding Facebook friends (13%) and the feeling of getting addicted to Facebook (6%). Facebook quitters were found to be more concerned about privacy, more addicted to the Internet and more conscientious.

Iphone 'Paper' App

Following the release of the Facebook iPhone app "Paper" at the beginning of February 2014, developer company FiftyThree sent a correspondence to the social media company regarding its own app, also entitled Paper and trademarked in 2012, asking Facebook to cease using an app name that they consider their own. In response, Facebook stated that it will continue to use the Paper title but conceded that it should have informed FiftyThree at an earlier point in time. FiftyThree articulated its desired outcome in a blog post: "There's a simple fix here. We think Facebook can apply the same degree of thought they put into the app into building a brand name of their own. An app about stories shouldn't start with someone else's story. Facebook should stop using our brand name."

Lane v. Facebook, Inc.

On March 2010, Judge Richard Seeborg issued an order approving the class settlement in *Lane v. Facebook, Inc.* This lawsuit charged that user's private information was being posted on Facebook without consent using Facebook's Beacon program.

User Influence Experiments

Academic and Facebook researchers have collaborated to test if the messages people see on Facebook can influence their behavior. For instance, in "A 61-Million-Person Experiment in Social Influence And Political Mobilization," during the 2010 elections, Facebook users were given the opportunity to "tell your friends you voted" by clicking on an "I voted" button. Users were 2% more likely to click the button if it was associated with friends who had already voted.

Much more controversially, a 2014 study of "Emotional Contagion Through Social Networks" manipulated the balance of positive and negative messages seen by 689,000 Facebook users. The researchers concluded that they had found "some of the first experimental evidence to support the controversial claims that emotions can spread throughout a network, [though] the effect sizes from the manipulations are small."

Unlike the "I voted" study, which had presumptively beneficial ends and raised few concerns, this study was criticized for both its ethics and methods/claims. As controversy about the study grew, Adam Kramer, a lead author of both studies and member of the Facebook data team, defended the work in a Facebook update. A few days later, Sheryl Sandburg, Facebook's COO, made a statement while traveling abroad. While at an Indian Chambers of Commerce event in New Delhi she stated that "This was part of ongoing research companies do to test different products, and that was what it was. It was poorly communicated and for that communication we apologize. We never meant to upset you."

Shortly thereafter, on July 3, 2014, USA Today reported that the privacy watchdog group Electronic Privacy Information Center (EPIC) had filed a formal complaint with the Federal Trade claiming that Facebook had broken the law when it conducted the study on the emotions of its users without their knowledge or consent. In its complaint, EPIC alleged that Facebook had deceived it users by secretly conducting a psychological experiment on their emotions: "At the time of the experiment, Facebook did not state in the Data Use Policy that user data would be used for research purposes. Facebook also failed to inform users that their personal information would be shared with researchers."

Beyond the ethical concerns, other scholars criticized the methods and reporting of the study's findings. John Grohol, writing at PsycCentral, argued that despite its title and claims of "emotional contagion," this study did not look at emotions at all. Instead, its authors used an application (called "Linguistic Inquiry and Word Count" or LIWC 2007) that simply counted positive and negative words in order to infer users' sentiments. He wrote that a shortcoming of the LIWC tool is that it does not understand negations. Hence, the tweet "I am not happy" would be scored as positive: "Since the LIWC 2007 ignores these subtle realities of informal human communication, so do the researchers." Grohol concluded that given these subtleties, the effect size of the findings are little more than a "statistical blip."

Kramer et al. (2014) found a 0.07% — that's not 7 percent, that's 1/15th of one percent!! — decrease in negative words in people's status updates when the number of negative posts on their Facebook news feed decreased. Do you know how many words you'd have to read or write before you've written one less negative word due to this effect? Probably thousands.

The consequences of the controversy are pending (be it FTC or court proceedings) but it did prompt an "Editorial Expression of Concern" from its publisher, the Proceedings of the National Academy of Sciences, as well as an blog posting from OkCupid that "We experiment on human beings!" In September 2014, law professor James Grimmelmann argued that the actions of both companies were "illegal, immoral, and mood-altering" and filed notices with the Maryland Attorney General and Cornell Institutional Review Board.

In the UK, the study was also criticised by the British Psychological Society which said, in a letter to *The Guardian*, "There has undoubtedly been some degree of harm caused, with many individuals affected by increased levels of negative emotion, with consequent potential economic costs, increase in possible mental health problems and burden on health services. The so-called 'positive' manipulation is also potentially harmful."

Real-Name Policy Controversy and Compromise

Facebook has a real-name system policy for user profiles. The real-name policy stems from the position "that way, you always know who you're connecting with. This helps keep our community safe." Facebook's real-name system does not allow adopted names or pseudonyms, and in its enforcement has suspended accounts of legitimate users, until the user provides identification indicating the name. Facebook representatives have described these incidents as very rare. A user claimed responsibility via the anonymous Android and iOS app Secret for reporting "fake names" which caused user profiles to be suspended, specifically targeting the stage names of drag queens. On October 1, 2014, Chris Cox, Chief Product Officer at Facebook, offered an apology: "In the two weeks since the real-name policy issues surfaced, we've had the chance to hear from many of you in these communities and understand the policy more clearly as you experience it. We've also come to understand how painful this has been. We owe you a better service and a better experience using Facebook, and we're going to fix the way this policy gets handled so everyone affected here can go back to using Facebook as you were."

On December 15, 2015, Facebook announced in a press release that it would be providing a compromise to its real name policy after protests from groups such as the gay/lesbian community and abuse-victims. The site is developing a protocol that will allow members to provide specifics as to their "special circumstance" or "unique situation" with a request to use pseudonyms, subject to verification of their true identities. At that time, this was already being tested in the U.S. Product manager Todd Gage and vice president of global operations Justin Osofsky also promised a new method for reducing the number of members who must go through ID verification while ensuring the safety of others on Facebook. The fake name reporting procedure will also be modified, forcing anyone who makes such an allegation to provide specifics that would be investigated and giving the accused individual time to dispute the allegation.

"Free Basics" Controversy in India

In February 2016, TRAI ruled against differential data pricing for limited services from mobile phone operators effectively ending zero-rating platforms in India. Zero rating provides access to limited number of websites for no charge to the end user. Net-neutrality supporters from India(SaveTheInternet. in) brought out the negative implications of Facebook Free Basic program and spread awareness to the public. Facebook's Free Basics program was a collaboration with Reliance Communications to launch Free Basics in India. The TRAI ruling against differential pricing marked the end of Free Basics in India.

Earlier, Facebook had spent $44 million USD in advertising and it implored all of its Indian users to send an email to the Telecom Regulatory Authority to support its program. TRAI later asked Facebook to provide specific responses from the supporters of Free Basics

Safety Check Bug

On March 27, 2016, following a bombing in Lahore, Pakistan, Facebook activated its "Safety Check" feature, which allows people to let friends and loved ones know they are okay following a crisis or natural disaster, to people who were never in danger, or even close to the Pakistan explosion. Some users as far as the US, UK and Egypt received notifications asking if they were okay.

U.s. Federal Tax Examination

On July 6, 2016, the U.S. Department of Justice filed a petition in the U.S. District Court in San Francisco, asking for a court order to enforce an administrative summons issued to Facebook, Inc., under Internal Revenue Code section 7602, in connection with an Internal Revenue Service examination of Facebook's year 2010 U.S. Federal income tax return.

Support for Terrorism Lawsuit

In July 2016, a civil action for $1 billion in damages was filed in the United States District Court for the Southern District of New York on behalf of the victims and family members of four Israeli-Americans and one US citizen killed since June 2014 by Hamas terrorists who had used Facebook.The government of the United States has designated Hamas as a Foreign Terrorist Organization and the suit alleges that Facebook provided Hamas with "material support" in violation of US Anti-Terrorism laws.

Stalking

At least one adolescent accused of serial rape was described as using Facebook to make friends of his victims.

Impact

Facebook on the Ad-tech 2010

Media Impact

In April 2011, Facebook launched a new portal for marketers and creative agencies to help them develop brand promotions on Facebook. The company began its push by inviting a select group of British advertising leaders to meet Facebook's top executives at an "influencers' summit" in February 2010. Facebook has now been involved in campaigns for *True Blood*, *American Idol*, and *Top Gear*. News and media outlets such as the Washington Post, Financial Times and ABC News have used aggregated Facebook fan data to create various infographics and charts to accompany their articles. In 2012, the beauty pageant Miss Sri Lanka Online was run exclusively using Facebook.

Social Impact

Facebook has affected the social life and activity of people in various ways. Facebook allows people using computers or mobile phones to continuously stay in touch with friends, relatives and other acquaintances wherever they are in the world, as long as there is access to the Internet. It has re-united lost family members and friends. It allows users to trade ideas, stay informed with local or global developments, and unite people with common interests and/or beliefs through open, closed and private groups and other pages.

Facebook's social impact has also changed how people communicate. Rather than having to reply to others through email, Facebook allows users to broadcast or share content to others, and thereby to engage others or be engaged with others' posts.

Facebook has been successful and more socially impactful than many other social media sites. David Kirkpatrick, technology journalist and author of *The Facebook Effect*, believes that Facebook is structured in a way that is not easily replaceable. He challenges users to consider how difficult it would be to move all the relationships and photos to an alternative. Facebook has let people participate in an atmosphere with the "over the backyard fence quality" of a small town, despite the move to larger cities. As per Pew Research Center survey, 44 percent of the overall population gets news through Facebook.

Emotional Health Impact

Recent studies have shown that Facebook causes negative effects on self-esteem by triggering feelings of envy, with vacation and holiday photos proving to be the largest resentment triggers. Other prevalent causes of envy include posts by friends about family happiness and images of physical beauty—such envious feelings leave people lonely and dissatisfied with their own lives. A joint study by two German universities discovered that one out of three people were more dissatisfied with their lives after visiting Facebook, and another study by Utah Valley University found that college students felt worse about their own lives following an increase in the amount of time spent on Facebook.

According to professor of psychology Susan Krauss Whitbourne, although Facebook has an upside of friending people, there is also the downside of having someone unfriend or reject another person. Whitbourne refers to unfriended persons on Facebook as victims of estrangement. Unfriending someone is seldom a mutual decision and the person often does not know they have been unfriended.

Political Impact

A man during the 2011 Egyptian protests carrying a card saying "Facebook,#jan25, The Egyptian Social Network".

In February 2008, a Facebook group called "One Million Voices Against FARC" organized an event in which hundreds of thousands of Colombians marched in protest against the Revolutionary Armed Forces of Colombia, better known as the FARC (from the group's Spanish name). In August 2010, one of North Korea's official government websites and the official news agency of the country, Uriminzokkiri, joined Facebook.

During the Arab Spring many journalists made claims that Facebook played a major role in generating the 2011 Egyptian revolution. On January 14, the Facebook page of "We are all khaled Said" was started by Wael Ghoniem Create Event to invite the Egyptian people to "peaceful demonstrations" on January 25. According to Mashable, in Tunisia and Egpyt, Facebook became the primary tool for connecting all protesters and led the Egyptian government of Prime Minister Nazif to ban Facebook, Twitter and another websites on January 26 then ban all mobile and Internet connections for all of Egypt at midnight January 28. After 18 days, the uprising forced President Mubarak to resign.

In Bahrain uprising which started on February 14, 2011, Facebook was utilized by the Bahraini regime as well as regime loyalists to identify, capture and prosecute citizens involved in the protests. A 20-year-old girl named Ayat Al Qurmezi was identified as a protester using Facebook, taken from her home by masked commandos and put in prison.

In 2011, Facebook filed paperwork with the Federal Election Commission to form a political action committee under the name *FB PAC*. In an email to *The Hill*, a spokesman for Facebook said "Facebook Political Action Committee will give our employees a way to make their voice heard in the political process by supporting candidates who share our goals of promoting the value of innovation to our economy while giving people the power to share and make the world more open and connected."

During the Syrian civil war, the YPG, a libertarian army for Rojava has recruited westerners through Facebook in its fight against ISIL. Dozens have joined its ranks for various reasons from religious to ideological. The Facebook page's name "The Lions of Rojava" comes from a Kurdish saying which translates as "A lion is a lion, whether it's a female or a male", reflecting the organisation's feminist ideology.

United States

Facebook's role in the American political process was demonstrated in January 2008, shortly before the New Hampshire primary, when Facebook teamed up with ABC and Saint Anselm College to allow users to give live feedback about the "back to back" January 5 Republican and Democratic debates. Facebook users took part in debate groups organized around specific topics, register to vote, and message questions.

Over a million people installed the Facebook application "US Politics on Facebook" in order to take part, and the application measured users' responses to specific comments made by the debating candidates. This debate showed the broader community what many young students had already experienced: Facebook as a popular and powerful new way to interact and voice opinions. A poll by CBS News, UWIRE and *The Chronicle of Higher Education* claimed to illustrate how the "Facebook effect" has affected youth voting rates, support by youth of political candidates, and general involvement by the youth population in the 2008 election.

The new social media, such as Facebook and Twitter, made use first of the personal computer and the Internet, and after 2010 of the smart phones to connect hundreds of millions of people, especially those under age 35. By 2008, politicians and interest groups were experimenting with systematic use of social media to spread their message among much larger audiences than they had previously reached.

Facebook is having an impact on local government as well. Justin Smith, a Colorado sheriff uses Facebook to disseminate his ideas on matters relating to local, state, and national concerns. He also publicizes crimes, particularly those that his department solves. He has seven thousand followers on the social medium, considered a large number. Smith said that he rarely goes out in public "when I don't get feedback from folks. ... Facebook is an interesting tool because I think it holds candidates and elected officials more accountable. Voters know where someone stands."

As American political strategists turn their attention to the 2016 presidential contest, they identify Facebook as an increasingly important advertising tool. Recent technical innovations have made possible more advanced divisions and subdivisions of the electorate. Most important, Facebook can now deliver video ads to small, highly targeted subsets. Television, by contrast, shows the same commercials to all viewers, and so cannot be precisely tailored.

Ban

In many countries the social networking sites and mobile apps have been blocked temporarily or permanently. In Bangladesh, the government has been blocking Facebook, WhatsApp, Tango, Viber and many other sites and apps since November 18, 2015.

In Popular Culture

Facebook parade float in San Francisco Pride 2014

- American author Ben Mezrich published a book in July 2009 about Zuckerberg and the founding of Facebook, titled *The Accidental Billionaires: The Founding of Facebook, A Tale of Sex, Money, Genius, and Betrayal*.

- *The Social Network*, a drama film directed by David Fincher and adapted from Mezrich's book, was released October 1, 2010. People portrayed in the movie, including Zuckerberg, have criticized its accuracy. However a search of IMDB will reveal this to be a movie produced as standard entertainment.

- In response to the Everybody Draw Mohammed Day controversy and the banning of the website in Pakistan, an Islamic version of the website was created, called MillatFacebook.

- "You Have 0 Friends", an April 2010 episode of the American animated comedy series, *South Park*, explicitly parodied Facebook.

- At age 102, Ivy Bean of Bradford, England joined Facebook in 2008, making her one of the oldest people ever on Facebook. At the time of her death in July 2010, she had 4,962 friends on Facebook and more than 56,000 followers on Twitter.

- On May 16, 2011, an Israeli couple named their daughter after the Facebook "like" feature.

- In July 2014, Shakira became the first celebrity to cross over 100 million likes, Cristiano Ronaldo is the second to reach 100 million likes, ahead of Rihanna and Eminem, who had 98 million and 89 million likes respectively. Mark Zuckerberg posted a congratulatory message on the artist's wall.

YouTube

The service was created by three former PayPal employees in February 2005. In November 2006, it was bought by Google for US$1.65 billion. YouTube now operates as one of Google's subsidiaries. The site allows users to upload, view, rate, share, and comment on videos, and it makes use of WebM, H.264/MPEG-4 AVC, and Adobe Flash Video technology to display a wide variety of user-generated and corporate media video. Available content includes video clips, TV clips, music videos, movie trailers, and other content such as video blogging, short original videos, and educational videos.

Most of the content on YouTube has been uploaded by individuals, but media corporations including CBS, the BBC, Vevo, Hulu, and other organizations offer some of their material via YouTube, as part of the YouTube partnership program. Unregistered users can watch videos, and registered users are permitted to upload an unlimited number of videos and add comments to videos. Videos deemed potentially offensive are available only to registered users affirming themselves to be at least 18 years old.

Company history

From left to right: Chad Hurley, Steve Chen, and Jawed Karim

YouTube was founded by Chad Hurley, Steve Chen, and Jawed Karim, who were all early employees of PayPal. Hurley had studied design at Indiana University of Pennsylvania, and Chen and Karim studied computer science together at the University of Illinois at Urbana-Champaign.

According to a story that has often been repeated in the media, Hurley and Chen developed the idea for YouTube during the early months of 2005, after they had experienced difficulty sharing videos that had been shot at a dinner party at Chen's apartment in San Francisco. Karim did not attend the party and denied that it had occurred, but Chen commented that the idea that YouTube was founded after a dinner party "was probably very strengthened by marketing ideas around creating a story that was very digestible".

The YouTube homepage as it appeared from April to June 2005

Karim said the inspiration for YouTube first came from Janet Jackson's role in the 2004 Super Bowl incident, when her breast was exposed during her performance, and later from the 2004 Indian Ocean tsunami. Karim could not easily find video clips of either event online, which led to the idea of a video sharing site. Hurley and Chen said that the original idea for YouTube was a video version of an online dating service, and had been influenced by the website Hot or Not.

The YouTube logo from launch until 2011, featuring its former slogan *Broadcast Yourself*

YouTube began as a venture-funded technology startup, primarily from a $11.5 million investment by Sequoia Capital between November 2005 and April 2006. YouTube's early headquarters were situated above a pizzeria and Japanese restaurant in San Mateo, California. The domain name www.youtube.com was activated on February 14, 2005, and the website was developed over the subsequent months.

The first YouTube video, titled *Me at the zoo*, shows co-founder Jawed Karim at the San Diego Zoo. The video was uploaded on April 23, 2005, and can still be viewed on the site.

YouTube offered the public a beta test of the site in May 2005. The first video to reach one million views was a Nike advertisement featuring Ronaldinho in September 2005. Following a $3.5 million investment from Sequoia Capital in November, the site launched officially on December 15, 2005, by which time the site was receiving 8 million views a day. The site grew rapidly, and in July 2006 the company announced that more than 65,000 new videos were being uploaded every day, and that the site was receiving 100 million video views per day. According to data published by market research company comScore, YouTube is the dominant provider of online video in the United States, with a market share of around 43% and more than 14 billion views of videos in May 2010.

In 2014 YouTube said that 300 hours of new videos were uploaded to the site every minute, three times more than one year earlier and that around three quarters of the material comes from outside the U.S. The site has 800 million unique users a month. It is estimated that in 2007 YouTube consumed as much bandwidth as the entire Internet in 2000. According to third-party web analytics providers, Alexa and SimilarWeb, YouTube is the third most visited website in the world, as of June 2015; SimilarWeb also lists YouTube as the top TV and video website globally, attracting more than 15 billion visitors per month.

The choice of the name www.youtube.com led to problems for a similarly named website, www.utube.com. The site's owner, Universal Tube & Rollform Equipment, filed a lawsuit against YouTube in November 2006 after being regularly overloaded by people looking for YouTube. Universal Tube has since changed the name of its website to www.utubeonline.com.

In October 2006, Google Inc. announced that it had acquired YouTube for $1.65 billion in Google stock, and the deal was finalized on November 13, 2006.

In March 2010, YouTube began free streaming of certain content, including 60 cricket matches of the Indian Premier League. According to YouTube, this was the first worldwide free online broadcast of a major sporting event.

On March 31, 2010, the YouTube website launched a new design, with the aim of simplifying the interface and increasing the time users spend on the site. Google product manager Shiva Rajaraman commented: "We really felt like we needed to step back and remove the clutter." In May 2010, it was reported that YouTube was serving more than two billion videos a day, which it described as "nearly double the prime-time audience of all three major US television networks combined". In May 2011, YouTube reported in its company blog that the site was receiving more than three billion views per day. In January 2012, YouTube stated that the figure had increased to four billion videos streamed per day.

YouTube's headquarters as of 2010 in San Bruno, California

In October 2010, Hurley announced that he would be stepping down as chief executive officer of YouTube to take an advisory role, and that Salar Kamangar would take over as head of the company.

In April 2011, James Zern, a YouTube software engineer, revealed that 30% of videos accounted for 99% of views on the site.

In November 2011, the Google+ social networking site was integrated directly with YouTube and the Chrome web browser, allowing YouTube videos to be viewed from within the Google+ interface.

In December 2011, YouTube launched a new version of the site interface, with the video channels displayed in a central column on the home page, similar to the news feeds of social networking sites. At the same time, a new version of the YouTube logo was introduced with a darker shade of red, the first change in design since October 2006.

In May 2013, YouTube launched a pilot program to begin offering some content providers the ability to charge $0.99 per month or more for certain channels, but the vast majority of its videos would remain free to view.

In February 2015, YouTube announced the launch of a new app specifically for use by children visiting the site, called YouTube Kids. It allows parental controls and restrictions on who can upload content, and is available for both Android and iOS devices. Later on August 26, 2015, YouTube Gaming was launched, a platform for video gaming enthusiasts intended to compete with Twitch.tv. 2015 also saw the announcement of a premium YouTube service titled YouTube Red, which provides users with both ad-free content as well as the ability to download videos among other features.

On August 10, 2015, Google announced that it was creating a new company, Alphabet, to act as the holding company for Google, with the change in financial reporting to begin in the fourth quarter of 2015. YouTube remains as a subsidiary of Google.

In January 2016, YouTube expanded its headquarters in San Bruno by purchasing an office park for $215 million. The complex has 554,000 square feet of space and can house up to 2,800 employees.

Features

Video Technology

Previously, viewing YouTube videos on a personal computer required the Adobe Flash Player plug-in to be installed in the browser.

In January 2010, YouTube launched an experimental version of the site that used the built-in multimedia capabilities of web browsers supporting the HTML5 standard. This allowed videos to be viewed without requiring Adobe Flash Player or any other plug-in to be installed. The YouTube site had a page that allowed supported browsers to opt into the HTML5 trial. Only browsers that supported HTML5 Video using the H.264 or WebM formats could play the videos, and not all videos on the site were available.

On January 27, 2015, YouTube announced that HTML5 will be the default playback method on supported browsers. Supported browsers include Google Chrome, Safari 8, and Internet Explorer 11.

YouTube experimented with Dynamic Adaptive Streaming over HTTP (MPEG-DASH), which is an adaptive bit-rate HTTP-based streaming solution optimizing the bitrate and quality for the available network. Currently they are using Adobe Dynamic Streaming for Flash.

Uploading

All YouTube users can upload videos up to 15 minutes each in duration. Users who have a good track record of complying with the site's Community Guidelines may be offered the ability to upload videos up to 12 hours in length, which requires verifying the account, normally through a mobile phone. When YouTube was launched in 2005, it was possible to upload long videos, but a ten-minute limit was introduced in March 2006 after YouTube found that the majority of videos exceeding this length were unauthorized uploads of television shows and films. The 10-minute limit was increased to 15 minutes in July 2010. If an up-to-date browser version is used, videos greater than 20 GB can be uploaded.

YouTube accepts videos uploaded in most container formats, including .AVI, .MKV, .MOV, .MP4, DivX, .FLV, and .ogg and .ogv. These include video formats such as MPEG-4, MPEG, VOB, and .WMV. It also supports 3GP, allowing videos to be uploaded from mobile phones. Videos with progressive scanning or interlaced scanning can be uploaded, but for the best video quality, YouTube suggests interlaced videos be deinterlaced before uploading. All the video formats on YouTube use progressive scanning.

Quality and Formats

YouTube originally offered videos at only one quality level, displayed at a resolution of 320×240 pixels using the Sorenson Spark codec (a variant of H.263), with mono MP3 audio. In June 2007, YouTube added an option to watch videos in 3GP format on mobile phones. In March 2008, a high-quality mode was added, which increased the resolution to 480×360 pixels.

In November 2008, 720p HD support was added. At the time of the 720p launch, the YouTube player was changed from a 4:3 aspect ratio to a widescreen 16:9. With this new feature, YouTube began a switchover to H.264/MPEG-4 AVC as its default video compression format. In November 2009, 1080p HD support was added. In July 2010, YouTube announced that it had launched a range of videos in 4K format, which allows a resolution of up to 4096×3072 pixels. In June 2015, support for 8K resolution was added, with the videos playing at 7680×4320 pixels.

In June 2014, YouTube introduced videos playing at 60 frames per second, in order to reproduce video games with a frame rate comparable to high-end graphics cards. The videos play back at a resolution of 720p or higher.

YouTube videos are available in a range of quality levels. The former names of standard quality (SQ), high quality (HQ) and high definition (HD) have been replaced by numerical values representing the vertical resolution of the video. The default video stream is encoded in the VP9 format with stereo Opus audio; if VP9/WebM is not supported in the browser/device or the browser's user agent reports Windows XP, then H.264/MPEG-4 AVC video with stereo AAC audio is used instead.

Comparison of YouTube media encoding options.

itag value	Default container	Video resolution	Video encoding	Video profile	Video bitrate (Mbit/s)	Audio encoding	Audio bitrate (kbit/s)
17	3GP	144p	MPEG-4 Visual	Simple	0.05	AAC	24
36	3GP	240p	MPEG-4 Visual	Simple	0.175	AAC	32
5	FLV	240p	Sorenson H.263	N/A	0.25	MP3	64
18	MP4	360p	H.264	Baseline	0.5	AAC	96
22	MP4	720p	H.264	High	2-3	AAC	192
43	WebM	360p	VP8	N/A	0.5	Vorbis	128

itag value	Default container	Video resolution	Video encoding	Video profile	Video bitrate (Mbit/s)
160		144p 15 fps			0.1
133		240p			0.2–0.3
134		360p			0.3–0.4
135		480p		Main	0.5–1
136		720p			1–1.5
298	MP4	720p HFR	H.264		3–3.5
137		1080p			2.5–3
299		1080p HFR			5.5
264		1440p		High	4–4.5
266		2160p–2304p			12.5–16
138		2160p–4320p			13.5–25
278		144p 15 fps			0.08
242		240p			0.1–0.2
243		360p			0.25
244		480p			0.5
247		720p			0.7–0.8
248		1080p			1.5
271	WebM	1440p	VP9	n/a	9
313		2160p			13–15
302		720p HFR			2.5
303		1080p HFR			5
308		1440p HFR			10
315		2160p HFR			20–25

itag value	Default container	Video resolution	Video encoding	Video profile	Video bitrate (Mbit/s)	Audio encoding	Audio bitrate (kbit/s)
82	MP4	360p	H.264	3D	0.5	AAC	96
83	MP4	240p	H.264	3D	0.5	AAC	96
84	MP4	720p	H.264	3D	2-3	AAC	192
85	MP4	1080p	H.264	3D	3-4	AAC	192
100	WebM	360p	VP8	3D	N/A	Vorbis	128

itag value	Default container	Audio encoding	Audio bitrate (kbit/s)
140	M4A	AAC	128
141	M4A	AAC	256
171	WebM	Vorbis	128
249	WebM	Opus	48
250	WebM	Opus	64
251	WebM	Opus	160

itag value	Default container	Video resolution	Video encoding	Video profile	Video bitrate (Mbit/s)	Audio encoding	Audio bitrate (kbit/s)
132	240p	H.264	Baseline	0.15–0.2	48		
151	72p	H.264	Baseline	0.05	24		
92	TS	240p	H.264	Main	0.15–0.3	AAC	48
93		360p	H.264	Main	0.5–1		128
94		480p	H.264	Main	0.8–1.25		128
95		720p	H.264	Main	1.5–3		256
96		1080p	H.264	High	2.5–6		256
127 / 128		Audio Only	N/A	N/A	N/A		96

3D videos

In a video posted on July 21, 2009, YouTube software engineer Peter Bradshaw announced that YouTube users can now upload 3D videos. The videos can be viewed in several different ways, including the common anaglyph (cyan/red lens) method which utilizes glasses worn by the viewer to achieve the 3D effect. The YouTube Flash player can display stereoscopic content interleaved in rows, columns or a checkerboard pattern, side-by-side or anaglyph using a red/cyan, green/magenta or blue/yellow combination. In May 2011, an HTML5 version of the YouTube player began supporting side-by-side 3D footage that is compatible with Nvidia 3D Vision.

360° videos

In January 2015, Google announced that 360° videos would be natively supported on YouTube. On March 13, 2015, YouTube enabled 360° videos which can be viewed from Google Cardboard.

Content Accessibility

YouTube offers users the ability to view its videos on web pages outside their website. Each YouTube video is accompanied by a piece of HTML that can be used to embed it on any page on the Web. This functionality is often used to embed YouTube videos in social networking pages and blogs. Users wishing to post a video discussing, inspired by or related to another user's video are able to make a "video response". On August 27, 2013, YouTube announced that it would remove video responses for being an underused feature. Embedding, rating, commenting and response posting can be disabled by the video owner.

YouTube does not usually offer a download link for its videos, and intends for them to be viewed through its website interface. A small number of videos, such as the weekly addresses by President Barack Obama, can be downloaded as MP4 files. Numerous third-party web sites, applications and browser plug-ins allow users to download YouTube videos. In February 2009, YouTube announced a test service, allowing some partners to offer video downloads for free or for a fee paid through Google Checkout. In June 2012, Google sent cease and desist letters threatening legal action against several websites offering online download and conversion of YouTube videos. In response, Zamzar removed the ability to download YouTube videos from its site. The default settings when uploading a video to YouTube will retain a copyright on the video for the uploader, but since July 2012 it has been possible to select a Creative Commons license as the default, allowing other users to reuse and remix the material if it is free of copyright.

Platforms

Most modern smartphones are capable of accessing YouTube videos, either within an application or through an optimized website. YouTube Mobile was launched in June 2007, using RTSP streaming for the video. Not all of YouTube's videos are available on the mobile version of the site.

Since June 2007, YouTube's videos have been available for viewing on a range of Apple products. This required YouTube's content to be transcoded into Apple's preferred video standard, H.264, a process that took several months. YouTube videos can be viewed on devices including Apple TV, iPod Touch and the iPhone. In July 2010, the mobile version of the site was relaunched based on HTML5, avoiding the need to use Adobe Flash Player and optimized for use with touch screen controls. The mobile version is also available as an app for the Android platform. In September 2012, YouTube launched its first app for the iPhone, following the decision to drop YouTube as one of the preloaded apps in the iPhone 5 and iOS 6 operating system. According to GlobalWebIndex, YouTube was used by 35% of smartphone users between April and June 2013, making it the third most used app.

A TiVo service update in July 2008 allowed the system to search and play YouTube videos. In January 2009, YouTube launched "YouTube for TV", a version of the website tailored for set-top boxes and other TV-based media devices with web browsers, initially allowing its videos to be viewed on the PlayStation 3 and Wii video game consoles. In June 2009, YouTube XL was introduced, which has a simplified interface designed for viewing on a standard television screen. YouTube is also available as an app on Xbox Live. On November 15, 2012, Google launched an official app for the Wii, allowing users to watch YouTube videos from the Wii channel. An app is also available for Wii U and Nintendo 3DS, and videos can be viewed on the Wii U Internet Browser using HTML5. Google made YouTube available on the Roku player on December 17, 2013 and in October 2014, the Sony PlayStation 4.

Localization

On June 19, 2007, Google CEO Eric Schmidt was in Paris to launch the new localization system.

The interface of the website is available with localized versions in 88 countries, one territory (Hong Kong) and a worldwide version.

Country	Language	Launch date
USA (and worldwide launch)	English	February 15, 2005
Brazil	Portuguese	June 19, 2007
France	French, and Basque	June 19, 2007
Ireland	English	June 19, 2007
Italy	Italian	June 19, 2007
Japan	Japanese	June 19, 2007
Netherlands	Dutch	June 19, 2007
Poland	Polish	June 19, 2007
Spain	Spanish, Galician, Catalan, and Basque	June 19, 2007
United Kingdom	English	June 19, 2007
Mexico	Spanish	October 11, 2007
Hong Kong	Chinese, and English	October 17, 2007
Taiwan	Chinese	October 18, 2007
Australia	English	October 22, 2007
New Zealand	English	October 22, 2007
Canada	French, and English	November 6, 2007
Germany	German	November 8, 2007
Russia	Russian	November 13, 2007
South Korea	Korean	January 23, 2008
India	Hindi, Bengali, English, Gujarati, Kannada, Malayalam, Marathi, Tamil, Telugu, and Urdu	May 7, 2008
Israel	Hebrew	September 16, 2008
Czech Republic	Czech	October 9, 2008
Sweden	Swedish	October 22, 2008
South Africa	Afrikaans, Zulu, and English	May 17, 2010
Argentina	Spanish	September 8, 2010
Algeria	French, and Arabic	March 9, 2011
Egypt	Arabic	March 9, 2011
Jordan	Arabic	March 9, 2011

Country	Language	Launch date
Morocco	French, and Arabic	March 9, 2011
Saudi Arabia	Arabic	March 9, 2011
Tunisia	French, and Arabic	March 9, 2011
Yemen	Arabic	March 9, 2011
Kenya	Swahili, and English	September 1, 2011
Philippines	Filipino, and English	October 13, 2011
Singapore	English, Malay, Chinese, and Tamil	October 20, 2011
Belgium	French, Dutch, and German	November 16, 2011
Colombia	Spanish	November 30, 2011
Uganda	English	December 2, 2011
Nigeria	English	December 7, 2011
Chile	Spanish	January 20, 2012
Hungary	Hungarian	February 29, 2012
Malaysia	Malay, and English	March 22, 2012
Peru	Spanish	March 25, 2012
United Arab Emirates	Arabic, and English	April 1, 2012
Greece	Greek	May 1, 2012
Indonesia	Indonesian, and English	May 17, 2012
Ghana	English	June 5, 2012
Senegal	French, and English	July 4, 2012
Turkey	Turkish	October 1, 2012
Ukraine	Ukrainian	December 13, 2012
Denmark	Danish	February 1, 2013
Finland	Finnish, and Swedish	February 1, 2013
Norway	Norwegian	February 1, 2013
Switzerland	German, French, and Italian	March 29, 2013
Austria	German	March 29, 2013
Romania	Romanian	April 18, 2013
Portugal	Portuguese	April 25, 2013
Slovakia	Slovak	April 25, 2013
Bahrain	Arabic	August 16, 2013
Kuwait	Arabic	August 16, 2013

Country	Language	Launch date
Oman	Arabic	August 16, 2013
Qatar	Arabic	August 16, 2013
Bosnia and Herzegovina	Bosnian, Croatian, and Serbian	March 17, 2014
Bulgaria	Bulgarian	March 17, 2014
Croatia	Croatian	March 17, 2014
Estonia	Estonian	March 17, 2014
Latvia	Latvian	March 17, 2014
Lithuania	Lithuanian	March 17, 2014
Macedonia	Macedonian, Serbian, and Turkish	March 17, 2014
Montenegro	Serbian, and Croatian	March 17, 2014
Serbia	Serbian	March 17, 2014
Slovenia	Slovenian	March 17, 2014
Thailand	Thai	April 1, 2014
Lebanon	Arabic	May 1, 2014
Puerto Rico	Spanish, and English	August 23, 2014
Iceland	Icelandic	?, 2014
Luxembourg	French, and German	?, 2014
Vietnam	Vietnamese	October 1, 2014
Libya	Arabic	February 1, 2015
Tanzania	Swahili, and English	June 2, 2015
Zimbabwe	English	June 2, 2015
Azerbaijan	Azerbaijani	October 12, 2015
Belarus	Russian	October 12, 2015
Georgia	Georgian	October 12, 2015
Kazakhstan	Kazakh	October 12, 2015
Nepal	Nepali	January 12, 2016
Pakistan	Urdu, and English	January 12, 2016
Sri Lanka	Sinhala, and Tamil	January 12, 2016

Country	Language	Launch date
Iraq	Arabic	?, 2016

The YouTube interface suggests which local version should be chosen on the basis of the IP address of the user. In some cases, the message "This video is not available in your country" may appear because of copyright restrictions or inappropriate content.

The interface of the YouTube website is available in 76 language versions, including Amharic, Albanian, Armenian, Bengali, Burmese, Khmer, Kyrgyz, Laotian, Mongolian, Persian and Uzbek, which do not have local channel versions.

Access to YouTube was blocked in Turkey between 2008 and 2010, following controversy over the posting of videos deemed insulting to Mustafa Kemal Atatürk and some material offensive to Muslims. In October 2012, a local version of YouTube was launched in Turkey, with the domain youtube.com.tr. The local version is subject to the content regulations found in Turkish law.

In March 2009, a dispute between YouTube and the British royalty collection agency PRS for Music led to premium music videos being blocked for YouTube users in the United Kingdom. The removal of videos posted by the major record companies occurred after failure to reach agreement on a licensing deal. The dispute was resolved in September 2009. In April 2009, a similar dispute led to the removal of premium music videos for users in Germany.

Youtube Red

YouTube Red is YouTube's premium subscription service. It offers advertising-free streaming, access to exclusive content, background and offline video playback on mobile devices, and access to the Google Play Music "All Access" service. YouTube Red was originally announced on November 12, 2014, as "Music Key", a subscription music streaming service, and was intended to integrate with and replace the existing Google Play Music "All Access" service. On October 28, 2015, the service was re-launched as YouTube Red, offering ad-free streaming of all videos, as well as access to exclusive original content.

Social Impact

Both private individuals and large production companies have used YouTube to grow audiences. Independent content creators have built grassroots followings numbering in the thousands at very little cost or effort, while mass retail and radio promotion proved problematic. Concurrently, old media celebrities moved into the website at the invitation of a YouTube management that witnessed early content creators accruing substantial followings, and perceived audience sizes potentially larger than that attainable by television. While YouTube's revenue-sharing "Partner Program" made it possible to earn a substantial living as a video producer—its top five hundred partners each earning more than $100,000 annually and its ten highest-earning channels grossing from $2.5 million to $12 million—in 2012 CMU business editor characterized YouTube as "a free-to-use... promotional platform for the music labels". In 2013 *Forbes'* Katheryn Thayer asserted that digital-era artists' work must not only be of high quality, but must elicit reactions on the YouTube platform and social media. In 2013, videos of the 2.5% of artists categorized as "mega", "mainstream" and "mid-sized" received 90.3% of the relevant views on YouTube and Vevo. By early 2013 *Billboard* had announced that it was factoring YouTube streaming data into calculation of the *Billboard* Hot 100 and related genre charts.

Observing that face-to-face communication of the type that online videos convey has been "fine-tuned by millions of years of evolution", TED curator Chris Anderson referred to several YouTube contributors and asserted that "what Gutenberg did for writing, online video can now do for face-to-face communication". Anderson asserted that it's not far-fetched to say that online video will dramatically accelerate scientific advance, and that video contributors may be about to launch "the biggest learning cycle in human history." In education, for example, the Khan Academy grew from YouTube video tutoring sessions for founder Salman Khan's cousin into what *Forbes'* Michael Noer called "the largest school in the world", with technology poised to disrupt how people learn.

Jordan Hoffner at the 68th Annual Peabody Awards accepting for YouTube

YouTube was awarded a 2008 George Foster Peabody Award, the website being described as a Speakers' Corner that "both embodies and promotes democracy." *The Washington Post* reported that a disproportionate share of YouTube's most subscribed channels feature minorities, contrasting with mainstream television in which the stars are largely white.

A Pew Research Center study reported the development of "visual journalism", in which citizen eyewitnesses and established news organizations share in content creation. The study also concluded that YouTube was becoming an important platform by which people acquire news.

YouTube has enabled people to more directly engage with government, such as in the CNN/YouTube presidential debates (2007) in which ordinary people submitted questions to U.S. presidential candidates via YouTube video, with a techPresident co-founder saying that Internet video was changing the political landscape. Describing the Arab Spring (2010-), sociologist Philip N. Howard quoted an activist's succinct description that organizing the political unrest involved using "Facebook to schedule the protests, Twitter to coordinate, and YouTube to tell the world." In 2012, more than a third of the U.S. Senate introduced a resolution condemning Joseph Kony 16 days after the "Kony 2012" video was posted to YouTube, with resolution co-sponsor Senator Lindsey Graham remarking that the video "will do more to lead to (Kony's) demise than all other action combined."

Leading YouTube content creators met at the White House with U.S. President Obama to discuss how government could better connect with the "YouTube generation".

Conversely, YouTube has also allowed government to more easily engage with citizens, the White House's official YouTube channel being the seventh top news organization producer on YouTube in 2012 and in 2013 a healthcare exchange commissioned Obama impersonator Iman Crosson's YouTube music video spoof to encourage young Americans to enroll in the Affordable Care Act (Obamacare)-compliant health insurance. In February 2014, U.S. President Obama held a meeting at the White House with leading YouTube content creators to not only promote awareness of Obamacare but more generally to develop ways for government to better connect with the "YouTube Generation". Whereas YouTube's inherent ability to allow presidents to directly connect with average citizens was noted, the YouTube content creators' new media savvy was perceived necessary to better cope with the website's distracting content and fickle audience.

Some YouTube videos have themselves had a direct effect on world events, such as *Innocence of Muslims* (2012) which spurred protests and related anti-American violence internationally.

TED curator Chris Anderson described a phenomenon by which geographically distributed individuals in a certain field share their independently developed skills in YouTube videos, thus challenging others to improve their own skills, and spurring invention and evolution in that field. Journalist Virginia Heffernan stated in *The New York Times* that such videos have "surprising implications" for the dissemination of culture and even the future of classical music.

The Legion of Extraordinary Dancers and the YouTube Symphony Orchestra selected their membership based on individual video performances. Further, the cybercollaboration charity video "We Are the World 25 for Haiti (YouTube edition)" was formed by mixing performances of 57 globally distributed singers into a single musical work, with *The Tokyo Times* noting the "We Pray for You" YouTube cyber-collaboration video as an example of a trend to use crowdsourcing for charitable purposes.

The anti-bullying It Gets Better Project expanded from a single YouTube video directed to discouraged or suicidal LGBT teens, that within two months drew video responses from hundreds including U.S. President Barack Obama, Vice President Biden, White House staff, and several cabinet secretaries. Similarly, in response to fifteen-year-old Amanda Todd's video "My story: Struggling, bullying, suicide, self-harm", legislative action was undertaken almost immediately after her suicide to study the prevalence of bullying and form a national anti-bullying strategy.

Revenue

Google does not provide detailed figures for YouTube's running costs, and YouTube's revenues in 2007 were noted as "not material" in a regulatory filing. In June 2008, a *Forbes* magazine article projected the 2008 revenue at $200 million, noting progress in advertising sales. In January 2012, it was estimated that visitors to YouTube spent an average of 15 minutes a day on the site, in contrast to the four or five hours a day spent by a typical U.S. citizen watching television. In 2012, YouTube's revenue from its ads program was estimated at 3.7 billion. In 2013 it nearly doubled and estimated to hit 5.6 billion dollars according to eMarketer, others estimated 4.7 billion,

The vast majority of videos on YouTube are free to view and supported by advertising. In May 2013, YouTube introduced a trial scheme of 53 subscription channels with prices ranging from $0.99 to $6.99 a month. The move was seen as an attempt to compete with other providers of online subscription services such as Netflix and Hulu.

Advertisement Partnerships

YouTube entered into a marketing and advertising partnership with NBC in June 2006. In November 2008, YouTube reached an agreement with MGM, Lions Gate Entertainment, and CBS, allowing the companies to post full-length films and television episodes on the site, accompanied by advertisements in a section for US viewers called "Shows". The move was intended to create competition with websites such as Hulu, which features material from NBC, Fox, and Disney. In November 2009, YouTube launched a version of "Shows" available to UK viewers, offering around 4,000 full-length shows from more than 60 partners. In January 2010, YouTube introduced an online film rentals service, which is available only to users in the US, Canada and the UK as of 2010. The service offers over 6,000 films.

Partnership with Video Creators

In May 2007, YouTube launched its Partner Program, a system based on AdSense which allows the uploader of the video to share the revenue produced by advertising on the site. YouTube typically takes 45 percent of the advertising revenue from videos in the Partner Program, with 55 percent going to the uploader. There are over a million members of the YouTube Partner Program. According to TubeMogul, in 2013 a pre-roll advertisement on YouTube cost advertisers on average $7.60 per 1000 views. Usually no more than half of eligible videos have a pre-roll advertisement, due to a lack of interested advertisers. Assuming pre-roll advertisements on half of videos, a YouTube partner would earn 0.5 X $7.60 X 55% = $2.09 per 1000 views in 2013.

Revenue to Copyright Holders

Much of YouTube's revenue goes to the copyright holders of the videos. In 2010 it was reported that nearly a third of the videos with advertisements were uploaded without permission of the copyright holders. YouTube gives an option for copyright holders to locate and remove their videos or to have them continue running for revenue. In May 2013, Nintendo began enforcing its copyright ownership and claiming the advertising revenue from video creators who posted screenshots of its games. In February 2015, Nintendo agreed to share the revenue with the video creators.

Community Policy

YouTube has a set of community guidelines aimed to reduce abuse of the site's features. Generally prohibited material includes sexually explicit content, videos of animal abuse, shock videos, content uploaded without the copyright holder's consent, hate speech, spam, and predatory behaviour. Despite the guidelines, YouTube has faced criticism from news sources for content in violation of these guidelines.

Copyrighted Material

At the time of uploading a video, YouTube users are shown a message asking them not to violate copyright laws. Despite this advice, there are still many unauthorized clips of copyrighted material on YouTube. YouTube does not view videos before they are posted online, and it is left to copyright holders to issue a DMCA takedown notice pursuant to the terms of the Online Copyright Infringement Liability Limitation Act. Any successful complaint about copyright infringement results in a YouTube copyright strike. Three successful complaints for copyright infringement against a user account will result in the account and all of its uploaded videos being deleted.

Organizations including Viacom, Mediaset, and the English Premier League have filed lawsuits against YouTube, claiming that it has done too little to prevent the uploading of copyrighted material. Viacom, demanding $1 billion in damages, said that it had found more than 150,000 unauthorized clips of its material on YouTube that had been viewed "an astounding 1.5 billion times". YouTube responded by stating that it *"goes far beyond its legal obligations in assisting content owners to protect their works"*.

During the same court battle, Viacom won a court ruling requiring YouTube to hand over 12 terabytes of data detailing the viewing habits of every user who has watched videos on the site. The decision was criticized by the Electronic Frontier Foundation, which called the court ruling "a setback to privacy rights". In June 2010, Viacom's lawsuit against Google was rejected in a summary judgment, with U.S. federal Judge Louis L. Stanton stating that Google was protected by provisions of the Digital Millennium Copyright Act. Viacom announced its intention to appeal the ruling.

On April 5, 2012, the United States Court of Appeals for the Second Circuit reinstated the case, allowing Viacom's lawsuit against Google to be heard in court again. On March 18, 2014, the lawsuit was settled after seven years with an undisclosed agreement.

In August 2008, a US court ruled in *Lenz v. Universal Music Corp.* that copyright holders cannot order the removal of an online file without first determining whether the posting reflected fair use of the material. The case involved Stephanie Lenz from Gallitzin, Pennsylvania, who had made a home video of her 13-month-old son dancing to Prince's song "Let's Go Crazy", and posted the 29-second video on YouTube.

In the case of *Smith v. Summit Entertainment LLC*, professional singer Matt Smith sued Summit Entertainment for the wrongful use of copyright takedown notices on YouTube. He asserted seven causes of action, and four were ruled in Smith's favor.

In April 2012, a court in Hamburg ruled that YouTube could be held responsible for copyrighted material posted by its users. The performance rights organization GEMA argued that YouTube had not done enough to prevent the uploading of German copyrighted music. YouTube responded by stating:

As of 2013, YouTube and GEMA have still not reached a licensing agreement. As a result, most videos containing copyrighted music have been blocked in Germany since 2009.

In April 2013, it was reported that Universal Music Group and YouTube have a contractual agreement that prevents content blocked on YouTube by a request from UMG from being restored, even if the uploader of the video files a DMCA counter-notice. When a dispute occurs, the uploader of the video has to contact UMG.

YouTube's owner Google announced in November 2015 that they would help cover the legal cost in select cases where they believe "fair use" laws apply.

Content ID

In June 2007, YouTube began trials of a system for automatic detection of uploaded videos that infringe copyright. Google CEO Eric Schmidt regarded this system as necessary for resolving lawsuits such as the one from Viacom, which alleged that YouTube profited from content that it did not have the right to distribute. The system, which became known as Content ID, creates an ID File for copyrighted audio and video material, and stores it in a database. When a video is uploaded, it is checked against the database, and flags the video as a copyright violation if a match is found.

When this occurs, the content owner has the choice of blocking the video to make it unviewable, tracking the viewing statistics of the video, or adding advertisements to the video. YouTube describes Content ID as "very accurate in finding uploads that look similar to reference files that are of sufficient length and quality to generate an effective ID File". Content ID accounts for over a third of the monetized views on YouTube.

An independent test in 2009 uploaded multiple versions of the same song to YouTube, and concluded that while the system was "surprisingly resilient" in finding copyright violations in the audio tracks of videos, it was not infallible. The use of Content ID to remove material automatically has led to controversy in some cases, as the videos have not been checked by a human for fair use. If a YouTube user disagrees with a decision by Content ID, it is possible to fill in a form disputing the decision. YouTube has cited the effectiveness of Content ID as one of the reasons why the site's rules were modified in December 2010 to allow some users to upload videos of unlimited length.

Controversial Content

YouTube has also faced criticism over the offensive content in some of its videos. The uploading of videos containing defamation, pornography, and material encouraging criminal conduct is prohibited by YouTube's terms of service. Controversial content has included material relating to Holocaust denial and the Hillsborough disaster, in which 96 football fans from Liverpool were crushed to death in 1989.

YouTube relies on its users to flag the content of videos as inappropriate, and a YouTube employee will view a flagged video to determine whether it violates the site's terms of service. In July 2008, the Culture and Media Committee of the House of Commons of the United Kingdom stated that it was "unimpressed" with YouTube's system for policing its videos, and argued that "proactive review of content should be standard practice for sites hosting user-generated content". YouTube responded by stating:

We have strict rules on what's allowed, and a system that enables anyone who sees inappropriate content to report it to our 24/7 review team and have it dealt with promptly. We educate our community on the rules and include a direct link from every YouTube page to make this process as easy as possible for our users. Given the volume of content uploaded on our site, we think this is by far the most effective way to make sure that the tiny minority of videos that break the rules come down quickly. (July 2008)

In October 2010, U.S. Congressman Anthony Weiner urged YouTube to remove from its website videos of imam Anwar al-Awlaki. YouTube pulled some of the videos in November 2010, stating they violated the site's guidelines. In December 2010, YouTube added "promotes terrorism" to the list of reasons that users can give when flagging a video as inappropriate.

User Comments

Most videos enable users to leave comments, and these have attracted attention for the negative aspects of both their form and content. In 2006, *Time* praised Web 2.0 for enabling "community and collaboration on a scale never seen before", and added that YouTube "harnesses the stupidity of crowds as well as its wisdom. Some of the comments on YouTube make you weep for the future of humanity just for the spelling alone, never mind the obscenity and the naked hatred". *The Guardian* in 2009 described users' comments on YouTube as:

In September 2008, *The Daily Telegraph* commented that YouTube was "notorious" for "some of the most confrontational and ill-formed comment exchanges on the internet", and reported on YouTube Comment Snob, "a new piece of software that blocks rude and illiterate posts". *The Huffington Post* noted in April 2012 that finding comments on YouTube that appear "offensive, stupid and crass" to the "vast majority" of the people is hardly difficult.

On November 6, 2013, Google implemented a new comment system that requires all YouTube users to use a Google+ account in order to comment on videos and making the comment system Google+ oriented. The changes are in large part an attempt to address the frequent criticisms of the quality and tone of YouTube comments. They give creators more power to moderate and block comments, and add new sorting mechanisms to ensure that better, more relevant discussions appear at the top. The new system restored the ability to include URLs in comments, which had previously been removed due to problems with abuse. In response, YouTube co-founder Jawed Karim posted the question "why the fuck do I need a google+ account to comment on a video?" on his YouTube channel to express his negative opinion of the change. The official YouTube announcement received 20,097 "thumbs down" votes and generated more than 32,000 comments in two days. Writing in the *Newsday* blog Silicon Island, Chase Melvin noted that "Google+ is nowhere near as popular a social media network as Facebook, but it's essentially being forced upon millions of YouTube users who don't want to lose their ability to comment on videos" and "Discussion forums across the Internet are already bursting with outcry against the new comment system". In the same article Melvin goes on to say:

On July 27, 2015, Google announced in a blog post that it would be removing the requirement to sign up to a Google+ account to post comments to YouTube.

View Counts

In December 2012, two billion views were removed from the view counts of Universal and Sony music videos on YouTube, prompting a claim by *The Daily Dot* that the views had been deleted due to a violation of the site's terms of service, which ban the use of automated processes to inflate view counts. This was disputed by *Billboard*, which said that the two billion views had been moved to Vevo, since the videos were no longer active on YouTube.

On August 5, 2015, YouTube removed the feature of the site which caused a video's view count to freeze at "301" (later "301+") until the actual count was verified to prevent view count fraud. YouTube view counts now update in real time.

Censorship and Filtering

As of September 2012, countries with standing national bans on YouTube include China, Iran, and Turkmenistan.

YouTube is blocked for a variety of reasons, including:

- limiting public exposure to content that may ignite social or political unrest;
- preventing criticism of a ruler, government, government officials, religion, or religious leaders;

- violations of national laws, including:

    o copyright and intellectual property protection laws;

    o violations of hate speech, ethics, or morality-based laws; and

    o national security legislation.

- preventing access to videos judged to be inappropriate for youth;

- reducing distractions at work or school; and

- reducing the amount of network bandwidth used.

In some countries, YouTube is completely blocked, either through a long term standing ban or for more limited periods of time such as during periods of unrest, the run-up to an election, or in response to upcoming political anniversaries. In other countries access to the website as a whole remains open, but access to specific videos is blocked. In cases where the entire site is banned due to one particular video, YouTube will often agree to remove or limit access to that video in order to restore service.

Businesses, schools, government agencies, and other private institutions often block social media sites, including YouTube, due to bandwidth limitations and the site's potential for distraction.

Several countries have blocked access to YouTube:

- Iran temporarily blocked access on December 3, 2006, to YouTube and several other sites, after declaring them as violating social and moral codes of conduct. The YouTube block came after a video was posted online that appeared to show an Iranian soap opera star having sex. The block was later lifted and then reinstated after Iran's 2009 presidential election. In 2012, Iran reblocked access, along with access to Google, after the controversial film *Innocence of Muslims'* trailer was released on YouTube.

- Thailand blocked access between 2006 and 2007 due to offensive videos relating to King Bhumibol Adulyadej.

- Some Australian state education departments block YouTube citing "an inability to determine what sort of video material might be accessed" and "There's no educational value to it and the content of the material on the site."

- China blocked access from October 15, 2007, to March 22, 2008, and again starting on March 24, 2009. Access remains blocked.

- Morocco blocked access in May 2007, possibly as a result of videos critical of Morocco's actions in Western Sahara. YouTube became accessible again on May 30, 2007, after *Maroc Telecom* unofficially announced that the denied access to the website was a mere "technical glitch".

- Turkey blocked access between 2008 and 2010 after controversy over videos deemed insulting to Mustafa Kemal Atatürk. In November 2010, a video of the Turkish politician Deniz Baykal caused the site to be blocked again briefly, and the site was threatened with a new shutdown if it did not remove the video. During the two and a half year block of YouTube, the video-sharing website remained the eighth most-accessed site in Turkey. In 2014, Turkey blocked the access for the second time, after "a high-level intelligence leak."

- Pakistan blocked access on February 23, 2008, because of "offensive material" towards the Islamic faith, including display of the Danish cartoons of Muhammad. This led to a near global blackout of the YouTube site for around two hours, as the Pakistani block was inadvertently transferred to other countries. On February 26, 2008, the ban was lifted after the website had removed the objectionable content from its servers at the request of the government. Many Pakistanis circumvented the three-day block by using virtual private network software. In May 2010, following the Everybody Draw Mohammed Day, Pakistan again blocked access to YouTube, citing "growing sacrilegious content". The ban was lifted on May 27, 2010, after the website removed the objectionable content from its servers at the request of the government. However, individual videos deemed offensive to Muslims posted on YouTube will continue to be blocked. Pakistan again placed a ban on YouTube in September 2012, after the site refused to remove the film *Innocence of Muslims*, with the ban still in operation as of September 2013. The ban was lifted in January 2016 after YouTube launched a Pakistan-specific version.

- Turkmenistan blocked access on December 25, 2009, for unknown reasons. Other websites, such as LiveJournal were also blocked.

- Libya blocked access on January 24, 2010, because of videos that featured demonstrations in the city of Benghazi by families of detainees who were killed in Abu Salim prison in 1996, and videos of family members of Libyan leader Muammar Gaddafi at parties. The blocking was criticized by Human Rights Watch. In November 2011, after the Libyan Civil War, YouTube was once again allowed in Libya.

- Afghanistan, Bangladesh, Russia, and Sudan blocked access in September 2012 following controversy over a 14-minute trailer for the film *Innocence of Muslims* which had been posted on the site.

- In Libya and Egypt, the *Innocence of Muslims* trailer was blamed for violent protests in September 2012. YouTube stated that "This video—which is widely available on the Web—is clearly within our guidelines and so will stay on YouTube. However, given the very difficult situation in Libya and Egypt we have temporarily restricted access in both countries."

Music Key Licensing

In May 2014, prior to the launch of YouTube's subscription-based Music Key service, the independent music trade organization Worldwide Independent Network alleged that YouTube was using non-negotiable contracts with independent labels that were "undervalued" in comparison to other streaming services, and that YouTube would block all music content from labels who do not reach a deal to be included on the paid service. In a statement to the *Financial Times* in June 2014, Robert Kyncl confirmed that YouTube would block the content of labels who do not negotiate deals to be included in the paid service "to ensure that all content on the platform is governed by its new contractual terms." Stating that 90% of labels had reached deals, he went on to say that "while we wish that we had [a] 100% success rate, we understand that is not likely an achievable goal and therefore it is our responsibility to our users and the industry to launch the enhanced music experience." The *Financial Times* later reported that YouTube had reached an aggregate deal with Merlin Network—a trade group representing over 20,000 independent labels, for their inclusion in the service. However, YouTube itself has not confirmed the deal.

April Fools

YouTube has featured an April Fools prank on the site on April 1 of every year since 2008:

- 2008: All the links to the videos on the main page were redirected to Rick Astley's music video "Never Gonna Give You Up", a prank known as "Rickrolling".

- 2009: When clicking on a video on the main page, the whole page turned upside down. YouTube claimed that this was a new layout.

- 2010: YouTube temporarily released a "TEXTp" mode, which translated the colors in the videos to random upper case letters. YouTube claimed in a message that this was done in order to reduce bandwidth costs by $1 per second.

- 2011: The site celebrated its "100th anniversary" with a "1911 button" and a range of sepia-toned silent, early 1900s-style films, including "Flugelhorn Feline", a parody of Keyboard Cat.

- 2012: Clicking on the image of a DVD next to the site logo led to a video about "The YouTube Collection", an option to order every YouTube video for home delivery on DVD, videocassette, Laserdisc, or Betamax tapes. The spoof promotional video touted "the complete YouTube experience completely offline."

- 2013: YouTube teamed up with newspaper satire company *The Onion* to claim that the video sharing website was launched as a contest which had finally come to an end, and would announce a winner of the contest when the site went back up in 2023. A video of two presenters announcing the nominees streamed live for twelve hours.

- 2014: YouTube announced that it was responsible for the creation of all viral video trends, and revealed previews of upcoming memes, such as "Clocking", "Kissing Dad", and "Glub Glub Water Dance".

- 2015: YouTube added a music button to the video bar that played samples from "Sandstorm" by Darude. Additionally, when users searched for a song title, a message would appear saying "Did you mean: Darude – Sandstorm by Darude".

- 2016: YouTube announced "SnoopaVision Beta", telling their users that soon they would have the option to watch every video on the platform in 360 degree mode with Snoop Dogg.

Viral Marketing

Viral marketing, viral advertising, or marketing buzz are buzzwords referring to marketing techniques that use pre-existing social networking services and other technologies to try to produce increases in brand awareness or to achieve other marketing objectives (such as product sales) through self-replicating viral processes, analogous to the spread of viruses or computer viruses (cf. Internet memes and memetics). It can be delivered by word of mouth or enhanced by the network effects of the Internet and mobile networks. Viral advertising is personal and, while coming from an identified sponsor, it does not mean businesses pay for its distribution. Most of the well-known viral ads circulating online are ads paid by a sponsor company, launched either on their own platform (company webpage or social media profile) or on social media websites such as YouTube. Consumers receive the page link from a social media network or copy the entire ad from a website and pass it along through e-mail or posting it on a blog, webpage or social media profile. Viral marketing may take the form of video clips, interactive Flash games, advergames, ebooks, brandable software, images, text messages, email messages, or web pages. The most commonly utilized transmission vehicles for viral messages include: pass-along based, incentive based, trendy based, and undercover based. However, the creative nature of viral marketing enables an "endless amount of potential forms and vehicles the messages can utilize for transmission", including mobile devices.

The ultimate goal of marketers interested in creating successful viral marketing programs is to create viral messages that appeal to individuals with high social networking potential (SNP) and that have a high probability of being presented and spread by these individuals and their competitors in their communications with others in a short period of time.

The term "Viral marketing" has also been used pejoratively to refer to stealth marketing campaigns—marketing strategies that advertise a product to people without them knowing they are being marketed to.

History

The emergence of "viral marketing," as an approach to advertisement, has been tied to the popularization of the notion that ideas spread like viruses. The field that developed around this notion, memetics, peaked in popularity in the 1990s. As this then began to influence marketing gurus, it took on a life of its own in that new context.

There is debate on the origination and the popularization of the specific term *viral marketing*, though some of the earliest uses of the current term are attributed to the Harvard Business School graduate Tim Draper and faculty member Jeffrey Rayport. The term was later popularized by Rayport in the 1996 *Fast Company* article "The Virus of Marketing," and Tim Draper and Steve Jurvetson of the venture capital firm Draper Fisher Jurvetson in 1997 to describe Hotmail's practice of appending advertising to outgoing mail from their users. An earlier attestation of the term is found in *PC User* magazine in 1989, but with a somewhat differing meaning.

Among the first to write about viral marketing on the Internet was the media critic Doug Rushkoff. The assumption is that if such an advertisement reaches a "susceptible" user, that user becomes "infected" (i.e., accepts the idea) and shares the idea with others "infecting them," in the viral analogy's terms. As long as each infected user shares the idea with more than one susceptible user on average (i.e., the basic reproductive rate is greater than one—the standard in epidemiology for qualifying something as an epidemic), the number of infected users grows according to an exponential curve. Of course, the marketing campaign may be successful even if the message spreads more slowly, if this user-to-user sharing is sustained by other forms of marketing communications, such as public relations or advertising.

Bob Gerstley was among the first to write about algorithms designed to identify people with high "social networking potential." Gerstley employed SNP algorithms in quantitative marketing research. In 2004, the concept of the *alpha user* was coined to indicate that it had now become possible to identify the focal members of any viral campaign, the "hubs" who were most influential. Alpha users could be targeted for advertising purposes most accurately in mobile phone networks, due to their personal nature.

In early 2013 the first ever Viral Summit was held in Las Vegas. It attempted to identify similar trends in viral marketing methods for various media.

Methods and Metrics

According to marketing professors Andreas Kaplan and Michael Haenlein, to make viral marketing work, three basic criteria must be met, i.e., giving the right message to the right messengers in the right environment:

1. Messenger: Three specific types of messengers are required to ensure the transformation of an ordinary message into a viral one: market mavens, social hubs, and salespeople. Market mavens are individuals who are continuously 'on the pulse' of things (information specialists); they are usually among the first to get exposed to the message and who transmit it to their immediate social network. Social hubs are people with an exceptionally large number of social connections; they often know hundreds of different people and have the ability to serve as connectors or bridges between different subcultures. Salespeople might be needed who receive the message from the market maven, amplify it by making it more relevant and persuasive, and then transmit it to the social hub for further distribution. Market mavens may not be particularly convincing in transmitting the information.

2. Message: Only messages that are both memorable and sufficiently interesting to be passed on to others have the potential to spur a viral marketing phenomenon. Making a message more memorable and interesting or simply more infectious, is often not a matter of major changes but minor adjustments. It should be unique and engaging with a main idea that

motivates the recipient to share it widely with friends – a "must-see" element.

3. Environment: The environment is crucial in the rise of successful viral marketing – small changes in the environment lead to huge results, and people are much more sensitive to environment. The timing and context of the campaign launch must be right.

Whereas Kaplan, Haenlein and others reduce the role of marketers to crafting the initial viral message and seeding it, futurist and sales and marketing analyst Marc Feldman, who conducted IMT Strategies' viral marketing study in 2001, carves a different role for marketers which pushes the 'art' of viral marketing much closer to 'science.'

Metrics

To clarify and organize the information related to potential measures of viral campaigns, the key measurement possibilities should be considered in relation to the objectives formulated for the viral campaign. In this sense, some of the key cognitive outcomes of viral marketing activities can include measures such as the number of views, clicks, and hits for specific content, as well as the number of shares in social media, such as likes on Facebook or retweets on Twitter, which demonstrate that consumers processed the information received through the marketing message. Measures such as the number of reviews for a product or the number of members for a campaign webpage quantify the number of individuals who have acknowledged the information provided by marketers. Besides statistics that are related to online traffic, surveys can assess the degree of product or brand knowledge, though this type of measurement is more complicated and requires more resources.

Related to consumers' attitudes toward a brand or even toward the marketing communication, different online and social media statistics, including the number of likes and shares within a social network, can be used. The number of reviews for a certain brand or product and the quality assessed by users are indicators of attitudes. Classical measures of consumer attitude toward the brand can be gathered through surveys of consumers. Behavioral measures are very important because changes in consumers' behavior and buying decisions are what marketers hope to see through viral campaigns. There are numerous indicators that can be used in this context as a function of marketers' objectives. Some of them include the most known online and social media statistics such as number and quality of shares, views, product reviews, and comments. Consumers' brand engagement can be measured through the K-factor, the number of followers, friends, registered users, and time spent on the website. Indicators that are more bottom-line oriented focus on consumers' actions after acknowledging the marketing content, including the number of requests for information, samples, or test-drives. Nevertheless, responses to actual call-to-action messages are important, including the conversion rate. Consumers' behavior is expected to lead to contributions to the bottom line of the company, meaning increase in sales, both in quantity and financial amount. However, when quantifying changes in sales, managers need to consider other factors that could potentially affect sales besides the viral marketing activities. Besides positive effects on sales, the use of viral marketing is expected to bring significant reductions in marketing costs and expenses.

Methods

Viral marketing often involves and utilizes:

- Customer participation and polling services

- Industry-specific organization contributions

- Web search engines and blogs

- Mobile smartphone integration

- Multiple forms of print and direct marketing

- Target marketing web services

- Search engine optimization (SEO)

- Social media optimization (SMO)

- Television and radio

Viral target marketing is based on three important principles:

1. Social profile gathering

2. Proximity market analysis

3. Real-time key word density analysis

By applying these three important disciplines to an advertising model, a VMS company is able to match a client with their targeted customers at a cost effective advantage.

The Internet makes it possible for a campaign to go viral very fast; it can, so to speak, make a brand famous overnight. However, the Internet and social media technologies themselves do not make a brand viral; they just enable people to share content to other people faster. Therefore, it is generally agreed that a campaign must typically follow a certain set of guidelines in order to potentially be successful:

- It must be appealing to most of the audience.

- It must be worth sharing with friends and family.

- A large platform, e.g. YouTube or Facebook must be used.

- An initial boost to gain attention is used, e.g. seeding, buying views, or sharing to Facebook fans.

- The content is of good quality.

Social Networking

The growth of social networks significantly contributed to the effectiveness of viral marketing. As of 2009, two thirds of the world's Internet population visits a social networking service or blog site at least every week. Facebook alone has over 1 billion active users. In 2009, time spent visiting social media sites began to exceed time spent emailing. A 2010 study found that 52% of people who view news online forward it on through social networks, email, or posts.

Notable Examples

Early in its existence, the television show *Mystery Science Theater 3000* had limited distribution. The producers encouraged viewers to make copies of the show on video tapes and give them to friends in order to expand viewership and increase demand for the fledgling Comedy Channel network. During this period the closing credits included the words "Keep circulating the tapes!"

Between 1996–1997, Hotmail was one of the first internet businesses to become extremely successful utilizing viral marketing techniques by inserting the tagline "Get your free e-mail at Hotmail" at the bottom of every e-mail sent out by its users. Hotmail was able to sign up 12 million users in 18 months. At the time, this was historically the fastest growth of any user based media company. By the time Hotmail reached "66 million users", the company was establishing "270,000 new accounts each day".

In 2000, Slate.com described TiVo's unpublicized gambit of giving free systems to web-savvy enthusiasts to create "viral" word of mouth, pointing out that a viral campaign differs from a publicity stunt.

Burger King has used several marketing campaigns. Its The Subservient Chicken campaign, running from 2004 until 2007, was an example of viral or word-of-mouth marketing.

The Blendtec viral video series *Will It Blend?* debuted in 2006. In the show, Tom Dickson, Blendtec founder and CEO, attempts to blend various unusual items in order to show off the power of his blender. *Will it Blend?* has been nominated for the 2007 YouTube award for Best Series, winner of .Net Magazine's 2007 Viral Video campaign of the year and winner of the Bronze level Clio Award for Viral Video in 2008. In 2010, Blendtec claimed the top spot on the AdAge list of "Top 10 Viral Ads of All Time." The Will It Blend page on YouTube currently shows over 200 million video views.

In 2007, World Wrestling Entertainment promoted the return of Chris Jericho with a viral marketing campaign using 15-second cryptic binary code videos. The videos contained hidden messages and biblical links related to Jericho, although speculation existed throughout WWE fans over whom the campaign targeted. The text "Save Us" and "2nd Coming" were most prominent in the videos. The campaign spread throughout the internet with numerous websites, though no longer operational, featuring hidden messages and biblical links to further hint at Jericho's return.

In 2007, Portuguese football club Sporting Portugal integrated a viral feature in their campaign for season seats. In their website, a video required the user to input his name and phone number before playback started, which then featured the coach Paulo Bento and the players waiting at the locker room while he makes a phone call to the user telling him that they just can't start the season until the user buys his season ticket.

The Big Word Project, launched in 2008, aimed to redefine the *Oxford English Dictionary* by allowing people to submit their website as the definition of their chosen word. The project, created to fund two Masters students' educations, attracted the attention of bloggers worldwide, and was featured on Daring Fireball and *Wired Magazine.*

Between December 2009 and March 2010 a series of seven videos were posted to YouTube under the name "iamamiwhoami" leading to speculation that they were a marketing campaign for a musician. In March 2010, an anonymous package was sent to an MTV journalist claiming to contain a code which if cracked would give the identity of the artist. The seventh video, entitled 'y', appears to feature the Swedish singer Jonna Lee.

On July 14, 2010, Old Spice launched the fastest growing online viral video campaign ever, garnering 6.7 million views after 24 hours, ballooning over 23 million views after 36 hours. Old Spice's agency created a bathroom set in Portland, OR and had their TV commercial star, Isaiah Mustafa, reply to 186 online comments and questions from websites like Twitter, Facebook, Reddit, Digg, YouTube and others. The campaign ran for 3 days.

Companies may also be able to use a viral video that they did not create for marketing purposes. A notable example is the viral video "The Extreme Diet Coke & Mentos Experiments" created by Fritz Grobe and Stephen Voltz of EepyBird. After the initial success of the video, Mentos were quick to offer their support. They shipped EepyBird thousands of mints for their experiments. Coke were slower to get involved.

On March 6, 2012, Dollar Shave Club launched their online video campaign. In the first 48hrs of their video debuting on YouTube they had over 12,000 people signing up for the service. The video cost just $4500 to make and as of November 2015 has had more than 21 million views. The video was considered as one of the best viral marketing campaigns of 2012 and won "Best Out-of-Nowhere Video Campaign" at the 2012 AdAge Viral Video Awards.

Internet Meme

An Internet meme (/miːm/ *MEEM*) is an activity, concept, catchphrase or piece of media which spreads, often as mimicry, from person to person via the Internet. Some notable examples include posting a photo of people lying down in public places (called "planking") and uploading a short video of people dancing to the Harlem Shake.

A meme is "an idea, behavior, or style that spreads from person to person within a culture". An Internet meme may take the form of an image, hyperlink, video, website, or hashtag. It may be just a word or phrase, including an intentional misspelling. These small movements tend to spread from person to person via social networks, blogs, direct email, or news sources. They may relate to various existing Internet cultures or subcultures, often created or spread on various websites, or by Usenet boards and other such early-internet communications facilities. Fads and sensations tend to grow rapidly on the Internet, because the instant communication facilitates word-of-mouth transmission.

The word *meme* was coined by Richard Dawkins in his 1976 book *The Selfish Gene,* as an attempt to explain the way cultural information spreads; *Internet* memes are a subset of this general meme concept specific to the culture and environment of the Internet. In 2013 Dawkins characterized an *Internet* meme as being a meme deliberately altered by human creativity—distinguished from biological genes and Dawkins' pre-Internet concept of a meme which involved mutation by random change and spreading through accurate replication as in Darwinian selection. Dawkins explained that Internet memes are thus a "hijacking of the original idea", the very idea of a meme having mutated and evolved in this new direction. Further, Internet memes carry an additional property that ordinary memes do not—Internet memes leave a footprint in the media through which they propagate (for example, social networks) that renders them traceable and analyzable.

Internet memes are a subset that Susan Blackmore called *temes*—memes which live in technological artifacts instead of the human mind.

Image macros are often confused with internet memes and are often miscited as such, usually by their creators. However, there is a key distinction between the two. Primarily this distinction lies within the subject's recognizability in internet pop-culture. While such an image may display an existing meme, or in fact a macro itself may even eventually become a meme, it does not qualify as one until it reaches approximately the same level of mass recognition as required for a person to be considered a celebrity.

History

In the early days of the Internet, such content was primarily spread via email or Usenet discussion communities. Messageboards and newsgroups were also popular because they allowed a simple method for people to share information or memes with a diverse population of internet users in a short period. They encourage communication between people, and thus between meme sets, that do not normally come in contact. Furthermore, they actively promote meme-sharing within the messageboard or newsgroup population by asking for feedback, comments, opinions, etc. This format is what gave rise to early internet memes, like the Hampster Dance. Another factor in the increased meme transmission observed over the internet is its interactive nature. Print matter, radio, and television are all essentially passive experiences requiring the reader, listener, or viewer to perform all necessary cognitive processing; in contrast the social nature of the Internet allows phenomena to propagate more readily. Many phenomena are also spread via web search engines, internet forums, social networking services, social news sites, and video hosting services. Much of the Internet's ability to spread information is assisted from results found through search engines, which can allow users to find memes even with obscure information.

Evolution and Propagation

An Internet meme may stay the same or may evolve over time, by chance or through commentary, imitations, parody, or by incorporating news accounts about itself. Internet memes can evolve and spread extremely rapidly, sometimes reaching world-wide popularity within a few days. Internet memes usually are formed from some social interaction, pop culture reference, or situations people often find themselves in. Their rapid growth and impact has caught the attention of both researchers and industry. Academically, researchers model how they evolve and predict which memes will survive and spread throughout the Web. Commercially, they are used in viral marketing where they are an inexpensive form of mass advertising.

One empirical approach studied meme characteristics and behavior independently from the networks in which they propagated, and reached a set of conclusions concerning successful meme propagation. For example, the study asserted that Internet memes not only *compete* for viewer attention generally resulting in a shorter life, but also, through user creativity, memes can *collaborate* with each other and achieve greater survival. Also, paradoxically, an individual meme that experiences a popularity peak significantly higher than its average popularity is not generally expected to survive unless it is unique, whereas a meme with no such popularity peak keeps being used together with other memes and thus has greater survivability.

Theoretical studies on media psychology and communication have aimed to characterise and analyse the concept and representations in order to make it accessible for the academic research. Thus, Internet memes can be regarded as a unit of information which replicates via internet. This unit can replicate or mutate. This mutation instead of being generational follows more a viral pattern, giving the Internet memes generally a short life. Other theoretical problems with the Internet memes are their behaviour, their type of change, and their teleology.

Writing for *The Washington Post* in 2013, Dominic Basulto asserted that with the growth of the Internet and the practices of the marketing and advertising industries, memes have come to transmit fewer snippets of human culture that could survive for centuries as originally envisioned by Dawkins, and instead transmit banality at the expense of big ideas.

Image Macros

Typical format for image macros.

An image macro meme is an Internet meme consisting of:

1. Text, typically in the font Impact, centered at the top and bottom of the image. White text with a black border is typically used because it is easily readable on almost any background color.

2. Image to be placed behind the text. These are typically drawn from a set of "known images" that are understood by many Internet users, such as Bad Luck Brian. However, by using the aforementioned typographic style, any image can take on the context or aesthetic of an image macro.

Marketing

Public relations, advertising, and marketing professionals have embraced Internet memes as a form of viral marketing and guerrilla marketing to create marketing "buzz" for their product or service. The practice of using memes to market products or services is known as memetic marketing. Internet memes are seen as cost-effective, and because they are a (sometimes self-conscious) fad, they are therefore used as a way to create an image of awareness or trendiness.

Marketers, for example, use Internet memes to create interest in films that would otherwise not generate positive publicity among critics. The 2006 film *Snakes on a Plane* generated much publicity via this method. Used in the context of public relations, the term would be more of an advertising buzzword than a proper Internet meme, although there is still an implication that the interest in the content is for purposes of trivia, ephemera, or frivolity rather than straightforward advertising and news.

Examples of memetic marketing include the FreeCreditReport.com singing ad campaign, the "Nope, Chuck Testa" meme from an advertisement for taxidermist Chuck Testa, and the Dumb Ways to Die public announcement ad campaign by Metro Trains Melbourne.

References

*   *Miller, Vincent (2011). Understanding digital culture. London: Sage Publications. sec. "Convergence and the contemporary media experience". ISBN 978-1-84787-497-9.*

*   *Gonzalez, Rafael, C; Woods, Richard E (2008). Digital Image Processing, 3rd Edition. Pearson Prentice Hall. p. 577. ISBN 978-0-13-168728-8.*

*   *Jähne, Bernd (1993). Spatio-temporal image processing, Theory and Scientific Applications. Springer Verlag. p. 208. ISBN 3-540-57418-2.*

*   *Chisholm, Roderick M (16 August 2004). Person And Object: A Metaphysical Study. Psychology Press. pp. 11–. ISBN 978-0-415-29593-2. Retrieved 12 April 2012.*

*   *Saylor, Michael (2012). The Mobile Wave: How Mobile Intelligence Will Change Everything. Vanguard Press. p. 124. ISBN 1-59315-720-7.*

*   *Neil Gaiman (1988). DON'T PANIC: The official Hitch-Hiker's Guide to the Galaxy companion. Titan Books. ISBN 1-85286-013-8. OCLC 24722438.*

*   *Day, B. H.; Wortman, W. A. (2000). Literature in English: A Guide for Librarians in the Digital Age. Chicago: Association of College and Research Libraries. p. 170. ISBN 0-8389-8081-3.*

*   *Pearson, David (2006). Bowman, J, ed. British Librarianship and Information Work 1991-2000: Rare book librarianship and historical bibliography. Aldershot: Ashgate Publishing Ltd. p. 178. ISBN 978-0-7546-4779-9.*

- *Saylor, Michael (2012). The Mobile Wave: How Mobile Intelligence Will Change Everything. Vanguard Press. p. 54. ISBN 1-59315-720-7.*

- *Keen, Andrew (2008). The Cult of the Amateur: How Today's Internet Is Killing Our Culture. New York: Nicholas Brealey Publishing. p. 3. ISBN 978-1857885200.*

- Firestone, Scott & Thiya Ramalingam, & Fry, Steve. Voice and Video Conferencing Fundamentals. Indianapolis, IN: Cisco Press, 2007, pg 10, ISBN 1-58705-268-7, ISBN 978-1-58705-268-2.

- *Turkle, S. (2012). Alone together: Why we expect more from technology and less from each other. New York, NY: Basic Books. ISBN 978-0-465-03146-7.*

- *Burke, Moira; Kraut, Robert; Marlow, Cameron (2011). "Social capital on Facebook: Differentiating uses and users" (PDF). Conference on Human Factors in Computing Systems. 7–9: 571–580. doi:10.1145/1978942.1979023. ISBN 978-1-4503-0228-9.*

- *Kirkpatrick, David (2010). The Facebook effect: the inside story of the company that is connecting the world. New York: Simon & Schuster. ISBN 978-1-4391-0980-9.*

- *Buettner, R. (2016). Getting a Job via Career-oriented Social Networking Sites: The Weakness of Ties. 49th Annual Hawaii International Conference on System Sciences. Kauai, Hawaii: IEEE. doi:10.13140/ RG.2.1.3249.2241.*

- *R., Miller, Carolyn; Dawn, Shepherd,. "Blogging as Social Action: A Genre Analysis of the Weblog". conservancy.umn.edu. Retrieved 2016-04-22.*

- *Wrigh, Donald (2008). "How blogs and social media are changing public relations and the way it is practiced" (PDF). Public relations journal. Retrieved 22 April 2016.*

- *Filer, Tanya; Fredheim, Rolf (2016). "Sparking debate? Political deaths and Twitter discourses in Argentina and Russia". Information, Communication & Society. 19 (11): 1539–1555. doi:10.1080/136911 8X.2016.1140805.*

Means of Digital Media and Communication

Communication helps in addressing a large audience at once using diverse mediums such as television, radio, etc. This chapter focuses on the digital means of communication which have revolutionized the field of communication. The topics elaborated herein include digital radio, internet, online newspaper, etc.

Digital Television

Digital television (DTV) is the transmission of audio and video by digitally processed and multiplexed signal, in contrast to the totally analog and channel separated signals used by analog television. Digital TV can support more than one program in the same channel bandwidth. It is an innovative service that represents the first significant evolution in television technology since color television in the 1950s. Several regions of the world are in different stages of adaptation and are implementing different broadcasting standards. Below are the different widely used digital television broadcasting standards (DTB):

- Digital Video Broadcasting (DVB) uses coded orthogonal frequency-division multiplexing (OFDM) modulation and supports hierarchical transmission. This standard has been adopted in Europe, Australia and New Zealand.

- Advanced Television System Committee (ATSC) uses eight-level vestigial sideband (8VSB) for terrestrial broadcasting. This standard has been adopted by six countries: United States, Canada, Mexico, South Korea, Dominican Republic and Honduras.

- Integrated Services Digital Broadcasting (ISDB) is a system designed to provide good reception to fixed receivers and also portable or mobile receivers. It utilizes OFDM and two-dimensional interleaving. It supports hierarchical transmission of up to three layers and uses MPEG-2 video and Advanced Audio Coding. This standard has been adopted in Japan and the Philippines. ISDB-T International is an adaptation of this standard using H.264/MPEG-4 AVC that been adopted in most of South America and is also being embraced by Portuguese-speaking African countries.

- Digital Terrestrial Multimedia Broadcasting (DTMB) adopts time-domain synchronous (TDS) OFDM technology with a pseudo-random signal frame to serve as the guard interval (GI) of the OFDM block and the training symbol. The DTMB standard has been adopted in the People's Republic of China, including Hong Kong and Macau.

- Digital Multimedia Broadcasting (DMB) is a digital radio transmission technology developed in South Korea as part of the national IT project for sending multimedia such as TV, radio and datacasting to mobile devices such as mobile phones, laptops and GPS navigation systems.

History

Digital TV's roots have been tied very closely to the availability of inexpensive, high performance computers. It wasn't until the 1990s that digital TV became a real possibility.

In the mid-1980s as Japanese consumer electronics firms forged ahead with the development of HDTV technology, and as the MUSE analog format proposed by NHK, a Japanese company, was seen as a pacesetter that threatened to eclipse U.S. electronics companies. Until June 1990, the Japanese MUSE standard—based on an analog system—was the front-runner among the more than 23 different technical concepts under consideration. Then, an American company, General Instrument, demonstrated the feasibility of a digital television signal. This breakthrough was of such significance that the FCC was persuaded to delay its decision on an ATV standard until a digitally based standard could be developed.

In March 1990, when it became clear that a digital standard was feasible, the FCC made a number of critical decisions. First, the Commission declared that the new ATV standard must be more than an enhanced analog signal, but be able to provide a genuine HDTV signal with at least twice the resolution of existing television images. Then, to ensure that viewers who did not wish to buy a new digital television set could continue to receive conventional television broadcasts, it dictated that the new ATV standard must be capable of being "simulcast" on different channels. The new ATV standard also allowed the new DTV signal to be based on entirely new design principles. Although incompatible with the existing NTSC standard, the new DTV standard would be able to incorporate many improvements.

The final standard adopted by the FCC did not require a single standard for scanning formats, aspect ratios, or lines of resolution. This outcome resulted from a dispute between the consumer electronics industry (joined by some broadcasters) and the computer industry (joined by the film industry and some public interest groups) over which of the two scanning processes—interlaced or progressive—is superior. Interlaced scanning, which is used in televisions worldwide, scans even-numbered lines first, then odd-numbered ones. Progressive scanning, which is the format used in computers, scans lines in sequences, from top to bottom. The computer industry argued that progressive scanning is superior because it does not "flicker" in the manner of interlaced scanning. It also argued that progressive scanning enables easier connections with the Internet, and is more cheaply converted to interlaced formats than vice versa. The film industry also supported progressive scanning because it offers a more efficient means of converting filmed programming into digital formats. For their part, the consumer electronics industry and broadcasters argued that interlaced scanning was the only technology that could transmit the highest quality pictures then (and currently) feasible, i.e., 1,080 lines per picture and 1,920 pixels per line. Broadcasters also favored interlaced scanning because their vast archive of interlaced programming is not readily compatible with a progressive format.

Technical Information

Formats and Bandwidth

Digital television supports many different picture formats defined by the broadcast television systems which are a combination of size and aspect ratio (width to height ratio).

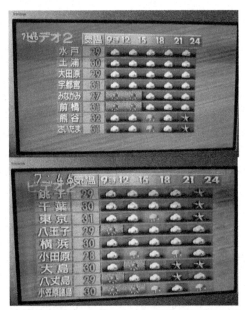

Comparison of image quality between ISDB-T (top) and NTSC (bottom)

With digital terrestrial television (DTT) broadcasting, the range of formats can be broadly divided into two categories: high definition television (HDTV) for the transmission of high-definition video and standard-definition television (SDTV). These terms by themselves are not very precise, and many subtle intermediate cases exist.

One of several different HDTV formats that can be transmitted over DTV is: 1280 × 720 pixels in progressive scan mode (abbreviated *720p*) or 1920 × 1080 pixels in interlaced video mode (*1080i*). Each of these uses a 16:9 aspect ratio. (Some televisions are capable of receiving an HD resolution of 1920 × 1080 at a 60 Hz progressive scan frame rate — known as 1080p.) HDTV cannot be transmitted over analog television channels because of channel capacity issues.

Standard definition TV (SDTV), by comparison, may use one of several different formats taking the form of various aspect ratios depending on the technology used in the country of broadcast. For 4:3 aspect-ratio broadcasts, the 640 × 480 format is used in NTSC countries, while 720 × 576 is used in PAL countries. For 16:9 broadcasts, the 720 × 480 format is used in NTSC countries, while 1024 × 576 is used in PAL countries. However, broadcasters may choose to reduce these resolutions to reduce bit rate (e.g., many DVB-T channels in the United Kingdom use a horizontal resolution of 544 or 704 pixels per line).

Each commercial broadcasting terrestrial television DTV channel in North America is permitted to be broadcast at a bit rate up to 19 megabits per second. However, the broadcaster does not need to use this entire bandwidth for just one broadcast channel. Instead the broadcast can use the channel to include PSIP and can also subdivide across several video subchannels (a.k.a. feeds) of varying quality and compression rates, including non-video datacasting services that allow one-way high-bit-rate streaming of data to computers like National Datacast.

A broadcaster may opt to use a standard-definition (SDTV) digital signal instead of an HDTV signal, because current convention allows the bandwidth of a DTV channel (or "multiplex") to be subdivided into multiple digital subchannels, (similar to what most FM radio stations offer with HD Radio), providing multiple feeds of entirely different television programming on the same channel. This ability to provide either a single HDTV feed or multiple lower-resolution feeds is often referred to as distributing one's "bit budget" or multicasting. This can sometimes be arranged automatically, using a statistical multiplexer (or "stat-mux"). With some implementations, image resolution may be less directly limited by bandwidth; for example in DVB-T, broadcasters can choose from several different modulation schemes, giving them the option to reduce the transmission bit rate and make reception easier for more distant or mobile viewers.

Receiving Digital Signal

There are several different ways to receive digital television. One of the oldest means of receiving DTV (and TV in general) is from terrestrial transmitters using an antenna (known as an *aerial* in some countries). This way is known as Digital terrestrial television (DTT). With DTT, viewers are limited to channels that have a terrestrial transmitter in range of their antenna.

Other ways have been devised to receive digital television. Among the most familiar to people are digital cable and digital satellite. In some countries where transmissions of TV signals are normally achieved by microwaves, digital MMDS is used. Other standards, such as Digital multimedia broadcasting (DMB) and DVB-H, have been devised to allow handheld devices such as mobile phones to receive TV signals. Another way is IPTV, that is receiving TV via Internet Protocol, relying on digital subscriber line (DSL) or optical cable line. Finally, an alternative way is to receive digital TV signals via the open Internet (Internet television), whether from a central streaming service or a P2P (peer-to-peer) system.

Some signals carry encryption and specify use conditions (such as "may not be recorded" or "may not be viewed on displays larger than 1 m in diagonal measure") backed up with the force of law under the World Intellectual Property Organization Copyright Treaty (WIPO Copyright Treaty) and national legislation implementing it, such as the U.S. Digital Millennium Copyright Act. Access to encrypted channels can be controlled by a removable smart card, for example via the Common Interface (DVB-CI) standard for Europe and via Point Of Deployment (POD) for IS or named differently CableCard.

Disadvantages

While poor signal analog TV quality could be evaluated by the user by the amount of noise on the screen, digital TV has no grey areas, it either works or does not depending on signal strength.

Protection Parameters for Terrestrial Dtv Broadcasting

Digital television signals must not interfere with each other, and they must also coexist with analog television until it is phased out. The following table gives allowable signal-to-noise and signal-to-interference ratios for various interference scenarios. This table is a crucial regulatory tool for controlling the placement and power levels of stations. Digital TV is more tolerant of interference than analog TV, and this is the reason a smaller range of channels can carry an all-digital set of television stations.

System Parameters (protection ratios)	Canada	USA	EBU ITU-mode M3	Japan & Brazil
C/N for AWGN Channel	+19.5 dB (16.5 dB)	+15.19 dB	+19.3 dB	+19.2 dB
Co-Channel DTV into Analog TV	+33.8 dB	+34.44 dB	+34 ~ 37 dB	+38 dB
Co-Channel Analog TV into DTV	+7.2 dB	+1.81 dB	+4 dB	+4 dB
Co-Channel DTV into DTV	+19.5 dB (16.5 dB)	+15.27 dB	+19 dB	+19 dB
Lower Adjacent Channel DTV into Analog TV	−16 dB	−17.43 dB	−5 ~ −11 dB	−6 dB
Upper Adjacent Channel DTV into Analog TV	−12 dB	−11.95 dB	−1 ~ −10	−5 dB
Lower Adjacent Channel Analog TV into DTV	−48 dB	−47.33 dB	−34 ~ −37 dB	−35 dB
Upper Adjacent Channel Analog TV into DTV	−49 dB	−48.71 dB	−38 ~ −36 dB	−37 dB
Lower Adjacent Channel DTV into DTV	−27 dB	−28 dB	−30 dB	−28 dB
Upper Adjacent Channel DTV into DTV	−27 dB	−26 dB	−30 dB	−29 dB

Interaction

People can interact with a DTV system in various ways. One can, for example, browse the electronic program guide. Modern DTV systems sometimes use a return path providing feedback from the end user to the broadcaster. This is possible with a coaxial or fiber optic cable, a dialup modem, or Internet connection but is not possible with a standard antenna.

Some of these systems support video on demand using a communication channel localized to a neighborhood rather than a city (terrestrial) or an even larger area (satellite).

1-segment Broadcasting

1seg (1-segment) is a special form of ISDB. Each channel is further divided into 13 segments. The 12 segments of them are allocated for HDTV and remaining segment, the 13th, is used for narrow-band receivers such as mobile television or cell phone.

Timeline of Transition

Comparison of Analog vs Digital

DTV has several advantages over analog TV, the most significant being that digital channels take up less bandwidth, and the bandwidth needs are continuously variable, at a corresponding reduction in image quality depending on the level of compression as well as the resolution of the transmitted image. This means that digital broadcasters can provide more digital channels in the same space, provide high-definition television service, or provide other non-television services such as multimedia or interactivity. DTV also permits special services such as multiplexing (more than one program on the same channel), electronic program guides and additional languages (spoken or subtitled). The sale of non-television services may provide an additional revenue source.

Digital and analog signals react to interference differently. For example, common problems with analog television include ghosting of images, noise from weak signals, and many other potential problems which degrade the quality of the image and sound, although the program material may still be watchable. With digital television, the audio and video must be synchronized digitally, so reception of the digital signal must be very nearly complete; otherwise, neither audio nor video will be usable. Short of this complete failure, "blocky" video is seen when the digital signal experiences interference.

Analog TV started off with monophonic sound, and later evolved to stereophonic sound with two independent audio signal channels. DTV will allow up to 5 audio signal channels plus a sub-woofer bass channel, with broadcasts similar in quality to movie theaters and DVDs.

Compression Artifacts and Allocated Bandwidth

DTV images have some picture defects that are not present on analog television or motion picture cinema, because of present-day limitations of bit rate and compression algorithms such as MPEG-2. This defect is sometimes referred to as "mosquito noise".

Because of the way the human visual system works, defects in an image that are localized to particular features of the image or that come and go are more perceptible than defects that are uniform and constant. However, the DTV system is designed to take advantage of other limitations of the human visual system to help mask these flaws, e.g. by allowing more compression artifacts during fast motion where the eye cannot track and resolve them as easily and, conversely, minimizing artifacts in still backgrounds that may be closely examined in a scene (since time allows).

Effects of Poor Reception

Changes in signal reception from factors such as degrading antenna connections or changing weather conditions may gradually reduce the quality of analog TV. The nature of digital TV results in a perfectly decodable video initially, until the receiving equipment starts picking up interference that overpowers the desired signal or if the signal is too weak to decode. Some equipment will show a garbled picture with significant damage, while other devices may go directly from perfectly decodable video to no video at all or lock up. This phenomenon is known as the digital cliff effect.

For remote locations, distant channels that, as analog signals, were previously usable in a snowy and degraded state may, as digital signals, be perfectly decodable or may become completely un-available. The use of higher frequencies will add to these problems, especially in cases where a clear line-of-sight from the receiving antenna to the transmitter is not available.

Effect on Old Analog Technology

Television sets with only analog tuners cannot decode digital transmissions. When analog broadcasting over the air ceases, users of sets with analog-only tuners may use other sources of programming (e.g. cable, recorded media) or may purchase set-top converter boxes to tune in the digital signals. In the United States, a government-sponsored coupon was available to offset the cost of an external converter box. Analog switch-off (of full-power stations) took place on December 11, 2006 in The Netherlands, June 12, 2009 in the United States for full-power stations, and later for Class-A Stations on September 1, 2016, July 24, 2011 in Japan, August 31, 2011 in Canada, February 13, 2012 in Arab states, May 1, 2012 in Germany, October 24, 2012 in the United Kingdom and Ireland, October 31, 2012 in selected Indian cities, and December 10, 2013 in Australia. Completion of analog switch-off is scheduled for December 31, 2017 in the whole of India, December 2018 in Costa Rica and around 2020 for the Philippines.

Disappearance of TV-Audio Receivers

Prior to the conversion to digital TV, analog television broadcast audio for TV channels on a separate FM carrier signal from the video signal. This FM audio signal could be heard using standard radios equipped with the appropriate tuning circuits.

However, after the transition of many countries to digital TV, no portable radio manufacturer has yet developed an alternative method for portable radios to play just the audio signal of digital TV channels. (DTV radio is not the same thing.)

Environmental Issues

The adoption of a broadcast standard incompatible with existing analog receivers has created the problem of large numbers of analog receivers being discarded during digital television transition. One superintendent of Public Works was quoted in 2009 as saying, "Some of the studies I've read in the trade magazines say up to a quarter of American households could be throwing a TV out in the next two years following the regulation change". In 2009, an estimated 99 million analog TV receivers were sitting unused in homes in the US alone and, while some obsolete receivers are being retrofitted with converters, many more are simply dumped in landfills where they represent a source of toxic metals such as lead as well as lesser amounts of materials such as barium, cadmium and chromium.

According to one campaign group, a CRT computer monitor or TV contains an average of 8 pounds (3.6 kg) of lead. According to another source, the lead in glass of a CRT varies from 1.08 lb to 11.28 lb, depending on screen size and type, but the lead is in the form of "stable and immobile" lead oxide mixed into the glass. It is claimed that the lead can have long-term negative effects on the environment if dumped as landfill. However, the glass envelope can be recycled at suitably equipped facilities. Other portions of the receiver may be subject to disposal as hazardous material.

Local restrictions on disposal of these materials vary widely; in some cases second-hand stores have refused to accept working color television receivers for resale due to the increasing costs of disposing of unsold TVs. Those thrift stores which are still accepting donated TVs have reported significant increases in good-condition working used television receivers abandoned by viewers who often expect them not to work after digital transition.

In Michigan in 2009, one recycler estimated that as many as one household in four would dispose of or recycle a TV set in the following year. The digital television transition, migration to high-definition television receivers and the replacement of CRTs with flatscreens are all factors in the increasing number of discarded analog CRT-based television receivers.

Digital Radio

Digital radio is the use of digital technology to transmit and/or receive across the radio spectrum. The may refer to digital transmission by radio waves, including digital broadcasting, and especially to Digital audio radio services.

The term is also applied to radio equipment using digital electronics to process analog radio signals.

Types

In digital broadcasting systems, the analog audio signal is digitized, compressed using formats such as MP2, and transmitted using a digital modulation scheme. The aim is to increase the number of radio programs in a given spectrum, to improve the audio quality, to eliminate fading problems in mobile environments, to allow additional datacasting services, and to decrease the transmission power or the number of transmitters required to cover a region. However, analog radio (AM and FM) is still more popular and listening to radio over IP (Internet Protocol) is growing in popularity.

In 2012 four digital wireless radio systems are recognized by the International Telecommunication Union: the two European systems Digital Audio Broadcasting (DAB) and Digital Radio Mondiale (DRM), the Japanese ISDB-T and the in-band on-channel technique used in the US and Arab world and branded as HD Radio.

An older definition, still used in communication engineering literature, is wireless digital transmission technologies, i.e. microwave and radio frequency communication standards where analog information signals as well as digital data are carried by a digital signal, by means of a digital modulation method. This definition includes broadcasting systems such as digital TV and digital radio broadcasting, but also two-way digital radio standards such as the second generation (2G) cell-phones and later, short-range communication such as digital cordless phones, wireless computer networks, digital micro-wave radio links, deep space communication systems such as communications to and from the two Voyager space probes, etc.

A less common definition is radio receiver and transmitter implementations that are based on digital signal processing, but may transmit or receive analog radio transmission standards, for example FM radio. This may reduce noise and distortion induced in the electronics. It also allows software radio implementations, where the transmission technology is changed just by selecting another piece of software. In most cases, this would however increase the energy consumption of the receiver equipment.

One-way (Broadcasting) Systems

Broadcast Standards

Digital audio broadcasting standards may provide terrestrial or satellite radio service. Digital radio broadcasting systems are typically designed for handheld mobile devices, just like mobile-TV systems, but as opposed to other digital TV systems which typically require a fixed directional antenna.

Some digital radio systems provide in-band on-channel (IBOC) solutions that may coexist with or simulcast with analog AM or FM transmissions, while others are designed for designated radio frequency bands. The latter allows one wideband radio signal to carry a multiplex consisting of several radio-channels of variable bitrate as well as data services and other forms of media. Some digital broadcasting systems allow single-frequency network (SFN), where all terrestrial transmitters in a region sending the same multiplex of radio programs may use the same frequency channel without self-interference problems, further improving the system spectral efficiency.

While digital broadcasting offers many potential benefits, its introduction has been hindered by a lack of global agreement on standards and many disadvantages. The DAB Eureka 147 standard for digital radio is coordinated by the World DMB Forum. This standard of digital radio technology was defined in the late 1980s, and is now being introduced in some European countries. Commercial DAB receivers began to be sold in 1999 and, by 2006, 500 million people were in the coverage area of DAB broadcasts, although by this time sales had only taken off in the UK and Denmark. In 2006 there are approximately 1,000 DAB stations in operation. There have been criticisms of the Eureka 147 standard and so a new 'DAB+' standard has been introduced.

The DRM standard has been used for several years to broadcast digitally on frequencies below 30 MHz (shortwave, mediumwave and longwave). Also there is now the extended standard DRM+ which make it possible to broadcast on frequencies above 30 MHz.This will make it possible to digitalize transmission on the FM-band. Successful tests of DRM+ has been made in several countries 2010-2012 as in Brazil, Germany, France, India, Sri Lanka, the UK, Slovakia and Italy (incl. the Vatican). DRM+ will be tested in Sweden 2012.

DRM+ is regarded as a more transparent and less costly standard than DAB+ and thus a better choice for local radio; commercial or community broadcasters. Although DAB+ has been introduced in Australia the government has concluded 2011 that a preference for DRM and DRM+ above HD Radio could be used to supplement DAB+ services in (some) local and regional areas.

All Digital Radio Broadcast system share many disadvantages which don't exist for Analogue to Digital TV changeover: About x20 more power consumption, Digital Cliff effect for Mobile use, very slow channel change, especially for a different DAB multiplex frequency, high transmission cost resulting poorer quality than FM and sometimes AM due to low bitrate (64K mono rather than 256K stereo), higher compression is more distorted for hearing aid users, usually poor user interfaces and Radio audio quality, not enough fill in stations for portable / mobile coverage (like 1950s UK FM). The Multiplex & SFN concepts are advantageous to State Broadcasters and Large Pan National Multi-channel companies and worse for all Local, Community and most Regional stations. In contrast almost all the aspects of Digital TV vs Analogue TV are positive with almost no negative effects. TVs could be used with a Set-box. Digital Radio requires replacement of all radios, though an awkward DAB receiver with FM output can be used with existing FM car Radios.

To date the following standards have been defined for one-way digital radio:

Digital Audio Broadcasting Systems

- Eureka 147 (branded as DAB)
- DAB+

- ISDB-TSB
- Internet radio (Technically not a true Broadcast system)
- FM band in-band on-channel (FM IBOC):
    - HD Radio (OFDM modulation over FM and AM band IBOC sidebands)
    - FMeXtra (FM band IBOC subcarriers)
    - Digital Radio Mondiale extension (DRM+) (OFDM modulation over AM band IBOC sidebands)
- AM band in-band on-channel (AM IBOC):
    - HD Radio (AM IBOC sideband)
    - Digital Radio Mondiale (branded as DRM) for the short, medium and long wave-bands
- Satellite radio:
    - WorldSpace in Asia and Africa
    - Sirius XM Radio in North America
    - MobaHo! in Japan and the Republic of (South) Korea
- Systems also designed for digital TV:
    - DMB
    - DVB-H
    - ISDB-T
- Low-bandwidth digital data broadcasting over existing FM radio:
    - Radio Data System (branded as RDS)
- Radio pagers:
    - FLEX
    - ReFLEX
    - POCSAG
    - NTT

Digital Television (DTV) Broadcasting Systems

- Digital Video Broadcasting (DVB)
- Integrated Services Digital Broadcasting (ISDB)
- Digital Multimedia Broadcasting (DMB)

- Digital Terrestrial Television (DTTV or DTT) to fixed mainly roof-top antennas:
    - DVB-T (based on OFDM modulation)
    - ISDB-T (based on OFDM modulation)
    - ATSC (based on 8VSB modulation)
    - T-DMB
- Mobile TV reception in handheld devices:
    - DVB-H (based on OFDM modulation)
    - MediaFLO (based on OFDM modulation)
    - DMB (based on OFDM modulation)
    - Multimedia Broadcast Multicast Service (MBMS) via the GSM EDGE and UMTS cellular networks
    - DVB-SH (based on OFDM modulation)
- Satellite TV:
    - DVB-S (for Satellite TV)
    - ISDB-S
    - 4DTV
    - S-DMB
    - MobaHo!

Status by Country

DAB Adopters

Digital Audio Broadcasting (DAB), also known as Eureka 147, has been under development since the early eighties, has been adopted by around 20 countries worldwide. It is based on the MPEG-1 Audio Layer II audio coding format and this has been co-ordinated by the WorldDMB.

WorldDMB announced in a press release in November 2006, that DAB would be adopting the HE-AACv2 audio coding format, which is also known as eAAC+. Also being adopted are the MPEG Surround format, and stronger error correction coding called Reed-Solomon coding. The update has been named DAB+. Receivers that support the new DAB standard began being released during 2007 with firmware updated available for some older receivers.

DAB and DAB+ cannot be used for mobile TV because they do not include any video codecs. DAB related standards Digital Multimedia Broadcasting (DMB) and DAB-IP are suitable for mobile radio and TV both because they have MPEG 4 AVC and WMV9 respectively as video coding formats. However a DMB video sub-channel can easily be added to any DAB transmission - as DMB was designed from the outset to be carried on a DAB subchannel. DMB broadcasts in Korea carry conventional MPEG 1 Layer II DAB audio services alongside their DMB video services.

United States

The United States has opted for the proprietary HD Radio technology, a type of in-band on-channel (IBOC) technology. According to iBiquity, "HD Radio" is the company's trade name for its proprietary digital radio system, but the name does not imply either high definition or "hybrid digital" as it is commonly incorrectly referenced.

Transmissions use orthogonal frequency-division multiplexing, a technique which is also used for European terrestrial digital TV broadcast (DVB-T). HD Radio technology was developed and is licensed by iBiquity Digital Corporation. It is widely believed that a major reason for HD radio technology is to offer some limited digital radio services while preserving the relative "stick values" of the stations involved and to insure that new programming services will be controlled by existing licensees.

The FM digital schemes in the U.S. provide audio at rates from 96 to 128 kilobits per second (kbit/s), with auxiliary "subcarrier" transmissions at up to 64 kbit/s. The AM digital schemes have data rates of about 48 kbit/s, with auxiliary services provided at a much lower data rate. Both the FM and AM schemes use lossy compression techniques to make the best use of the limited bandwidth.

Lucent Digital Radio, USA Digital Radio (USADR), and Digital Radio Express commenced tests in 1999 of their various schemes for digital broadcast, with the expectation that they would report their results to the National Radio Systems Committee (NRSC) in December 1999. Results of these tests remain unclear, which in general describes the status of the terrestrial digital radio broadcasting effort in North America. Some terrestrial analog broadcast stations are apprehensive about the impact of digital satellite radio on their business, while others plan to convert to digital broadcasting as soon as it is economically and technically feasible.

While traditional terrestrial radio broadcasters are trying to "go digital", most major US automobile manufacturers are promoting digital satellite radio. HD Radio technology has also made inroads in the automotive sector with factory-installed options announced by BMW, Ford, Hyundai, Jaguar, Lincoln, Mercedes, MINI, Mercury, Scion, and Volvo.

Satellite radio is distinguished by its freedom from FCC censorship in the United States, its relative lack of advertising, and its ability to allow people on the road to listen to the same stations at any location in the country. Listeners must currently pay an annual or monthly subscription fee in order to access the service, and must install a separate security card in each radio or receiver they use.

Ford and Daimler AG are working with Sirius Satellite Radio, previously CD Radio, of New York City, and General Motors and Honda are working with XM Satellite Radio of Washington, D.C. to build and promote satellite DAB radio systems for North America, each offering "CD quality" audio and about a hundred channels.

Sirius Satellite Radio launched a constellation of three Sirius satellites during the course of 2000. The satellites were built by Space Systems/Loral and were launched by Russian Proton boosters. As with XM Satellite Radio, Sirius implemented a series of terrestrial ground repeaters where satellite signal would otherwise be blocked by large structures including natural structures and high-rise buildings.

XM Satellite Radio has a constellation of three satellites, two of which were launched in the spring of 2001, with one following later in 2005. The satellites are Boeing 702 comsats, and were put into orbit by Sea Launch boosters. Back-up ground transmitters (repeaters) will be built in cities where satellite signals could be blocked by big buildings.

On February 19, 2007, Sirius Satellite Radio and XM Satellite Radio merged, to form Sirius XM Radio.

The FCC has auctioned bandwidth allocations for satellite broadcast in the S band range, around 2.3 GHz.

The perceived wisdom of the radio industry is that the terrestrial medium has two great strengths: it is free and it is local. Satellite radio is neither of these things; however, in recent years, it has grown to make a name for itself by providing uncensored content (most notably, the crossover of Howard Stern from terrestrial radio to satellite radio) and commercial-free, all-digital music channels that offer similar genres to local broadcast favorites.

The "HD Radio" signal of an FM broadcast station in the US has a limited listening distance from the broadcast tower site. FCC regulations currently limit the power of the digital part of the station's transmission to 10% of the existing analog power permitted the station. Even at this power level, the presence of the digital signal right next to the station's analog signal can result in older radios picking up noise due to trouble rejecting the adjacent digital signal. "There are still some concerns that HD Radio on FM will increase interference between different stations even though HD Radio at the 10% power level fits within the FCC spectral mask." HD Radio HD Radio#cite note-14. "HD Radio" allows each existing broadcast station to add additional "channels" in the USA by transmitting a digital signal just outside of their analog signal, on both sides just beyond their existing analog Frequency Modulation signal. The HD Radio signal occupies the 0.1 MHz that begins 0.1 MHz above and below the carrier frequency station. For instance, if a station's analog signal's carrier frequency is 93.3 MHz, the digital signal will fill 92.1 - 92.2 MHz and 93.4 MHz - 93.5 MHz within the FM Broadcast Band. Several digital audio streams, or "subchannels", can be carried within this single digital data stream, with the number of audio of subchannels and the percentage of the overall bandwidth allocated to each stream up to the choice of the station. On the radio tuner, these will appear as (in the above case) "92.3-2" , "92.3-3", and so on. The frequencies that are used do not change as more channels are added to the one radio station (93.3 MHz in the example above). Instead, a fixed total amount of bandwidth is simply reallocated across the audio streams such that each now receives less bandwidth, and therefore lower audio quality, than before.

Canada

Canada has begun allowing experimental HD Radio broadcasts and digital audio subchannels on a case-by-case basis, with the first stations in the country being CFRM-FM in Little Current, CING-FM in Hamilton, and CJSA-FM in Toronto (with a fourth, CFMS-FM in the Toronto suburb of Markham applying to operate HD Radio technology), all within the province of Ontario.

United Kingdom

In the United Kingdom, 44.3% of the population now has a DAB digital radio set and 34.4% of listening is to different digital platforms.

26 million people, or 50% of the population, now tune into digital radio each week, up 2.6 million year on year, according to RAJAR in Q1 2013. But FM listening has increased to 61% and DAB decreased to 21% DAB listeners may also use AM & FM too.

The UK currently has the world's biggest digital radio network, with 103 transmitters, two nationwide DAB ensembles and 48 local and regional DAB ensembles, broadcasting over 250 commercial and 34 BBC radio stations; 51 of these stations are broadcast in London. On DAB digital radio most listeners can receive around 20 additional stations, in addition to the analogue stations available on digital. The frequency band used is 217.5 to 230 MHz.

Some areas of the country are not yet covered by DAB but the BBC has announced plans to build out national coverage to 92% by the end of 2011 with 40 new transmitters being launched in 2011. The Government will make a decision on a radio switchover subject to listening and coverage criteria being met. A digital radio switchover would maintain FM as a platform, while moving some services to DAB-only distribution. Digital radio stations are also broadcast on digital television platforms such as Sky, Virgin Media and Freeview, as well as internet radio.

Germany

The first DAB station network was deployed in Bavaria since 1995 until full coverage in 1999. Other states had funded a station network but the lack of success led them to scrap the funding - the MDR switched off in 1998 already and Brandenburg declared a failure in 2004. Instead Berlin/Brandenburg began to switch to digital radio based on an audio-only DVB-T mode given the success of the DVB-T standard in the region when earlier analogue television was switched off in August 2003 (being the first region to switch in Germany). During that time the DVB-H variant of the DVB family was released for transmission to mobile receivers in 2004. During 2005 most radio stations left the DAB network with only one public service broadcaster ensemble to remain in the now fully state-funded station network. At last the KEF (*commission to determine the financial needs of broadcasters*) blocked federal funding on 15. July 2009 until economic viability of DAB broadcasting would be proven - and pointing to DVB-T as a viable alternative.

Digital radio deployment was rebooted during 2011 - a joint commission of public and private radio broadcasters decided upon "DAB+" as the new national standard in December 2010. The new station network started as planned on 1. August 2011 with 27 stations with 10 kW each giving a coverage of 70% across the nation. A single "Bundesmux" ("fed-mux" short of "federal multiplex") was created on band 5C as a single-frequency network with the band 5C to cross over to neighbouring countries. Berlin/Brandenburg joined the DAB+ broadcasting in January 2012 but other dark regions remain in Eastern Germany. With the initial market success of DAB + the contractors decided on an expansion of the digital radio station network in November 2012. With DAB being available across Belgium, Netherlands, Switzerland and Northern Italy there is good coverage across the European Backbone area indicating a sufficient momentum on the market.

Australia

Australia commenced regular digital audio broadcasting using the DAB+ standard in May 2009, after many years of trialling alternative systems. Normal radio services operate on the AM and FM bands, as well as four stations (ABC and SBS) on digital TV channels. The services are currently operating in the five state capital cities: Adelaide, Brisbane, Melbourne, Perth and Sydney, and is being trialled in Canberra and Darwin.

Japan

Japan has started terrestrial sound broadcasting using ISDB-Tsb and MobaHO! 2.6 GHz Satellite Sound digital broadcasting

Korea

On 1 December 2005 South Korea launched its T-DMB service which includes both television and radio stations. T-DMB is a derivative of DAB with specifications published by ETSI. More than 110,000 receivers had been sold in one month only in 2005.

Developing Nations

Digital radio is now being provided to the developing world. A satellite communications company named WorldSpace was setting up a network of three satellites, including "AfriStar", "AsiaStar", and "AmeriStar", to provide digital audio information services to Africa, Asia, and Latin America. AfriStar and AsiaStar are in orbit. AmeriStar cannot be launched from the United States as Worldspace transmits on the L-band and would interfere with USA military as mentioned above in its heyday provided service to over 170,000 subscribers in eastern and southern Africa, the Middle East, and much of Asia with 96% coming from India. Timbre Media along with Saregama India plan to relaunch the company. As of 2013 Worldspace is defunct, but two satellites are in orbit which still have a few channels.

Each satellite provides three transmission beams that can support 50 channels each, carrying news, music, entertainment, and education, and including a computer multimedia service. Local, regional, and international broadcasters were working with WorldStar to provide services.

A consortium of broadcasters and equipment manufacturers are also working to bring the benefits of digital broadcasting to the radio spectrum currently used for terrestrial AM radio broadcasts, including international shortwave transmissions. Over seventy broadcasters are now transmitting programs using the new standard, known as Digital Radio Mondiale (DRM), and / commercial DRM receivers are available (though there are few models on the DRM website and some are discontinued). DRM's system uses the MPEG-4 based standard aacPlus to code the music and CELP or HVXC for speech programs. At present these are priced too high to be affordable by many in the third world, however. Take-up of DRM has been minuscule and many traditional Shortwave broadcasters now only stream on Internet, use fixed satellite (TV set-boxes) or Local Analogue FM relays to save on costs. Very few (expensive) DRM radio sets are available and some Broadcasters (RTE in Ireland on 252 kHz) have ceased trials without launching a service.

Low-cost DAB radio receivers are now available from various Japanese manufacturers, and WorldSpace has worked with Thomson Broadcast to introduce a village communications center known as a Telekiosk to bring communications services to rural areas. The Telekiosks are self-contained and are available as fixed or mobile units

Two-way Digital Radio Standards

The key breakthrough or key feature in digital radio transmission systems is that they allow lower transmission power, they can provide robustness to noise and cross-talk and other forms of interference, and thus allow the same radio frequency to be reused at shorter distance. Consequently, the spectral efficiency (the number of phonecalls per MHz and base station, or the number of bit/s per Hz and transmitter, etc.) may be sufficiently increased. Digital radio transmission can also carry any kind of information whatsoever — just as long at it has been expressed digitally. Earlier radio communication systems had to be made expressly for a given form of communications: telephone, telegraph, or television, for example. All kinds of digital communications can be multiplexed or encrypted at will.

- Digital cellular telephony (2G systems and later generations):
    - GSM
    - UMTS (sometimes called W-CDMA)
    - TETRA
    - IS-95 (cdmaOne)
    - IS-136 (D-AMPS, sometimes called TDMA)
    - IS-2000 (CDMA2000)
    - iDEN
- Digital Mobile Radio:
    - Project 25 a.k.a. "P25" or "APCO-25"
    - TETRA
    - TETRAPOL
    - NXDN
    - DMR
- Wireless networking:
    - Wi-Fi
    - HIPERLAN
    - Bluetooth
    - DASH7
    - ZigBee
    - 6LoWPAN

- Military radio systems for Network-centric warfare

    o   JTRS (Joint Tactical Radio System- a flexible software-defined radio)

    o   SINCGARS (Single channel ground to air radio system)

- Amateur packet radio:

    o   AX.25

- Digital modems for HF:

    o   PACTOR

- Satellite radio:

    o   Satmodems

- Wireless local loop:

    o   Basic Exchange Telephone Radio Service

- Broadband wireless access:

    o   IEEE 802.16

Internet

The Internet is the global system of interconnected computer networks that use the Internet protocol suite (TCP/IP) to link devices worldwide. It is a *network of networks* that consists of private, public, academic, business, and government networks of local to global scope, linked by a broad array of electronic, wireless, and optical networking technologies. The Internet carries an extensive range of information resources and services, such as the inter-linked hypertext documents and applications of the World Wide Web (WWW), electronic mail, telephony, and peer-to-peer networks for file sharing.

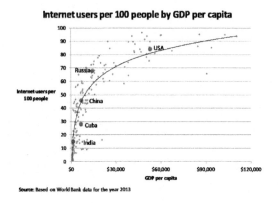

Internet users per 100 population members and GDP per capita for selected countries.

The origins of the Internet date back to research commissioned by the United States federal government in the 1960s to build robust, fault-tolerant communication via computer networks. The primary precursor network, the ARPANET, initially served as a backbone for interconnection of regional academic and military networks in the 1980s. The funding of the National Science Foundation Network as a new backbone in the 1980s, as well as private funding for other commercial extensions, led to worldwide participation in the development of new networking technologies, and the merger of many networks. The linking of commercial networks and enterprises by the early 1990s marks the beginning of the transition to the modern Internet, and generated a sustained exponential growth as generations of institutional, personal, and mobile computers were connected to the network. Although the Internet was widely used by academia since the 1980s, the commercialization incorporated its services and technologies into virtually every aspect of modern life.

Internet use grew rapidly in the West from the mid-1990s and from the late 1990s in the developing world. In the 20 years since 1995, Internet use has grown 100-times, measured for the period of one year, to over one third of the world population. Most traditional communications media, including telephony, radio, television, paper mail and newspapers are being reshaped or redefined by the Internet, giving birth to new services such as email, Internet telephony, Internet television music, digital newspapers, and video streaming websites. Newspaper, book, and other print publishing are adapting to website technology, or are reshaped into blogging, web feeds and online news aggregators. The entertainment industry was initially the fastest growing segment on the Internet. The Internet has enabled and accelerated new forms of personal interactions through instant messaging, Internet forums, and social networking. Online shopping has grown exponentially both for major retailers and small businesses and entrepreneurs, as it enables firms to extend their "bricks and mortar" presence to serve a larger market or even sell goods and services entirely online. Business-to-business and financial services on the Internet affect supply chains across entire industries.

The Internet has no centralized governance in either technological implementation or policies for access and usage; each constituent network sets its own policies. Only the overreaching definitions of the two principal name spaces in the Internet, the Internet Protocol address space and the Domain Name System (DNS), are directed by a maintainer organization, the Internet Corporation for Assigned Names and Numbers (ICANN). The technical underpinning and standardization of the core protocols is an activity of the Internet Engineering Task Force (IETF), a non-profit organization of loosely affiliated international participants that anyone may associate with by contributing technical expertise.

Terminology

The term *Internet*, when used to refer to the specific global system of interconnected Internet Protocol (IP) networks, is a proper noun and may be written with an initial capital letter. In common use and the media, it is often not capitalized, viz. *the internet*. Some guides specify that the word should be capitalized when used as a noun, but not capitalized when used as an adjective. The Internet is also often referred to as *the Net*, as a short form of *network*. Historically, as early as 1849, the word *internetted* was used uncapitalized as an adjective, meaning *interconnected* or *interwoven*. The designers of early computer networks used *internet* both as a noun and as a verb in shorthand form of internetwork or internetworking, meaning interconnecting computer networks.

The Internet Messenger by Buky Schwartz in Holon, Israel

The terms *Internet* and *World Wide Web* are often used interchangeably in everyday speech; it is common to speak of *"going on the Internet"* when invoking a web browser to view web pages. However, the World Wide Web or *the Web* is only one of a large number of Internet services. The Web is a collection of interconnected documents (web pages) and other web resources, linked by hyperlinks and URLs. As another point of comparison, Hypertext Transfer Protocol, or HTTP, is the language used on the Web for information transfer, yet it is just one of many languages or protocols that can be used for communication on the Internet. The term *Interweb* is a portmanteau of *Internet* and *World Wide Web* typically used sarcastically to parody a technically unsavvy user.

History

Research into packet switching started in the early 1960s, and packet switched networks such as the ARPANET, CYCLADES, the Merit Network, NPL network, Tymnet, and Telenet, were developed in the late 1960s and 1970s using a variety of protocols. The ARPANET project led to the development of protocols for internetworking, by which multiple separate networks could be joined into a single network of networks. ARPANET development began with two network nodes which were interconnected between the Network Measurement Center at the University of California, Los Angeles (UCLA) Henry Samueli School of Engineering and Applied Science directed by Leonard Kleinrock, and the NLS system at SRI International (SRI) by Douglas Engelbart in Menlo Park, California, on 29 October 1969. The third site was the Culler-Fried Interactive Mathematics Center at the University of California, Santa Barbara, followed by the University of Utah Graphics Department. In an early sign of future growth, fifteen sites were connected to the young ARPANET by the end of 1971. These early years were documented in the 1972 film *Computer Networks: The Heralds of Resource Sharing*.

Early international collaborations on the ARPANET were rare. European developers were concerned with developing the X.25 networks. Notable exceptions were the Norwegian Seismic Array (NORSAR) in June 1973, followed in 1973 by Sweden with satellite links to the Tanum Earth Station and Peter T. Kirstein's research group in the United Kingdom, initially at the Institute of Computer Science, University of London and later at University College London. In December 1974, RFC 675 (*Specification of Internet Transmission Control Program*), by Vinton Cerf, Yogen Dalal, and Carl Sunshine, used the term *internet* as a shorthand for *internetworking* and later RFCs repeated this use. Access to the ARPANET was expanded in 1981 when the National Science Foundation (NSF) funded the Computer Science Network (CSNET). In 1982, the Internet Protocol Suite (TCP/IP) was standardized, which permitted worldwide proliferation of interconnected networks.

NSFNET T3 Network 1992

T3 NSFNET Backbone, c. 1992.

TCP/IP network access expanded again in 1986 when the National Science Foundation Network (NSFNet) provided access to supercomputer sites in the United States for researchers, first at speeds of 56 kbit/s and later at 1.5 Mbit/s and 45 Mbit/s. Commercial Internet service providers (ISPs) emerged in the late 1980s and early 1990s. The ARPANET was decommissioned in 1990. By 1995, the Internet was fully commercialized in the U.S. when the NSFNet was decommissioned, removing the last restrictions on use of the Internet to carry commercial traffic. The Internet rapidly expanded in Europe and Australia in the mid to late 1980s and to Asia in the late 1980s and early 1990s. The beginning of dedicated transatlantic communication between the NSFNET and networks in Europe was established with a low-speed satellite relay between Princeton University and Stockholm, Sweden in December 1988. Although other network protocols such as UUCP had global reach well before this time, this marked the beginning of the Internet as an intercontinental network.

Slightly over a year later in March 1990, the first high-speed T1 (1.5 Mbit/s) link between the NSFNET and Europe was installed between Cornell University and CERN, allowing much more robust communications than were capable with satellites. Six months later Tim Berners-Lee would begin writing WorldWideWeb, the first web browser after two years of lobbying CERN management. By Christmas 1990, Berners-Lee had built all the tools necessary for a working Web: the HyperText Transfer Protocol (HTTP) 0.9, the HyperText Markup Language (HTML), the first Web browser (which was also a HTML editor and could access Usenet newsgroups and FTP files), the first HTTP server software (later known as CERN httpd), the first web server (http://info.cern.ch), and the first Web pages that described the project itself. Public commercial use of the Internet began in mid-1989 with the connection of MCI Mail and Compuserve's email capabilities to the 500,000 users of the Internet. Just months later on January 1, 1990, PSInet launched an alternate Internet backbone for commercial use; one of the networks that would grow into the commercial Internet we know today. In 1991 the Commercial Internet eXchange was founded, allowing PSInet to communicate with the other commercial networks CERFnet and Alternet. Since 1995 the Internet has tremendously impacted culture and commerce, including the rise of near instant communication by email, instant messaging, telephony (Voice over Internet Protocol or VoIP), two-way interactive video calls, and the World Wide Web with its discussion forums, blogs, social networking, and online shopping sites. Increasing amounts of data are transmitted at higher and higher speeds over fiber optic networks operating at 1-Gbit/s, 10-Gbit/s, or more.

The Internet continues to grow, driven by ever greater amounts of online information and knowledge, commerce, entertainment and social networking. During the late 1990s, it was estimated that traffic on the public Internet grew by 100 percent per year, while the mean annual growth in the number of Internet users was thought to be between 20% and 50%. This growth is often attributed to the lack of central administration, which allows organic growth of the network, as well as the non-proprietary nature of the Internet protocols, which encourages vendor interoperability and prevents any one company from exerting too much control over the network. As of 31 March 2011, the estimated total number of Internet users was 2.095 billion (30.2% of world population). It is estimated that in 1993 the Internet carried only 1% of the information flowing through two-way telecommunication, by 2000 this figure had grown to 51%, and by 2007 more than 97% of all telecommunicated information was carried over the Internet.

Governance

The Internet is a global network comprising many voluntarily interconnected autonomous networks. It operates without a central governing body. The technical underpinning and standardization of the core protocols (IPv4 and IPv6) is an activity of the Internet Engineering Task Force (IETF), a non-profit organization of loosely affiliated international participants that anyone may associate with by contributing technical expertise. To maintain interoperability, the principal name spaces of the Internet are administered by the Internet Corporation for Assigned Names and Numbers (ICANN). ICANN is governed by an international board of directors drawn from across the Internet technical, business, academic, and other non-commercial communities. ICANN coordinates the assignment of unique identifiers for use on the Internet, including domain names, Internet Protocol (IP) addresses, application port numbers in the transport protocols, and many other parameters. Globally unified name spaces are essential for maintaining the global reach of the Internet. This role of ICANN distinguishes it as perhaps the only central coordinating body for the global Internet.

ICANN headquarters in the Playa Vista neighborhood of Los Angeles, California, United States.

Regional Internet Registries (RIRs) allocate IP addresses:

- African Network Information Center (AfriNIC) for Africa

- American Registry for Internet Numbers (ARIN) for North America

- Asia-Pacific Network Information Centre (APNIC) for Asia and the Pacific region

- Latin American and Caribbean Internet Addresses Registry (LACNIC) for Latin America and the Caribbean region

- Réseaux IP Européens – Network Coordination Centre (RIPE NCC) for Europe, the Middle East, and Central Asia

The National Telecommunications and Information Administration, an agency of the United States Department of Commerce, continues to have final approval over changes to the DNS root zone. The Internet Society (ISOC) was founded in 1992 with a mission to *"assure the open development, evolution and use of the Internet for the benefit of all people throughout the world"*. Its members include individuals (anyone may join) as well as corporations, organizations, governments, and universities. Among other activities ISOC provides an administrative home for a number of less formally organized groups that are involved in developing and managing the Internet, including: the Internet Engineering Task Force (IETF), Internet Architecture Board (IAB), Internet Engineering Steering Group (IESG), Internet Research Task Force (IRTF), and Internet Research Steering Group (IRSG). On 16 November 2005, the United Nations-sponsored World Summit on the Information Society in Tunis established the Internet Governance Forum (IGF) to discuss Internet-related issues.

Infrastructure

The communications infrastructure of the Internet consists of its hardware components and a system of software layers that control various aspects of the architecture.

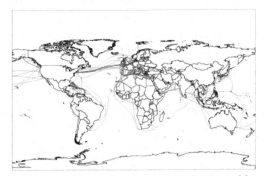

2007 map showing submarine fiberoptic telecommunication cables around the world.

Routing and Service Tiers

Internet service providers establish the worldwide connectivity between individual networks at various levels of scope. End-users who only access the Internet when needed to perform a function or obtain information, represent the bottom of the routing hierarchy. At the top of the routing hierarchy are the tier 1 networks, large telecommunication companies that exchange traffic directly with each other via peering agreements. Tier 2 and lower level networks buy Internet transit from other providers to reach at least some parties on the global Internet, though they may also engage in peering. An ISP may use a single upstream provider for connectivity, or implement multihoming to achieve redundancy and load balancing. Internet exchange points are major traffic exchanges with physical connections to multiple ISPs. Large organizations, such as academic institutions, large enterprises, and governments, may perform the same function as ISPs, engaging in peering and purchasing transit on behalf of their internal networks. Research networks tend to interconnect with large subnetworks such as GEANT, GLORIAD, Internet2, and the UK's national research and education network, JANET. Both the Internet IP routing structure and hypertext links of the World Wide Web are examples of scale-free networks. Computers and routers use routing tables in their operating system to direct IP packets to the next-hop router or destination. Routing tables are maintained by manual configuration or automatically by routing protocols. End-nodes typically use a default route that points toward an ISP providing transit, while ISP routers use the Border Gateway Protocol to establish the most efficient routing across the complex connections of the global Internet.

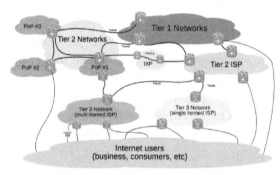

Packet routing across the Internet involves several tiers of Internet service providers.

Access

Common methods of Internet access by users include dial-up with a computer modem via telephone circuits, broadband over coaxial cable, fiber optics or copper wires, Wi-Fi, satellite and cellular telephone technology (3G, 4G). The Internet may often be accessed from computers in libraries and Internet cafes. Internet access points exist in many public places such as airport halls and coffee shops. Various terms are used, such as *public Internet kiosk, public access terminal*, and *Web payphone*. Many hotels also have public terminals, though these are usually fee-based. These terminals are widely accessed for various usages, such as ticket booking, bank deposit, or online payment. Wi-Fi provides wireless access to the Internet via local computer networks. Hotspots providing such access include Wi-Fi cafes, where users need to bring their own wireless devices such as a laptop or PDA. These services may be free to all, free to customers only, or fee-based.

Grassroots efforts have led to wireless community networks. Commercial Wi-Fi services covering large city areas are in place in New York, London, Vienna, Toronto, San Francisco, Philadelphia, Chicago and Pittsburgh. The Internet can then be accessed from such places as a park bench. Apart from Wi-Fi, there have been experiments with proprietary mobile wireless networks like Ricochet, various high-speed data services over cellular phone networks, and fixed wireless services. High-end mobile phones such as smartphones in general come with Internet access through the phone network. Web browsers such as Opera are available on these advanced handsets, which can also run a wide variety of other Internet software. More mobile phones have Internet access than PCs, though this is not as widely used. An Internet access provider and protocol matrix differentiates the methods used to get online.

Structure

Many computer scientists describe the Internet as a "prime example of a large-scale, highly engineered, yet highly complex system". The structure was found to be highly robust to random failures, yet, very vulnerable to intentional attacks. The Internet structure and its usage characteristics have been studied extensively and the possibility of developing alternative structures has been investigated.

Protocols

While the hardware components in the Internet infrastructure can often be used to support other software systems, it is the design and the standardization process of the software that characterizes the Internet and provides the foundation for its scalability and success. The responsibility for the architectural design of the Internet software systems has been assumed by the Internet Engineering Task Force (IETF). The IETF conducts standard-setting work groups, open to any individual, about the various aspects of Internet architecture. Resulting contributions and standards are published as *Request for Comments* (RFC) documents on the IETF web site. The principal methods of networking that enable the Internet are contained in specially designated RFCs that constitute the Internet Standards. Other less rigorous documents are simply informative, experimental, or historical, or document the best current practices (BCP) when implementing Internet technologies.

The Internet standards describe a framework known as the Internet protocol suite. This is a model architecture that divides methods into a layered system of protocols, originally documented in RFC 1122 and RFC 1123. The layers correspond to the environment or scope in which their services operate. At the top is the application layer, space for the application-specific networking methods used in software applications. For example, a web browser program uses the client-server application model and a specific protocol of interaction between servers and clients, while many file-sharing systems use a peer-to-peer paradigm. Below this top layer, the transport layer connects applications on different hosts with a logical channel through the network with appropriate data exchange methods.

Underlying these layers are the networking technologies that interconnect networks at their borders and hosts via the physical connections. The Internet layer enables computers to identify and locate each other via Internet Protocol (IP) addresses, and routes their traffic via intermediate (transit) networks. Last, at the bottom of the architecture is the link layer, which provides connectivity between hosts on the same network link, such as a physical connection in the form of a local area network (LAN) or a dial-up connection. The model, also known as TCP/IP, is designed to be independent of the underlying hardware, which the model, therefore, does not concern itself with in any detail. Other models have been developed, such as the OSI model, that attempt to be comprehensive in every aspect of communications. While many similarities exist between the models, they are not compatible in the details of description or implementation; indeed, TCP/IP protocols are usually included in the discussion of OSI networking.

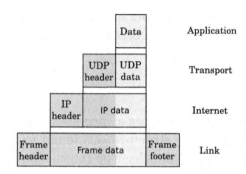

As user data is processed through the protocol stack, each abstraction layer adds encapsulation information at the sending host. Data is transmitted *over the wire* at the link level between hosts and routers. Encapsulation is removed by the receiving host. Intermediate relays update link encapsulation at each hop, and inspect the IP layer for routing purposes.

The most prominent component of the Internet model is the Internet Protocol (IP), which provides addressing systems (IP addresses) for computers on the Internet. IP enables internetworking and, in essence, establishes the Internet itself. Internet Protocol Version 4 (IPv4) is the initial version used on the first generation of the Internet and is still in dominant use. It was designed to address up to ~4.3 billion (10^9) Internet hosts. However, the explosive growth of the Internet has led to IPv4 address exhaustion, which entered its final stage in 2011, when the global address allocation pool was exhausted. A new protocol version, IPv6, was developed in the mid-1990s, which provides vastly larger addressing capabilities and more efficient routing of Internet traffic. IPv6 is currently in growing deployment around the world, since Internet address registries (RIRs) began to urge all resource managers to plan rapid adoption and conversion.

IPv6 is not directly interoperable by design with IPv4. In essence, it establishes a parallel version of the Internet not directly accessible with IPv4 software. Thus, translation facilities must exist for internetworking or nodes must have duplicate networking software for both networks. Essentially all modern computer operating systems support both versions of the Internet Protocol. Network infrastructure, however, is still lagging in this development. Aside from the complex array of physical connections that make up its infrastructure, the Internet is facilitated by bi- or multi-lateral commercial contracts, e.g., peering agreements, and by technical specifications or protocols that describe the exchange of data over the network. Indeed, the Internet is defined by its interconnections and routing policies.

Services

The Internet carries many network services, most prominently mobile apps such as social media apps, the World Wide Web, electronic mail, multiplayer online games, Internet telephony, and file sharing services.

World Wide Web

Many people use the terms *Internet* and *World Wide Web*, or just the *Web*, interchangeably, but the two terms are not synonymous. The World Wide Web is the primary application that billions of people use on the Internet, and it has changed their lives immeasurably. However, the Internet provides many other services. The Web is a global set of documents, images and other resources, logically interrelated by hyperlinks and referenced with Uniform Resource Identifiers (URIs). URIs symbolically identify services, servers, and other databases, and the documents and resources that they can provide. Hypertext Transfer Protocol (HTTP) is the main access protocol of the World Wide Web. Web services also use HTTP to allow software systems to communicate in order to share and exchange business logic and data.

This NeXT Computer was used by Tim Berners-Lee at CERN and became the world's first Web server.

World Wide Web browser software, such as Microsoft's Internet Explorer, Mozilla Firefox, Opera, Apple's Safari, and Google Chrome, lets users navigate from one web page to another via hyperlinks embedded in the documents. These documents may also contain any combination of computer data, including graphics, sounds, text, video, multimedia and interactive content that runs while the user is interacting with the page. Client-side software can include animations, games, office applications and scientific demonstrations. Through keyword-driven Internet research using search engines like Yahoo! and Google, users worldwide have easy, instant access to a vast and diverse amount of online information. Compared to printed media, books, encyclopedias and traditional libraries, the World Wide Web has enabled the decentralization of information on a large scale.

The Web has also enabled individuals and organizations to publish ideas and information to a potentially large audience online at greatly reduced expense and time delay. Publishing a web page, a blog, or building a website involves little initial cost and many cost-free services are available. However, publishing and maintaining large, professional web sites with attractive, diverse and up-to-date information is still a difficult and expensive proposition. Many individuals and some companies and groups use *web logs* or blogs, which are largely used as easily updatable online diaries. Some commercial organizations encourage staff to communicate advice in their areas of specialization in the hope that visitors will be impressed by the expert knowledge and free information, and be attracted to the corporation as a result.

One example of this practice is Microsoft, whose product developers publish their personal blogs in order to pique the public's interest in their work. Collections of personal web pages published by large service providers remain popular and have become increasingly sophisticated. Whereas operations such as Angelfire and GeoCities have existed since the early days of the Web, newer offerings from, for example, Facebook and Twitter currently have large followings. These operations often brand themselves as social network services rather than simply as web page hosts.

Advertising on popular web pages can be lucrative, and e-commerce or the sale of products and services directly via the Web continues to grow. Online advertising is a form of marketing and advertising which uses the Internet to deliver promotional marketing messages to consumers. It includes email marketing, search engine marketing (SEM), social media marketing, many types of display advertising (including web banner advertising), and mobile advertising. In 2011, Internet advertising revenues in the United States surpassed those of cable television and nearly exceeded those of broadcast television. Many common online advertising practices are controversial and increasingly subject to regulation.

When the Web developed in the 1990s, a typical web page was stored in completed form on a web server, formatted in HTML, complete for transmission to a web browser in response to a request. Over time, the process of creating and serving web pages has become dynamic, creating a flexible design, layout, and content. Websites are often created using content management software with, initially, very little content. Contributors to these systems, who may be paid staff, members of an organization or the public, fill underlying databases with content using editing pages designed for that purpose while casual visitors view and read this content in HTML form. There may or may not be editorial, approval and security systems built into the process of taking newly entered content and making it available to the target visitors.

Communication

Email is an important communications service available on the Internet. The concept of sending electronic text messages between parties in a way analogous to mailing letters or memos predates the creation of the Internet. Pictures, documents, and other files are sent as email attachments. Emails can be cc-ed to multiple email addresses.

Internet telephony is another common communications service made possible by the creation of the Internet. VoIP stands for Voice-over-Internet Protocol, referring to the protocol that underlies all Internet communication. The idea began in the early 1990s with walkie-talkie-like voice applications for personal computers. In recent years many VoIP systems have become as easy to use and as convenient as a normal telephone. The benefit is that, as the Internet carries the voice traffic, VoIP can be free or cost much less than a traditional telephone call, especially over long distances and especially for those with always-on Internet connections such as cable or ADSL. VoIP is maturing into a competitive alternative to traditional telephone service. Interoperability between different providers has improved and the ability to call or receive a call from a traditional telephone is available. Simple, inexpensive VoIP network adapters are available that eliminate the need for a personal computer.

Voice quality can still vary from call to call, but is often equal to and can even exceed that of traditional calls. Remaining problems for VoIP include emergency telephone number dialing and reliability. Currently, a few VoIP providers provide an emergency service, but it is not universally available. Older traditional phones with no "extra features" may be line-powered only and operate during a power failure; VoIP can never do so without a backup power source for the phone equipment and the Internet access devices. VoIP has also become increasingly popular for gaming applications, as a form of communication between players. Popular VoIP clients for gaming include Ventrilo and Teamspeak. Modern video game consoles also offer VoIP chat features.

Data Transfer

File sharing is an example of transferring large amounts of data across the Internet. A computer file can be emailed to customers, colleagues and friends as an attachment. It can be uploaded to a website or File Transfer Protocol (FTP) server for easy download by others. It can be put into a "shared location" or onto a file server for instant use by colleagues. The load of bulk downloads to many users can be eased by the use of "mirror" servers or peer-to-peer networks. In any of these cases, access to the file may be controlled by user authentication, the transit of the file over the Internet may be obscured by encryption, and money may change hands for access to the file. The price can be paid by the remote charging of funds from, for example, a credit card whose details are also passed – usually fully encrypted – across the Internet. The origin and authenticity of the file received may be checked by digital signatures or by MD5 or other message digests. These simple features of the Internet, over a worldwide basis, are changing the production, sale, and distribution of anything that can be reduced to a computer file for transmission. This includes all manner of print publications, software products, news, music, film, video, photography, graphics and the other arts. This in turn has caused seismic shifts in each of the existing industries that previously controlled the production and distribution of these products.

Streaming media is the real-time delivery of digital media for the immediate consumption or enjoyment by end users. Many radio and television broadcasters provide Internet feeds of their live audio and video productions. They may also allow time-shift viewing or listening such as Preview, Classic Clips and Listen Again features. These providers have been joined by a range of pure Internet "broadcasters" who never had on-air licenses. This means that an Internet-connected device, such as a computer or something more specific, can be used to access on-line media in much the same way as was previously possible only with a television or radio receiver. The range of available types of content is much wider, from specialized technical webcasts to on-demand popular multimedia services. Podcasting is a variation on this theme, where – usually audio – material is downloaded and played back on a computer or shifted to a portable media player to be listened to on the move. These techniques using simple equipment allow anybody, with little censorship or licensing control, to broadcast audio-visual material worldwide.

Digital media streaming increases the demand for network bandwidth. For example, standard image quality needs 1 Mbit/s link speed for SD 480p, HD 720p quality requires 2.5 Mbit/s, and the top-of-the-line HDX quality needs 4.5 Mbit/s for 1080p.

Webcams are a low-cost extension of this phenomenon. While some webcams can give full-frame-rate video, the picture either is usually small or updates slowly. Internet users can watch animals around an African waterhole, ships in the Panama Canal, traffic at a local roundabout or monitor their own premises, live and in real time. Video chat rooms and video conferencing are also popular with many uses being found for personal webcams, with and without two-way sound. YouTube was founded on 15 February 2005 and is now the leading website for free streaming video with a vast number of users. It uses a flash-based web player to stream and show video files. Registered users may upload an unlimited amount of video and build their own personal profile. YouTube claims that its users watch hundreds of millions, and upload hundreds of thousands of videos daily. Currently, YouTube also uses an HTML5 player.

Social Impact

The Internet has enabled new forms of social interaction, activities, and social associations. This phenomenon has given rise to the scholarly study of the sociology of the Internet.

Users

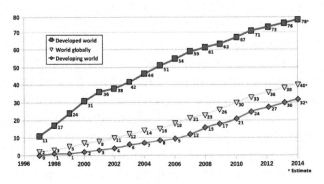

Internet users per 100 inhabitants

Source: International Telecommunications Union.

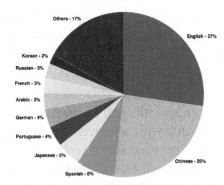

Internet users by language[69]

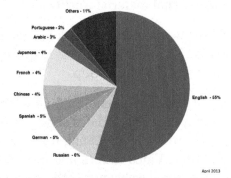

Website content languages[70]

Internet usage has seen tremendous growth. From 2000 to 2009, the number of Internet users globally rose from 394 million to 1.858 billion. By 2010, 22 percent of the world's population had access to computers with 1 billion Google searches every day, 300 million Internet users reading blogs, and 2 billion videos viewed daily on YouTube. In 2014 the world's Internet users surpassed 3 billion or

43.6 percent of world population, but two-thirds of the users came from richest countries, with 78.0 percent of Europe countries population using the Internet, followed by 57.4 percent of the Americas.

The prevalent language for communication on the Internet has been English. This may be a result of the origin of the Internet, as well as the language's role as a lingua franca. Early computer systems were limited to the characters in the American Standard Code for Information Interchange (ASCII), a subset of the Latin alphabet.

After English (27%), the most requested languages on the World Wide Web are Chinese (25%), Spanish (8%), Japanese (5%), Portuguese and German (4% each), Arabic, French and Russian (3% each), and Korean (2%). By region, 42% of the world's Internet users are based in Asia, 24% in Europe, 14% in North America, 10% in Latin America and the Caribbean taken together, 6% in Africa, 3% in the Middle East and 1% in Australia/Oceania. The Internet's technologies have developed enough in recent years, especially in the use of Unicode, that good facilities are available for development and communication in the world's widely used languages. However, some glitches such as *mojibake* (incorrect display of some languages' characters) still remain.

In an American study in 2005, the percentage of men using the Internet was very slightly ahead of the percentage of women, although this difference reversed in those under 30. Men logged on more often, spent more time online, and were more likely to be broadband users, whereas women tended to make more use of opportunities to communicate (such as email). Men were more likely to use the Internet to pay bills, participate in auctions, and for recreation such as downloading music and videos. Men and women were equally likely to use the Internet for shopping and banking. More recent studies indicate that in 2008, women significantly outnumbered men on most social networking sites, such as Facebook and Myspace, although the ratios varied with age. In addition, women watched more streaming content, whereas men downloaded more. In terms of blogs, men were more likely to blog in the first place; among those who blog, men were more likely to have a professional blog, whereas women were more likely to have a personal blog.

According to forecasts by Euromonitor International, 44% of the world's population will be users of the Internet by 2020. Splitting by country, in 2012 Iceland, Norway, Sweden, the Netherlands, and Denmark had the highest Internet penetration by the number of users, with 93% or more of the population with access.

Several neologisms exist that refer to Internet users: Netizen (as in as in "citizen of the net") refers to those actively involved in improving online communities, the Internet in general or surrounding political affairs and rights such as free speech, Internaut refers to operators or technically highly capable users of the Internet, digital citizen refers to a person using the Internet in order to engage in society, politics, and government participation.

Usage

The Internet allows greater flexibility in working hours and location, especially with the spread of unmetered high-speed connections. The Internet can be accessed almost anywhere by numerous means, including through mobile Internet devices. Mobile phones, datacards, handheld game consoles and cellular routers allow users to connect to the Internet wirelessly. Within the limitations imposed by small screens and other limited facilities of such pocket-sized devices, the services of the Internet, including email and the web, may be available. Service providers may restrict the services offered and mobile data charges may be significantly higher than other access methods.

Educational material at all levels from pre-school to post-doctoral is available from websites. Examples range from CBeebies, through school and high-school revision guides and virtual universities, to access to top-end scholarly literature through the likes of Google Scholar. For distance education, help with homework and other assignments, self-guided learning, whiling away spare time, or just looking up more detail on an interesting fact, it has never been easier for people to access educational information at any level from anywhere. The Internet in general and the World Wide Web in particular are important enablers of both formal and informal education. Further, the Internet allows universities, in particular, researchers from the social and behavioral sciences, to conduct research remotely via virtual laboratories, with profound changes in reach and generalizability of findings as well as in communication between scientists and in the publication of results.

The low cost and nearly instantaneous sharing of ideas, knowledge, and skills have made collaborative work dramatically easier, with the help of collaborative software. Not only can a group cheaply communicate and share ideas but the wide reach of the Internet allows such groups more easily to form. An example of this is the free software movement, which has produced, among other things, Linux, Mozilla Firefox, and OpenOffice.org. Internet chat, whether using an IRC chat room, an instant messaging system, or a social networking website, allows colleagues to stay in touch in a very convenient way while working at their computers during the day. Messages can be exchanged even more quickly and conveniently than via email. These systems may allow files to be exchanged, drawings and images to be shared, or voice and video contact between team members.

Content management systems allow collaborating teams to work on shared sets of documents simultaneously without accidentally destroying each other's work. Business and project teams can share calendars as well as documents and other information. Such collaboration occurs in a wide variety of areas including scientific research, software development, conference planning, political activism and creative writing. Social and political collaboration is also becoming more widespread as both Internet access and computer literacy spread.

The Internet allows computer users to remotely access other computers and information stores easily from any access point. Access may be with computer security, i.e. authentication and encryption technologies, depending on the requirements. This is encouraging new ways of working from home, collaboration and information sharing in many industries. An accountant sitting at home can audit the books of a company based in another country, on a server situated in a third country that is remotely maintained by IT specialists in a fourth. These accounts could have been created by home-working bookkeepers, in other remote locations, based on information emailed to them from offices all over the world. Some of these things were possible before the widespread use of the Internet, but the cost of private leased lines would have made many of them infeasible in practice. An office worker away from their desk, perhaps on the other side of the world on a business trip or a holiday, can access their emails, access their data using cloud computing, or open a remote desktop session into their office PC using a secure virtual private network (VPN) connection on the Internet. This can give the worker complete access to all of their normal files and data, including email and other applications, while away from the office. It has been referred to among system administrators as the Virtual Private Nightmare, because it extends the secure perimeter of a corporate network into remote locations and its employees' homes.

Social Networking and Entertainment

Many people use the World Wide Web to access news, weather and sports reports, to plan and book vacations and to pursue their personal interests. People use chat, messaging and email to make and stay in touch with friends worldwide, sometimes in the same way as some previously had pen pals. Social networking websites such as Facebook, Twitter, and Myspace have created new ways to socialize and interact. Users of these sites are able to add a wide variety of information to pages, to pursue common interests, and to connect with others. It is also possible to find existing acquaintances, to allow communication among existing groups of people. Sites like LinkedIn foster commercial and business connections. YouTube and Flickr specialize in users' videos and photographs. While social networking sites were initially for individuals only, today they are widely used by businesses and other organizations to promote their brands, to market to their customers and to encourage posts to "go viral". "Black hat" social media techniques are also employed by some organizations, such as spam accounts and astroturfing.

A risk for both individuals and organizations writing posts (especially public posts) on social networking websites, is that especially foolish or controversial posts occasionally lead to an unexpected and possibly large-scale backlash on social media from other Internet users. This is also a risk in relation to controversial *offline* behavior, if it is widely made known. The nature of this backlash can range widely from counter-arguments and public mockery, through insults and hate speech, to, in extreme cases, rape and death threats. The online disinhibition effect describes the tendency of many individuals to behave more stridently or offensively online than they would in person. A significant number of feminist women have been the target of various forms of harassment in response to posts they have made on social media, and Twitter in particular has been criticised in the past for not doing enough to aid victims of online abuse.

For organizations, such a backlash can cause overall brand damage, especially if reported by the media. However, this is not always the case, as any brand damage in the eyes of people with an opposing opinion to that presented by the organization could sometimes be outweighed by strengthening the brand in the eyes of others. Furthermore, if an organization or individual gives in to demands that others perceive as wrong-headed, that can then provoke a counter-backlash.

Some websites, such as Reddit, have rules forbidding the posting of personal information of individuals (also known as doxxing), due to concerns about such postings leading to mobs of large numbers of Internet users directing harassment at the specific individuals thereby identified. In particular, the Reddit rule forbidding the posting of personal information is widely understood to imply that all identifying photos and names must be censored in Facebook screenshots posted to Reddit. However, the interpretation of this rule in relation to public Twitter posts is less clear, and in any case, like-minded people online have many other ways they can use to direct each other's attention to public social media posts they disagree with.

Children also face dangers online such as cyberbullying and approaches by sexual predators, who sometimes pose as children themselves. Children may also encounter material which they may find upsetting, or material which their parents consider to be not age-appropriate. Due to naivety, they may also post personal information about themselves online, which could put them or their families at risk unless warned not to do so. Many parents choose to enable Internet filtering, and/or supervise their children's online activities, in an attempt to protect their children from inappropriate material on the Internet. The most popular social networking websites, such as Facebook and Twitter, commonly forbid users under the age of 13. However, these policies are typically trivial to circumvent by registering an account with a false birth date, and a significant number of children aged under 13 join such sites anyway. Social networking sites for younger children, which claim to provide better levels of protection for children, also exist.

The Internet has been a major outlet for leisure activity since its inception, with entertaining social experiments such as MUDs and MOOs being conducted on university servers, and humor-related Usenet groups receiving much traffic. Today, many Internet forums have sections devoted to games and funny videos. Over 6 million people use blogs or message boards as a means of communication and for the sharing of ideas. The Internet pornography and online gambling industries have taken advantage of the World Wide Web, and often provide a significant source of advertising revenue for other websites. Although many governments have attempted to restrict both industries' use of the Internet, in general, this has failed to stop their widespread popularity.

Another area of leisure activity on the Internet is multiplayer gaming. This form of recreation creates communities, where people of all ages and origins enjoy the fast-paced world of multiplayer games. These range from MMORPG to first-person shooters, from role-playing video games to online gambling. While online gaming has been around since the 1970s, modern modes of online gaming began with subscription services such as GameSpy and MPlayer. Non-subscribers were limited to certain types of game play or certain games. Many people use the Internet to access and download music, movies and other works for their enjoyment and relaxation. Free and fee-based services exist for all of these activities, using centralized servers and distributed peer-to-peer technologies. Some of these sources exercise more care with respect to the original artists' copyrights than others.

Internet usage has been correlated to users' loneliness. Lonely people tend to use the Internet as an outlet for their feelings and to share their stories with others, such as in the "I am lonely will anyone speak to me" thread.

Cybersectarianism is a new organizational form which involves: "highly dispersed small groups of practitioners that may remain largely anonymous within the larger social context and operate in relative secrecy, while still linked remotely to a larger network of believers who share a set of practices and texts, and often a common devotion to a particular leader. Overseas supporters provide funding and support; domestic practitioners distribute tracts, participate in acts of resistance, and share information on the internal situation with outsiders. Collectively, members and practitioners of such sects construct viable virtual communities of faith, exchanging personal testimonies and engaging in the collective study via email, on-line chat rooms, and web-based message boards." In particular, the British government has raised concerns about the prospect of young British Muslims being indoctrinated into Islamic extremism by material on the Internet, being persuaded to join terrorist groups such as the so-called "Islamic State", and then potentially committing acts of terrorism on returning to Britain after fighting in Syria or Iraq.

Cyberslacking can become a drain on corporate resources; the average UK employee spent 57 minutes a day surfing the Web while at work, according to a 2003 study by Peninsula Business Services. Internet addiction disorder is excessive computer use that interferes with daily life. Psychologist, Nicolas Carr believe that Internet use has other effects on individuals, for instance improving skills of scan-reading and interfering with the deep thinking that leads to true creativity.

Electronic Business

Electronic business (*e-business*) encompasses business processes spanning the entire value chain: purchasing, supply chain management, marketing, sales, customer service, and business relationship. E-commerce seeks to add revenue streams using the Internet to build and enhance relationships with clients and partners. According to International Data Corporation, the size of worldwide e-commerce, when global business-to-business and -consumer transactions are combined, equate to $16 trillion for 2013. A report by Oxford Economics adds those two together to estimate the total size of the digital economy at $20.4 trillion, equivalent to roughly 13.8% of global sales.

While much has been written of the economic advantages of Internet-enabled commerce, there is also evidence that some aspects of the Internet such as maps and location-aware services may serve to reinforce economic inequality and the digital divide. Electronic commerce may be responsible for consolidation and the decline of mom-and-pop, brick and mortar businesses resulting in increases in income inequality.

Author Andrew Keen, a long-time critic of the social transformations caused by the Internet, has recently focused on the economic effects of consolidation from Internet businesses. Keen cites a 2013 Institute for Local Self-Reliance report saying brick-and-mortar retailers employ 47 people for every $10 million in sales while Amazon employs only 14. Similarly, the 700-employee room rental start-up Airbnb was valued at $10 billion in 2014, about half as much as Hilton Hotels, which employs 152,000 people. And car-sharing Internet startup Uber employs 1,000 full-time employees and is valued at $18.2 billion, about the same valuation as Avis and Hertz combined, which together employ almost 60,000 people.

Telecommuting

Telecommuting is the performance within a traditional worker and employer relationship when it is facilitated by tools such as groupware, virtual private networks, conference calling, videoconferencing, and voice over IP (VOIP) so that work may be performed from any location, most conveniently the worker's home. It can be efficient and useful for companies as it allows workers to communicate over long distances, saving significant amounts of travel time and cost. As broadband Internet connections become commonplace, more workers have adequate bandwidth at home to use these tools to link their home to their corporate intranet and internal communication networks.

Crowdsourcing

The Internet provides a particularly good venue for crowdsourcing, because individuals tend to be more open in web-based projects where they are not being physically judged or scrutinized and thus can feel more comfortable sharing.

Collaborative Publishing

Wikis have also been used in the academic community for sharing and dissemination of information across institutional and international boundaries. In those settings, they have been found useful for collaboration on grant writing, strategic planning, departmental documentation, and committee work. The United States Patent and Trademark Office uses a wiki to allow the public to collaborate on finding prior art relevant to examination of pending patent applications. Queens, New York has used a wiki to allow citizens to collaborate on the design and planning of a local park. The English Wikipedia has the largest user base among wikis on the World Wide Web and ranks in the top 10 among all Web sites in terms of traffic.

Politics and Political Revolutions

The Internet has achieved new relevance as a political tool. The presidential campaign of Howard Dean in 2004 in the United States was notable for its success in soliciting donation via the Internet. Many political groups use the Internet to achieve a new method of organizing for carrying out their mission, having given rise to Internet activism, most notably practiced by rebels in the Arab Spring. *The New York Times* suggested that social media websites, such as Facebook and Twitter, helped people organize the political revolutions in Egypt, by helping activists organize protests, communicate grievances, and disseminate information.

Banner in Bangkok during the 2014 Thai coup d'état, informing the Thai public that 'like' or 'share' activities on social media could result in imprisonment (observed June 30, 2014).

The potential of the Internet as a civic tool of communicative power was explored by Simon R. B. Berdal in his 2004 thesis:

As the globally evolving Internet provides ever new access points to virtual discourse forums, it also promotes new civic relations and associations within which communicative power may flow and accumulate. Thus, traditionally ... national-embedded peripheries get entangled into greater, international peripheries, with stronger combined powers... The Internet, as a consequence, changes the topology of the "centre-periphery" model, by stimulating conventional peripheries to interlink into "super-periphery" structures, which enclose and "besiege" several centres at once.

Berdal, therefore, extends the Habermasian notion of the *public sphere* to the Internet, and underlines the inherent global and civic nature that interwoven Internet technologies provide. To limit the growing civic potential of the Internet, Berdal also notes how "self-protective measures" are put in place by those threatened by it:

If we consider China's attempts to filter "unsuitable material" from the Internet, most of us would agree that this resembles a self-protective measure by the system against the growing civic potentials of the Internet. Nevertheless, both types represent limitations to "peripheral capacities". Thus, the Chinese government tries to prevent communicative power to build up and unleash (as the 1989 Tiananmen Square uprising suggests, the government may find it wise to install "upstream measures"). Even though limited, the Internet is proving to be an empowering tool also to the Chinese periphery: Analysts believe that Internet petitions have influenced policy implementation in favour of the public's online-articulated will ...

Incidents of politically motivated Internet censorship have now been recorded in many countries, including western democracies.

Philanthropy

The spread of low-cost Internet access in developing countries has opened up new possibilities for peer-to-peer charities, which allow individuals to contribute small amounts to charitable projects for other individuals. Websites, such as DonorsChoose and GlobalGiving, allow small-scale donors to direct funds to individual projects of their choice. A popular twist on Internet-based philanthropy is the use of peer-to-peer lending for charitable purposes. Kiva pioneered this concept in 2005, offering the first web-based service to publish individual loan profiles for funding. Kiva raises funds for local intermediary microfinance organizations which post stories and updates on behalf of the borrowers. Lenders can contribute as little as $25 to loans of their choice, and receive their money back as borrowers repay. Kiva falls short of being a pure peer-to-peer charity, in that loans are disbursed before being funded by lenders and borrowers do not communicate with lenders themselves.

However, the recent spread of low-cost Internet access in developing countries has made genuine international person-to-person philanthropy increasingly feasible. In 2009, the US-based nonprofit Zidisha tapped into this trend to offer the first person-to-person microfinance platform to link lenders and borrowers across international borders without intermediaries. Members can fund loans for as little as a dollar, which the borrowers then use to develop business activities that improve their families' incomes while repaying loans to the members with interest. Borrowers access the Internet via public cybercafes, donated laptops in village schools, and even smart phones, then create their own profile pages through which they share photos and information about themselves and their businesses. As they repay their loans, borrowers continue to share updates and dialogue with lenders via their profile pages. This direct web-based connection allows members themselves to take on many of the communication and recording tasks traditionally performed by local organizations, bypassing geographic barriers and dramatically reducing the cost of microfinance services to the entrepreneurs.

Security

Internet resources, hardware, and software components are the target of criminal or malicious attempts to gain unauthorized control to cause interruptions, commit fraud, engage in blackmail or access private information. Such attempts include computer viruses which copy with the help of humans, computer worms which copy themselves automatically, denial of service attacks, ransomware, botnets, and spyware that reports on the activity and typing of users. Usually, these activities constitute cybercrime. Defense theorists have also speculated about the possibilities of cyber warfare using similar methods on a large scale.

Surveillance

The vast majority of computer surveillance involves the monitoring of data and traffic on the Internet. In the United States for example, under the Communications Assistance For Law Enforcement Act, all phone calls and broadband Internet traffic (emails, web traffic, instant messaging, etc.) are required to be available for unimpeded real-time monitoring by Federal law enforcement agencies. Packet capture is the monitoring of data traffic on a computer network. Computers communicate over the Internet by breaking up messages (emails, images, videos, web pages, files, etc.) into small chunks called "packets", which are routed through a network of computers, until they reach their destination, where they are assembled back into a complete "message" again. Packet Capture Appliance intercepts these packets as they are traveling through the network, in order to examine their contents using other programs. A packet capture is an information *gathering* tool, but not an *analysis* tool. That is it gathers "messages" but it does not analyze them and figure out what they mean. Other programs are needed to perform traffic analysis and sift through intercepted data looking for important/useful information. Under the Communications Assistance For Law Enforcement Act all U.S. telecommunications providers are required to install packet sniffing technology to allow Federal law enforcement and intelligence agencies to intercept all of their customers' broadband Internet and voice over Internet protocol (VoIP) traffic.

The large amount of data gathered from packet capturing requires surveillance software that filters and reports relevant information, such as the use of certain words or phrases, the access of certain types of web sites, or communicating via email or chat with certain parties. Agencies, such as the Information Awareness Office, NSA, GCHQ and the FBI, spend billions of dollars per year to develop, purchase, implement, and operate systems for interception and analysis of data. Similar systems are operated by Iranian secret police to identify and suppress dissidents. The required hardware and software was allegedly installed by German Siemens AG and Finnish Nokia.

Censorship

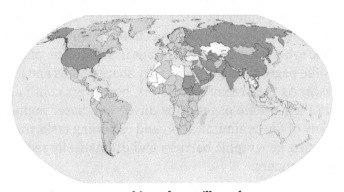

Internet censorship and surveillance by country

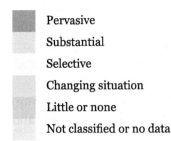

Pervasive

Substantial

Selective

Changing situation

Little or none

Not classified or no data

Some governments, such as those of Burma, Iran, North Korea, the Mainland China, Saudi Arabia and the United Arab Emirates restrict access to content on the Internet within their territories, especially to political and religious content, with domain name and keyword filters.

In Norway, Denmark, Finland, and Sweden, major Internet service providers have voluntarily agreed to restrict access to sites listed by authorities. While this list of forbidden resources is supposed to contain only known child pornography sites, the content of the list is secret. Many countries, including the United States, have enacted laws against the possession or distribution of certain material, such as child pornography, via the Internet, but do not mandate filter software. Many free or commercially available software programs, called content-control software are available to users to block offensive websites on individual computers or networks, in order to limit access by children to pornographic material or depiction of violence.

Performance

As the Internet is a heterogeneous network, the physical characteristics, including for example the data transfer rates of connections, vary widely. It exhibits emergent phenomena that depend on its large-scale organization.

Outages

An Internet blackout or outage can be caused by local signalling interruptions. Disruptions of submarine communications cables may cause blackouts or slowdowns to large areas, such as in the 2008 submarine cable disruption. Less-developed countries are more vulnerable due to a small number of high-capacity links. Land cables are also vulnerable, as in 2011 when a woman digging for scrap metal severed most connectivity for the nation of Armenia. Internet blackouts affecting almost entire countries can be achieved by governments as a form of Internet censorship, as in the blockage of the Internet in Egypt, whereby approximately 93% of networks were without access in 2011 in an attempt to stop mobilization for anti-government protests.

Energy Use

In 2011, researchers estimated the energy used by the Internet to be between 170 and 307 GW, less than two percent of the energy used by humanity. This estimate included the energy needed to build, operate, and periodically replace the estimated 750 million laptops, a billion smart phones and 100 million servers worldwide as well as the energy that routers, cell towers, optical switches, Wi-Fi transmitters and cloud storage devices use when transmitting Internet traffic.

Online Newspaper

An online newspaper is the online version of a newspaper, either as a stand-alone publication or as the online version of a printed periodical.

Going online created more opportunities for newspapers, such as competing with broadcast journalism in presenting breaking news in a more timely manner. The credibility and strong brand recognition of well-established newspapers, and the close relationships they have with advertisers, are also seen by many in the newspaper industry as strengthening their chances of survival. The movement away from the printing process can also help decrease costs.

Online newspapers are much like hard-copy newspapers and have the same legal boundaries, such as laws regarding libel, privacy and copyright, also apply to online publications in most countries, such as in the UK. Also in the UK the Data Protection Act applies to online newspapers and news pages, as well as the PCC rules in the UK. But the distinction was not very clear to the public in the UK as to what was a blog or forum site and what was an online newspaper. In 2007, a ruling was passed to formally regulate UK based online newspapers, news audio, and news video websites covering the responsibilities expected of them and to clear up what is, and what isn't, an online publication.

News reporters are being taught to shoot video and to write in the succinct manner necessary for the Internet news pages. Many are learning how to implement blogs and the ruling by the UK's PCC should help this development of the internet. Some newspapers have attempted to integrate the internet into every aspect of their operations, i.e., reporters writing stories for both print and online, and classified advertisements appearing in both media; others operate websites that are more distinct from the printed newspaper. The Newspaper National Network LP is an online advertising sales partnership of the Newspaper Association of America and 25 major newspaper companies.

History

An early example of an "online only" newspaper or magazine is "News Report", an online newspaper created by Bruce Parrello in 1974 on the PLATO system at the University of Illinois. Beginning in 1987, the Brazilian newspaper Jornaldodia ran on the state owned Embratel network, moving to the internet in the 1990s. By the late 1990s, hundreds of U.S. newspapers were publishing online versions, but did not yet offer much interactivity. One example is Britain's Weekend City Press Review, which provided a weekly news summary online beginning in 1995.

Examples

Very few newspapers in 2006 claimed to have made money from their websites, which were mostly free to all viewers. Declining profit margins and declining circulation in daily newspapers forced executives to contemplate new methods of obtaining revenue from websites, without charging for subscription. This has been difficult. Newspapers with specialized audiences such as *The Wall Street Journal* and *The Chronicle of Higher Education* successfully charge subscription fees. Most newspapers have an online edition, including *The Los Angeles Times, The Washington Post, USA Today, Mid Day,* and *The New York Times.*

The Guardian experimented with new media in 2005, offering a free twelve part weekly podcast series by Ricky Gervais. Another UK daily to go online is *The Daily Telegraph.*

In Australia, some newspapers corporations offer an online version to let their readers read the news online, such as The Australian, Sydney Morning Herald.

Online-only Newspapers

The true online only paper is a paper that does not have any hard copy connections. An example of this is an independent web-only newspaper, introduced in the UK in 2000, called the *Southport Reporter*. It is a weekly regional newspaper that is not produced or run in any format other than 'soft-copy' on the internet by its publishers, PCBT Photography. Unlike blog sites and other news websites, it is run as a newspaper and is recognized by media groups in the UK, such as the NUJ and/or the IFJ. They fall under the UK's PCC rules. Another example is the *Atlantic Highlands Herald*, a New Jersey-based web-only daily newspaper published in the US since 1999.

allNovaScotia is an online newspaper based in Halifax, Nova Scotia, Canada that publishes business and political news six days a week. The website was the first online-only newspaper in Atlantic Canada and has been behind a paywall since starting in 2001.

As of 2009, the collapse of the tradition-al business model of print newspapers has led to various attempts to establish local, regional or national online-only newspapers - publications that do original reporting, rather than just com-mentary or summaries of reporting from other publications. An early major example in the U.S. is the *Seattle Post-Intelligencer*, which stopped publishing after 149 years in March 2009 and went online only. In Scotland, in 2010, *Caledonian Mercury* became Scotland's first online-only news-paper, with the same aims as *Southport Reporter* in the UK, with *The Yorkshire Times* following suit and becoming Yorkshire's first online-only paper in 2011.

In the US, technology news websites such as CNET, TechCrunch, and ZDNet started as web publications and enjoy comparable readership to the conventional newspapers. Also, with the ever-rising popularity of online media, veteran publications like the *U.S. News & World Report* are abandoning print and going online-only. Another example of an online-only English daily newspaper is the Arabian Post, focussing on the Middle East's current affairs and business. There are a few niche online-only news websites such as Engadget, Mashable, Nagina News Portal, Polygon, Aperture Games and Game Rant.

News Aggregators

News aggregation technology helps to consolidate many online newspapers into one page or application that can show the new or updated information from many online news sources. News aggregators like Feedly and Flipboard show users stories from a user defined list of RSS feeds. Others like Google news and Newsprompt are able to cluster similar stories and show top news from across many leading news sites.

Trends

In 2015 the percentage of people who reported that print was their preferred method for reading a newspaper, down nearly 4% from 2014. The methods people use to get their news from digital means was at 28%, as opposed to 20% of people attaining the news through print newspapers. These trends indicate an increase in digital consumption of newspapers, as opposed to print. Today, ad revenue for digital forms of newspapers is nearly 25%, while print is constituting the remaining 75%. Contrastingly, ad revenue for digital methods was 5% in 2006.

Hybrid Newspapers

Hybrid newspapers are predominantly focused on its online content, but also produce a print form. Trends in online newspapers indicate publications may switch to digital methods, especially online newspapers in the future. The New York Times is an example of this model of newspaper as it provides both a home delivery print subscription and a digital one as well.There are some newspapers which are predominantly online, but also provide limited hard copy publishing An example is annarbor.com, which replaced the Ann Arbor News in the summer of 2009. It is primarily an online newspaper, but publishes a hard copy twice a week. Other trends indicate that this business model is being adopted by many newspapers with the growth of digital media.

Use

In 2013, the Reuters Institute commissioned a cross-country survey on news consumption, and gathered data related to online newspaper use that emphasize the lack of use of paid online newspaper services. The countries surveyed were France, German, Denmark, Spain, Italy, Japan, Brazil, the United States, and the United Kingdom. All samples within each country were nationally representative. Half of the sample reportedly paid for a print newspaper in the past 7 days, and only one-twentieth of the sample paid for online news in the past 7 days. That only 5% of the sample had recently paid for online newspaper access is likely because most people access news that is free. People with portable devices, like tablets or smartphones, were significantly more likely to subscribe to digital news content. Additionally, younger people—25- to 34-year-olds—are more willing to pay for digital news than older people across all countries. This is in line with the Pew Research Center's finding in a survey of U.S. Americans that the Internet is a leading source of news for people less than 50.

Digital Photography

Digital photography is a form of photography that uses cameras containing arrays of electronic photodetectors to capture images focused by a lens, as opposed to an exposure on photographic film. The captured images are digitized and stored as a computer file ready for further digital processing, viewing, digital publishing or printing.

Nikon D700 — a 12.1-megapixel full-frame DSLR

The Canon PowerShot A95

Until the advent of such technology, photographs were made by exposing light sensitive photographic film and paper, which were processed in liquid chemical solutions to develop and stabilize the image. Digital photographs are typically created solely by computer-based photoelectric and mechanical techniques, without wet bath chemical processing.

Digital photography is one of several forms of digital imaging. Digital images are also created by non-photographic equipment such as computer tomography scanners and radio telescopes. Digital images can also be made by scanning other printed photographic images or negatives.

The first consumer digital cameras were marketed in the late 1990s. Professionals gravitated to digital slowly, and were won over when their professional work required using digital files to fulfill the demands of employers and/or clients, for faster turn-around than conventional methods would allow. Starting around 2007, digital cameras were incorporated in cellphones and in the following years cellphone cameras became widespread, particularly due to their connectivity to social media websites and email. Since 2010, the digital point-and-shoot and DSLR formats have also seen competition from the mirrorless digital camera format, which typically provides better image quality than the point-and-shoot or cellphone formats but comes in a smaller size and shape than the typical DSLR. Many mirrorless cameras accept interchangeable lenses and have advanced features through an electronic viewfinder, which replaces the through-the-lens finder image of the SLR format.

The Digital Camera

History

The first flyby spacecraft image of Mars was taken from Mariner 4 on July 15, 1965 with a camera system designed by NASA/JPL. It used a video camera tube followed by a digitizer, rather than a mosaic of solid state sensor elements, so it was not what we usually define as a digital camera, but it produced a digital image that was stored on tape for later slow transmission back to earth.

The first recorded attempt at building a digital camera was in 1975 by Steven Sasson, an engineer at Eastman Kodak. It used the then-new solid-state CCD (charge-coupled device, a high-speed semiconductor) image sensor chips developed by Fairchild Semiconductor in 1973. The camera weighed 8 pounds (3.6 kg), recorded black and white images to a cassette tape, had a resolution of 0.01 megapixels (10,000 pixels), and took 23 seconds to capture its first image in December 1975. The prototype camera was a technical exercise, not intended for production.

The first true digital camera that recorded images as a computerized file was likely the Fuji DS-1P of 1988, which recorded to a 16 MB internal memory card that used a battery to keep the data in memory. This camera was never marketed internationally, and has not been confirmed to have shipped even in Japan.

The first commercially available digital camera was the 1990 Dycam Model 1; it also sold as the Logitech Fotoman. It used a CCD image sensor, stored pictures digitally, and connected directly to a computer for downloading images.

Sensors

Image sensors read the intensity of light, and digital memory devices store the digital image information as RGB color space or as raw data.

The two main types of sensors are charge-coupled devices (CCD), in which the photocharge is shifted to a central charge-to-voltage converter, and CMOS or active pixel sensors.

Multifunctionality and Connectivity

Except for some linear array type of cameras at the highest-end and simple web cams at the lowest-end, a digital memory device (usually a memory card; floppy disks and CD-RWs are less common) is used for storing images, which may be transferred to a computer later.

Digital cameras can take pictures, and may also record sound and video. Some can be used as webcams, some can use the PictBridge standard to connect to a printer without using a computer, and some can display pictures directly on a television set. Similarly, many camcorders can take still photographs, and store them on videotape or on flash memorycards with the same functionality as digital cameras.

Digital photography is one of the most exceptional instances of the shift from converting conventional analog information to digital information. This shift is so tremendous because it was a chemical and mechanical process and became an all digital process with a built in computer in all digital cameras.

Performance Metrics

The quality of a digital image is a composite of various factors, many of which are similar to those of film cameras. Pixel count (typically listed in megapixels, millions of pixels) is only one of the major factors, though it is the most heavily marketed figure of merit. Digital camera manufacturers advertise this figure because consumers can use it to easily compare camera capabilities. It is not, however, the major factor in evaluating a digital camera for most applications. The processing system inside the camera that turns the raw data into a color-balanced and pleasing photograph is usually more critical, which is why some 4+ megapixel cameras perform better than higher-end cameras.

Resolution in pixels is not the only measure of image quality. A larger sensor with the same number of pixels generally produces a better image than a smaller one. One of the most important differences is an improvement in image noise. This is one of the advantages of digital SLR (single-lens reflex) cameras, which have larger sensors than simpler cameras (so-called point and shoot cameras) of the same resolution.

Image at left has a higher pixel count than the one to the right, but lower spatial resolution.

- Lens quality: resolution, distortion, dispersion.

- Capture medium: CMOS, CCD, negative film, reversal film etc.

- Capture format: pixel count, digital file type (RAW, TIFF, JPEG), film format (135 film, 120 film, 5x4, 10x8).

- Processing: digital and / or chemical processing of 'negative' and 'print'.

Pixel Counts

The number of pixels n for a given maximum resolution (w horizontal pixels by h vertical pixels) is the product $n = w \times h$. This yields e. g. 1.92 megapixels (1,920,000 pixels) for an image of 1600 × 1200. The majority of compact as well as some DSLR cameras have a 4:3 aspect ratio, i.e. $w/h = 4/3$. According to *Digital Photography Review*, the 4:3 ratio is because "computer monitors are 4:3 ratio, old CCDs always had a 4:3 ratio, and thus digital cameras inherited this aspect ratio."

The pixel count quoted by manufacturers can be misleading as it may not be the number of full-color pixels. For cameras using single-chip image sensors the number claimed is the total number of single-color-sensitive photosensors, whether they have different locations in the plane, as with the Bayer sensor, or in stacks of three co-located photosensors as in the Foveon X3 sensor. However, the images have different numbers of RGB pixels: Bayer-sensor cameras produce as many RGB pixels as photosensors via demosaicing (interpolation), while Foveon sensors produce uninterpolated image files with one-third as many RGB pixels as photosensors. Comparisons of megapixel ratings of these two types of sensors are sometimes a subject of dispute.

The relative increase in detail resulting from an increase in resolution is better compared by looking at the number of pixels across (or down) the picture, rather than the total number of pixels in the picture area. For example, a sensor of 2560 × 1600 sensor elements is described as "4 megapixels" (2560 × 1600 = 4,096,000). Increasing to 3200 × 2048 increases the pixels in the picture to 6,553,600 (6.5 megapixels), a factor of 1.6, but the pixels per cm in the picture (at the same image size) increases by only 1.25 times. A measure of the comparative increase in linear resolution is the square root of the increase in area resolution, i.e., megapixels in the entire image.

Dynamic Range

Practical imaging systems both digital and film, have a limited "dynamic range": the range of luminosity that can be reproduced accurately. Highlights of the subject that are too bright are rendered as white, with no detail; shadows that are too dark are rendered as black. The loss of detail is not abrupt with film, or in dark shadows with digital sensors: some detail is retained as brightness moves out of the dynamic range. "Highlight burn-out" of digital sensors, however, can be abrupt, and highlight detail may be lost. And as the sensor elements for different colors saturate in turn, there can be gross hue or saturation shift in burnt-out highlights.

Some digital cameras can show these blown highlights in the image review, allowing the photographer to re-shoot the picture with a modified exposure. Others compensate for the total contrast of a scene by selectively exposing darker pixels longer. A third technique is used by Fujifilm in its FinePix S3 Pro digital SLR. The image sensor contains additional photodiodes of lower sensitivity than the main ones; these retain detail in parts of the image too bright for the main sensor.

High dynamic range imaging (HDR) addresses this problem by increasing the dynamic range of images by either

- increasing the dynamic range of the image sensor or

- by using exposure bracketing and post-processing the separate images to create a single image with a higher dynamic range.

HDR images curtail burn-outs and black-outs.

Storage

Many camera phones and most digital cameras use memory cards having flash memory to store image data. The majority of cards for separate cameras are SD (Secure Digital) format; many are CompactFlash (CF) and the other formats are rare. XQD card format was the last new form of card, targeted at high-definition camcorders and high-resolution digital photo cameras. Most modern digital cameras also use internal memory for a limited capacity for pictures that can be transferred to or from the card or through the camera's connections; even without a memory card inserted into the camera.

Memory cards can hold vast numbers of photos, requiring attention only when the memory card is full. For most users, this means hundreds of quality photos stored on the same memory card. Images may be transferred to other media for archival or personal use. Cards with high speed and capacity are suited to video and burst mode (capture several photographs in a quick succession).

Because photographers rely on the integrity of image files, it is important to take proper care of memory cards. Common advocacy calls for formatting of the cards after transferring the images onto a computer. However, since all cameras only do quick formatting of cards, it is advisable to carry out a more thorough formatting using appropriate software on a PC once in a while. Effectively, this involves scanning of the cards to search for possible errors.

Market Impact

In late 2002, 2-megapixel cameras were available in the United States for less than $100, with some 1-megapixel cameras for under $60. At the same time, many discount stores with photo labs introduced a "digital front end", allowing consumers to obtain true chemical prints (as opposed to ink-jet prints) in an hour. These prices were similar to those of prints made from film negatives. However, because digital images have a different aspect ratio than 35 mm film images, people have started to realize that 4x6 inch prints crop some of the image off the print. Some photofinishers have started offering prints with the same aspect ratio as the digital cameras record.

In July 2003, digital cameras entered the disposable camera market with the release of the Ritz Dakota Digital, a 1.2-megapixel (1280 x 960) CMOS-based digital camera costing only $11 (USD). Following the familiar single-use concept long in use with film cameras, Ritz intended the Dakota Digital for single use. When the pre-programmed 25-picture limit is reached, the camera is returned to the store, and the consumer receives back prints and a CD-ROM with their photos. The camera is then refurbished and resold.

Since the introduction of the Dakota Digital, a number of similar single-use digital cameras have appeared. Most single-use digital cameras are nearly identical to the original Dakota Digital in specifications and function, though a few include superior specifications and more advanced functions (such as higher image resolutions and LCD screens). Most, if not all these single-use digital cameras cost less than $20 (USD), not including processing. However, the huge demand for complex digital cameras at competitive prices has often caused manufacturing shortcuts, evidenced by a large increase in customer complaints over camera malfunctions, high parts prices, and short service life. Some digital cameras offer only a 90-day warranty.

Since 2003, digital cameras have outsold film cameras. Prices of 35mm compact cameras have dropped with manufacturers further outsourcing to countries such as China. Kodak announced in January 2004 that they would no longer sell Kodak-branded film cameras in the developed world. In January 2006, Nikon followed suit and announced they would stop production of all but two models of their film cameras. They will continue to produce the low-end Nikon FM10, and the high-end Nikon F6. In the same month, Konica Minolta announced it was pulling out of the camera business altogether. The price of 35mm and APS (Advanced Photo System) compact cameras have dropped, probably due to direct competition from digital and the resulting growth of the offer of second-hand film cameras. Pentax have reduced production of film cameras but not halted it. The technology has improved so rapidly that one of Kodak's film cameras was discontinued before it was awarded a "camera of the year" award later in the year. The decline in film camera sales has also led to a decline in purchases of film for such cameras. In November 2004, a German division of Agfa-Gevaert, AgfaPhoto, split off. Within six months it filed for bankruptcy. Konica Minolta Photo Imaging, Inc. ended production of Color film and paper worldwide by March 31, 2007. In addition, by 2005, Kodak employed less than a third of the employees it had twenty years earlier. It is not known if these job losses in the film industry have been offset in the digital image industry. Digital cameras have decimated the film photography industry through declining use of the expensive film rolls and development chemicals previously required to develop the photos. This has had a dramatic effect on companies such as Fuji, Kodak, and Agfa. Many stores that formerly offered photofinishing services or sold film no longer do, or have seen a tremendous decline. In 2012, Kodak filed for bankruptcy after struggling to adapt to the changing industry.

In addition, digital photography has resulted in some positive market impacts as well. The increasing popularity of products such as digital photo frames and canvas prints is a direct result of the increasing popularity of digital photography.

Digital camera sales peaked in March 2012 averaging about 11 million units a month, but sales have declined significantly ever since. By March 2014, about 3 million were purchased each month, about 30 percent of the peak sales total. The decline may have bottomed out, with sales average hovering around 3 million a month. The main competitor is smartphones, most of which have built-in digital cameras, which routinely get better. They also offer the ability to record videos.

Social Impact

Until the advent of the digital camera, amateur photographers could either buy print or slide film for their cameras. Slides could be developed and shown to an audience using a slide projector. Digital photography revolutionized the industry by eliminating the delay and cost. The ease of viewing, transferring, editing and distributing allowed consumers to manage their digital photos with ordinary home computers rather than specialized equipment.

Camera phones, being the majority of cameras, have arguably the largest impact. The user can set their Smartphones to upload their products to the Internet, preserving them even if the camera is destroyed or the images deleted. Some high street photography shops have self-service kiosks that allow images to be printed directly from smartphones via Bluetooth technology.

Archivists and historians have noticed the transitory nature of digital media. Unlike film and print, which are tangible and immediately accessible to a person, digital image storage is ever-changing, with old media and decoding software becoming obsolete or inaccessible by new technologies. Historians are concerned that we are creating a historical void where information and details about an era would have been lost within either failed or inaccessible digital media. They recommend that professional and amateur users develop strategies for digital preservation by migrating stored digital images from old technologies to new. Scrapbookers who may have used film for creating artistic and personal memoirs may need to modify their approach to digital photo books to personalize them and retain the special qualities of traditional photo albums.

The web has been a popular medium for storing and sharing photos ever since the first photograph was published on the web by Tim Berners-Lee in 1992 (an image of the CERN house band Les Horribles Cernettes). Today photo sharing sites such as Flickr, Picasa and PhotoBucket, as well as social Web sites, are used by millions of people to share their pictures.

Recent Research and Innovation

Research and development continues to refine the lighting, optics, sensors, processing, storage, display, and software used in digital photography. Here are a few examples.

- 3D models can be created from collections of normal images. The resulting scene can be viewed from novel viewpoints, but creating the model is very computationally intensive. An example is Microsoft's Photosynth, which provides some models of famous places as examples.

- Panoramic photographs can be created directly in camera without the need for any external processing. Some cameras feature a 3D Panorama capability, combining shots taken with a single lens from different angles to create a sense of depth.

- High dynamic range cameras and displays are commercially available. Sensors with dynamic range in excess of 1,000,000:1 are in development, and software is also available to combine multiple non-HDR images (shot with different exposures) into an HDR image.

- Motion blur can be dramatically removed by a flutter shutter (a flickering shutter that adds a signature to the blur, which postprocessing recognizes). It is not yet commercially available.

- Advanced bokeh techniques use a hardware system of 2 sensors, one to take the photo as usual while the other records depth information. Bokeh effect and refocusing can then be applied to an image after the photo is taken.

- In advanced camera or camcorders, manipulating the sensitivity of the sensor not one, but 2 or more neutral density filters are available.

- An object's specular reflection can be captured using computer-controlled lights and sensors. This is needed to create attractive images of oil paintings, for instance. It is not yet commercially available, but some museums are starting to use it.

- Dust reduction systems help keep dust off of image sensors. Originally introduced only by a few cameras like Olympus DSLRs, have now become standard in most models and brands of detachable lens camera, except the low-end/cheap ones.

Other areas of progress include improved sensors, more powerful software, advanced camera processors (sometimes using more than one processor, e.g., the Canon 7d camera has 2 Digic 4 processors), enlarged gamut displays, built in GPS & WiFi, and computer-controlled lighting.

Comparison with Film Photography

Advantages Already in Consumer Level Cameras

The primary advantage of consumer-level digital cameras is the low recurring cost, as users need not purchase photographic film. Processing costs may be reduced or even eliminated. Digicams tend also to be easier to carry and to use, than comparable film cameras. They more easily adapt to modern use of pictures. Some, particularly those that are smartphones, can send their pictures directly to e-mail or web pages or other electronic distribution.

Advantages of Professional Digital Cameras

Manufacturers such as Nikon and Canon have promoted the adoption of digital single-lens reflex cameras (DSLRs) by photojournalists. Images captured at 2+ megapixels are deemed of sufficient quality for small images in newspaper or magazine reproduction. Eight- to 24-megapixel images, found in modern digital SLRs, when combined with high-end lenses, can approximate the detail of film prints from 35 mm film based SLRs.

The Golden Gate Bridge retouched for painterly light effects

- Immediate image review and deletion is possible; lighting and composition can be assessed immediately, which ultimately conserves storage space.

- High volume of images to medium ratio; allowing for extensive photography sessions without changing film rolls. To most users a single memory card is sufficient for the lifetime of the camera whereas film rolls are a re-incurring cost of film cameras.

- Faster workflow: Management (colour and file), manipulation and printing tools are more versatile than conventional film processes. However, batch processing of RAW files can be time consuming, even on a fast computer.

- Precision and reproducibility of processing: since processing in the digital domain is purely numerical, image processing using deterministic (non-random) algorithms is perfectly reproducible and eliminates variations common with photochemical processing that make many image processing techniques difficult if not impractical.

- Digital manipulation: A digital image can be modified and manipulated much easier and faster than with traditional negative and print methods. The digital image to the right was captured in Raw image format, processed and output in 3 different ways from the source RAW file, then merged and further processed for color saturation and other special effects to produce a more dramatic result than was originally captured with the RAW image.

Disadvantages of Digital Cameras

- High ISO image noise may manifest as multicolored speckles in digital images, rather than the less-objectionable "grain" of high-ISO film. While this speckling can be removed by noise-reduction software, either in-camera or on a computer, this can have a detrimental effect on image quality as fine detail may be lost in the process.

- As with any sampled signal, the combination of regular (periodic) pixel structure of common electronic image sensors and regular (periodic) structure of (typically man-made) objects being photographed can cause objectionable aliasing artefacts, such as false colors when using cameras using a Bayer pattern sensor. Aliasing is also present in film, but typically manifests itself in less obvious ways (such as increased granularity) due to the stochastic grain structure (stochastic sampling) of film.

For many consumers, the advantages of digital cameras outweigh the disadvantages. Some professional photographers still prefer film. Concerns that have been raised by professional photographers include: editing and post-processing of RAW files can take longer than 35mm film, downloading a large number of images to a computer can be time-consuming, shooting in remote sites requires the photographer to carry a number of batteries, equipment failure—while all cameras may fail, some film camera problems (e.g., meter or rangefinder problems, failure of only some shutter speeds) can be worked around. As time passes, it is expected that more professional photographers will switch to digital.

Equivalent Features

Image noise / grain

Noise in a digital camera's image may sometimes be visually similar to film grain in a film camera.

Speed of use

Turn of the century digital cameras had a long start-up delay compared to film cameras, i.e., the delay from when they are turned on until they are ready to take the first shot, but this is no longer the case for modern digital cameras with start-up times under 1/4 seconds.

Frame rate

While some film cameras could reach up to 10 fps, like the Canon EOS-1V HS, professional digital SLR cameras can take still photographs at highest frame rates. While the Sony SLT technology allows rates of up to 12 fps, the Canon EOS-1Dx can take stills at a 14 fps rate. The Nikon F5 is limited to 36 continuous frames (the length of the film) while the Canon EOS-1D Mark III is able to take about 110 high definition JPEG images before its buffer must be cleared and the remaining space on the storage media can be used.

Image longevity

Depending on the materials and how they are stored, analog photographic film and prints may fade as they age. Similarly, the media on which digital images are stored or printed can decay or become corrupt, leading to a loss of image integrity.

Colour reproduction

Colour reproduction (gamut) is dependent on the type and quality of film or sensor used and the quality of the optical system and film processing. Different films and sensors have different color sensitivity; the photographer needs to understand his equipment, the light conditions, and the media used to ensure accurate colour reproduction. Many digital cameras offer RAW format (sensor data), which makes it possible to choose color space in the development stage regardless of camera settings.

Even in RAW format, however, the sensor and the camera's dynamics can only capture colors within the gamut supported by the hardware. When that image is transferred for reproduction on any device, the best possible gamut is the gamut that the end device supports. For a monitor, it is the gamut of the display device. For a photographic print, it is the gamut of the device that prints the image on a specific type of paper. Color gamut or Color space is an abstract term that describes an area where points of color fit in a three-dimensional space.

Professional photographers often use specially designed and calibrated monitors that help them to reproduce color accurately and consistently.

Frame Aspect Ratios

Most digital point & shoot cameras have an aspect ratio of 1.33 (4:3), the same as analog television or early movies. However, a 35 mm picture's aspect ratio is 1.5 (3:2). Several digital cameras take photos in either ratio, and nearly all digital SLRs take pictures in a 3:2 ratio, as most can use lenses designed for 35 mm film. Some photo labs print photos on 4:3 ratio paper, as well as the existing 3:2. In 2005 Panasonic launched the first consumer camera with a native aspect ratio of 16:9, matching HDTV. This is similar to a 7:4 aspect ratio, which was a common size for APS film. Different aspect ratios is one of the reasons consumers have issues when cropping photos. An aspect ratio of 4:3 translates to a size of 4.5"x6.0". This loses half an inch when printing on the "standard" size of 4"x6", an aspect ratio of 3:2. Similar cropping occurs when printing on other sizes, i.e., 5"x7", 8"x10", or 11"x14".

Digital Library

A digital library is a special library with a focused collection of digital objects that can include text, visual material, audio material, video material, stored as electronic media formats (as opposed to print, microform, or other media), along with means for organizing, storing, and retrieving the files and media contained in the library collection. Digital libraries can vary immensely in size and scope, and can be maintained by individuals, organizations, or affiliated with established physical library buildings or institutions, or with academic institutions. The digital content may be stored locally, or accessed remotely via computer networks. An electronic library is a type of information retrieval system.

Software Implementation

Institutional repository software is designed for archiving, organizing, and searching a library's content. Popular open-source solutions include DSpace, EPrints, Digital Commons, and Fedora Commons-based systems Islandora and Hydra.

History

Early projects centered on the creation of an electronic card catalogue known as Online Public Access Catalog (OPAC). By the 1980s, the success of these endeavors resulted in OPAC replacing the traditional card catalog in many academic, public and special libraries. This permitted libraries to undertake additional rewarding co-operative efforts to support resource sharing and expand access to library materials beyond an individual library.

An early example of a digital library is the Education Resources Information Center (ERIC) which was "born digital" in 1966.

Terminology

The term *digital libraries* was first popularized by the NSF/DARPA/NASA Digital Libraries Initiative in 1994. These draw heavily on Vannevar Bush's essay *As We May Think* (1945), which set out a vision not in terms of technology, but user experience. The term *virtual library* was initially used interchangeably with *digital library,* but is now primarily used for libraries that are virtual in other senses (such as libraries which aggregate distributed content). In the early days of digital libraries, there was discussion of the similarities and differences among the terms *digital, virtual,* and *electronic.*

In the context of the DELOS, a Network of Excellence on Digital Libraries, and DL.org, a Coordination Action on *Digital Library Interoperability, Best Practices and Modelling Foundations,* Digital Library researchers and practitioners and software developer produced a Digital Library Reference Model which defines a digital library as: "A potentially virtual organization, that comprehensively collects, manages and preserves for the long depth of time rich digital content, and offers to its targeted user communities specialized functionality on that content, of defined quality and according to comprehensive codified policies."

A distinction is often made between content that was created in a digital format, known as born-digital, and information that has been converted from a physical medium, e.g. paper, through digitization. It should also be noted that not all electronic content is in digital data format. The term hybrid library is sometimes used for libraries that have both physical collections and electronic collections. For example, American Memory is a digital library within the Library of Congress.

Some important digital libraries also serve as long term archives, such as arXiv and the Internet Archive. Others, such as the Digital Public Library of America, seek to make digital information from various institutions widely accessible online.

Academic Repositories

Many academic libraries are actively involved in building institutional repositories of the institution's books, papers, theses, and other works which can be digitized or were 'born digital'. Many of these repositories are made available to the general public with few restrictions, in accordance with the goals of open access, in contrast to the publication of research in commercial journals, where the publishers often limit access rights. Institutional, truly free, and corporate repositories are sometimes referred to as digital libraries.

Digital Archives

Physical archives differ from physical libraries in several ways. Traditionally, archives are defined as:

1. Containing primary sources of information (typically letters and papers directly produced by an individual or organization) rather than the secondary sources found in a library (books, periodicals, etc.).

2. Having their contents organized in groups rather than individual items.

3. Having unique contents.

The technology used to create digital libraries is even more revolutionary for archives since it breaks down the second and third of these general rules. In other words, "digital archives" or "online archives" will still generally contain primary sources, but they are likely to be described individually rather than (or in addition to) in groups or collections. Further, because they are digital, their contents are easily reproducible and may indeed have been reproduced from elsewhere. The Oxford Text Archive is generally considered to be the oldest digital archive of academic physical primary source materials.

Archives differ from libraries in the nature of the materials held. Libraries collect individual published books and serials, or bounded sets of individual items. The books and journals held by libraries are not unique, since multiple copies exist and any given copy will generally prove as satisfactory as any other copy. The material in archives and manuscript libraries are "the unique records of corporate bodies and the papers of individuals and families".

A fundamental characteristic of archives is that they have to keep the context in which their records have been created and the network of relationships between them in order to preserve their informative content and provide understandable and useful information over time. The fundamental characteristic of archives resides in their hierarchical organization expressing the context by means of the archival bond. Archival descriptions are the fundamental means to describe, understand, retrieve and access archival material. At the digital level, archival descriptions are usually encoded by means of the Encoded Archival Description XML format. The EAD is a standardized electronic representation of archival description which makes it possible to provide union access to detailed archival descriptions and resources in repositories distributed throughout the world.

Digital libraries benefit from the existence of sophisticated formal models, such as The 5S Framework: Streams, Structures, Spaces, Scenarios and Societies, which allow us to formally describe them and to prove their properties and features.

Given the importance of archives, a dedicated formal model, called NEsted SeTs for Object Hierarchies (NESTOR), built around their peculiar constituents, has been defined. NESTOR is based on the idea of expressing the hierarchical relationships between objects through the inclusion property between sets, in contrast to the binary relation between nodes exploited by the tree. NESTOR has been used to formally extend the 5S model to define a digital archive as a specific case of digital library able to take into consideration the peculiar features of archives.

The Future

Large scale digitization projects are underway at Google, the Million Book Project, and Internet Archive. With continued improvements in book handling and presentation technologies such as optical character recognition and development of alternative depositories and business models, digital libraries are rapidly growing in popularity. Just as libraries have ventured into audio and video collections, so have digital libraries such as the Internet Archive. Google Books project recently received a court victory on proceeding with their book-scanning project that was halted by the Authors' guild. This helped open the road for libraries to work with Google to better reach patrons who are accustomed to computerized information.

According to Larry Lannom, Director of Information Management Technology at the nonprofit Corporation for National Research Initiatives (CNRI), "all the problems associated with digital libraries are wrapped up in archiving." He goes on to state, "If in 100 years people can still read your article, we'll have solved the problem." Daniel Akst, author of The Webster Chronicle, proposes that "the future of libraries — and of information — is digital." Peter Lyman and Hal Variant, information scientists at the University of California, Berkeley, estimate that "the world's total yearly production of print, film, optical, and magnetic content would require roughly 1.5 billion gigabytes of storage." Therefore, they believe that "soon it will be technologically possible for an average person to access virtually all recorded information."

Searching

Most digital libraries provide a search interface which allows resources to be found. These resources are typically deep web (or invisible web) resources since they frequently cannot be located by search engine crawlers. Some digital libraries create special pages or sitemaps to allow search engines to find all their resources. Digital libraries frequently use the Open Archives Initiative Protocol for Metadata Harvesting (OAI-PMH) to expose their metadata to other digital libraries, and search engines like Google Scholar, Yahoo! and Scirus can also use OAI-PMH to find these deep web resources.

There are two general strategies for searching a *federation* of digital libraries: distributed searching and searching previously harvested metadata.

Distributed searching typically involves a client sending multiple search requests in parallel to a number of servers in the federation. The results are gathered, duplicates are eliminated or clustered, and the remaining items are sorted and presented back to the client. Protocols like Z39.50 are frequently used in distributed searching. A benefit to this approach is that the resource-intensive tasks of indexing and storage are left to the respective servers in the federation. A drawback to this approach is that the search mechanism is limited by the different indexing and ranking capabilities of each database; therefore, making it difficult to assemble a combined result consisting of the most relevant found items.

Searching over previously harvested metadata involves searching a locally stored index of information that has previously been collected from the libraries in the federation. When a search is performed, the search mechanism does not need to make connections with the digital libraries it is searching - it already has a local representation of the information. This approach requires the creation of an indexing and harvesting mechanism which operates regularly, connecting to all the digital libraries and querying the whole collection in order to discover new and updated resources. OAI-PMH is frequently used by digital libraries for allowing metadata to be harvested. A benefit to this approach is that the search mechanism has full control over indexing and ranking algorithms, possibly allowing more consistent results. A drawback is that harvesting and indexing systems are more resource-intensive and therefore expensive.

Software

There are a number of software packages for use in general digital libraries. Institutional repository software, which focuses primarily on ingest, preservation and access of locally produced documents, particularly locally produced academic outputs, can be found in Institutional repository software. This software may be proprietary, as is the case with the Library of Congress which uses Digiboard and CTS to manage digital content.

Digitization

In the past few years, procedures for digitizing books at high speed and comparatively low cost have improved considerably with the result that it is now possible to digitize millions of books per year. Google book-scanning project is also working with libraries to offer digitize books pushing forward on the digitize book realm.

Advantages

The advantages of digital libraries as a means of easily and rapidly accessing books, archives and images of various types are now widely recognized by commercial interests and public bodies alike.

Traditional libraries are limited by storage space; digital libraries have the potential to store much more information, simply because digital information requires very little physical space to contain it. As such, the cost of maintaining a digital library can be much lower than that of a traditional library. A physical library must spend large sums of money paying for staff, book maintenance, rent, and additional books. Digital libraries may reduce or, in some instances, do away with these fees. Both types of library require cataloging input to allow users to locate and retrieve material. Digital libraries may be more willing to adopt innovations in technology providing users with improvements in electronic and audio book technology as well as presenting new forms of communication such as wikis and blogs; conventional libraries may consider that providing online access to their OP AC catalog is sufficient. An important advantage to digital conversion is increased accessibility to users. They also increase availability to individuals who may not be traditional patrons of a library, due to geographic location or organizational affiliation.

- No physical boundary. The user of a digital library need not to go to the library physically; people from all over the world can gain access to the same information, as long as an Internet connection is available.

- Round the clock availability A major advantage of digital libraries is that people can gain access 24/7 to the information.

- Multiple access. The same resources can be used simultaneously by a number of institutions and patrons. This may not be the case for copyrighted material: a library may have a license for "lending out" only one copy at a time; this is achieved with a system of digital rights management where a resource can become inaccessible after expiration of the lending period or after the lender chooses to make it inaccessible (equivalent to returning the resource).

- Information retrieval. The user is able to use any search term (word, phrase, title, name, subject) to search the entire collection. Digital libraries can provide very user-friendly interfaces, giving click able access to its resources.

- Preservation and conservation. Digitization is not a long-term preservation solution for physical collections, but does succeed in providing access copies for materials that would otherwise fall to degradation from repeated use. Digitized collections and born-digital objects pose many preservation and conservation concerns that analog materials do not.

- Space. Whereas traditional libraries are limited by storage space, digital libraries have the potential to store much more information, simply because digital information requires very little physical space to contain them and media storage technologies are more affordable than ever before.

- Added value. Certain characteristics of objects, primarily the quality of images, may be improved. Digitization can enhance legibility and remove visible flaws such as stains and discoloration.

- Easily accessible.

Digital Preservation

Digital preservation aims to ensure that digital media and information systems are still interpretable into the indefinite future. Each necessary component of this must be migrated, preserved or emulated. Typically lower levels of systems (floppy disks for example) are emulated, bit-streams (the actual files stored in the disks) are preserved and operating systems are emulated as a virtual machine. Only where the meaning and content of digital media and information systems are well understood is migration possible, as is the case for office documents. However, at least one organization, the Wider Net Project, has created an offline digital library, the e Granary, by reproducing materials on a 4 TB hard drive. Instead of a bit-stream environment, the digital library contains a built-in proxy server and search engine so the digital materials can be accessed using an Internet browser. Also, the materials are not preserved for the future. The e Granary is intended for use in places or situations where Internet connectivity is very slow, non-existent, unreliable, unsuitable or too expensive. But, it also pose for the risk of online hazards which could be disastrous as the physical natural calamities. Effective ways of prevention like that of maintaining a backup system are hence very much essential.

Copyright and Licensing

Digital libraries are hampered by copyright law because, unlike with traditional printed works, the laws of digital copyright are still being formed. The republication of material on the web by libraries may require permission from rights holders, and there is a conflict of interest between libraries and the publishers who may wish to create online versions of their acquired content for commercial purposes. In 2010, it was estimated that twenty-three percent of books in existence were created before 1923 and thus out of copyright. Of those printed after this date, only five percent were still in print as of 2010. Thus, approximately seventy-two percent of books were not available to the public.

There is a dilution of responsibility that occurs as a result of the distributed nature of digital resources. Complex intellectual property matters may become involved since digital material is not always owned by a library. The content is, in many cases, public domain or self-generated content only. Some digital libraries, such as Project Gutenberg, work to digitize out-of-copyright works and make them freely available to the public. An estimate of the number of distinct books still existent in library catalogues from 2000 BC to 1960, has been made.

The Fair Use Provisions (17 USC § 107) under the Copyright Act of 1976 provide specific guidelines under which circumstances libraries are allowed to copy digital resources. Four factors that constitute fair use are "Purpose of the use, Nature of the work, Amount or substantiality used and Market impact."

Some digital libraries acquire a license to lend their resources. This may involve the restriction of lending out only one copy at a time for each license, and applying a system of digital rights management for this purpose.

The Digital Millennium Copyright Act of 1998 was an act created in the United States to attempt to deal with the introduction of digital works. This Act incorporates two treaties from the year 1996. It criminalizes the attempt to circumvent measures which limit access to copyrighted materials. It also criminalizes the act of attempting to circumvent access control. This act provides an exemption for nonprofit libraries and archives which allows up to three copies to be made, one of which may be digital. This may not be made public or distributed on the web, however. Further, it allows libraries and archives to copy a work if its format becomes obsolete.

Copyright issues persist. As such, proposals have been put forward suggesting that digital libraries be exempt from copyright law. Although this would be very beneficial to the public, it may have a negative economic effect and authors may be less inclined to create new works.

Another issue that complicates matters is the desire of some publishing houses to restrict the use of digit materials such as e-books purchased by libraries. Whereas with printed books, the library owns the book until it can no longer be circulated, publishers want to limit the number of times an e-book can be checked out before the library would need to repurchase that book. "[HarperCollins] began licensing use of each e-book copy for a maximum of 26 loans. This affects only the most popular titles and has no practical effect on others. After the limit is reached, the library can repurchase access rights at a lower cost than the original price." While from a publishing perspective, this sounds like a good balance of library lending and protecting themselves from a feared decrease in book sales, libraries are not set up to monitor their collections as such. They acknowledge the increased demand of digital materials available to patrons and the desire of a digital library to become expanded to include best sellers, but publisher licensing may hinder the process...

Metadata Creation

In traditional libraries, the ability to find works of interest is directly related to how well they were cataloged. While cataloging electronic works digitized from a library's existing holding may be as simple as copying or moving a record from the print to the electronic form, complex and born-digital works require substantially more effort. To handle the growing volume of electronic publications, new tools and technologies have to be designed to allow effective automated semantic classification and searching. While full text search can be used for some items, there are many common catalog searches which cannot be performed using full text, including:

- finding texts which are translations of other texts

- differentiating between editions/volumes of a text/periodical

- inconsistent descriptors(especially subject headings)

- missing, deficient or poor quality taxonomy practices

- linking texts published under pseudonyms to the real authors (Samuel Clemens and Mark Twain, for example)

- differentiating non-fiction from parody (*The Onion* from *The New York Times*)

Disadvantages

Digital libraries, or at least their digital collections, unfortunately also have brought their own problems and challenges in areas such as: There are many large scale digitisation projects that perpetuate this problem.

- User authentication for access to collections

- Copyright

- Digital preservation

- Equity of access

- Interface design

- Interoperability between systems and software

- Information organization

- Inefficient or non existent taxomomy practices (especially with historical material)

- Training and development

- Quality of Metadata

References

- *Kim, Byung-Keun (2005). Internationalising the Internet the Co-evolution of Influence and Technology. Edward Elgar. pp. 51–55. ISBN 1845426754.*

- *Hafner, Katie (1998). Where Wizards Stay Up Late: The Origins Of The Internet. Simon & Schuster. ISBN 0-684-83267-4.*

- *Mueller, Milton L. (2010). Networks and States: The Global Politics of Internet Governance. MIT Press. p. 61. ISBN 978-0-262-01459-5.*

- Reips, U.-D. (2008). How Internet-mediated research changes science. In A. Barak (Ed.), Psychological aspects of cyberspace: Theory, research, applications (pp. 268-294). Cambridge: Cambridge University Press. ISBN 978-0-521-69464-3. Retrieved 22 July 2014.

- *The Shallows: What the Internet Is Doing to Our Brains*, Nicholas Carr, W. W. Norton, 7 June 2010, 276 pp., ISBN 0-393-07222-3, ISBN 978-0-393-07222-8

- *MM Wanderley; D Birnbaum; J Malloch (2006). New Interfaces For Musical Expression. IRCAM – Centre Pompidou. p. 180. ISBN 2-84426-314-3.*

- *Access Controlled: The Shaping of Power, Rights, and Rule in Cyberspace*, Ronald J. Deibert, John G. Palfrey, Rafal Rohozinski, and Jonathan Zittrain (eds), MIT Press, April 2010, ISBN 0-262-51435-4, ISBN 978-0-262-51435-4

- *Bell, Suzanne (2015). Librarian's Guide to Online Searching: Cultivating Database Skills for Research and Instruction, 4th Edition: Cultivating Database Skills for Research and Instruction. p. 69. ISBN 1610699998.*

- *Ross, Seamus (2006), "Approaching Digital Preservation Holistically", in Moss, Michael; Currall, James, Information Management and Preservation, Oxford: Chandos Press, pp. 115–153, ISBN 1-84334-186-7*

- Mossberger, Karen. "Digital Citizenship – The Internet, Society and Participation" By Karen Mossberger, Caroline J. Tolbert, and Ramona S. McNeal." 23 Nov. 2011. ISBN 978-0-8194-5606-9

- *Alzner, Belina. "A paywall success story: AllNovaScotia.com". J-Source: The Canadian Journalism Project. J-Source. Retrieved 13 April 2016.*

- *Castagné, Michel. "Institutional repository software comparison: DSpace, EPrints, Digital Commons, Islandora and Hydra". open.library.ubc.ca. Retrieved 2016-04-25.*

- ICT Facts and Figures 2005, 2010, 2014, Telecommunication Development Bureau, International Telecommunication Union (ITU). Retrieved 24 May 2015.

- "Individuals using the Internet 2005 to 2014", Key ICT indicators for developed and developing countries and the world (totals and penetration rates), International Telecommunication Union (ITU). Retrieved 25 May 2015.

- "Internet users per 100 inhabitants 1997 to 2007", ICT Data and Statistics (IDS), International Telecommunication Union (ITU). Retrieved 25 May 2015.

- "Special Report: The Telecom Consumer in 2020", Pavel Marceux, Euromonitor International, 27 August 2013. Retrieved 7 June 2015.

- *Harris, Michael (January 2, 2015). "Book review: 'The Internet Is Not the Answer' by Andrew Keen". Washington Post. Retrieved 25 January 2015.*

- "Internet Enemies", *Enemies of the Internet 2014: Entities at the heart of censorship and surveillance*, Reporters Without Borders (Paris), 11 March 2014. Retrieved 24 June 2014.

- *"The Difference Between the Internet and the World Wide Web". Webopedia.com. QuinStreet Inc. 2010-06-24. Retrieved 2014-05-01.*

Permissions

Index

CPSIA information can be obtained
at www.ICGtesting.com
Printed in the USA
BVOW07*1308020218
506942BV00028B/133/P